Do You Think That's Wise?

Graham McCann is the bestselling and critically acclaimed author of *Bounder! The Biography of Terry-Thomas* (also published by Aurum), *Dad's Army*, *Spike & Co.*, *Fawlty Towers* and *Morecambe & Wise*.

For
Joan and Robin

Do You Think That's Wise?

The Life of John Le Mesurier

By
Graham McCann

First published 2010 by
Aurum Press Limited
7 Greenland Street
London NW1 0ND
www.aurumpress.co.uk

Paperback edition first published in 2012 by Aurum Press

A catalogue record for this book is available from the British Library.

ISBN 978 1 84513 790 8

10 9 8 7 6 5 4 3 2 1
2017 2016 2015 2014 2013 2012

Typeset by SX Composing DTP, Rayleigh, Essex

Printed and bound by CPI Group (UK) Ltd, Croydon, CR0 4YY

Contents

Acknowledgements

Many people have helped in a variety of ways during the writing of this book. First and foremost, I would like to thank Joan Le Mesurier and Robin Le Mesurier for their kind co-operation, encouragement, understanding and support.

I would also like to thank everyone else who agreed to interviews, committed their memories to paper or provided information and memorabilia. I am extremely grateful to all of them, including David Croft, Jimmy Perry, Ian Lavender, Bill Pertwee, Frank Williams, Colin Bean, Sir Paul Fox, Richard Briers, John Howard Davies, John Ammonds, Jonathan Cecil, Vince Powell, Brian Culcheth, Harry Fielder, Barry Took, Sir David Jason, Annette Crosbie and Lord Tollemache.

I must also record my thanks to the staff of the following institutions: the BBC Written Archives Centre (especially Trish Hayes); the National Archives; the London Metropolitan Archives; the British Library, Newspaper Library and Sound Archive; *The Stage*; the Theatre Museum; the Margaret Herrick Library; the National Film and Sound Archive of Australia; the British Film Institute Library; and the University of Cambridge Library. The excerpt by Alec Waugh from *The Loom of Youth* (© Alec Waugh, 1917) is reproduced by permission of PFD on behalf of the Estate of Alec Waugh. My original editor at Aurum, Karen Ings, and my agent, Mic Cheetham, initiated the project, and Graham Coster oversaw its conclusion. I am pleased to acknowledge, in addition, the assistance of several other people at Aurum – including Lydia Harley, Barbara Phelan and Sarah Whale – as well as Steve Gove, Sharon Gregory, Richard McCann, Irene Melling, Christopher Potter and Andrea Thompson.

Finally, my heartfelt thanks go, as always, to my wonderful mother, Vera McCann, Dick Geary and Silvana Dean. Their kindness, company and good humour helped me see the project all the way through to its conclusion.

Prologue

Oh how the ghost of you clings
These foolish things
Remind me of you.

_____

How awfully nice to see you.

On one more drab and damp autumn morning back in 1983, countless British people, browsing through their newspapers over breakfast, came across the following announcement tucked away in the classified pages of *The Times*:

> **John Le Mesurier** Wishes it to be known that he conked out on November 15th. He sadly misses family and friends.[1]

From such a self-effacing celebrity, the farewell, though unconventional, could hardly have seemed more apt.

The actor known affectionately as 'Le Mez' had never been guilty of taking himself too seriously. From the early days of his career as a seemingly ever-present, uncomfortable-looking authority figure in the British movies of the fifties and early sixties, to his prime time on television as the dreamy and sweetly teasing Sergeant Arthur Wilson in the hugely popular sitcom *Dad's Army*, John Le Mesurier had never been anything other, in his own eyes, than an ordinary 'jobbing actor' – moving from one role to another as he simply tried to ply an honest sort of trade. 'I couldn't care less,' he always said, 'if my name is billed above or below the title.'[2] Even when, in 1971, he won great critical acclaim in the form of a Best Actor BAFTA for his portrayal of a disgraced double agent in Dennis Potter's BBC1 play *Traitor*, he merely thanked everyone politely, strolled back home and started using the award as a humble door stop.

It came as no great surprise, therefore, that he ended up even making light of his own death, eschewing all thoughts of dimmed theatrical lights, solemn eulogies and fragrant floral displays in favour of a comically low-key and prosaic-sounding little message about having 'conked out'. That, however, was one of the reasons why John Le Mesurier was destined to be so keenly and sincerely missed. He would have been horrified by the kind of crass accoutrements that come with today's brand of exaggerated fame: the tittle-tattle tabloid tales, the over-exposed chat show expatiations, the ill-informed political disquisitions and the private lives made all too shamelessly public. All he used to say, even at the height of his own success, was that he felt very lucky to be paid for doing what he loved to do, and that he was flattered by any applause that his efforts elicited.

He might not have realised how good he really was – but his audience certainly did, and they admired him even more for his old-fashioned but deeply appealing sense of modesty. He stood for something rather special. He still does.

What words best sum up the public's perception of a man like John Le Mesurier? 'Charming', yes, undeniably so; 'urbane' and 'gentlemanly', again, undoubtedly; 'shy', 'diffident' and 'dry', almost certainly; and, following on from all of that (and in spite of the foreign-sounding surname), 'English', profoundly and indubitably. John Le Mesurier seemed, indeed, like the most admirable type of Englishman around: kind and polite; rooted yet worldly; well brought up but most definitely not snobbish; interesting yet self-deprecating; and, lurking discreetly beneath the sang-froid surface, a thoroughly and endearingly playful sort of presence.

He was, on the stage and the screen, a strange hybrid of star and supporting player, in the sense that, more often than not, whatever character he portrayed seemed very much like his own increasingly familiar public persona. His grudgingly dutiful judges, barristers and clerks of the court always looked as though they would much rather be back at their club nursing another large glass of cognac by the fire; his twitchy bureaucrats appeared to be waiting anxiously for someone or something to turn up and free them from the terrible tedium of their long-term jobs; and his absent-minded aristocrats seemed a little envious of any less class-bound, but still subtly sybaritic, kind of modern democratic lifestyle. Few actors, in short, were better at embodying that peculiarly English brand of wistful hedonism that opened the eyes while pursing the lips.

He was a rather different person behind the scenes, in private, where his best friends cherished the chance to share some of his hard-earned leisure hours. He would call them up early on in the spare evenings and, in that wonderfully soft, snug and languorous tone of his, enquire conspiratorially, 'Play time . . .?' before tempting them with 'the pleasurable anticipation of late night adventures'.[3] He loved to unwind at jazz clubs, race meetings and cocktail bars. He relished fine wine, good food and great company. He adored having harmless, but worthwhile, fun. He never hid from the fact that he worked in order to live rather than lived in order to work.

As a professional performer, however, he was far more artful and effective than he ever cared to suggest. 'You should always try to play the same character and, when possible, wear the same suit,'[4] he used to say, and 'never turn anything down',[5] but, in practice, he was a quiet master of his own particular aspect of the acting craft. True, he did not really 'do' action or accents, nor did he do much emoting or camera-catching animation, but, then again, such qualities were seldom required for the kind of characterisations that he was asked to convey. What John Le Mesurier did do so well, in his own subtle way, was to appear so unobtrusively 'normal' and casually, but memorably, authentic.

People knew in real life of grudgingly dutiful judges, barristers and clerks of the court, and twitchy bureaucrats and absent-minded aristocrats (and dreamy, sweetly teasing, Arthur Wilsons), just like the ones that he portrayed. People understood what he seemed to be thinking and feeling without having to strain to make sense of his presence. Every good British screen comedy, for that reason, needed someone as good, sensitive, intelligent and unselfish as John Le Mesurier in its cast. He supplied the reassuring watermark of realism on every crisp new comic print.

By the time, however, that *Dad's Army* had established itself in the seventies as the nation's favourite current sitcom, he had come to mean something even more remarkable still: he now seemed like a close personal friend of the family – everyone's family. As Sergeant Wilson, he struck a sure chord with the broad British public: with each furtive chuckle, each reluctant but dutiful nod, each embarrassed glance up at the heavens, each anxiously polite 'Would you mind terribly . . .?' and 'Thank you so much . . .' he summed up slightly more sharply than before what it so often felt like to be someone like one of us. Long after the actor conked out, therefore, the vivid kindred spirit that he created continues to connect with new generations of amused and appreciative viewers.

What, though, do his admirers really know of the real person they lost? The answer, so far, is: precious little. There were very few interviews or public appearances, and he always made it clear that he had no wish to be the recipient of a televised *This Is Your Life* tribute. He did, in addition to his playful little message in absentia, bequeath us a short and posthumously published volume of memoirs, but, true to form, this failed to reveal much more than the extent of his own humility. He ridiculed his own looks: 'I felt as if I possessed every physical defect known to humanity';[6] he described the attraction of acting in the theatre as hinging on the fact that 'you don't have to get up early in the morning';[7] he dismissed much of his work on film as a bit of a bore: 'I used sometimes to hope while driving to the studios that they might burn down . . . in order that I should not have to perform';[8] he belittled any reputation he had as a box-office draw when it came to being placed in any new project: 'I am inclined to say to myself, "Why couldn't they have got So-and-So?';[9] and he seemed to delight in casting doubt on the extent of his own achievements: 'Did I really deserve it, I kept asking myself.'[10] Even his sometimes painfully complicated and emotionally draining love life was reduced to a few tactful passages that were very kind to his partners while more than a little cruel to himself.

The real man known as 'Le Mez', therefore, has remained a benign but intriguingly distant figure, still in need of a proper, thorough biographical tribute – which is why this book now exists. In what follows, while respecting the many echoes of his famous question – 'Do you think that's wise?' – we will endeavour to learn rather more about the man behind the shy smile.

CHAPTER I

Master John

Don't fuss, please!

Life began for John Le Mesurier – or rather, to give him his full and proper name, John Elton Le Mesurier Halliley – in the early hours of a fine but breezy Friday on 5 April 1912 in the clean, compact and quiet East Anglian market town of Bedford. Apart from the fact that his head was judged to be 'a trifle oversized',[1] he looked more or less like any other healthy newborn baby boy of the time.

This child, however, had arrived into a family that possessed an unusually colourful and impressive-sounding pedigree. Although both parents were also Bedford-born (his father in 1881, his mother in 1878), each of them had a distinguished line of descent that stretched out far and wide within and beyond the British Empire.

John's father, Charles Elton Halliley (he preferred to be addressed by his middle name), came from an eminently comfortable upper-middle-class background long associated with the legal and public service professions. A well-regarded solicitor himself, Elton's own father, Charles Bailey Halliley, had been born and raised under British colonial rule at Trincomalee in Ceylon (now Sri Lanka) – where his own father, William, was stationed as the senior civil servant in charge of the Customs Department – before being taken back in 1858 to his family's roots in Britain, marrying a young woman from Bristol in 1878 called Emma Mary Elton, and forging a successful career in Bedford as a solicitor as one half of the firm Halliley & Stimson at 26 Mill Street. Now in his sixties and semi-retired, he managed his various property investments in and around the town, including an ambitious but ill-advised attempt to revive the local Turkish Baths[2], bought a second home at Burleigh in Somerset,[3] and spent most of his spare time either gambling on horses at major race meetings or just relaxing at home regaling his family with long and rambling stories about his improbably eventful life. There were many other related Hallileys still in positions of power and influence in various locations around the world, including a number ranked high up in the armed forces, several more making key decisions in the colonies and one or two others whispering into the right ears in Whitehall, but the vast majority tended to favour the low-key style and demeanour of the *éminence grise* rather than stray too far into the spotlight.

Baby John's mother, Amy Michelle, whose maiden name, Le Mesurier (rhyming with 'treasurer'), was an ancient Guernsey surname of Norman-French origin, hailed from an even grander family (much more centre stage than back stage), descended from the Hereditary Governors of Alderney.[4] Among her many illustrious ancestors were great-grand-uncles Captain Frederick Le Mesurier, the very brave and adventurous but 'most amiable' and 'modest' commander of the East India Company ship the *Ponsborne*,[5] the Right Honourable Paul Le Mesurier, who served as Tory MP for Southwark (1784–96) and both City Sheriff and Lord Mayor of London as well as helped to oversee the sailing of the first convict fleet to Australia,[6] and the bright and ambitious Havilland Le Mesurier, who made a large sum through profiteering in the War of American Independence from 1774 to 1783 before distinguishing himself back in Britain as a strong and progressive Commissary-General of the Army.[7] There were also first cousins twice-removed Thomas Le Mesurier, who was Archdeacon of Malta for thirty-four years during the mid- to late nineteenth century, and Edward Le Mesurier, a Lieutenant in the Royal Navy who settled eventually in Italy and became acquainted there with the likes of Lord Byron. More recently, there were her second cousins once removed, Edward Algernon Le Mesurier, a banker who served as the British Consul at Genoa in Italy, and Colonel Cecil Brooke Le Mesurier of the Royal Artillery, a much-decorated veteran of the Afghan War and other conflicts who came up with the concept of the 'screw gun',[8] was made Companion of the Order of the Bath by the British Government, honoured abroad with the Gold Cross of the Order of the Saviour of Greece and married the Contessa Nicolina Zancarol of Corfu. Through her aunt Rachel, Amy was also a cousin of Sir Denys de Saumarez Bray KCSI, KCIE, CBE, sometime Foreign Secretary to the Government of India and Indian delegate to the

League of Nations during the British colonial period. Her three older brothers, Arthur Swynfer, Cecil Andros and Paul Dobrée Le Mesurier, had emigrated together to Canada in the 1890s, where they joined several other self-styled English gentlemen homesteaders near the Moose Mountains of Saskatchewan at a place called Cannington Manor (a tiny self-contained utopian community built on strict Victorian upper-class social and cultural values, complete with thoroughbred horse racing, fox hunts, dramatic societies, poetry clubs, croquet, cricket, rugby and tennis, all supported – for a while at least – by an intensive agricultural economy).[9]

Amy's Alderney-born great-grandfather (himself the son of a Hereditary Governor), was a Winchester and Oxford-educated academic-turned-cleric named the Rev. Thomas Le Mesurier, who had not only been a Rector first of Newton Longville in Buckinghamshire and later of Haughton-le-Skerne in the diocese of County Durham, but also served as a somewhat Machiavellian private chaplain to the former Tory Prime Minister Lord Sidmouth. The Rev. Le Mesurier and his wife, Margaret (née Bandinel), had no fewer than fifteen children in rapid succession from 1801 onwards,[10] and the increasing strain that this had on their finances soon ruined their health as well. Thomas died in 1822 and Margaret the following year, leaving their many orphaned offspring (fourteen had outlived their parents) to be divided up and placed in the care of a variety of relations, family friends and philanthropic strangers. One of the oldest of these unfortunate children was Amy's grandfather, Henry Le Mesurier, who nonetheless overcame his early hardship to graduate from New College, Oxford, and find some much-needed stability and security in the dual role of clergyman and second master of a local public school in Bedford,[11] where he settled in the mid-1830s with his Canadian-born wife, Eliza Margaret Andrews. Undaunted by his parents' harrowing fate (and buoyed by an inheritance from one of his wealthy relations back in Alderney), Henry went on to have ten children: Una, John, Henry Jr, Mary, Anne, Bulkeley, Rachel, Mabel, Thomas Arthur and Paul.

Immensely proud of his family's heritage (concentrating on the great and the good while ignoring the naughty and bad), the very moral-minded Henry (the school song that he penned, 'Domus Pater', implored the good Lord to direct the pupils' footsteps 'day by day' and 'drive all evil things away'[12]) brought up all his children with a keen sense of what was expected of a Le Mesurier: one was to become a well-educated, upright, distinguished member of society, serving the public good in some pertinent capacity while advancing and expressing oneself as a distinctive individual. Some, as a consequence, carved out a career for themselves in one or another of the high status professions at home, while others, including John (Amy's father) and Henry Jr, elected to serve their country abroad (the former in the Army, the latter in the Navy) by defending and extending the Empire. By the latter part of the Victorian era, therefore, there seemed to be a rather impressive number of people named Le Mesurier occupying positions of influence, authority and power.

Both of Amy's parents – her father, John, and Dessa-born mother, Georgina (née Moyle) – spent much of their early adult years in India as part of British Raj military communities based in or around Bombay, before meeting and marrying (in Karachi in 1868) and then moving to Britain (first, briefly, to Torquay before being reunited with their extended family back in John's home town of Bedford). Georgina, who died, aged 49, in 1900, was a good-looking and very positive-natured woman who raised four children (three sons and a daughter) and maintained an orderly household during her husband's many periods away pursuing various military matters. The strong, serious and 'madly efficient' John, a proud career soldier (as well as a keen swordsman, marksman and horseman) who had risen fairly rapidly to the lofty rank of Major-General in the Royal Engineers, remained an extremely intimidating figure far beyond his retirement (marked by the award of the honorary rank of Lieutenant-General) in 1887, blustering on about old battles and former foes inside a cluster of cosy Bedford clubs and pubs and commanding a degree of respect sometimes bordering on fear from most of those whom he met until his death, at the age of sixty-nine, in 1903. 'I am quite glad never to have come across him,' his grandson would later confess with a hint of a nervous twitch. 'I don't think I'd have survived the encounter.'[13]

Such characters could certainly have seemed like a hard act to follow, but, by 1912, neither Amy nor Elton was feeling unduly burdened by the weight of so great a tradition. As a young married couple, they were now in a reassuringly secure material position themselves, with not only Elton's relatively high income as a solicitor (at his own firm of Halliley & Morrison) on which to rely but also a pension and extra annuity Amy had inherited from her father. They had a daughter, Michelle (born in 1909), and their baby son, John, and were looking forward as a family to an encouragingly propitious future.

The Halliley family's home, at the time of John's birth, was a rather cold but commodious red and beige-bricked Victorian property called 'Covenant House', situated at 26 Chaucer Road, Bedford, a conveniently short distance away from both the town centre and the railway station (itself, in those days, only an hour's train ride away from London). Domestic staff consisted of one live-in servant and another who came in for a few hours each day, and one more local woman was hired as a nanny for the two young children (who would always be addressed by her respectfully as 'Miss Michelle' and 'Master John'). A couple of pet dachshunds (named Nipper and Patience) were soon acquired, and domestic life went on in broad accordance with a traditional Edwardian English routine. Elton went out into town each morning to start work at his busy office; Amy supervised the housekeeping, planned the meals and met socially on occasion with a small group of female friends. Except on those days when Elton was obliged to stay out late attending to various civic matters (he was, like his father before him, a keen and prominent member of several community-spirited local committees), the family spent the evenings relaxing quietly together at home. Apart from the sound of a certain amount of commotion on the streets outside, ten days after Master John's birth, as Bedford people rushed back and forth from the station newsstands reacting to shocking reports that the luxury passenger liner *Titanic* had struck an iceberg off the Grand Banks of Newfoundland, those first few months as a complete family unit passed by calmly without any undue intrusion from the outside world.

The odd worrying word about, among other things, the 'German menace' reached the family every now and then from the various Le Mesuriers and Hallileys who were currently serving their country abroad, but, within the relatively cosseted confines of Bedford, life seemed, for the immediate future, reassuringly safe and secure. The town boasted some of the best primary and secondary schools in the area, numerous sporting activities and opportunities (ranging from the nearby Oakley Hunt to the newly opened Borough Bowling Club), a steady supply of seasonal outdoor affairs (including the well-attended 'pleasure fairs' in April and October) and, at least by the provincial standards of the time, plenty of cultural attractions and events. Amy, in particular, relished any opportunity to venture out and sample the local arts, making regular visits to such venues as the Town Hall, the Corn Exchange and the Royal County Theatre for concerts, exhibitions, lectures and plays, and, as a keen reader of literature, she also made full use of the large public library in Harpur Street. Her husband Elton, when free from his routine duties as a solicitor, was by no means devoid of healthy cultural interests himself, displaying a particular enthusiasm for music (a national magazine article of the time singled him out for praise as the 'indefatigable' honorary treasurer of Bedford Musical Society[14]), but his real passion, at this stage in his life, was for politics.

Politics – and, more specifically, Tory politics – had always been in his blood. His father, Charles, had acted for many years as a part-time Conservative Party agent in what was then the North Beds Division, and he had brought up Elton to follow in his footsteps, taking him out on the campaign trail during his teenage years and eventually helping him to become a part-time agent himself, for Bedford Borough, in his mid-twenties. Having recently turned thirty, Elton now felt that the time was right to act on his most heartfelt of ambitions ('I enjoyed law, but I loved politics'[15]) and turn what was currently not much more than an absorbing hobby into a proper professional career.

A thoughtful and progressive kind of Conservative who liked to stand back every now and then and scrutinise the system as a whole, he had come to the conclusion, after reflecting on recent election campaigns as well as studying a range of parliamentary and local debates, that the time had arrived to modernise the mechanics of representation – and he wanted to play his part. The practical business of being a political actor, he reasoned, was now far too complicated and time-consuming to still be conducted in the manner of a well-meaning Victorian amateur. What the average modern politician required, he believed, was the assistance of a genuinely professional administrative and advisory team headed by someone with sound managerial expertise.

One problem with the current role of the political agent, he acknowledged rather ruefully, was that it was so often performed by people like his father and himself: in other words, solicitors. Thanks to the 1883 Corrupt and Illegal Practices Act[16] – introduced to bring an end to the bribing and intimidation of voters – candidates, agents and electors alike were so anxious to avoid being caught breaking any of the new rules and regulations that they started ceding more and more power and authority to those figures who could be trusted to understand 'the niceties of the law'.[17] Such figures usually took the form of the local solicitor, who, in addition to his own full-time legal practice, was paid a retaining fee between elections to do relatively little as well as a substantial sum to act as agent whenever a campaign was called. This, argued Elton Halliley, was one reason why the existing system was still so frustratingly unsatisfactory: although the Conservative Party now had its own National Society of agents (formed in 1891),[18] the solicitors who controlled it still seemed far more interested in discussing the law (often over long lunches, dinners and suppers[19]) than they were in analysing and influencing politics. Worse still, as far as Elton was concerned, was the fact that, as there was no formal examination process to qualify as an agent, the Society had already developed into a depressingly smug and self-perpetuating elite, with older solicitors recruiting younger solicitors in the manner of a clubbable 'old pals' act.

Another problem was that these solicitors (who were now enjoying an income boosted by sources that were 'two-thirds law and one-third politics'[20]) were only serving as agents in their spare time – and Elton Halliley was one of those activists who now regarded this as hopelessly outdated and impractical. Citing his own experience as a part-time agent in Bedford, he would later explain: 'In the day time I was engaged on drafting conveyances, examining abstracts of title and dealing with other legal conundrums, and in the evenings I was doing political work'.[21] In the brave and bold new age of mass politics, he reasoned, such a perfunctory approach could not possibly cope with the growing scope and complexity of basic party business, let alone the chaos and controversies of an election campaign. The time had thus arrived, he declared, for the creation of the full-time professional political agent, and he was eager to become a prominent member of this new breed.

The immediate problem, however, as far as his own personal ambitions were concerned, was that he now found himself based in a town that was shifting its allegiance from the Conservatives to the Liberals. Captain Charles Guy Pym – a good friend of the Hallileys – had held the seat for the Tories from 1895 to 1906, but since then, apart from the brief and ill-fated interlude of Walter Attenborough's spell at Westminster between the two General Elections of 1910, the

Liberals had held on strongly to power in Bedford, and the borough's current MP, Frederick George Kellaway, was looking a formidably durable political presence (indeed, he was to remain in the seat from the end of 1910 to November 1922). Fortunately for Elton Halliley, however, a far more promising-sounding alternative soon presented itself some sixty miles away across East Anglia, in the Suffolk town of Bury St Edmunds, where the man who had been its MP since 1907, Walter Guinness, was now looking for a new agent and ally.[22]

A suave, worldly, energetic and public-spirited young man, the Irish-born Guinness (who hailed from the prominent and prosperous family of brewers in Dublin, and would later be ennobled in Britain as the first Baron Moyne) met the rather sombre and reserved but smart and good-natured Elton Halliley at a local Conservative Club function and the pair seemed to bond straight from the start. It therefore did not take long before Guinness invited Halliley to assume primary responsibility for managing his political affairs, initially on a part-time basis but ultimately, as soon as his other commitments as a solicitor could be rearranged, full time. Elton duly talked the matter over with his wife, who understood how much the opportunity meant to him; shortly after their son John was born, he accepted and became an official political agent. Although he would continue to maintain his involvement in the family firm of Halliley & Morrison in Bedford, he knew that, from this moment on, he would have to immerse himself in the minutiae of day-to-day political life, working as closely as possible with his newly adopted MP.

Fond though he was of Bedford, therefore, Elton felt that he had no choice but to move his family to Bury St Edmunds, and so, when baby John was little more than one year old, the Hallileys had a new home. Having fallen in love with a remarkably peaceful, private and elegant little area called St Mary's Square[23] (a short walk away from the site of Walter Guinness's own sumptuous manor house on Honey Hill), they took on the tenancy of a stunning-looking low white country Queen Anne house situated grandly on its own in a corner at number 8. Elton found a suitable office to serve as his political HQ (at 3 Abbeygate Street[24]),while Amy supervised elaborate plans for the interior redecorations, and together they began structuring a new basic routine with an enlarged set of staff. In addition to the children's nanny, who had accompanied the family from Bedford, the Halliley domestic household was now bolstered by two new live-in servants as well as a weekly washerwoman and a somewhat gruff and eccentric gardener called Miss Cooke (who came by a couple of times a week from her cottage in the nearby village of Risby, arriving on a battered old bicycle and wearing a pair of dusty breeches, ill-fitting leggings and ancient leather boots). Life in Bury promised to be busy and interesting.

Before the family had a proper chance to settle in, however, two distressing crises – one personal, the other political – had to be overcome. First, on 4 August 1914, war broke out between Britain and Germany; then, within a few days of the formal announcement, both Elton and baby John were struck down with double pneumonia. A terrified Amy brought in two nurses during the days and two more for the nights, barely slept herself and tried to keep her young daughter calm and happy while anxiously monitoring the condition of her ailing husband and son. The next fortnight was a harrowing time for all the family. At one stage, Elton became so delirious because of his fever that he had to be prevented forcibly from hurling himself out through his bedroom window, while John was often to be heard either screaming with pain or wheezing and coughing violently, but then their fever seemed to descend just as quickly as it had risen, and both of them were eased back to health.

Although all was soon serene again within the Halliley home, the war outside raged on, and several of Master John's earliest memories would be prompted by the sights and sounds of conflict. There were many days, for example, when his nanny took him for an outing around the town in his pram. On these excursions he became increasingly aware of the clamour of the soldiers from the 7th Battalion of the Suffolk Regiment marching through St Mary's Square, looking strange and striking with their fancy caps, tight tunics, puttees and boots, their bodies emitting a strong smell of stale sweat that the baby boy would never be able to forget. There was also one eerie night, shortly after his third birthday at the end of April 1915, when he was woken abruptly by the sound of pheasants squawking a warning in the grounds around the house. After his nanny had plucked him up from his cot and taken him over to the window, he was intrigued to see what appeared to be a 'remarkable giant cigar moving slowly like a shadow through the clouds' – the sight, in fact, of a Zeppelin preparing to drop its clutch of bombs over Bury St Edmunds.[25]

Not all of his formative memories were so grim and unnerving. One incident, in particular, would bring a wry smile to his face whenever it crept back into mind in later years. Out once again being pushed by his nanny in the pram, he came to focus on four 'unlikely looking people' – two tall men sporting large black hats and long dark coats complete with full and lush astrakhan collars, and two slim-hipped, pale-necked, bob-haired women who seemed much more extravagantly dressed and strongly scented than any female encountered back at home – and so he felt compelled to ask who on earth these exotic creatures were. His nanny, speeding up the passage of the pram, tut-tutted and replied: 'They are theatricals, Master John, and you should have absolutely nothing to do with them.'

His curiosity, however, had been aroused, and it was stimulated further a few days later when, in the middle of the evening, he was stopped from slipping off to sleep by the rumbling of several horse-drawn wagons moving slowly through the Square: the circus was arriving in town. Although he was deemed too young, on that early occasion, to be taken to see the subsequent action unfold, the sense of wonder and anticipation caused by the mere glimpse of its containers was sufficient to convince him that the seasonal event 'promised great things'.[26]

Such high excitement was something of an exception, in those days, in a place like Bury St Edmunds. The town had always tended to elicit one of two common emotions from those who spent some time wandering through its streets: either warm affection for its aura of cosy continuity or niggling irritation at its suggestion of sleepy timidity. During the nineteenth century, for example, the radical critic William Cobbett had dubbed Bury 'a very pretty place' that was 'extremely clean and neat',[27] and Charles Dickens had praised it in similar terms as 'a handsome little town of thriving and cleanly appearance',[28] whereas novelist and former resident Maria Louise Ramé – hiding behind her pen name of 'Ouida' – had dismissed the town acidly as, at best, 'an old maid dressed for a party' and, at worst, 'that slowest and dreariest of boroughs' where 'the inhabitants are driven to ring their own door-bells lest they should rust from disuse'.[29] For a typically playful, inquisitive and potentially mischievous little boy like Master John, finding himself part of such a quiet and close-knit community could often seem rather dull and boring, but, as he grew and explored the area, he came to cherish its calm and subtle charms.

Richly endowed with a variety of historic monuments (including, not far from John's home, the ruins of an eleventh-century Benedictine abbey and a large and striking ancient church that had recently been elevated to the status of a cathedral), a lively but appealingly intimate shopping area (with its medieval street pattern still largely intact) and plenty of green and open rural areas such as the nearby Hardwick Heath, Bury offered a wide enough range of distractions if one made an effort to seek them out. In terms of more formal cultural fare, there was often something interesting on offer, just a short walk down the road from St Mary's Square, inside the light and wonderfully elegant little William Wilkins-designed Theatre Royal – one of the last Regency-era playhouses in England – as well as, not much further on, the impressive-looking Athenaeum, the imposingly turreted Guildhall and the grandly porticoed Corn Exchange. Socially, too, with its tensely class-conscious concatenation of struggling labourers, ambitious tradesmen and haughty gentry, the town's commercial centre was not without its own array of characterful daily dramas.

The Halliley home itself was quite a privileged environment within which a child could grow and play, with several large and welcoming rooms, a number of curious nooks and crannies and, out and about in the grounds, a private tennis court, a paddock and a large garden shielded by a smart row of chestnut trees. Young Master John used to take particular pleasure in watching the gardener Miss Cooke go about her horticultural duties during the warmer spring and summer afternoons, sometimes coaxing from her the odd muttered response (like being 'spoken to by an old hat', as Philip Larkin would have put it[30]). He sympathised with her whenever she was made to scream by the sudden appearance of a muddy-green frog: 'I am still uneasy in the presence of small, squashy amphibians,' he would later admit, 'and can't walk through a damp meadow on a May morning with any peace of mind.'[31] Although he would never really develop much of a rapport with his sister Michelle – upon whom, by his own admission, he tended to inflict some of the worst outbursts associated with 'the typical behaviour of the younger and slightly spoilt child'[32] – he did at least enjoy being taught by her how to ride a bicycle as she guided him patiently around and around the edges of the immaculately manicured lawn. The two of them also shared a fair amount of fun looking after what by this time was a greatly expanded menagerie of pets, the two dachshunds from Bedford having been joined by three spaniels, two pekes, a Scottish Terrier and a slightly anxious cat.

Probably the most important influence on him during these early years was his nanny. Even though he would never call her – or remember her – by any name more personal than that of 'Nanny', and she would never dream of dropping the 'Master' and address him directly as 'John', the pair would form an emotional bond that would never be completely broken. He would lie in his cot and watch her with innocent fascination as she dressed herself each morning, pulling up her stockings and struggling with her lace-up corset, sometimes resorting to her favourite exclamation – 'Oh, bust the thing!' – whenever she missed an eye or a hook. He relied on her for his regular excursions around the town, first pushed in his shiny black pram and then walking by her side holding tightly on to her hand, and trusted her to answer all of the many questions that an inquisitive child might ask.

As he grew a little older and more aware, he would be unnerved by her infrequent but always highly dramatic departures when, seemingly disturbed by 'the time of the full moon', she stuck on her best black bonnet, picked up her bags and bounded off to Bury train station. Apparently so distressed, depressed and confused in her pre-menstrual state that she had convinced herself that someone or other within the Halliley household had been 'stealing' her belongings ('Strangely she never accused me of anything,' John would recall, 'not even wetting the bed, which at this period I was inclined to do'), she would stay for a few days with her sister in Bedford and then return 'as if nothing untoward had happened'.[33] While the rest of the family therefore had reason to feel that their relationship with Nanny – though generally warm – was sometimes rather fraught and fragile, Master John's deep affection for her would go on undiminished.

His attitude to his own parents, at this early stage, was rather more complicated. Like many children of the time born into conventional upper-middle-class families, he found that his mother, though clearly affectionate, delegated much of his everyday care to Nanny, while his busy father was rarely available for an intimate audience. Both figures could often therefore seem somewhat aloof. 'I was closest to my mother both in temperament and interests,' John would recall, and he savoured those relatively rare times that they shared together alone at home, with her playing the grand piano in the elegant drawing-room while he attempted to sing such popular songs of the time as the sentimental music-hall turn 'Tommy, Lad' ('Tommy, lad! Tommy, lad!/Oh! a man you soon will be,/And you'll fight for the right/Be a better man than me') or the proudly patriotic 'Drake's Drum' ('Take my drum to England, hang et by the shore/Strike et when your powder's runnin' low;/If the Dons sight Devon, I'll quit the port o' Heaven,/An' drum them up the Channel as we drummed them long ago').[34] Her playful habit of allowing him, from the age of about six,[35] to sip a little from her post-prandial glass of sherry would inadvertently awaken in him a lifelong appetite for alcohol, and, rather more deliberately, her taste for the finer things in life certainly had a pronounced influence on the development of his own aesthetic preferences and expectations. He would also have reason to be grateful to her for introducing him to the world of theatre, because, in spite of Nanny's notorious warnings about the profession, Amy eventually decided that it would be safe enough, one matinée at Christmas, to treat him to a visit inside the Theatre Royal: 'I saw Robin Hood in panto, and I was very soon hooked.'[36]

As for his father, John would later admit, with typical tact and politeness: 'I suppose I never really got to know him very well.'[37] Halliley Sr by this time very much looked the part of the authoritative and somewhat intimidating political boss, gliding around town displaying the kind of countenance that suggested not so much that he feared he had left the gas on at home, but rather that he feared that you had left your gas on at home, and he was valued greatly by Walter Guinness as he kept the local Tory troops firmly on their toes. Acknowledging the authenticity of Elton's increasingly intense political passions (which would eventually earn him the OBE[38]), John reflected sincerely if rather coolly:

He was always out in the evenings, attending political meetings: it seemed to me an unnecessary chore since Bury was a rock solid Conservative seat. I was left to have dinner with my mother and sister. Sometimes we went to the pictures and my father would pick us up in his noisy Citroën. This was our opportunity to tell him of the delights he had missed – the early Chaplins, Harry Langdon, Pola Negri, Vilma Banky, Rod le Rocque and the D.W. Griffith epics. I know that he cared for us and that he inspired great affection within the family and his profession.[39]

On those rare occasions when Elton did find enough time to sit and talk to his young son, he tried to engage with him via a love of literature, encouraging him to explore and enjoy English not only as it was written but also spoken. Some of the serials, short stories and poems that Elton recited had such an impact that John would still recall them fondly many decades later. One piece in particular, entitled 'My Financial Career' – a dry little comic tour de force by the Canadian humorist Stephen Leacock about a nervous young man attempting to open his first bank account in the presence of the tetchy manager – remained such a great favourite that, in addition to noting its nuances during certain TV tête-à-tête exchanges, he would go on to record it for an album that he released in the mid-1970s.[40]

Another important cultural influence on Master John during this period was the young classical pianist Kathleen Long,[41] a good friend of the family who resided, in those days, just around the corner from St Mary's Square in Sparhawk Street. As a music-loving couple, Elton and Amy had first come into contact with Long through their involvement in Bedford's various cultural events and societies, and Amy, in particular, had struck up such a sure rapport with her that she had not hesitated before asking the musician to be godmother to her newly born son. Still in her early twenties when John was a young boy, she doted on him, providing him with an alternative source of comfort and reassurance whenever there were real or imagined problems at home. She also cultivated in him a wide range of deep-rooted musical interests, beginning with the gift of a gramophone record – featuring a rendition of 'The Song of the Volga Boatmen' – which he would always treasure. Making the most of her contacts as one of Herbert Sharpe's students at the Royal College of Music, she sometimes collaborated with Amy to organise special soirées for the more culturally curious burghers of Bury, always making sure that her godson felt properly involved in the build-up to the elegant event. John would recall:

> Artists came all the way from London (it seemed so remote in those days) to perform string quartets at the Guildhall – Mozart, Haydn – then they would come back to our house and sometimes even stay the night. Our guests had names I still take pride in dropping like André Mangeot, John Barbirolli and John Birley whom I recall putting on the wireless to listen attentively to the music of Hal Payne at the Hotel Cecil in the Strand.[42]

Perhaps the most significant influence of all, in terms of Master John's future theatrical ventures, came from the ongoing procession of relations in and out of the Halliley home. Some other keen-eyed character actors and comic performers – including Charles Laughton and Tony Hancock – spent their formative years as residents of their parents' own hotels, where the daily exposure to a richly varied and constantly changing cast of individuals taught them to notice in a snapshot the tiny telling details that made each guest seem distinctive, thus providing them with an invaluable private memory bank of authentic human types. John Le Mesurier, to much the same effect, grew up in that large house in Bury observing the to-ing and fro-ing of so many of his distinguished family's memorably grand, bland, suave, stern and downright odd VIPs. When the time arrived, he would find himself eminently well-prepared to play just about any type of Establishment figure with rare authority and precision.

Among the Hallileys, for example, Master John was increasingly fascinated by his grandfather, Charles, who used to come to stay on a regular basis. Recognising, from an early age, that he was in the presence of a master of the dubious art of orotund windbaggery, he came to take a perverse kind of pleasure in sitting at the great man's feet and studying the bluster: 'The way he told his stories always made me laugh, but the laughter was not always for the reasons he hoped. Sometimes I would have to hide under the table at mealtimes before my mother said, in desperate tones, "Come out, John, and don't make things more difficult than they need be".'[43]

Charles's appearance alone – with his carefully curved Edward VII-style beard, starched wing collar, drooping silk bow tie, ancient tailored jacket and a pair of eccentric-looking trousers that were always creased sideways 'like pyjamas' – was enough to make his grandson break out in what he hoped would be mistaken for an innocently welcoming smile, but it was the habit of speaking at great length 'in a loud and clear voice even when he was talking utter rubbish'[44] that really caused such perverse delight. One of Charles's most-repeated anecdotes, concerning the sea voyage made by his mother, his two brothers, and himself from Ceylon to England in 1858 on board the *Star of the East*, had grown over the years from a relatively short summary of the basic details into a positive epic of *Moby-Dick*-like proportions. 'The time occupied for the passage,' the story began, very slowly and portentously, 'was three months and fifteen days . . .', and it involved hair-raising close encounters with much bigger sailing vessels, some harrowing bouts of stormy weather, the historic sighting of Donati's Comet and the moment when the entire crew gathered on deck to celebrate the arrival of Charles's eighth birthday with a generous tot of rum. He was so proud of this particular tale that he ended up writing a letter about it to *The Times*.[45] Master John sniggered a little more each time a new version was aired.

Another memorable member of the Halliley clan was the redoubtable Aunt Connie, who could always be relied on to provide John with an unwittingly entertaining demonstration of that remarkable upper-middle-class trick: how to accumulate grandeur and gravitas simply by association. She would always arrive, take the most comfortable seat in the room and, in tones of unbrookable authority, launch straight into a loud recitation of every recent adventure and achievement experienced by anyone she happened to know in the Navy. She then sat back and accepted all of the polite praise and admiration very graciously on their behalf. John would later joke that she really should have been in the service herself: 'She was a dead ringer for an admiral with her granite jaw, ramrod spine and far-away look in her eyes which suggested an unhappy experience in an open boat but was, in fact, caused by an addiction to pink gin.'[46]

The majority of the visiting Le Mesuriers tended to inspire rather more respect, and Master John stayed dutifully seen but not heard as a succession of his mother's well-connected uncles and cousins drifted in for a drink and a chat. Some of them sported high-ranking military uniforms, others were smartly turned-out in tailored pinstripe or off-duty tweed, and quite a few also happened to be called 'John'. Most significantly, however, almost all of them acted and sounded as if nature had brought them expressly into being in order to assume their lofty roles. Master John looked and listened closely as each one came and went, appreciating the personal variations on the theme of noblesse oblige, and he gradually acquired an unusually sure sense of what made each particular type tock and tick.

He did not yet realise that a career could be made out of imitating such characters, but he did already have a strong inkling that his parents expected him to emulate them in some way. It would be different for his sister Michelle, who, by the patriarchal conventions of the time, would be left merely to complete her good but limited private education and then marry a 'respectable' man (which, at the tender age of twenty in 1929, she did – becoming the wife of Archibald Willington, a Northern Irish soldier serving in the Suffolk

Regiment, whom John would dismiss as 'a rather humourless Army officer' with a moustache 'which didn't grow properly'[47]). John, however, was the son, and, going as far back as either parent could remember, any son of a Halliley and certainly of a Le Mesurier seemed destined at least either to achieve greatness or else to have greatness thrust upon him. It came as no real surprise, therefore, when, following a pleasant enough spell at the local kindergarten – which was run by two elderly spinster sisters known to pupils and parents alike simply as 'The Misses Underwood' (both of whom, Master John had soon decided, 'smelt of hot milk, petit-beurres biscuits and ever so slightly damp mackintoshes'[48]) – he learned that the decision had been made to send him away to stay at a suitable preparatory school to start realising his full potential. What did come as quite a shock, however, was the kind of place that had been deemed most acceptable.

'The choice of institution,' John would later say with more than a little residual bitterness, 'was determined by a friend of my parents, the owner of the local Greene King brewery, who, being rich and influential, obviously knew a thing or two about where a young man could best have the nonsense knocked out of him.'[49] The school in question was the relatively new but already quite well-regarded Grenham House, some 130 miles away from Bury at Birchington-on-Sea in Kent. Built in 1910 on land bought from St John's College, Cambridge, this cold and compact place of learning was indeed fast acquiring a reputation for achieving high academic standards in an environment of 'character-forming' discipline and controlled austerity. One former pupil of the institution – which was demolished in 1987 – would look back with a shudder and describe it as a place characterised by 'homesickness, freezing swims, sadistic teachers and meagre and disgusting meals';[50] another branded it bluntly as a school 'run by bastards';[51] and a third simply judged it 'monstrous'.[52] Though these were by no means universally shared impressions, they certainly match the one that Master John Halliley came to form. He hated the place.

'It is strange,' he would say, 'that my parents, both sensitive people, should have thought that dispatching their offspring to [such] an establishment . . . would somehow bring out the best in him. But it was the thing to do and my father was certainly not one to buck the system.'[53] He did try to resist, complaining that he was in the grip of some mystery illness, but to no avail: at the start of the autumn of 1921, he was taken to Victoria Station and, 'blubbing slightly', was placed on the school train.[54] He sat there all on his own, gazing out glumly at the place names flashing by – Rochester, Chatham, Sittingbourne, Faversham, Whitstable, Herne Bay – until, after three long hours, his dreaded destination came into sight. Clutching a small leather case containing a sponge bag, a change of underwear, some pictures of his family and a favourite volume of Zane Grey Western stories, he was collected from Birchington-on-Sea station and taken a short distance away to the school. Its Victorian-style red-bricked and turreted design struck him like a dark and scary illustration from *The Strand*, and the strong smell inside of moist carbolic soap made him feel sick. Taking ownership of his allotted bed next to the window in the small and narrow dormitory, he changed into his pyjamas, pulled the blanket over his head and sobbed himself to sleep.

It was an unfortunate time for any British child to start their serious schooling. So many from an entire generation of fine teachers had been lost in the Great War, and certainly at Grenham House the majority of those now taking charge of lessons were either rehabilitated pensioners with failing faculties or, as John would put it, a selection of 'life's misfits searching for an escape from their own terrible frustrations'.[55] Among the latter category was a disturbingly sadistic middle-aged man who not only managed, in his capacity as maths teacher, to extinguish any interest his pupils might have had in that subject but also, in his ancillary capacity as sports master, to terrorise countless young boys by pinching their bare legs with tweezers whenever he judged them to have made a mistake. John loathed him and most of his other teachers, and found solace only in the regular games of cricket.

Cricket was a sport for which John was unusually well-prepared, thanks to the private coaching sessions his father had arranged back in Bury with the former first-class player for Essex, Walter Mead. A talented slow right-arm bowler whose combination of thick sweaters with a lugubriously moustachioed face made him look as though he had just returned from trying to track down Captain Oates at the South Pole, Mead proved himself to be a rather unorthodox kind of tutor – according to John, 'he was only at his best when he was slightly intoxicated – which happened to be most of the time'[56], but he did well enough to ensure that his pupil arrived at Grenham House armed not only with a sound batting technique and one or two crafty bowling tricks but also with a strong and sincere belief that cricket was 'always the finest sport'.[57]

It was because of cricket, bizarrely enough, that John would acquire his first sexual experience. Following a jape that had backfired badly at the crease, when he dropped his bat and caught his own partner's soft 'dolly' shot, he had been ordered off the field (supposedly 'retired hurt') by an apoplectic umpire who, once the innings was over, marched back to his office and gave his victim six violent strokes of the cane. A little later, however, a still rather tearful John (now genuinely 'retired hurt') was consoled by Matron in her room. As with Nanny before her, he would never know the first name of the woman he only ever called 'Matron', but he did know that she was an attractive twenty-eight-year-old who, after feeding him Earl Grey tea and shortcake biscuits by way of consolation, started slowly 'disarranging' his clothes. Before he quite understood what was actually happening, he found himself lying next to her naked in bed, where, for the first time, he was able to 'explore the softness and warmth of the female body'.[58] Although the encounter would not be repeated (Matron, belatedly, knew best), the memory of it burned away in his brain for many more years, and it certainly remained the one great highlight of his time at Grenham House.

So much of his stay there was miserable that he had to fight hard to preserve any real individual spirit. A frequent wearer of the dunce's cap – which was a real dunce's cap, white and pointed with a big black 'D' painted on its side – he was often teased by his fellow pupils as well as shouted at and smacked by the staff. The only thing he really learned during his time at Grenham House was the art of passive resistance: realising that he could not take on an entire institution and hope to win, he settled instead for the kind of well-mannered obduracy that obliged his tormentors to work extra hard merely to make him go through the motions. 'I decided at a very early age,' he later explained, 'to pretend to know fuck all about anything.'[59] When things seemed particularly hard and hazardous, he would go into what he later termed 'hedgehog mode' – curling up and withdrawing into himself until the immediate danger had passed.[60]

There had always been something naturally melancholic about his countenance: an early photograph of him, aged just three, showed a sad-eyed little boy with dark hair curling down over his forehead like a lonely teardrop and a mouth pushed up and out like a slightly sullen pout. Now, as the shades of the prison-house seemed to close ever more tightly around him, he resembled the kind of desperately woebegone figure whom P.G. Wodehouse described as 'one who has searched for the leak in life's gas-pipe with a lighted candle'.[61] Although he had been sent to the school in part to help cement his lofty class identity by mixing with other similarly privileged young boys, the experience was having the opposite effect, turning him into something of a disaffected loner. 'I hated the snobbishness of the place,' he would say, angrily recalling 'the persistent interrogation on family claims to social distinction – what does your father do? How many servants have you got? How big is your car?'[62] It was not the kind of silly game that he wanted to play.

He did find a few kindred spirits lurking on the periphery of this class-conscious crowd, and took some comfort from the discovery that he was rather good, when he was in the right mood, at making them laugh. Impressions turned out to be his forte, capturing especially well the cheerfully clipped tones of the actor Jack Hulbert and the croaky-fruitiness of the master farceur Robertson ('Oh, calamity!') Hare, as well as providing amusing parodies of the most notorious members of staff. His pièce de résistance was his imitation of the school's head, a very tall and broad authoritarian figure burdened with a comically high-pitched voice; John somehow managed to 'borrow' a spare pair of his size twelve boots and started clodhopping up and down the dormitory in them while squeaking out an angry tirade. The sound of the cheers and applause restored at least a little of his much-needed self-esteem, and made him more eager than ever to show off on a regular basis. Another way of ingratiating himself with the more good-natured of his peers was by sharing the copies of *The Tatler* and *Illustrated Sporting and Dramatic News* that were sent to him each month by his mother. He would hold on to each one until he had absorbed all of the latest information concerning the likes of Noël Coward, Ivor Novello, Beverly Nichols and Lady Diana Cooper, and then, with the rather precious warning that they must be returned in pristine condition because he was 'planning to have them bound', he would distribute them among his most favoured friends.

It was still a huge relief when each term finally came to an end. The family holidays that followed were usually spent somewhere or other on the Norfolk coast, often in hotels or rented homes at Sheringham, Cromer or Hunstanton, and it was on such pleasant seaside excursions that John could relax, play and recover some of the self-confidence that had been slapped and shouted out of him at school.

As time went by, however, the carefree happiness of these occasions became somewhat compromised, as far as John was concerned, by the fact that the family (not just Elton and Amy but also, it seemed, both sides of their large and prominent clan) was starting to ponder where he should spend the next, critical stage of his education. The majority opinion among the Le Mesuriers seemed to be that John should be groomed for a grand career in the Royal Navy, whereas most of those Hallileys consulted considered, unsurprisingly, a life in the Law to be his most appropriate vocation now that imperial administration was well on the wane (although the husband of Elton's sister Marjorie, Brigadier Arthur Allan Shakespear Younger, DSO, made a forceful case for pointing the boy – in the nicest possible sense – in the direction of the Royal Artillery). Eventually, after much discussion, the Le Mesuriers won, and John's name was put down for the Royal Naval College at Dartmouth.

If the family had thought to ask John himself, he probably would have confessed that he was already sick and tired of toeing the line at Grenham House and was hardly in the right frame of mind to go and win a place in another fiercely disciplined organisation, even if it was what his 'type' was supposed to do. His own opinion, however, was not solicited, so he just groaned inwardly and did what he was told. Summoned to London for an interview with four florid-faced Admiralty officials, he was not overly surprised to find that one of them knew his father and two of the others knew various relations of his mother, so the preliminary conversation proved pleasantly relaxed and convivial. Once the formal discussion began, however, John seemed to lose his focus, mumbling awkwardly but apologetically at each invitation to speak while stroking his thick dark hair, rubbing his face or fiddling absentmindedly with the cuffs on his jacket. Alarmed that this young man, from such a promising background, appeared so bemused by the most straightforward of questions, one of his exasperated interrogators finally asked him, 'How many steps did you climb up from the Main Entrance to this room?' Instead of taking a wild guess, John merely sighed, rolled his eyes and replied, with a precocious sense of ennui, that he was terribly sorry but he really had absolutely no idea whatsoever how many steps there had been outside, nor, to be completely honest, had he felt any inclination to count them as he climbed them. That, as far as his interviewers were concerned, was it: even the best class of family sometimes chips too thin a flake off the old block. He was sent out the door with the parting advice to try and count the steps on his way back down to the street.

Strolling off in the direction of the nearest theatre where he hoped to take in a matinée, John realised that he had badly underperformed, and blamed his strangely eviscerated behaviour on the fact that he had decided to 'relax' himself before the ordeal ('I seem to remember masturbating somewhere outside Faversham on my way to Victoria'[63]). In truth, his failure had far more to do with his total lack of enthusiasm for a life spent out at sea.

Having not so much jumped through the hoops held up for him as merely glanced at them grudgingly before wandering idly away, he returned to school that night without feeling the slightest tinge of regret. He did not know what he wanted to do – or what he was best suited to do – but he knew that it did not involve the Navy. A telegram came a few days later confirming his rejection – 'How extraordinary,' exclaimed the master who read it, not used to seeing a pupil held back from rising up the ranks – and his embarrassed parents were forced to think about his future all over again.

Meanwhile, life back at Grenham House was not quite as wretched as it had once been for John. Now outgrowing the mild but tiresome attacks of acne that had embarrassed him in earlier years, he felt rather better about himself, and, as one of the older boys at the school, he was a smarter, smoother operator when it came to avoiding the usual types of trouble. He was also starting, by this stage, to be aware that he possessed the kind of natural charm that seemed to make other people want to do the most menial of tasks on his behalf, and so, as he waited patiently for news to arrive of his next educational destination, he began to conserve his energy by delegating – very politely – a growing number of his duties. 'How very kind of you,' he would always say, 'you've just saved my life.'[64] There was, for example, the old carpentry master who found himself, without ever quite knowing why, making cabinets and pipe stands for John to present as his own efforts when he next went home to his parents, and the fellow pupil who sat happily cleaning John's cricket boots while he was taken to lunch by the headmaster's pretty young wife. Although, therefore, he was looking increasingly aimless academically, he was now drifting along in quite some style.

The relaxed impasse ended abruptly after a month or so when his parents announced that they had decided to send him on to a prestigious public school, Sherborne in Dorset. John responded to this news by promptly failing the Common Entrance exam, but his parents had a discreet word with the head of Grenham House, Henry Jeston, who had a close friend on the staff at Sherborne, and, in spite of his failure, John found himself summoned to Dorset for an interview. He was greeted there by the Bursar, who wore an old tweed suit and a faded MCC tie and behaved with unforced bonhomie. Playing 'Blue Skies' on his gramophone throughout their meeting, he chatted away cheerfully to his young visitor and concluded by assuring him that, despite his current areas of academic weakness, there would indeed be a place for him at Sherborne.

A slightly dazed John thanked him very politely, made his way back to the station, took a seat on the train and reflected on what had just happened. Diffidence, it seemed, was no match for destiny if one was a Le Mesurier or a Halliley. He was still on course for precisely the kind of life that he had never, ever craved.

Feeling somewhat confused and vaguely depressed, he stopped off in London on his way back to Kent to take in another of his favourite Aldwych farces. His spirits were lifted a little when he managed to snatch a brief meeting backstage with some of the stars, before, with a sigh, he boarded another train and resumed his journey to Birchington-on-Sea. As if things could not have gone any worse for this most unambitious of young scholars, soon after arriving back at Grenham House he went down with mumps. As term was coming to an end, the other pupils were starting to depart, so he found himself left behind in miserable isolation in one of the dormitories. Lying in bed one lonely evening as the shadows crept into the room, he shut his eyes and reflected sadly on the fact that, after spending more than four long years there, his stay was ending just as it had started: with him on his own in tears.

Once he was well on his way to recovery, however, he discovered that plans had been made to ensure that he would at least leave the old school in fine style: he was wrapped up warmly, deposited on the back seat of Walter Guinness's gleaming Rolls-Royce and driven up to London by the politician's smart chauffeur, where Guinness proceeded to treat him and his father to a long and sumptuous celebratory lunch. Sherborne, both men assured Master John, was going to be a hugely rewarding experience. The young boy smiled and nodded politely in agreement, without being entirely sure they would be proven right.

CHAPTER II

Sherborne

Not for me the dubious heaven
Of being some prefect's protégé.

The date was Monday 3 May 1926. Many people alive in Britain at the time would later remember it as the date of the outbreak of the ten-day General Strike. John Le Mesurier, on the other hand, would always recall it as the date that he started at Sherborne.

He had spent much of that spring at home in Bury St Edmunds, waiting with a mounting sense of anticipation as the day of his move to Dorset crept closer and closer. Bits and pieces of information about the institution had been fed to him, during that anxious little period of freedom, by various well-meaning friends, relations and administrators. He had learned, for example, that Sherborne was one of Britain's original public schools; that its motto was '*Dieu et mon droit*' ('God and my right'); that its alumni included such impressive-sounding figures as the politician William Cecil, the philosopher Alfred North Whitehead and the writer John Cowper Powys; that it was now organised along the lines of a collegiate-style 'house system' (comprised in those days of School, Abbey, The Green, The Retreat, Abbeylands, Lyon and Westcott); and that he himself would soon be taking up residence in Lyon House. Such details piqued his curiosity without completely placating his concerns. He was still not sure about Sherborne.

He was not really sure about anything to do with his schooling – apart from the fact that he was glad to be gone from Grenham House. Knowing, however, that he had to go somewhere to complete his education, and appreciating the sacrifices his parents were prepared to make in order to get him somewhere as grand and expensive as

Sherborne, he tried to face his fate in the right frame of mind. At least, he kept telling himself, it will be better than Grenham House. It was not the most positive of responses but, as the clock kept on ticking, it was the best that he could provide.

When the time to go finally arrived early one crisp but fine morning in May, his parents, responding stoically to the stationary nature of the strike-bound trains, packed his belongings into the back of their car and set off with their nervous-looking fourteen-year-old son on the long and draining 225-mile diagonal drive from eastern to south-western England. Looking out through the window as they motored slowly through the well-manicured lanes around Newmarket, he saw the racehorses out on their morning exercise, the steam rising from their smooth chestnut-brown flanks as they made their way back to the stables, and, in spite of his best efforts to be positive, he wished more keenly than ever that he did not really have to leave. A stop for an extended lunch at the Mitre in Oxford only heightened his unspoken desire to slip away and retreat back to his beloved Bury, but, once his parents were ready to resume, the journey went on, and on, and on, until, in the darkness of the evening, they finally arrived at Sherborne.

It was so late in the day that they found the front door of Lyon House bolted – thus giving John cause to hope, however faintly, that his parents might turn around and take him back home with them – but, after what seemed like an achingly long delay, the bell was finally answered by a sleepy-eyed (and clearly none-too-pleased) housemaster, and John was led away to a junior dormitory while his parents departed for the nearby Digby Hotel. Instructed to make his way quietly in the dark until he came to an empty bed, he did as he was told, undressed as quickly as he could because of the cold and, groping for the space between the sheets, slipped straight in under the covers. Too tired for any fears or tears on this particular occasion, he soon drifted off to sleep.

His first impression the following morning, once he was out and about in the daylight, was one of awe. This was, without any doubt, an extraordinary place to be: the neat semi-monastic huddle of buildings in the shadow of the strikingly handsome abbey, the shadowy cloisters, the rich and golden Ham Hill stone and the bright and airy courtyard, the lush lawns and well-tended playing fields, the dreamy medieval glamour of it all – he wandered around, like so many other nervous newcomers, in a strange but warm sort of daze. Lyon House itself was a large and modern red-brick building (founded in 1910) overlooking an attractively designed private garden, and, as only the second of Sherborne's seven houses to be designed expressly for resident students, it appeared rather more welcoming than some of the older, colder constructions. John could not stop walking and exploring, looking up and around like a deeply impressed young tourist.

There was more time for such casual sightseeing than the start of a new term normally afforded. Thanks to the impact of the General Strike, the school was currently in a state of chaos, with some of its 400 pupils still stranded somewhere or other en route, a number of others arriving at certain stages during the first day via various modes of transport and many more already in situ but still waiting to be reunited with their luggage. John, once his parents had said their goodbyes and set off on the long drive back to Bury, was able to unpack and observe the ongoing commotion from a standpoint of relative placidity. Fellow new faces were noted, brief introductions were made and a sense of momentum developed. It would not be long, he realised, before this new life at Sherborne began to unfold.

Once it did, however, some doubts were not slow to creep in. Snobbish-sounding conversations were overheard both inside the dormitories and out in the courtyard ('What does your father do? How many servants have you got? How big is your car?'); slaps and smacks were witnessed in the classrooms; and orders seemed to be barked from the early morning right through until the night. It all seemed unnervingly familiar to John. He was still not sure about Sherborne.

It did not help that Sherborne was suffering currently from what would these days be termed an 'image problem'. A novel called *The Loom of Youth* had been written by a former pupil of the school – Alec Waugh, the older brother of Evelyn – back in 1916, a short time after he had been expelled for having been caught indulging in 'homosexual practices' (in other words, kissing another boy), and published the following year. Featuring a supposedly imaginary academic establishment, 'Fernhurst', clearly recognisable as his own alma mater, the book – which chronicled the slow but inexorable moral corruption of a character called Gordon Carruthers as he scaled the school's social ladder – had sold many copies and created quite a national scandal. Impassioned letters about its 'perniciousness' flooded in for months to the London press (correspondence filling three or four pages an issue ran for ten solid weeks in *The Spectator* alone). Waugh was publicly humiliated and ostracised by many of his friends, and the outraged governors of Sherborne promptly banned the book from the premises; it would be a caning offence, at the very least, to be found with it in one's possession. In John's time, however, 'everyone seemed to have a copy' and, as he furtively read the forbidden text himself, he found much in the fiction that rang true.

Bitterly critical of the romanticisation of Britain's 'backward', 'wasteful' and 'wretched' public school system, some passages read almost like a sobering admonitory letter to the next generation of freshmen:

> Most boys have at their preparatory schools been so carefully looked after that they have never learnt to think for themselves. They take everything as a matter of course. They believe implicitly what their masters tell them about what is right and wrong. Life is divided up into so many rules. But when the boy reaches his Public School he finds himself in a world where actions are regulated not by conscience, but by caprice. Boys do what they know is wrong; then invent a theory to prove it is right; and finally persuade themselves that black is white. It is pure chance what the Public School system will make of a boy. During the years of his apprenticeship, so to speak, he merely sits quiet, listening and learning; then comes the middle period, the period in which he is gradually changing into manhood. In it all his former experiences are jumbled hopelessly together, his life is in itself a paradox. He does things without thinking. There is no consistency in his actions. Then finally the threads are unravelled, and out of the disorder of conflicting ideas and emotions the tapestry is woven on the wonderful loom of youth.
>
> The average person comes through all right. He is selfish, easy-going, pleasure-loving, absolutely without a conscience, for the simple reason that he never thinks. But he is a jolly good companion; and the Freemasonry of a Public School is amazing. No man who has been through a good school can be an outsider. He may hang round the Empire bar, he may cheat at business; but you can be certain of one thing, he will never let you down. Very few Public School men ever do a mean thing to their friends. And for a system that produces such a spirit there is something to be said after all.
>
> But for the boy with a personality school is very dangerous. Being powerful, he can do nothing by halves; his actions influence not only himself, but many others. On his surroundings during the time of

transition from boyhood to manhood depend to a great extent the influence that man will work in the world. He will do whatever he does on a large scale, and people are bound to look at him. He may stand at the head of the procession of progress; he may dash himself to pieces fighting for a worthless cause; and by the splendour of his contest draw many to him. More likely he will be like Byron, a wonderful, irresponsible creature, who at one time plumbed the depths, and at another swept the heavens – a creature irresistibly attractive, because he is irresistibly human.[1]

John, on reading this, felt nothing but trepidation as he considered his own potential future. Other sections in the book – reflecting on not only the hypocrisy concerning homosexuality but also the neurotic fixation on athleticism, the pharisaic nature of the obligatory religious instruction, the shoddy standard of teaching in general and the shameless acceptance of cribbing, as well as the countless cases of cruelty and the hierarchy of meddlesome cliques – were depressingly believable. Although the contemporary reality did not strike John as 'quite as awful'[2] as the world Waugh had described, the difference seemed merely a matter of degree, and John was already starting to experience similar things during the course of his own daily routine.

The fagging system, for example, was one problem covered by Waugh that clearly continued to fester, with endless instances of bigger boys picking on smaller boys as if the school was intent on preserving and promoting some kind of perverse private chain of being. The strangely shrill and desperate macho spirit was another enduring source of disenchantment. Worse still, as far as John was concerned, was the poor attitude, as well as the sheer incompetence, of the majority of the teaching staff, although he could see, beyond the failings of certain individuals, that it was the system as a whole (which seemed, in his eyes, to require 'the teachers to be sillier than their pupils'[3]) that was most responsible for spawning such an unhappily uninspiring generation of so-called mentors. 'Many of them had spent their boyhood at Sherborne before taking modest degrees at Oxford or Cambridge whence they embarked on a cultural tour of the continent as a fashionable preliminary to a return to Sherborne, where they settled down to spend the rest of their lives teaching from text books. No wonder they behaved like overgrown kids.'[4]

John's own housemaster – a gruff, arrogant and rather aggressive middle-aged man called Alexander Hamelin ('A.H.') Trelawny-Ross – certainly wasted little time before establishing himself firmly as a demoralisingly negative presence in the new boy's everyday life. Notorious for his misogynistic and racist inclinations – apart from the many derogatory remarks about the dangers of those 'dames' who dared to step down from their 'pedestals' and become 'He-women', he was often to be heard urging colleagues to read Lothrop Stoddard's wildly right-wing disquisition, *The Rising Tide of Colour Against White World-Supremacy*[5] – the Plymouth-born and Sherborne- and Oxford-educated Trelawny-Ross was a stern foe of all forms of 'slackness' who viewed the growth of democracy as the main cause of the supposed decline in manners and morals. One of the first things he told John and the other boys in Lyon House was that it 'is no good having a wish-bone where your back-bone ought to be', warning them that it was vital they learnt as soon as possible such essential skills as 'self-nursing', 'saving life in fire or water' and 'self-defence by Boxing or Ju-jitsu' (because 'without such a man may be at a great disadvantage in a crisis').[6]

Describing him as 'a rulebook teacher who confused discipline with bullying', John would later complain that this tiresome martinet 'held to the therapeutic value of long country runs and cold baths in all seasons and urged us to adopt his fanaticism for rugger, a game I loathed'.[7] The 'solution' to any supposed problem, as far as Trelawny-Ross was concerned, was always a session of strenuous physical exercise. If one spoke at the wrong time, if one failed to speak at the right time, or produced a substandard piece of work, or made too many spelling mistakes, or was caught getting up to some mild bit of mischief, the belief seemed to be that running around until one was sick was the best way to make one mature and improve. John merely grew fitter but more miserable and resentful as each week passed slowly by.

There were a few minor but still precious personal triumphs. One came early on in the first term when all of the new boys were obliged to recite something in front of an audience all too eager to respond with a barrage of jeers and an assortment of improvised missiles. John chose to reprise an old Jack Hulbert monologue he knew by heart, and so strong and sure was his delivery that he muted the mob and even elicited a clap or two from some of his peers. He also managed to earn himself some credit by making his way up the scale as a cricketer, usually either opening the batting or else coming on at the fall of the first wicket. This achievement – which would eventually see him win a place in the very competitive First XI – not only impressed the sports-obsessed masters but also, more importantly, enabled John to spend some time away from the school, facing the likes of Radley, Westminster, Tonbridge, Clifton, Blundell's and Downside on some of the best-kept private playing fields in England.

Most of the time, however, he just struggled to keep out of trouble. A bid to brighten his days by collecting autographs, for example, ended after a promising start when his housemaster intercepted an envelope bearing a Los Angeles postmark and found that it contained a signed scantily clad portrait of the bisexual Hollywood star Tallulah Bankhead. John was punished for requesting such an item by having to stand and watch as his tormentor tore up this and all the rest of his special collection – and then he was beaten to make absolutely sure that the message sank in.

Within a matter of months, John had come to hate Sherborne more than he had ever hated Grenham House. 'I resented Sherborne for its closed mind, its collective capacity for rejecting anything that did not conform to the image of manhood as portrayed in the ripping yarns of a scouting manual,' he would say.[8] It all seemed so bitterly ironic: living in such beautiful ancient buildings but leading such a cultureless modern existence. Gone, it seemed, was the avuncular old bursar who had chatted away so amiably while a jaunty recording of 'Blue Skies' promised a 'sun shining so bright' and 'days hurrying by' while things were 'going so right'. Here instead was a hard-hearted housemaster barking out instructions while, more often than not, his own favourite recording – Harry Lauder's laboured anthem 'Keep Right On to the End of the Road' – droned on dauntingly in the background about the 'tired and weary' with 'big stout hearts' marching up 'long steep hills'. John could not help feeling cheated.

Backward-looking and brutally intolerant (another disaffected alumnus would capture the combination with the images of 'woodworm' and 'a whipping block'[9]), Sherborne was, said John, a profoundly miserable place to be. Every morning he would wake up and dress in his cold and over-ventilated dormitory, forcing his freezing fingers to fasten his hard collar studs, and then set off to endure the same old regimented and rod-ruled routine that appeared to have far more to do with testing his physical limits than it ever did with extending his intellectual abilities. Nobody seemed truly to think, or imagine, or experiment; nobody seemed to doubt (unless the doubt was to do with his aptitude for being one more high-class cog in the social machine).

Individualism per se appeared to be regarded as little more than mere impudence (or, as the in-house term put it, 'being ticklish'[10]); one was meant to 'stand out' only in the sense of being an exemplar of some universal quality, an embodiment of the classical notion of good citizenship, so as to better serve the Sherborne ideal of esprit de corps. As all of the boys were told each year during one of the headmaster's standard sermons: 'In form-room and hall and dormitory, on the field and on parade, in your relations with us masters and in the scale of seniority among yourselves, you have become familiar with the ideas of authority and obedience, of cooperation and loyalty, of putting the house and the school above your personal desires . . .'[11] Trelawny-Ross echoed the sentiment in his own predictably Kiplingesque address to John and his fellow residents of Lyon House: 'It is [here] that boys meet with triumph and disaster, learn to take the rough with the smooth, to face ridicule or accept praise as men should do; [here], in short, that they learn the art of living together and build up a spirit of service.'[12] Treating each pupil as though he was pre-programmed to assume a conventional position of power and influence somewhere in the adult world, the focus seemed to be on simply making sure that he would arrive in the job sporting the right kind of straight-backed, smooth-browed and stiff-lipped stoical attitude to keep the great tradition ticking on.

John would later see a funny side to all of this, when he watched another famous Old Shirburnian (as the school's alumni were termed), the actor Roland Young, a pupil there from 1902 to 1906, sending up the stereotype in countless Hollywood comedies of the era. Usually playing a sober little mouse of a man with an upper lip so stiff that, like the almost equally stiff lower one, it would barely move when he spoke, Young appeared as various figures who, in true Sherborne style, had been smacked, prodded and shouted at until they had been tamed for release into some or other branch of the Establishment. Probably his most memorable incarnation would be as the meek and quietly desperate little bank manager, Cosmo Topper, in the delightful 1937 Cary Grant and Constance Bennett screwball comedy *Topper*: here he captured perfectly the personality of the type of methodically dutiful

Englishman who secretly longed to run instead of walk every once in a while ('like a silly chicken'), be a minute or so early or late instead of always predictably right on time, go for a wild drive in a fast and 'flashy' sports car, dance and drink champagne and pink ladies, maybe even sing the odd popular song, and perhaps one day see his very proper wife wear a pair of fancy French knickers, but who, without some kind of magical intervention, was destined to remain stuck in his terribly respectable little rut. Every time John saw Young mutter and mumble on the screen he would smile, roll his eyes a little and think, 'Sherborne!' He would also, of course, go on to make similar fun of the type himself once he, too, became an actor.

In the here and now of the late 1920s, however, the prevailing mood, as far as John was concerned, was one of enervating boredom. The outdoor chores were bad enough: the daily grind of mid-morning physical training (or 'toughing up' as it was more often termed), followed every Friday afternoon by the even more monotonous Officers' Training Corps (OTC) parade, accompanied by the shrieking voice of their regular Army instructor, Sergeant-Major Longmore, seemed designed to drain every last drop of enthusiasm from each grudgingly obedient boy. The indoor drudgery, however, was even worse, with a depressingly narrow and uninspiring curriculum weighted heavily towards the classics.

One exact contemporary of John's at Sherborne was the future mathematician, logician, wartime Enigma code-breaker and computer science pioneer Alan Turing, a scruffy and gauche but very bright little boy who found himself similarly frustrated by the over-policed parameters of his current education. Although there is no firm evidence that the two teenagers spent any significant amount of time socialising together, both certainly attended several of the same classes and felt unnecessarily constrained by the old-fashioned nature of the limited range of lessons (and both of them had to endure the exceptionally archaic academic prejudices of the curmudgeonly A.H. Trelawny-Ross, who dismissed scientific subjects as 'low cunning' and would often enter a classroom, sniff the air and snarl, 'This room smells of mathematics! Go and fetch a disinfectant spray!' before launching into yet another extended session of Latin translation).[13]

The school's long-serving headmaster, Nowell Smith, was actually a rather cultured individual with a relatively broad range of personal artistic tastes and intellectual interests (and a scholarly fondness for some of the Romantic poets), but, as a professional educator, he remained a fierce advocate of keeping classics at the core of the curriculum, raging against the 'blind materialism' of the modern age and arguing that 'Hellenic studies in general, and the study of Greek in particular' were more relevant than ever to the cultivation of the civically virtuous and responsible young adult. He added that 'there is no subject nearly so valuable as Greek for combining the educational benefits of intellectual discipline and spiritual enrichment. A great deal of the "flood of modern subjects" flows over and round our youth with very little effect; but Greek, owing partly to the effort required to master it, partly to the vitality inherent in the language, has a power of penetrating and influencing the spiritual life of intelligent boys to a higher degree than any other subject.'[14]

The situation soon went from bad to worse when Nowell Smith (known affectionately as well as by convention as 'The Chief') retired and a man called Charles Boughey became the new headmaster. Boughey was even surer than his predecessor had been about Sherborne's special strengths, and so during the rest of John's time there the school would become more dogmatic than ever about its set of pedagogic principles. It was hardly surprising, therefore, that the only thing to which John looked forward each year was the moment when he could go home to Bury St Edmunds.

Even Bury St Edmunds, however, now seemed a little strange to him. His home, for example, was now on the opposite side of the road from its old location in St Mary's Square, as his parents had just moved the very short distance from their old property at number 8 to a tall and handsome red-brick Georgian town house at number 6.[15] Another reason why, upon his return, he felt somewhat disoriented was the imminent departure of his sister, Michelle, who was preparing to marry her soldier fiancé, Archie – who by this time had risen to the rank of Lieutenant-Colonel – and travel with him back to his home town of Castlerock in Northern Ireland. Ironically, therefore, the reassuringly static image of the family environment about which he had been dreaming in the dormitory was no longer there in reality. Life, unsentimentally, had moved on during the young man's absence.

One thing that did seem the same was the fact that there was rarely any sign of his father. Elton Halliley – now in his late forties, silver at the temples and looking very much the traditional *éminence grise* – was busier than ever on the local political circuit, not only attending to current matters but also planning for his Party's mid- to long-term future. Walter Guinness was coming to the end of his distinguished House of Commons career (after which he would, as the newly elevated Baron Moyne, play an influential role in the House of Lords), and John's father was already grooming a suitable successor: an ambitious young man named Frank Heilgers, who would duly become the town's next Conservative MP in 1931 (and, thanks in part to the organisational bedrock that had been established by Elton Halliley, the steady procession of Bury's Tory MPs would stretch on interrupted all the way through to the start of the next millennium).

In addition to his myriad local activities, however, Elton was also starting to make quite a name for himself behind the scenes (in true Halliley style) on the national political stage through his contribution to the National Society of Conservative and Unionist Agents, becoming not only a representative on its governing council but also its secretary, as well as the editor of its official journal. It was during this period that he was immersed in an admirable campaign that would end up as his chief political legacy: after first proposing a resolution in 1922 calling for the introduction of a proper qualifying examination for all prospective political agents, he would continue to fight for the change until, at long last, it was voted into a formal rule in 1932.[16] As a bid to help modernise and democratise the Tory Party's creaky machinery, his efforts had already caught the eye of many of the grandees at Central Office, and won him some very influential admirers among the progressive wing of the Party. He was thus excelling as a major political agent, even though that meant, as an unintended effect, that he was still under-performing as a parent.

At least Amy Halliley was able to spend some time in the summer with her son (who was now edging up to six foot tall and suddenly looking disarmingly 'grown-up'), although she, too, had her distractions, with a seemingly endless list of tasks to attend to around the new home as well as another local musical event to plan with her great friend Kathleen Long. Sensing that John regretted the lack of any real opportunity to discuss his recent experiences man-to-man with his father (and somewhat bemused herself by the fact that many of Trelawny-Ross's routine reports on John's progress, or lack of it, had been dispatched to her composed in doggerel 'as a sort of relief from letter-writing'[17]), Amy made a concerted effort to be a good and patient confidante, listening carefully to all of his mumbled concerns about Sherborne and doing her best to convince him that things would soon be better. Although her words did not really work, John appreciated hearing them and was genuinely grateful for her sympathy and support. He quickly came to the conclusion, however, that it was best not to think too much about the future; he just wanted to make the most of his current vacation.

Delighted to be back in the region of England to which he would always refer as his 'womb',[18] he proceeded to take great pleasure in reacquainting himself with his favourite old places in and around the town. Most of these excursions tended to be frustratingly solitary, as so many of his childhood friends had now moved on and away, but he still enjoyed the sense of nostalgia as he either roamed the streets or sat in the centre and watched the tourists pass by. Although Trelawny-Ross had declared that it was quite acceptable to be 'interested' in girls 'of your own class' during the holidays (so long as one did not go on to 'cheapen it all by chatter'[19]), the chances of any brief romantic encounters would prove to be few and far between. Delighted though he was to be free for a while from the boys-only environment of Sherborne, it did not help that such spells tended to be so short in their duration. What made things worse, from his perspective, was the fact that most of the girls of his age who were still around in the town struck him as 'rather hearty and jolly hockey stick types', and therefore not really his cup of tea.[20] The earlier furtive tryst with the fragrant Matron at Grenham House had left him with a strong preference for older and more experienced women, and so, with his parents still in close proximity, there was little hope of him doing more than admiring the odd fetching figure from afar.

Summer trips away from Bury remained a keenly anticipated annual treat, although the combination of the Great Depression and Elton Halliley's local political commitments meant that John and his parents would rarely stray beyond the boundaries of Britain. Aside from a few brief visits to various members of the Le Mesurier clan in the Channel Islands, the family continued to favour the convenience and familiarity of the Norfolk coast, a fortnight in a large rented home in Sheringham being Halliley Sr's equivalent of Mr Pooter's 'Good old Broadstairs!'[21] John never really hankered after more exotic kinds of vacation; he was happy enough wandering around the English countryside, gazing lazily out at the sea and sharing some precious days alone with his parents.

The other highlights of this and subsequent summers consisted of whatever visits he could engineer to the theatre, whether the productions were local (apart from his own town's elegant venues, he was also very fond of Norwich's Theatre Royal) or in London. It did not much matter to him if what was on offer was a play, a musical or a Variety show; he just adored the experience of being there in the auditorium when the lights went down to watch another evening's entertainment unfold. Among his West End experiences during such periods were a trio of Ben Travers farces – *Thark*, *Plunder* and *A Cup of Kindness* – at the Aldwych; the first production of *Show Boat* at the Theatre Royal Drury Lane; Gladys Cooper in *The Secret Flame* at the Playhouse; and the Jack Buchanan musical *That's a Good Girl* at the Hippodrome. He also managed to take in rougher and readier affairs such as a vaudeville bill at the Coliseum headed by the vivacious Miss Fannie Ward ('Sixty-one years old, yet looks and acts like sixteen') and a knockabout revue at the Alhambra Leicester Square, and he even witnessed a woman apparently being sawn in half by Horace Goldin, 'The Royal Illusionist', at the Metropolitan, Edgware Road.

He also seized on every chance that he had to visit Bury's 'flea pit to beat all flea pits' – the Central Cinema, just around the corner from his father's office, in Hatter Street, where the auditorium was still lit by gaslight and the projectionist would commence each event by emerging from behind the screen and walking slowly up the stairs towards his booth, turning down all of the lights as he progressed, thus leaving behind an audience in total darkness waiting excitedly for 'our dose of glorious escapism'.[22] Favourite features of the time included such late silent movies as Alfred Hitchcock's dark 1927 thriller *The Lodger* (starring matinée idol Ivor Novello as the suspicious stranger), Fritz Lang's hauntingly futuristic fantasy (released later the same year) *Metropolis*, Raoul Walsh's rather 'racy' adaptation of Somerset Maugham's short story *Sadie Thompson* (John was drawn especially to the alluring performance of Gloria Swanson in the title role) and E.A. Dupont's glamorous 1929 melodrama *Piccadilly*, as well as such early 'talkies' as Hitchcock's 1929 suspense *Blackmail* and, the same year, the dashing Ronald Colman star-vehicle *Bulldog Drummond*. John found himself increasingly fascinated by the stellar performers in these various spectacles: he studied their styles and personalities, their distinctive skills and sources of appeal, and he would fantasise a little more each summer about one day emulating their achievements.

Once the holidays were over, however, such bright dreams were brusquely dimmed as John made his way reluctantly back to Sherborne. There would never be any sense of progression as the next academic year began. There was just the same old gnawing realisation that he had enjoyed his time away, but was now facing yet another long and hard slog back at school.

He did form a few friendships there, but none of them were particularly close; the initial loneliness never really went away, and he much preferred being the discreetly affable outsider to immersing himself in any of the close-knit little cliques. There were several extra-curricular House societies, and one or two of them focused on literary and dramatic concerns: 'The Snuffer Club', for example, was an exclusive twelve-member group that met regularly in the house-master's study to read the plays of Richard Brinsley Sheridan 'in an old-fashioned atmosphere with snuffers and old candlesticks and an empty punch bowl on the table'.[23] As usual, however, there was a rigid pecking-order to ascend before one qualified as eligible for such dubious privileges, and John simply lacked the will to persevere.

He did get the odd chance to act whenever a play or operetta – usually something by Shakespeare or Gilbert & Sullivan – was staged, but even these occasional treats tended to be tarnished by the countless neurotic interventions of Trelawny-Ross, who was worried that the need for some boys to play roles intended for females ('cissy parts', as he called them) would encourage some of them to 'make themselves attractive and develop the airs and graces of sophisticated members of the opposite sex'. Even if such play-acting had 'a bad influence on one in ten', he declared, 'it stands condemned'.[24] The prospect of regular weekend film shows did lift John's spirits briefly, only for them to sag straight back down again when the headmaster ruled that viewing such entertainments too frequently might lead to 'intellectual apathy and laziness'.[25]

Most of the time, therefore, John had to devise his own ways of amusing himself. He managed, for example, to smuggle in to his study a portable gramophone, which he padded with an old sock to muffle the volume as he listened to a few scratchy recordings ranging from Louis Armstrong to Thomas Beecham. He also restarted his autograph collection, guarding against any unwelcome intervention this time around by arranging for his mother to receive any replies and send them on to him sandwiched between copies of *The Tatler* and *Horse & Hound*. Informal games of tennis (which he played, rather well, with one hand slotted casually inside his trouser pocket) and golf (at which he was still very much an enthusiastic novice) became a welcome source of further fun, even though the frivolous nature of his approach was frowned upon by those masters who stopped by every now and then to watch. He kept on hoping that his genuine enjoyment of, and expertise in, cricket would be enough to serve as compelling evidence of his commitment to the all-embracing sporting obsessions of the school. Apart from relishing the matches, he was keen to continue exploiting every opportunity to sink a pint or two in the buffet at Waterloo on his way back from playing away.

Such minor and irregular pleasures became all the more precious as the dreaded Trelawny-Ross became increasingly irascible and eccentric. The housemaster had never been known for his compassion: he seemed to find it hugely amusing, for example, when one of John's fellow pupils, the somewhat incontinent R.W. 'Pongo' Patterson, ran with such force straight into a plate glass dormitory door one dark and chilly night that he sliced off his nose and had to be rushed to hospital ('It was a good nose, too, with a Roman air'[26]). Now he appeared to be getting more cruel and callous as each new term went by, while monitoring the weekly letters home to ensure that no great complaints escaped beyond the boundaries of the school: 'When a small boy gets a pen in his hand and starts to think of home he is capable of the wildest and palpably untrue statements . . .'[27]

Some speculated that the recent antics of another of John's contemporaries, Claude de Crespigny, had nudged him a little nearer to the edge of sanity. The daring de Crespigny had attempted to strike a blow for those who were normally punished for oversleeping by climbing up the Abbey Tower one night and pushing the clock back by twenty precious minutes. Trelawny-Ross, once alerted to this deception, promptly ordered all of the boys to parade out in the quadrangle in their shorts while he bent down and searched for someone with incriminatingly scarred knees. When he failed to find any – as de Crespigny had already slipped away to freedom – he raged about the incident for days.

Whether or not this had genuinely been the catalyst for the marked advance in crankiness, it was certainly evident that the housemaster was now keener than ever to crack the whip. He had always been eager to introduce his own 'fortifying' schemes ('The Scoutmasters' Training Course', for example, was his personal homage to the teachings of Baden-Powell), but it was when he came up with something called 'Ginger Week' that John and more than a few others felt that their strained patience was finally about to snap.

'Ginger Week' was Trelawny-Ross's idea of a 'bracer-up'[28] – seven consecutive days of even stricter discipline, and grimmer austerity, than usual in order to tighten the sinews, shrink the stomachs, sharpen the mind and generally toughen the spirit ('It is better for us all to learn to bite granite than to suck jujubes'[29]). Inspired by 'Kitchener's Test' – the notorious trial of endurance that forced British soldiers serving in India to march for miles and miles through the heat and dust without any man dropping down and out from exhaustion – Trelawny-Ross would devise different physical and mental challenges each year for his boys. Just before the ordeal began, he would scribble down – so excitedly that, in spite of the fact that one of his other jobs was to teach English grammar and composition, he sometimes struggled to make much sense – a set of more prosaic instructions to be displayed as the following house rules:

> Doubling to all meals as far as Dining Hall door. No dirty collars, shoes, hands; no loitering in passages, illegal dress, elbows on table, messiness. Whole Dormitory call me if even a second late in putting out lights. No changing for O.T.C. in any room except Changing Room. Dormitory and Study Inspections daily. Scrupulous tidiness essential as regards beds, slippers, all belongings. Bedclothes to be neatly turned back. Towels tidily hung. Any untidiness punishable, or overcrowding of floor-space or tables. No billiards or ping pong. Everyone will be required to state on his honour that, unless exempted, he has done his daily quarter of an hour of 'toughing up'. Cold water only for washing at night. Hot baths only 5 minutes. [The Kipling poem] 'IF' to be known by end of week. No lime juice or stout! Five minutes only allowed for changing after leaving showers. Regular 'second hall' for those who stay up.[30]

John, predictably, loathed 'Ginger Week' with a deep and abiding passion, considering it to be the most egregious example so far of his housemaster's overzealous pursuit of his outdated and misguided ideals, but at least it never arrived without the proper prior warning. Some of Trelawny-Ross's other 'life lessons', however, proved even more unnerving because they seemed designed to take one entirely by surprise.

During John's final year, for example, his and others' failure to heed the rules and keep the study window near the front door firmly shut each evening so enraged Trelawny-Ross that he devised a typically idiosyncratic form of retribution. Enlisting the assistance of a younger colleague, he waited until the following night and then proceeded to stage a burglary, climbing through the window of his own building and, as he later admitted with evident pride, 'turning the place into a shambles'. Tables were upturned, chair legs were snapped, cups and saucers were smashed and papers and books were scattered all over the floor. He then tiptoed up to the Senior Dormitory, where John and three other boys were fast asleep, and shook them awake with anxious whispers about the supposed break-in below. Ordering them to get up and into their dressing-gowns and arm themselves with hockey sticks or pokers, he made them follow him quietly back downstairs, where – although they were greatly relieved to find that the so-called intruders had flown – they were stunned by the terrible mess that had been made of their study. Trelawny-Ross shook his head, told them to put everything back in order 'lest the servants should panic in the morning', and gave them 'a restrained lecture on the risks of leaving windows open' before sending them back up to bed. Far from coming to regret the incident, he would always boast about it as a fine demonstration of how he always achieved the desired results: 'I am unrepentant.'[31]

John responded to such antics in the only way that he knew: by being his usual passive-aggressive self. He allowed his superiors to feel a sense of achievement simply from making him do no more than go through the motions, and he sat back and watched the clock, kept an eye on the calendar, and counted down the days. He was done with the school long before the school was done with him.

When, after four utterly miserable years, the time finally came – in 1930 – for John to leave, he could not get away fast enough. There was not the slightest feeling of sadness, just a deep sense of regret at having taken so little that was positive from such a privileged education.

Not all of the twenty other boys in his year had been so unhappy there. Indeed, some would later claim not only to have enjoyed it greatly, but also to have benefited from the unorthodox methods employed by Trelawny-Ross[32] – and, it must be acknowledged, most of them went on to enjoy precisely the kind of solid and respectable careers that had always been predicted (including seven businessmen, three teachers, two priests and a solicitor as well as, in the case of Alan Turing, a very eminent Cambridge don). Sherborne had clearly been the wrong sort of place, however, for someone like John Halliley. Years later, when comparing notes with his fellow former public schoolboy, Robert Morley (an Old Wellingtonian), he agreed with his friend that the only way he would ever consent to making a return visit to his old school would be with 'a sub-machine gun and a fully armed platoon'.[33]

Back in 1930, as he travelled home to Bury by train, he merely breathed the deepest of sighs of relief. It was over. There would be no more cross-country runs, no more ice-cold baths, no more beatings and no more mind-numbing studies. What memories he had would be left to fade away from his mind. There was no point in looking back. He just wanted to look forward to what he hoped would be a far more enjoyable future.

CHAPTER III

Delaying Tactics

If you are not too long, I will wait here for you all my life.

'On looking back,' John Le Mesurier would come to say, 'it seems that most of the mistakes in my life have been delaying tactics.'[1] In his early years, as John Halliley, he certainly exhibited a weakness for a wide variety of curiously dilatory techniques.

It did not help that the loose strands of his nascent personality had been woven tightly into a pattern shaped by the warp of English conservatism and the weft of that country's reserve. Both sides of the family tended to be old-style Tory types who saw no reason to tamper with their own great tradition, and both sides were firm believers in the idea that emotions were the kind of things that were generally best kept pent-up and politely private. Young John, therefore, developed into a predictably reactive sort of character, moving dutifully along in the direction that had been designated for him by others, but doing so as sluggishly as seemed humanly possible, still harbouring the secret hope that something – anything – would turn up to 'force' him to wander off course.

The problem was that, by 1930, the tracks looked as straight and as true as ever. He had suffered in silence at not one but two schools that he had hated, completing an expensive education that he now deemed to be more or less worthless. Aged eighteen, he continued to find himself doggedly on course to commence the very kind of adult life that he had not the slightest desire to endure.

His parents, however, were very pleased with how things appeared to have turned out: they now had a nice young Old Shirburnian on their hands, who acted properly and spoke properly and seemed all set to follow in the footsteps of his many distinguished forebears by doing something special in society. They did realise, after the Royal Naval College débâcle, that he was unlikely ever to excel in the armed services, but they could still see him making a name for himself in the Law, and perhaps some position high up in the Conservative Party, thus becoming, in their eyes, an admirable Establishment figure. John, by this stage, had only a sweet dream of trying his luck one day as some kind of entertainer, but, true to form, he said nothing and simply waited for something to happen. 'I was diffident about expressing an ambition which my family would not welcome,' he later explained, 'and so, not having an easy alternative to suggest, allowed myself to be guided ever so gently into the occupation my parents knew best.'[2]

Elton Halliley thus duly pulled some strings and a place was found for John as an articled clerk to a highly respected and long-established firm of solicitors in Bury St Edmunds called Greene & Greene. Founded in 1893 by John Wollaston Greene, one of the family whose members would also include Kenneth (his younger brother and co-director), Benjamin (a Governor of the Bank of England), Edward (a Tory MP), Raymond (an Everest mountaineer and physician), Hugh (a Director-General of the BBC) and the author Graham Greene, as well as the original owners of the local brewery, Greene King, the firm could hardly have offered John a more suitable start as a budding provincial solicitor. Based, in those days, at 58 Abbeygate Street,[3] it was only a short walk away from his home in St Mary's Square, and boasted a very experienced team of lawyers on its books and a large and loyal client base. If he could not learn there, it was felt, he would probably not learn anywhere.

The problem was that John did not really want to learn there or anywhere. Once again, he was doing the wrong thing for himself just to please other people. He tried his best to look for positives, and did at least like the 'feel' and the 'sound' of the place: 'In Greene & Greene the sense of family continuity and thus dependability was reinforced by a name that was easily memorable yet distinguished from the common run of Greens by the addition of a single vowel. Perfect.'[4] He failed, however, to summon up any real enthusiasm for his new supposed vocation.

Most of the paperwork, for example, struck him as unnecessarily pedantic and repetitive. 'Why,' he enquired politely of his superiors, '[does] everything have to be written out at such laborious length and copied (in my best handwriting) so often?'[5] When told that the purpose was to make fully transparent the intricacies of the English law, he wondered to himself why, if that was indeed the case, the process was merely adding to his own chronic sense of confusion. The discomfort that came from having to deal with piles of paperwork, however, paled into insignificance when compared to the excruciating embarrassment that he felt whenever he was sent out to serve someone with a writ. He particularly hated having to 'do the dreadful deed' on any member of his beloved horse-racing community, such as the glum occasion when he was dispatched to stables just outside Newmarket: 'The victim was in a paddock schooling a two-year-old. I went up, thrust the document into his hand, mumbled my apologies and made one of the quickest exits of my career. But I was not fast enough to avoid seeing his hangdog look of total defeat.' Such prosaically harrowing sights would haunt him for the rest of his life.[6]

The one aspect of the job that he did find that he enjoyed involved visiting the local courts, especially the periodic Assizes (when the circuit judge came to town to try the more serious kinds of criminal cases). It was during such occasions that John came to appreciate the ways in which the skills of the barrister overlapped with those of the actor, watching intently as a commanding presence, a polished delivery and a keen sense of timing combined to gain a crucial advantage in many a fiercely contested case. The subtle idiosyncrasies of each visiting judge, which could be discerned from the manner whereby they laboured through the solemn adumbration of elementary principles and reacted calmly, testily or playfully to certain ear-catching assertions, provided another illuminating insight into the various ways that character could blend with cliché. He also found the procession of defendants – who ranged from the most unnerving of murderers to the more mildly aggressive of misdemeanants – endlessly fascinating, studying each one's background and personality as well as their behaviour under interrogation. '[I]f their dramas failed to teach me much about the law,' he later reflected, 'they certainly kept alive my interest in the theatre.'[7]

Most days, however, were spent going through the motions in the office, watching the clock until it was time to escape and relax via a variety of recreations. He played cricket for the Gents of Suffolk, worked on improving his golf handicap and toned up his general fitness with a few casual games of tennis. Piano playing was another enjoyable activity, although, as much as he loved it, he already knew that he would never be good enough to pursue it as a proper profession. He also frequented the local race meetings as often as possible, beginning a lifelong habit of supporting the sport's economy with his 'over-generous backing of tired horses'.[8] Dances were another welcome distraction; John attended several of them at the Athenaeum in Bury in the company of his mother, he formally attired in white tie and tails, she resplendent in full evening dress. They were certainly very diverting affairs for the area, featuring a fixed sequence of formal dances – first the Foxtrot, then the Quickstep, then the Waltz – accompanied by music performed by such leading London bands as Ambrose and his Orchestra, followed by a spirited 'John Peel' march around the dance floor and then a mass exodus to the Supper Room for champagne and bacon and eggs. Amy would sometimes nudge her son into dancing with some well-scrubbed Joan Hunter Dunn type who she had spotted was 'sitting this one out', but, although John – as usual – did as he was told, he was really looking to meet someone very different from the parentally approved sort of feminine norm.

He found her, eventually, on an occasion when he went to a dance – one of the rather grand Suffolk County Balls – on his own. She was tall and slim, with large green eyes, and – just like Matron – much older than John (thirty-six to his eighteen). She was also much, much worldlier, with a disarmingly direct manner of speaking and an excitingly flirtatious sense of fun. He was entranced by her right from the start: 'my goodness, the romance that attached to that girl'.[9] Shy and inadequate though he felt in her presence, he plucked up enough courage to ask her for a dance, did his best to engage her in conversation and managed to depart at the end of the evening with her telephone number, determined to see her again.

In later years, when recalling this person, he would make a point of never naming her. Judging from the few hints he did give – 'the child of a wealthy brewing family' who kept her 'in fine style in a moated house deep in the country'[10] – it might be tempting to assume that she was related to one of his bosses at Greene & Greene, but there was another Suffolk family around at the time that fitted the bill rather more neatly. The aristocratic Tollemache family also owned a local brewery – the Ipswich-based Tollemache's Breweries, which would later merge with Cobbold & Co. to form Tollemache & Cobbold, now much better known as Tolly Cobbold – and lived in fine style in a historic moated manor house in the country – Helmingham Hall in

Helmingham, a village about fourteen miles outside Stowmarket. It seems more than likely, therefore, that this mystery woman was actually one of the Tollemaches.

One has, of course, to be circumspect about indulging in any speculation as to the woman's identity, but, of all the female members of that family who were in the area at the time, the most plausible candidate is the Hon. Dorothy Clare Tollemache. Born in Bury St Edmunds in 1895, she would have been exactly the right age and would have been living in the right region of England in 1931. Although she had been married (to a man named Arthur Durling) for a decade, she was now estranged from her husband and was back on the high-class party circuit both in London and out and about in the country, where she usually used Helmingham Hall as her main base.[11] Later divorced, she would remarry on two more occasions and settle down eventually in Mayfair, where she died in 1949, aged just fifty-four, from a brain tumour. If this glamorous, green-eyed and very self-confident character was indeed John's mystery woman, she would certainly have fitted the image of the alluringly mature female figure of his teenage dreams.

John's parents, upon learning of this sudden infatuation, were quick to voice their disapproval. She had evidently acquired a certain 'reputation' in polite Bury society for drinking champagne 'as if it were going out of fashion', for being 'arrogantly outspoken' and 'none too discreet in her associations'. For a while, however, nothing could dampen his ardour for this 'dangerous' older woman. They met again at a number of local dances, and as the weeks went by, became sufficiently comfortable in each other's company to arrange more intimate assignations in clubs and restaurants out of town.

Pulsatingly post-pubescent, John longed to turn the fledgling romance into his first real sexual affair, but such hopes were frustrated by two troublesome facts: first, it was still considered in those days that one only properly 'came of age' when one reached twenty-one, and second, even if she agreed to something so deliciously 'illicit' as a tryst with a man still technically considered a minor, it would be hard to find a place where they could keep it appropriately clandestine. John knew that there was little prospect of her smuggling him over the drawbridge and into her bedroom at Helmingham Hall, and there was certainly no chance at all of him taking her back to his disapproving parents' house in St Mary's Square. At least for the moment, therefore, any advances had to remain trapped within a deeply tantalising daydream.

When a chance did finally come along one unusually warm early autumn weekend, John would find to his chagrin that his desire was no match for his diffidence. He had just bought himself his first car – a smart little second-hand bullnosed Morris – and was making good use of it travelling around the county playing cricket in his spare time for the Gents of Suffolk. Following close of play at a little ground on the coast, he felt in the mood, having hit more than his fair share of boundaries, to do something daring. He got into his car and drove straight off to the nearby hotel – the Felix, on the Promenade in Felixstowe – where he knew that the object of his affections kept a permanent suite ('because her family had built the place'[12]). Relieved to find her there on her own and, unusually, still free for the rest of the evening, he took her to dinner, flirted for longer than ever before, and then waited in vain for her to get up, take his hand and guide him up to her bed.

She failed, however, to be quite as 'forward' as her reputation had suggested, while he failed to summon up the nerve to make a move of his own. He drained the last drop of his brandy, bid her an awkward and reluctant farewell and got back into his car. The vehicle, however, broke down soon after he had departed, and, not knowing what else to do in the circumstances, he made his way back in the dark to the hotel and up to the door of her suite. Somewhat surprised but amused by his return, she took him in, gave him a drink and chatted to him for an hour or so. After once again waiting in vain for something to happen and being too nervous to respond to any possible signs, he settled down on a sofa and drifted off slowly to sleep.

Feeling deeply disappointed with himself the following morning, John fixed his car, kissed her goodbye and drove slowly home to Bury to face a frosty reception from his parents. 'I couldn't quite understand it,' he would say, 'as I had done nothing wrong. Or so it seemed to me. But parental disapproval – all the worse for remaining unspoken – troubled my conscience.'[13] He was greatly relieved, in the circumstances, to be obliged to leave again soon after in order to play in a two-day cricket match in Colchester against a team of soldiers from the Black Watch. The outing went rather well: opening the innings, he scored a total of fifty-three runs, joined the others for a sumptuous formal dinner in a grand country house and then got very, very drunk.

When, once again, he returned to St Mary's Square, he found that the mood of chilly disapproval had warmed up slightly into one of discreetly pink-cheeked curiosity: a very expensive-looking hat box from Lock's of St James's was waiting for him in a prominent position on the hallstand. Upon opening it, he found a grey trilby inside, along with a note from his female friend, inviting him to wear it in memory of her father, who had always sported one just like it. Two days later, another, even more surprising, gift from her arrived: a glamorous-looking, silky-coated, black-eyed Saluki dog, delivered directly from Bury station, who promptly took up residence in front of the fire in the drawing room, with her long and slender legs crossed elegantly rather like a canine version of Lady Diana Cooper. John named her 'Vanity', because, like the woman who had sent her, she seemed so calmly aware of her own beauty, and he let her sleep at the foot of his bed.

The messages that accompanied these gifts, though clearly kind and affectionate, made him realise that the dalliance would never develop into anything like a full-blown affair. He wondered whether she had been testing him, seeing how precocious he might prove himself to be, or perhaps she had never really wanted to do more than have some harmless fun with a much younger man, but, whatever the reason for the failure of a few hugs and kisses to lead to something more memorably and meaningfully intimate, John treated the gifts as a sign that it was time, at least in her eyes, for the two of them to move on. Sure enough, she soon started spending more and more of her time in London, where she already had an apartment, and, after a period of regretful introspection, he returned to escorting his mother to the local dances.

It would be seven long years before he set eyes on the woman of his dreams again, in 1938, but, even then, his diffidence conspired to defeat him: 'She was walking in the park near Rotten Row with a mixed assembly of dogs,' he would recall. 'She still looked beautiful, though slightly deranged. But shyness and confusion deterred me from speaking to her. She seemed entirely alone with her animals. I hope she had some kind of happiness within herself'.[14]

It was a sad and lonely time for John, back in Bury St Edmunds towards the end of 1931, but, to those around him, he stayed his usual stoical self, never giving anything away apart from the odd hint as to the depths of his inner ennui. He grew rather more cavalier about his health, drinking more beer and a wider range of spirits during his leisure hours and (exacerbating what was destined to become another one of his lifelong habits) smoking as many as ninety-two cigarettes a day. He also started suffering intermittently from psoriasis – a fairly non-contagious skin condition, causing rapid skin cell reproduction resulting in red, dry patches of thickened skin, usually affecting the elbows, knees and scalp – which, he would later say with typically mordant wit, tended to be triggered by two things in particular: 'working and not working'.[15] He was still only nineteen years of age, but suddenly he looked older; some of his youthfulness seemed to have drained away.

Trying hard to put up with the daily grind at Greene & Greene, dragging himself through deed after deed, drafting basic contracts, considering minor cases of tort or malfeasance, processing the odd *nolle prosequi* and delivering bundles of documents to court, he drifted on, much as he had done at school, without drawing on more than the minimum amount of energy or enthusiasm. Ironically, however, his indolence was helped, in this environment, by the fact that his slow-moving and somewhat saturnine demeanour rather suited the role of a solicitor. It lent him an aura of seriousness and sobriety, even gravitas, that suggested he was always thinking deep and troublingly complicated thoughts even when, which was the case more often than not, he was actually pondering which horse to back in the 3.45 at Newmarket. Being an articled clerk was, in a way, his first role as an actor. Even though he did not really understand the part, he none-theless wore the right clothes, said the right kind of things in the right kind of tones and generally did enough to make any potential doubters around him suspend their disbelief.

The idea of acting – 'proper' acting – was something that he simply could not shake out of his head. It had crept up on him slowly but steadily when he was still at school at Sherborne – the sheer enjoyment of being a spectator at the theatre or cinema had bred first a keen respect for his favourite performers and then a nagging desire to join them – and the dull routine at Greene & Greene served only to intensify the secret ambition. His ears certainly pricked up when he heard that another local solicitor, a wealthy man named John Baxter-Somerville (known to all in the business as 'JB'), was becoming increasingly active as a theatrical entrepreneur, founding a repertory company in Croydon and investing in a wide variety of other dramatic ventures, but, much to his frustration, the opportunities to meet such an excitingly hybrid figure proved few and far between. He remained, nonetheless, undaunted in spite of his isolation, attending as many plays as he could, watching all of the new movies and devouring every last detail in all of the latest magazines devoted to the stage and the screen. The fascination, though furtive, was fierce as he tried to envision the kind of figure, in such a world, that he might one day become.

A variety of potential templates were pondered as he ploughed on through the piles of paperwork. There was the tall, dark and handsome British matinée idol, typified by the likes of Ivor Novello, Owen Nares, Gerald du Maurier and Jack Buchanan, as well as affable character actors such as Nigel Bruce and A.E. Matthews, and crafty West End farceurs like one of his current favourites, Tom Walls. In truth, he was still not sure what kind of actor he wanted to be, or, more pointedly, what kind of actor he had the capacity to be. He just knew what he liked, and had a vague sense of what might suit him. The problem was that he lacked any opportunity to assess his own potential. A modest local amateur dramatic society would have been an ideal place for him to sample the art and the atmosphere and see how things developed, but, although Bury St Edmunds did boast such an organisation (Reginald Hall – the father of Sir Peter – was an enthusiastic current member), he was advised by his parents not to take part until properly 'settled' in his day job as a solicitor.

His parents, in their usual discreet way, were actually somewhat concerned about him. As much as they wanted him to succeed as a solicitor, they could see that he was far from passionate about the profession. Both father Elton and grandfather Charles had begun their legal careers brightly and briskly, rising rapidly up the ranks as they impressed colleagues and clients alike with their calm competence and clear thinking. John, in contrast, seemed strangely languid, which some people took for a sign of preternatural self-assurance, but which struck his parents as worrying evidence of his ongoing aimlessness. The Halliley household, however, had never been an environment in which such problems were dealt with head-on; it was far more normal for all concerned to keep on circling each other slowly and cautiously, prodding and probing gently and politely for hints of any troubles that might lurk somewhere or other within. There were therefore no tense interventions over the breakfast table, and no anxious inquisitions over sherry after work. Amy and Elton merely continued to ask John how 'things' were going, and John continued to respond with a pleasant-sounding but non-committal reply.

Elton, still hoping to glimpse something of the budding Conservative activist in his son, tried to engage with him on the safer, impersonal level of contemporary party politics, inviting his opinions on such topics as the rise in unemployment, the problems facing first the Labour Government and then (following on from the inconclusive 1931 General Election) the coalition National Government, the best policy regarding the future economic unity of the Empire, the drafting of the Land Utilisation Bill, the prominent role of press barons like the Lords Beaverbrook and Rothermere, and the various strengths and weaknesses of Stanley Baldwin as a Tory leader. Once again, however, John seemed disinclined to respond with much more than a pleasant-sounding but non-committal reply. Although Elton did manage to persuade his son to accompany him to the odd Tory event – including a valedictory drinks party in honour of the outgoing leader of the local Conservative Association, who happened to be a gentleman named Arthur Wilson[16] – he waited in vain for John to undergo some kind of life-changing political epiphany.

He would be a little more open with his godmother, Kathleen Long, who was now based in London and working as a teacher at the Royal College of Music as well as performing professionally as a concert pianist. Having always been a kind and trusted confidante, rather less ready than the Hallileys to regard any expression of emotion as 'bad form', she was happy now to have John visit whenever he wished. Attending a number of her public appearances – there were several recitals at the Wigmore Hall as well as recording sessions for the BBC and a role at one of Henry Wood's annual Proms – he relaxed a little in her company. As he chatted with uncharacteristic animation about her career in particular and artists and entertainers in general, she began to sense where his real interests might reside. Although he did not go so far as to admit an ambition to become part of this rich and exciting metropolitan culture, there was enough brightness in his eyes as he spoke to make her suspect that such a dream was hovering somewhere close within. She did not think to interfere – it was not the done thing – but she monitored her restless but dutiful godson discreetly from a distance, hoping that a positive, and painless, solution could somehow still be found.

It was a case, once again, of waiting patiently for something to happen. After enduring his first full year at the solicitor's office, John seemed to withdraw into himself more deeply than ever, 'lying doggo' whenever possible and drifting through each day in a heavy-lidded daze. Among his current ostensible concerns at Greene & Greene were a long-running tenancy dispute at a farm just outside town, an infuriatingly complicated query relating to the position and rights of a tithe owner in the nearby village of Long Melford and, no less sensationally, an alleged contravention of the Wart Disease of Potatoes Order of 1923 by a small local firm of seed potato merchants.[17] None of them left much of a trace on the brain as they passed through his eyes and his ears. He was far too preoccupied with thoughts of how Noël Coward's play *Private Lives* was faring on its debut run on Broadway, why the critics had been so cool about Alfred Hitchcock's new movie *Rich and Strange*, why the MCC had recently increased the regulation height of stumps by another inch and how the England cricket team might best win back the Ashes.

Another whole year crawled by like this. Only then, early in 1933,[18] did the quietly desperate John finally decide that not even he could wait indefinitely for Fate to intervene. After weeks of anxious prevarication, often mumbling the odd revealing comment before abruptly interrupting himself, he did what for such a long time he had half dreamed and half dreaded doing: 'I summoned the courage to tell my parents that the law was about to lose an unpromising recruit.'[19] He confessed to them that, grateful though he was for all of their help and support in funding his education and finding him a career, he was simply not suited to being a solicitor. Hesitantly, he went on to admit that, as rash and as wild as it might sound, a career in acting was what he really craved. He wanted to train, he wanted to learn the craft and he wanted to see how far whatever talent he possessed would take him. He acknowledged that it was probably imprudent and immature, and most certainly not what a typical Halliley or Le Mesurier was traditionally supposed to do. He stressed, however, that it was what he felt a need to do, and he just hoped that his parents would indulge him.

Elton and Amy sat listening to all of this in silence. While it was not what they had wanted to hear, they had been fearing something like it for quite some time. Although greatly disappointed, they were also realistic enough to know, deep down, that their son was never going to be happy – or, indeed, especially successful – as a solicitor, and, for all of their very conservative habits and expectations, they were most keen to see him find a genuinely engaging vocation. He was about to turn twenty-one and 'come of age', so, they reasoned, it was probably

the right time to accede, however nervously, to his most heartfelt of
wishes. Much to John's relief, therefore, they appeared to receive the
news calmly, exhibiting, he would later say, nothing more revealing in
terms of emotional judgement than a 'weary stoicism'.[20]

With their blessing, he duly resigned from Greene & Greene and,
for the first time in his life, prepared to set off in a direction of his own
design. The many delays, detours and deviations of the past three years
were, at least for now, at an end: he was finally going to try to be an
actor.

CHAPTER IV

Drama School

Hopefulness and nervousness struggling within you,
Dreading that familiar phrase: 'Thank you dear, no more.'

It was late in the summer of 1933 when John Halliley set off to London to begin the great adventure of training to become an actor. His parents, still rather worried about seeing him suddenly veer so far away from the course of a conventional career, had found him relatively cheap but reassuringly salubrious lodgings at 48 Wellington Road, St John's Wood – very close, he was pleased to see, to Lord's cricket ground as well as the appealing open spaces of Regent's Park and Primrose Hill – and he arrived there on a warm and sunny day in the very best of spirits. This, he thought to himself, was what he had always wanted.

The first thing that he did, once unpacked and reasonably settled, was to venture out and take in as many new plays and movies as the West End of London had to offer. There was one of his old role models, Owen Nares, at the Lyric in a sophisticated romantic comedy called *When Ladies Meet*; Robert Douglas and Maisie Darrell at the Haymarket in a popular suspense drama known as *Ten Minute Alibi*; and Edith Evans and Cedric Hardwick at the St James's in a dark little comedy entitled *The Late Christopher Bean*. He also saw the striking cinematic spectacle of a scantily clad Fay Wray wriggling in the palm of a huge hairy hand in the recently released *King Kong* at the Coliseum; the artful German film star Emil Jannings dominating every scene in *The Merry Monarch* at the Empire, Leicester Square; Fredric March, Cary Grant and Carole Lombard in the wartime aviation drama *The Eagle and the Hawk* at the Plaza; and the 'silly ass' specialist Ralph Lynn in Herbert Wilcox's big screen adaptation of the

P.G. Wodehouse story *Summer Lightning* at the Adelphi. Other memorably entertaining events included an open-air performance of *A Midsummer Night's Dream* at the Botanical Gardens, featuring a cast that included Phyllis Neilson-Terry, Jessica Tandy, Robert Atkins and a rather craggy and well-worn thirty-six-year-old Scot called John Laurie; a high-class music hall revue at the Lyceum headed by the self-styled 'Prime Minister of Mirth', George Robey; and, at the Little Theatre in John Adam Street, the debut appearance in Britain of the great radical Italian comic actor Ettore Petrolini.

He enjoyed himself immensely, relishing the richness and immediacy of life in London. For the first time in years, he felt wide awake and eager to make the most of every single day. Suddenly, John Halliley was in a hurry.

He certainly wasted no time in finding a suitable acting school. Having taken advice from friends both of his family and his god-mother Kathleen Long, he decided to audition for the Fay Compton Studio of Dramatic Art rather than the more prestigious Royal Academy of Dramatic Art (RADA) on the grounds that it was smaller, less competitive and 'offered more individual attention to absolute beginners like myself'.[1] Fay Compton – a distinguished and versatile stage and screen performer in her own right, having worked with the likes of Noël Coward, John Gielgud, Ivor Novello and John Barrymore – had set up the studio in 1927 in order to train a wide range of young hopefuls, from budding public speakers to ambitious classical actors. While she continued with her own career (she was starring alongside Ivor Novello at the time in a play called *Proscenium*), her sister, Viola, took primary responsibility for the day-to-day running of the institution. Based at 63 Baker Street, it boasted plenty of celebrity supporters – including several of John's current idols – and an encouragingly high rate of success in terms of students who went on to establish themselves as professionals (about 95 per cent, it was claimed, of each year's intake[2]).

John went there at the end of August to audition before five judges, together with about forty other young hopefuls. He performed his short set of carefully rehearsed pieces, which included his tried and tested Jack Hulbert monologue and a Noël Coward poem, and, to his relief and great delight, was awarded a place on the course. There was little time to celebrate, however, because the first term was due to begin soon after, on Monday 4 September 1933, so he did little but visit a couple more theatres in the West End, wondering as he watched if he, too, was now on his way to the stage.

When the big day arrived, he woke up feeling full of anticipation, rose immediately, washed and dressed as quickly as he could, had a few quick, nervous puffs on a cigarette and then raced out and bounded on to a bus from Wellington Road to Baker Street station. Realising that, even for a keen new student, he was still unfashionably early, he went into a nearby café, where he sat sipping coffee, gazing out through the window and thinking to himself, 'Well, here I am. Whatever happens, I must make the best of it.'[3] Once enough time had passed, he went back out, walked up Baker Street and entered the Studio, where he was greeted by Viola Compton and two of her teacher colleagues, Charles Hickman (an experienced director of straight plays, revues and musical comedies) and Mollie Hartley-Milburn (a somewhat eccentric minor character actor who wore a monocle and rarely stopped talking about her Roman Catholic faith). Of John's twenty-four fellow new students, one was a thin, pale, rather worried-looking man named Alec Guinness, another a taller and considerably more confident and charming individual called Dennis Edwards, and the other twenty-two were young women of various shapes, sizes and personalities. John was excited just to be among them and part of it all. His dream was at last becoming a reality.

The first few weeks seemed to race by as the standard lessons commenced. Each day was shaped by the same basic structure: the mornings were devoted mainly to studying aspects of revue and musical comedy along with such physical skills as tap dancing and mime, and the afternoons tended to focus primarily on understanding and performing Shakespeare and Greek tragedies. The schedule also accommodated regular exercises designed to improve diction, voice production and accents as well as some fencing sessions to prepare the men (and some of the women) for possible action scenes. Not everything suited everyone, but most found something of value even in those elements that seemed to hold the least appeal – students who disliked the dancing, for example, came to appreciate how it might help them with balance and posture – and the general working atmosphere was encouragingly positive. John, although still essentially the same quiet and diffident character that he had been before, began to grow more self-confident and at least a little more outgoing, relishing the challenge that each new exercise posed.

As he worked and socialised with the other students, he became particularly intrigued by Alec Guinness. A big-eared, sad-eyed former advertising copywriter who had only turned to the Fay Compton Studio after a scholarship to RADA had fallen through, he looked like an undernourished version of Stan Laurel – jam sandwiches and baked beans appeared to be his only regular source of sustenance. He seemed, moreover, startlingly impoverished for someone so well-spoken, sometimes arriving barefoot to save wear and tear on his one pair of smart leather shoes. Once the real work began, however, the great extent of his potential was undeniable. Guinness, in turn, was very impressed by what he saw of John's efforts, later recalling those initial performances as 'brilliant and accomplished': 'He was a delightful actor, with a lighter and wittier touch than anyone I can think of.'[4] As actors, the two men differed markedly in their approach to a role: whereas Guinness seemed to lose himself in a character, divining alien qualities in a quietly inscrutable manner, John seemed to find and fix on an aspect of himself, seeking connections and accentuating common traits in a calm and logical process. The difference produced a complement instead of a clash, with Guinness bringing to scenes something slyly and beguilingly exotic, and John supplying something believably typical and familiar. Guinness, for example, found that the bitter isolation of his Shylock worked well when pitted against the bland authority of John's Antonio during a session in which the pair worked together on dialogue from *The Merchant of Venice*. They were not, in other words, rivals; they were more like a subtle kind of double-act, each one enriching the other's brand of realism, and it was inevitable, as a consequence, that a deep sense of mutual respect should progress throughout the course of the academic year.

They also developed as friends, finding that they had almost as much in common as people as they had in contrast as performers. The London-born Guinness was two years younger than John and hailed from nothing like as rich and grand a family background, yet he still identified with the same kind of British upper-middle-class culture and values. He had endured a modest sort of prep school (Pembroke Lodge in Surrey) and then a minor public school (Roborough in Eastbourne), and had observed enough of the mores of the upper classes to draft an image of the 'proper gentleman' that he strove to emulate. What made the budding relationship rather more intriguing was that John was the very kind of figure that Alec, at that stage in his life, could not quite manage to be. Whereas John was very much the 'real deal' as far as class and pedigree were concerned, Alec, the illegitimate son of an unknown father, remained something of a social enigma even to himself. Christened Alec Guinness de Cuffe, he had later been known as Alec Stiven or Alec de Cuffe before assuming the surname of Guinness on the grounds, according to one version of a much-debated story, that he believed his mother might once have slept with Elton Halliley's great friend and political colleague, Walter Guinness;[5] hence he was as insecure about his 'real' identity as John seemed subtly but solidly assured. Both men, therefore, had something to learn from, and admire about, each other. Sharing a dry and mischievous wit as well as a somewhat reserved demeanour, they relaxed fairly easily in each other's company.

The only other man in the troupe, Dennis Edwards, represented no real threat to the other two. Not only was he younger, being Alec's junior by two years and John's by four, but he also seemed a little more limited in terms of his abilities, and his eminently affable nature made him a well-liked supporting player. Among the numerically dominant female contingent, an attractive young woman named Marcia Franklin tended to interact most effectively with her male counterparts, while another couple of performers called Betty Dennis and Juliet Minchin showed some promise as versatile character actors, but most of the others struggled to find a character or context with which they could truly impress. The three men, as a minority, were therefore more or less guaranteed prominent roles in every exercise, and, as a consequence, they tended to dominate most of the sessions.

John found the whole experience, week in, week out, extremely absorbing. Lessons on film technique – involving such basic procedures as blocking (choreographing one's movements in relation to the camera positions and shooting script), projecting for microphones and dealing with cuts, reaction shots and close-ups – fascinated him, as did the instruction he received on the distinct skills required for different sizes and types of theatrical environments. He even had fun when he was struggling with certain tasks, such as the tap-dance routine from *42nd Street* that he performed, rather awkwardly, alongside Alec Guinness, later commenting drily: 'We were not too good.'[6] The positive impact that the training was having on him – not only as a performer but also as a person – was evident to his parents when he visited them during a brief mid-term break. He not only looked healthier and happier, but there was also now a calmness about him, a clarity of purpose, that seemed such a pleasant contrast to the mumbling and frustratingly evasive character who used to clock in and out each day at Greene & Greene.

This particular visit, however, unfortunately overlapped with the announcement that Elton's father, Charles, had just passed away in his eighty-third year, on 15 March 1934, at his home in Bruton in Somerset. Although John had always found his grandfather's weakness for tall tales very amusing, he was genuinely saddened by the news. Accompanying his parents to the West Country for the funeral, he regretted the fact that whatever accomplishments he might now achieve would not go on to be exaggerated and embellished by the most memorable storyteller of his youth. There was barely any time for mourning, however, as he was due back in London the following day, with plenty of lines to learn before resuming his studies, and so, apologising for his haste, he paid his respects to his grandmother and other relations and then raced off to catch the next train bound for Paddington.

Back at the Fay Compton Studio, the work was growing increasingly intense as winter gave way to spring, with the students starting to concentrate on trying to master the various speeches, scenes and special routines that were designed to assess how far, by the end of their first year, each of them had progressed. Probably the most substantial of John's exercises was a role in a scene from John Balderston's 1929 time-travel-themed play *Berkeley Square*, playing a character who had recently been brought to life first on Broadway and then in a Hollywood adaptation by the very urbane English leading man Leslie Howard. Feeling fairly comfortable in this context (as he felt rather similar to Howard both in looks and demeanour), he rehearsed the piece for several weeks until he was quietly confident it was set to impress ('I thought at the time I was quite good in this'[7]). He was far more apprehensive about the singing role he had been handed in an excerpt from John Gay's eighteenth-century operetta *Polly*, playing the bass part of a pirate named Vanderbluff, but, once again, he laboured long and hard until the performance seemed much better than he had first expected. His confidence in general increased steadily as the sessions continued, and, as the day of his debut in front of a 'proper' audience drew near, the sense of optimism was encouragingly strong.

The Studio's rather glamorous and well-advertised annual public matinée duly took place on 19 July 1934. It was a nerve-wracking but also an exhilarating experience for each of the students who took part, because, as in previous years, Fay Compton had persuaded an impressive range of influential friends to attend, including a number of famous actors, directors and musicians whom all of the participants had long admired. Here then was a chance to catch the eye of one's idols, perhaps even to impress them enough to win a personal introduction and, just possibly, an invaluable recommendation. Here was also the opportunity to compete for a range of 'official' prizes and plaudits that were guaranteed to improve any budding performer's CV. This was, in short, the first great moment for those who felt that they had the talent to step out into the spotlight and prove that they really were actors.

Alec Guinness and John Halliley were two of those who, according to contemporary reports, proceeded to do just that, exhibiting enough of the poise, the power and the personality to suggest they might possess the potential to progress further. There were no slip-ups or stumbles; they, along with one or two of their female counterparts, seemed to grow as performers as the production went on. As they joined the rest of the company to take their final bows, they looked relieved but also excited. The applause was long and loud. People seemed to believe in them. They now seemed to believe in themselves. A few days later, John, like Alec, received his first mention (multiple mentions in fact) in the press as an actor in a detailed review of the event that appeared in the trade newspaper *The Stage*:

Miss Jessie Matthews, Mr Leslie Henson, Miss C.L. Anthony, Mr John Gielgud, Mr Ronald Adam, Mr Alfred Hitchcock and Mr Ivor Novello were among the judges at the annual public performance by the students of the Fay Compton Studio of Dramatic Art at the Rudolf Steiner Hall last Thursday afternoon. There was a large audience, and the proceedings lasted more than four hours. . . .

As is usual on these occasions, the programme had been devised to show off the full quality of the students' training in stage and screen, and even Variety work. Nor was the auxiliary art of fencing forgotten, an excellent sixteenth century rapier and dagger fight (Mary Hudson – Jasmine Budd) being included. The list of items covered a wide field, starting off, as it did, with an excerpt from Gay's comic opera *Polly*, and finishing with musical comedy numbers – in which Beryl Ellis did notably well in a *contredanse*. An excerpt from Greek Epic, Hector's Farewell to Andromache, was capitally done, with Dennis Edwards and Audrey Olorenshaw in the chief parts, and Rosemary Cameron-Rose and Marcia Franklin distinguishing themselves in the classic chorus as spoken thoughts.

John Halliley (Vanderbluff), Marcia Franklin (Jenny Diver) and Eileen Forman (Polly) put in good work in the *Polly* excerpt; and Juliet Minchin was funny as the Irish servant in the one-act comedy *The Fourteenth Guest*. We liked, too, the expressive work of Alec Guinness and Diana King in a little mime tragedy *The Showman*, built on a story by Compton Mackenzie. A short sketch, *A la Gare du Nord*, played in French, gave evidence of good accent and Gallic gesticulation; while eighteenth century elegance in manner and costume were pleasingly displayed in the first act of *Berkeley Square*.

Dennis Edwards (Tom), Jasmine Budd (Miss Pettigrew), Alec Guinness (Mr Throstle), Eleanor de Vesian, Rosemary Cameron Rose, John Halliley, Reno Spencer and others acted very naturally in this, and the change of period was well done. In the first act of *Romeo and Juliet*, Mr Guinness, as Mercutio, gave an excellent performance of the Queen Mab speech. Miss Olorenshaw was a pretty, well-spoken Juliet, and Mr Edwards a picturesque Romeo. Eleanor de Vesian followed the Terry tradition as the Nurse, and other praiseworthy performances came from Betty Dennis (a capital chorus), Jasmine Budd, John Halliley, Joan Evans, Mary Dunne, Juliet Minchin (Tybalt) and Audrey Ortner.

Prominent among the other items was the second act of *The Street Singer*, with clever Betty Dennis in the part of Marie. John Halliley (Bonni), Mary Hudson, Mr Guinness, Mr Edwards, Mary Dunne and Dennis Venables were among others in a quite sound performance. . . .

For the rest, Susan Ward pleased everybody in a song and step hornpipe, and the Misses Ortner, Dennis, Hudson and Eileen Ritchings danced artistically. Betty England was another good dancer in a tarantella. The performance, as a whole, was notably free from amateurishness, and another good point was that the performers could be distinctly heard. Both elocution and enunciation were eminently praiseworthy. Miss Viola Compton had arranged the varied programme, which was no light task. Certificates of Fellowship: Mary Hudson, R. Cameron-Rose, Juliet Minchin, Marcia Franklin, Myrtle

Yapp, Mary Dunne, John Halliley, Betty Dennis, Alec Guinness. Certificates of Merit: Joan Evans, Jasmine Budd, Diana King, Joan Butchart, Dennis Edwards. The special Fay Compton prize for the best all-round performance of the afternoon was won by Alec Guinness. Certificates of Fellowship are awarded to those members whose merits in the judges' opinion entitle them to undertake professional engagements.[8]

Once the sense of exhilaration associated with the event had dissipated, it was time for each performer to sit down in a cool hour, reflect on the feedback and consider what the future might hold. Some started to suffer from self-doubt; others from misplaced faith. Those who had been deemed to be as good, if not better, than they thought they were would now have to weigh up their options. It was a time of difficult decisions for students and teachers alike.

Most of the young women in that Fay Compton production would end up fading fairly quickly from view as far as the acting world was concerned, but the men fared much better. Dennis Edwards would go on to carve out a long and steady career for himself treading the boards in the theatre, and would also make the odd contribution to movies (including a minor role, as 'head valet', in the Marilyn Monroe–Laurence Olivier vehicle *The Prince and the Showgirl*) as well as numerous appearances on television as a guest in such popular series as *Z Cars*, *The Avengers*, *Doctor Who*, *Grange Hill*, *Bergerac* and *Minder*.[9] There would also, eventually, be an ironic change of career for one of the teaching staff: after falling on hard times as an actor and tutor during the early 1950s, Mollie Hartley-Milburn ended up being hired (partly out of pity) by Alec Guinness as his secretary (or, as her long-suffering employer often preferred to put it, 'alleged' secretary[10]).

Alec Guinness and John Halliley, on the other hand, had emerged from the process as the two main stars of the show. Both of them, due in part to the pull of ambition and in part to the prospect of poverty, decided to leave the Studio immediately and launch themselves straight into full-time professional acting. Alec, emboldened by the end of term prize (a miniature edition of Shakespeare's collected works donated by Jessie Matthews) and the encouragement of John Gielgud, started out as an understudy in a West End play before being recruited by Gielgud himself to play the relatively minor but by no means irrelevant role of Osric in his new production of *Hamlet*. John, meanwhile, received a tip from one of his old teachers that there was a place open for him in a repertory company – the Millicent Ward Repertory Players – based in Edinburgh, and so, feeling full of enthusiasm, he packed his bags, boarded a train and travelled up to Scotland.

Now he really was on his way. He was going to work as an actor.

CHAPTER V

A Jobbing Actor

Old situations,
New complications,
Nothing portentous or polite;
Tragedy tomorrow,
Comedy tonight!

John arrived in Edinburgh early in the autumn of 1934. Although fully aware that he was still very much the unfinished article, he believed that he would now learn faster 'on the job' rather than sitting in the classroom. A run in repertory was, he felt sure, the break for which he had been waiting.

The repertory system, which had taken shape in the latter part of the previous century, was a common way in those days for budding actors to get a decent chance to blossom. While providing a local community with a steady succession of plays, the system also enabled each actor to shake off that normal layer of social self-consciousness, become absorbed in the practical minutiae of the art and acquire the degree of discipline required to power a proper career. John could hardly wait for the experience to commence.

His company, the Millicent Ward Repertory Players, was relatively new on the scene (having been established in 1932) and was associated usually – though not exclusively – with Edinburgh's Palladium Theatre in East Fountainbridge. Millicent Ward, a native of the city, had learned her craft under the supervision of Sir Frank Benson, a distinguished English actor-manager who had been one of the pioneers of the repertory movement, before moving to Canada in 1914, where she had a spell as a member of the Empress Stock Company in Vancouver. She later travelled widely across North America, acquiring further practical experience both as a performer and producer in vaudeville as well as conventional theatre. Having returned to Edinburgh at the start of the 1930s, she worked for the city's innovative Studio Theatre group (which was much admired for its readiness to nurture creativity and diversity as well as for its aim to establish a closer relationship with its audience) before setting up a company of her own.

The Millicent Ward company, like the typical repertory troupe, was a very compact and close-knit unit in which everybody's contribution was really made to count. It consisted of just seven resident members: a middle-aged leading man and leading lady, a male and female 'juvenile' for the younger parts, an experienced male and female character actor for the older parts and a soubrette for sundry other roles (Millicent Ward herself would sometimes appear if an additional performer was required). The dominant figure in this particular company was an actor called Henry Ford – one of those loveable rogues known informally as 'Actor Laddies' – who was notorious for his booming delivery, wicked sense of humour and sure grasp of every scene-stealing trick in the book. The artistic director who presided over the group was a man named Patrick Desmond, who was noted for his distinctive style of dress – bespoke plus-fours and yellow woollen stockings – and his briskly efficient approach to staging plays in rapid succession. John, now aged twenty-two, had been recruited to be one of the resident juveniles, and no time was wasted before he was put to work helping to perform four new plays every month in return for a wage of £3 10s a week.

Being a new member of a repertory company in an unfamiliar town often entailed having to brave some distinctly basic, if not downright dilapidated, temporary living conditions in one of the area's local guest houses. Stories of such cheap and cheerless places would be common among those actors who went through the ordeal during their early days on the stage. Bernard Miles, for example, would recall staying at the kind of digs in which the substitute for a proper lavatory was a humble china bowl hidden beneath the bed: 'Please don't replace the chamber pot after use,' his host requested loudly as he prepared to retire on his first night in situ, 'as the steam rusts the springs.'[1] Another rep-ripened performer, Arthur Lane, would recount the time when he returned to his accommodation unexpectedly one afternoon in order to pick up a forgotten prop for an imminent matinée, only to find his landlady sprawled stark naked on the kitchen table with a milkman poured on top: 'I do apologise,' she later told him as she was serving supper. 'You must think I'm a terrible flirt!'[2] John was fortunate in comparison, finding a room in a small but comfortable guest house in Lauriston Place, situated conveniently a mere couple of streets away from the Palladium, where the friendly landlady spoilt him with three cooked meals each day for the modest all-in charge of thirty-five shillings a week. 'Perhaps,' he later reasoned, 'it was my helpless look . . .'[3] The only negative was the landlady's husband, a frequently inebriated Glaswegian who sometimes rolled up his sleeves and threatened to assault her; she usually kept him firmly in check by hurling that great Scottish speciality, a plate of hot fried bread, full in his face.

Even if he had ended up in much worse accommodation, John would no doubt have felt that any hardship was more than worth it. In those days, being in a repertory company meant regular employment, a modest but steady wage and the invaluable chance to acquire far more practical experience of the ups and downs of being an actor than one could have hoped to get in years of trying to graduate from understudy jobs in the West End of London. The standard preparatory schedule in rep for the conventional three-act play involved an initial read-through, plotting of moves and basic direction on a Tuesday, followed on Wednesday by a run-through of the first act and a blocking of the second act, on Thursday by a run-through of the second act and a blocking of the final act, and on Friday by a run-through of the final act and then the play as a whole. There would be another full run-through over the weekend (usually in casual clothes to avoid any wear and tear on the costumes), a proper dress rehearsal on Monday afternoon and then, at about 8 pm on the same day, the opening night. This process was repeated each subsequent week for the next play while the current one was being performed every evening, along with a matinée every Wednesday. The season as a whole would normally stretch out over the course of a six-month period, but could easily be extended for much of the year.

It was, therefore, a very intensive and draining process that demanded real and consistent discipline from all of the actors involved, but it was also a remarkably effective way for a young performer to master the basic elements of his or her profession. New lines had to be memorised as rapidly as possible (about forty minutes' worth, or more, each day) while old ones were wiped away, a fresh set of movements had to be mapped out methodically and each new characterisation had to be captured and crystallised within a matter of a couple of days. There was simply no time for serious neuroses to develop or nagging doubts to intrude. There was always another play to plan, another challenge to overcome, another opportunity to improve.

Perhaps the most valuable aspect of all in practical terms was the chronic obligation to overcome all kinds of unwelcome obstacles on stage in front of a very attentive audience. There were, for example, a wide range of scenery and prop malfunctions, most often involving doors that either would not open or failed to shut, door knobs that either refused to turn or came straight off in one's hand, and guns that either jammed or went off without so much as an ineffectual 'phut'. Then there were the human errors, including 'drying' and 'corpsing' (when another actor either forgot a line or simply lost concentration and started to giggle uncontrollably) or, more challengingly, a torturous phenomenon known as 'looping the loop' (which was prompted by one actor, usually through fatigue, accidentally missing out a chunk of dialogue and leaping straight ahead to a page or so later in the script, thus prompting his or her colleague to try to intervene, improvise a way to slip the absent details back into the play and then resume the scripted dialogue without repeating what had already been said). Rep would teach young actors such as John to take these trials in their stride. It was one of the reasons why he was so eager to throw himself into his first season.

Contrary to many common accounts,[4] which have suggested that John changed his surname from Halliley to Le Mesurier immediately upon becoming a professional actor, it would actually be three years before he adopted his mother's maiden name for the stage. He was thus billed as plain 'John Halliley' when he made his debut as a professional at the Palladium, in a play (the title of which has long been forgotten) in October 1934. The first published critical notice he would receive in rep came at the start of the following year, on 31 January 1935, in a brief review in the pages of *The Stage*:

> *While Parents Sleep* provides lively entertainment this week [at the Palladium], and is played in spirited style by Millicent Ward's excellent company. Patrick Desmond and John Halliley play in quite the proper spirit as the lively young men, and Dorothy Primrose and

Ruita Dagmar are equally successful. Molly Tapper and Henry Ford are also well in the picture.[5]

He went on to cover more or less every genre during this early run: comedies and tragedies, thrillers and fantasies, tense courtroom dramas and frenzied farces, Shakespeare and Ibsen, Sheridan and Wilde, Molière and Shaw, Congreve and Coward. The range was remarkable and, just as significantly, so was the eclectic nature of the schedule, forcing the actors to suddenly change gear, style and mood on a weekly basis.

John relished the sense of variety. There was never enough time to get bored. Some roles, and some types of play, suited him snugly, and some did not, but he was learning how to keep going, through difficult times as well as good, hiding his weaknesses while accentuating his strengths. It was precisely the kind of education that he had always craved.

Things seemed to get even better when the apparent misfortune of an unplanned break during the long repertory season (caused by complications both legal and logistical following a change in ownership of the Palladium's lease[6]) turned out to be something of a blessing in disguise, because it allowed him to accept an exciting short-term engagement. John had the great chance to work, as his friend Alec Guinness was already doing, for John Gielgud, who, following the huge critical and commercial success of his long-running London production of *Hamlet* (which had been described by one contemporary critic as 'the key Shakespearean revival of its period'[7]), was now taking the play out on tour. Unsurprisingly, there was no prominent role for John – he was hired merely to walk on and off holding a spear, as well as, more dauntingly, to be understudy to Anthony Quayle as Guildenstern – but he was thrilled just to be part of such an illustrious dramatic production. Beginning at Streatham in the spring of 1935, the tour went on to Manchester, Edinburgh and Leeds, among other places, playing to full houses night after night and attracting another great wave of critical plaudits. Throughout every performance, John would stand at the side of the stage and watch Gielgud work, marvelling at his 'cello-like voice' and elegant gestures, and admiring how, when he did make a rare error, he recovered so quickly and with such poise that only an 'insider' would notice. The whole spectacle, in fact, was always fascinating to study, and there were plenty of sound little practical lessons to be learned: 'Apart from observing the mighty and their occasional failings, I acquired some basic knowledge like where to stand before an entrance without being observed from the Upper Circle and how to project the voice beyond the front row when performing in the open air.'[8]

He returned to Edinburgh at the start of the summer, therefore, a rather more thoughtful and technically proficient performer, even if, after sampling some of the glamour that surrounded such a high-profile production, he felt a little flat when he resumed the rushed routine of weekly rep. John had never been much of a fan of the Palladium (which was an old converted cinema) as a building – regarding it as a 'down-at-heel establishment which offended my youthful sense of professional pride by not having a stage door'[9] – and now, having spent some time in a number of the biggest and best venues in Britain, he could not help noticing a few more of its physical flaws. The pressure of work, however, stopped him from dwelling on such matters. Within days of his arrival, he was back on stage: this time in a minor role in a production of J.B. Priestley's latest play, *Dangerous Corner* (the first night of which was brightened by Henry Ford 'whispering' stage directions at his under-prepared colleagues such as: 'Get off, boy, for God's sake; and if the door's not working, try the fireplace!'[10]).

John continued to enjoy his time as part of the company, and only when the season edged towards an end did thoughts of moving on begin to intrude. He sought advice from Patrick Desmond, his director, who suggested that he apply to Oldham Rep. This mystified John; even he knew that Oldham Rep specialised at that time in the kind of 'North Country' plays in which most of the characters spoke in broad regional dialects, something he regarded as 'not at all my forte'.[11] He was willing to try anything, however, so he duly applied and, much to his amazement, was hired.

The large industrial town of Oldham represented something of a culture shock to a young man who had been brought up in the green and pleasant land of the gentle Suffolk countryside. He looked at all of the long and dark sett or cobblestoned terraced streets, one end seeming to lead straight to the mill and the other to the cemetery – 'They seemed to bury a lot of people in Oldham',[12] he later noted – and wondered why on earth he was there. It took just one week for his employers to wonder the same thing. Cast in a small role in a rather saucy little light comedy by Wilson Collison called *Up in Mabel's Room*, he struggled anxiously through the first couple of days (performing twice nightly) before the lines began to flow more easily and he started to relax. After morning rehearsals on the Thursday, he went to take in a local wrestling match, drank a few beers and returned to his digs for a late lunch followed by a rest, asking his landlady to wake him at 5 pm 'at the latest' to prepare for the next performance. Predictably enough, she forgot; when he did eventually wake up and race off frantically to the theatre, he only arrived in time to hear the stage manager reading out his lines in a very testy-sounding monotone. There was nothing for him to do but sit in his dressing room until the performance was over and wait for the inevitable dismissal. Noël Coward, when told about this incident at a much later date, would merely remark, 'A very sensible choice of play to sleep through, dear boy,'[13] but at the time, as John fled ashen-faced from the scene of his no-show, it felt like a humiliation.

He went back to Bury St Edmunds, retreating into the bosom of his family until the emotional wounds started to heal. There he sat, 'resting', as he listened to his father ponder the future ambitions of another man who had once been thrown out of Oldham – its former Liberal MP, Winston Churchill, who now represented Epping and Woodford for Elton's beloved Tories – and heard his mother recall how enjoyable Kathleen Long's recent pianoforte recital had been when it had been broadcast on the wireless by the BBC.[14] Although he knew that neither parent would ever be so impolite as to chastise him overtly with an audible 'I told you so,' John still dreaded the prospect of one of them (probably his father) casting him a mildly admonitory glance about his idleness, so he did his best to convince both of them – as well as himself – that he was still just an actor between engagements rather than a former solicitor who had tried but failed to escape from the old profession.

After a couple more weeks scouring the ads in *The Stage*, therefore, John finally spotted something that seemed broadly suitable: a manager was looking for actors to help him relaunch a relatively large but struggling repertory company in Sheffield. Eager to resume his fledgling career (remembering the horse-loving Le Mesurier family's advice about remounting as soon as possible after a fall), he sent off an application. After passing a perfunctory audition in a grubby little office in Soho, he set off to South Yorkshire to join his new colleagues on the encouraging wage of £7 per week.

The reconstituted company duly made its debut on 2 September 1935, on its own premises, and received the following laboured but broadly encouraging review in the press:

> The Sheffield Repertory Theatre, in which marked structural improvements have been made, opened last Monday with a company of eight professionals and two amateurs. One of the professionals, Evelyn Allen, is specially engaged for this week; another, Horace Wentworth, is stage manager and well known to Sheffield audiences; the other six are new members of the company. The play was *Mary, Mary, Quite Contrary*, by St John Ervine; the producer was Leslie Harcourt. The leading part of the temperamental Mary Westlake was taken with spirit and humour by Phyllis Gadsden, Fernando Perredita made an excellent impression as the impulsive and susceptible Geoffrey, and Angus Adams gave good quiet comedy as the clergyman; while Evelyn Allen was placidly humorous as his wife. Patricia Pellowe made the most of her opportunities as the jealous niece. Eadie Palfrey had the comic part of the Cockney manager, and John Halliley and two amateurs had small parts. The piece was heartily received, and the season, which was formally opened by the Lord Mayor of Sheffield, has begun well.[15]

They went on to perform most of the standard safe shows (the ones that had already proven their copper-bottomed commercial appeal somewhere or other in the West End of London), along with the odd sample from Shakespeare, and John began to attract a number of favourable reviews in both *The Stage* and the local *Yorkshire Post*. Buoyed artificially every now and then by Benzedrine – such stimulants were a fairly common way for actors to battle both the boredom and fatigue in rep – he pushed himself on and continued to make an impact. Even when he felt that he had fallen far short of his highest standards, such as when he played the part of Malvolio in *Twelfth Night* ('I was quite dreadful'[16]), the critics tended to be relatively kind; he was praised by one for portraying that particular role 'in a restrained vein'.[17]

When the excitement of being back in rep started to recede as the sheer grind of the schedule took over, his spirits were lifted by a brief but enjoyable romance with an attractive young local woman who happened to be the great-great-granddaughter of Joseph Hansom, the inventor of the hansom cab. Sundays were the only free days for actors in rep, and, due to the rapid succession of shows and the discipline required to keep learning each fresh set of lines, the only reliable time for drinking and socialising was late on Saturday nights, so any tryst tended to be limited to a once-weekly treat. Making the most of such meetings, John took his good-looking female friend to nearby restaurants, pubs and cinemas, went for walks and picnics in the local Botanical Gardens and the odd drive out of town to take in some of the naturally beautiful scenes on show in various parts of the Peak District. It was all fairly innocent fun, but, nonetheless a very pleasant way to spend what rare leisure time there was to be had.

John was, however, feeling increasingly restless in Sheffield. In stark contrast to the chronic dilatoriness that he had shown as an adolescent, he now appeared in a hurry to progress. 'Had I known it was going to take so long,' he later reflected, 'I might well have given the whole thing up.'[18] Ideally, he would catch the attention of an influential impresario and be snapped up by a company in London. Night after night he went out on stage, did his best and hoped that someone, seated somewhere out there in the darkness of the auditorium, was taking note of his potential. Nothing seemed to happen – there were certainly no unexpected knocks on his dressing-room door – but the belief would remain that a lucky break was imminent. A steady decline in the standard of the company's productions, however, gradually convinced him that such a break would surely be more imminent if he was working somewhere else, and preferably somewhere in the south.

At this point, in his own recollections, John would misremember the proper chronological order of his career. In his memoirs, he would say that he moved on from Sheffield first to Glasgow and then to Croydon. The reality was actually the reverse. As the press coverage of the time confirms, he went first to Croydon.[19]

John Baxter-Somerville, the Suffolk solicitor whose theatrical interests had intrigued John back in his days as an articled clerk, was by this time making quite a name for himself as an enthusiastic patron of the art. Having started modestly in 1931 as the publicity officer of Croydon's Greyhound Theatre, he had gone on the following year to found a repertory theatre there, in Wellesley Road, also investing in a number of one-off London productions. Most recently, in 1935, he had not only become managing director of another repertory company based at the Theatre Royal in Brighton, but had also begun negotiations that would soon secure him control of the historic little Festival Theatre in Cambridge. John made contact with the man known as 'JB', mentioned as many mutual friends and acquaintances as he could remember from his days at Greene & Greene, and managed to get himself a new job (paying £5 per week) at Croydon Rep. Although he would have much preferred to have headed straight to the bright lights of London, he reassured himself that nearby Croydon at least represented a clear step in the right direction.

He started there in the autumn of 1936, just in time for the commencement of the company's fifth season. He had decided, thinking optimistically about his future prospects, to base himself in London, taking a room in a boarding house at 147 Ebury Street, which was close enough to Victoria station to allow him easy access to the direct line to East Croydon. The boarding house, which was run by a mousey little creature with the unlikely-sounding name of Olga Titoff, was full of 'theatricals', including a young German-born character actor called Ferdy Mayne (who would go on to enjoy a very long stage and screen career specialising in playing continental cads) and his then girlfriend Beryl Measor (who would also forge a steady career capped in 1957 by a Tony award nomination for her portrayal on Broadway of a put-upon hotelier in the Terence Rattigan play *Separate Tables*). John felt very much at home among such youthful kindred spirits.

He also felt reinvigorated by Croydon Rep. The theatre itself – 'built to the specifications,' moaned John, 'of a second rank village hall'[20] – made a poor first impression, but the people had a vastly more positive impact. The company boasted by far the best group of actors that John had thus far encountered. Such future leading lights as Maurice Denham, Mark Dignam and Carla Lehmann were already members, and Dennis Price would arrive a few months later. The troupe also included K. Hamilton Price (who was to play Prince Charles Stuart in the 1937 movie *The Vicar of Bray*), Michael Balfour (later a very familiar figure in 1950s British cinema), Anna Wing (who would find fame in the 1980s as the matriarch Lou Beale in *EastEnders*), Desmond Keith (soon to be a stalwart of pre-war TV), Richard Wattis (another future fixture of home-grown comic features) and a talented young woman called Pamela Ostrer (who was then dating – and would end up marrying – one of the company's former leading men, James Mason). The resident director was a bright and inventive twenty-five-year-old named Michael Barry – who would himself go on to become one of BBC TV's most successful and influential Heads of Drama (commissioning such groundbreaking productions as the *Quatermass* science-fiction series and an adaptation of George Orwell's *Nineteen Eighty-Four*). This, John realised, was precisely the kind of place where he needed to be.

Every aspect of the company's activity seemed much more polished and professional. More effort went into rehearsals, more advice was given to each performer, the direction in general was far more thoughtful and constructive, the overall standard of acting was very impressive and, most important of all, the actual productions were of a consistently high quality. If metropolitan critics and impresarios were going to take a serious interest in the output of any repertory company, Croydon's looked to be one of the likeliest candidates.

John was soon made to feel part of the troupe. The senior actors were quick to take him under their wing and advise him, while the junior ones were similarly prompt in striking up a more playful sort of rapport. All of the women recognised his potential as a handsome young leading man – 'He was divine,' one of them would recall. 'Absolutely stunning. He had blue-black hair, beautiful dark eyes. Incredibly good-looking. People pined away for him!'[21] – and the men soon warmed to his witty and self-effacing personality. He grew to be particularly fond of Desmond Keith for his sheer mischievousness. Never one to take himself too seriously, Keith – in stark contrast to the other members of the troupe – would pretend not to bother with scripts beyond flicking through the pages in a comically perfunctory fashion. 'Talks a lot, doesn't he?' he would mutter of his latest allotted character. 'Never mind, I'll have a look at it after tea.'[22] During performances, he would always try to 'corpse' John by whispering something sarcastic just before the two of them were due to make an entrance.

John grew even fonder – much fonder, in fact – of Carla Lehmann. Aged just nineteen, the Canadian-born, RADA-trained performer was five years younger than John, but he was soon drawn both to her looks (long brown hair, a slim but shapely body and a Garbo-graceful face) and her personality (very bright, inquisitive, witty and vivacious). He would later say that he was 'much in love with her',[23] although neither he nor she would ever reveal how close they had actually been. What is clear is that, throughout their time together in Croydon, she would remain his closest companion.

As usual, however, in rep, there was rarely much time for socialising, let alone anything more intimate, as the workload was always so great. The company's season began on Monday 7 September 1936 with an epic drama entitled *Peace In Our Time*. Billed, somewhat pompously, as a 'world première', the play (written by Douglas Walshe and Nigel Balchin) was an earnest tale of 'strife and chicanery in the commercial world', starring K. Hamilton Price as an iron-jawed business bully and another senior member of the company, Shirra Bailey, as a persecuted Jewish entrepreneur. John had only a minor role as a peripheral character called Mr Platt. Running for a fortnight, it was a strange choice to start the season; a slow-moving and self-conscious so-called 'parable' that seemed unsure not only of its tone but also of its own subject matter, rarely threatening to move beyond an old-fashioned and simplistic view of the amoral nature of modern capitalism. The critics, predictably enough, were underwhelmed, sneering at the ill-informed references to certain laws and legal procedures and bemoaning the numerous holes in the plot, and not even the actors themselves (although they did garner some praise) seemed very fond of this particular fiction. John, who had been reprimanded during rehearsals for sniggering at some of the clumsier lines, judged the event to have been 'a modest fiasco', and he was relieved, for once, not to have featured prominently enough to have attracted any attention.[24]

Things improved once the debut was done, rolling on with the usual company conveyor belt of varied fare – including the light-hearted crime thriller *Dusty Ermine*, George Bernard Shaw's political satire *The Apple Cart*, J.B. Priestley's 'farcical tragedy' *Bees on the Boat Deck*, Eugene O'Neill's sardonic take on small-town American life *Ah! Wilderness*, the adaptation by Basil Dean of Margaret Kennedy's romantic melodrama *The Constant Nymph* and the venerable farce (first performed forty-four years before at the Theatre Royal in Bury St Edmunds) *Charley's Aunt* – drawing in large and appreciative audiences all the way through to the end of the year. John's participation in these plays ranged from one or two fairly substantial characterisations to a few relatively modest supporting roles, but he seems to have enjoyed himself in most of the productions, growing in confidence as the autumn progressed.

The only time during this early period when he really struggled was when he was called on to appear in *The Constant Nymph* as a character called Lewis Dodd. This was the role that no lesser figure than Noël Coward had played in the original 1926 production. Although a great success, the strain of the part drove the already overworked Coward over the edge into a nervous breakdown – he collapsed on stage and had to be replaced by John Gielgud. John (who was feeling rather tired himself) was, therefore, rather anxious right from the start. The character of Dodd was a brilliant but impoverished young composer who pursues a haughty older woman while barely noticing the younger, nicer woman who adores him. The actor who played him was supposed to look handsome but elegantly dishevelled, be able to either play or fake playing the piano and sound as though music was deep in his heart and soul.

John found it easy enough to walk around in a slightly ill-fitting suit looking 'bohemian', but, like Coward before him, he found it hard to master the unfamiliar stage craft of holding and smoking a pipe (threatening on several occasions during rehearsals to set fire to his hair or tip tobacco all over his jacket). When it came to sitting at the piano and crooning a 'haunting melody' called 'When Thou Art Dead', he protested that this 'fiendish task' was beyond him, as he only knew one key and it was the wrong one, and 'the piano was out of tune'.[25] He nonetheless got through it all somehow, and, although there was no night when he seemed more than merely competent, he emerged with his enthusiasm as strong as ever. He could now survive the slap of failure just as well as he could savour the kiss of success. He felt 'grown-up' as an actor in Croydon. He finally felt like a proper professional.

It was perhaps symbolic of this sense of having 'come of age' (at twenty-four) as an actor that early the following year – 1937 – he decided to adopt 'Le Mesurier' as his new name for the stage. Although he never bothered, at least in public, to explain the reason for his decision, the change certainly had nothing to do with any supposed desire to 'protect' the name of Halliley from the possible negative publicity associated with having a 'theatrical' in the family. If that had indeed been the case, the Le Mesurier name would surely have had considerably more lustre to lose. It was not prompted, either, by the belief that his mother's name would be easier than his father's for theatregoers to pronounce; if anything, the opposite was actually the case. The later admission that he had always felt 'closer to my mother both in temperament and interests'[26] could, perhaps, be construed as a sign that he preferred to be linked a little more closely to Amy than to Elton, but it would have been wildly out of character for such a polite and dutiful son to have snubbed his father in so petty and public a fashion. It seems much more likely that John simply liked the sound of 'Le Mesurier' more than he did that of 'Halliley'. After all, Sir Gerald du Maurier, who had died three years before, had always struck John as a very glamorous theatrical figure (an aspirational upmarket brand of cigarettes, which John sometimes smoked, had been named in his honour), so it is not inconceivable that the similar sound of 'John Le Mesurier' might have suited the young actor's own ambitions for his future public image. Whatever the truth of the matter, however, the alteration met with no resistance within the company and the name 'John Le Mesurier' duly started to appear on the posters and among the regular credits.[27]

It was a year of steady improvement for John, with a growing number of rewardingly challenging roles in some well-received productions, and he attracted an increasingly large following (mostly female) among the local theatregoers. By the autumn, however, when he was even finding the task of appearing in such gritty social dramas as *Love on the Dole* fairly undemanding, a certain degree of restlessness returned and he started to look around for the next potential progression.

He thought he had found it, early the following year, when news reached him that an enterprising actor-manager called Ronald Adam, who ran the Embassy Theatre in Hampstead, had just extended his empire to Scotland, assuming control of two very handsome Victorian venues – the Lyceum Theatre in Edinburgh and the Theatre Royal in Glasgow – with the intention of linking them together via a brand new repertory company. Although the West End of London was still where John longed to be, this high-profile enterprise looked to him, as a relatively short-term engagement, a realistic way to further advance his career. Adam (who would later find greater fame on film playing the very kind of characters – lawyers, bankers, clerks and clergymen – that John would also be offered) was a very affable, and very shrewd, impresario who genuinely cared about quality and was very adept at promoting it. Having known this particular young man's work ever since he had been one of the judges at the Fay Compton end-of-year showcase back in 1934, he saw enough talent in John to sign him up for a season in Scotland.

No one at Croydon Rep wanted him to go, but, as its owner John

Baxter-Somerville seemed to acknowledge at the time, the company had perhaps been slow to spot just how strong his ambition had grown, and so could now only wish him well:

> Dear John,
>   Thank you for your letter. I tried to have a word with you the other night but as always you were surrounded by people.
>   We have very much enjoyed having you with us and I am bitterly sorry to be losing you now. Had I known that you wanted a change I could have offered you something by the sea but I suppose that the die is irrevocably cast by now. If at any time you would like to return, do let us know and I can assure you that no one will be more delighted to have you back again than me.
>   Yours sincerely,
>   JB[28]

Before he left London, John's old director from Croydon, Michael Barry (who had just started working for the BBC as a producer), gave him his television debut, playing (for a fee of five guineas[29]) Seigneur de Miolans in a play called *The Marvellous History of St Bernard*, which was shot at Alexandra Palace and broadcast on 17 April 1938. Barry would also arrange for him to make a second small screen appearance at the end of the year, playing Sir John Montague in another costume drama entitled *Richard of Bordeaux*, but, in those days, television was still very much in its experimental phase as a potentially popular medium (although the range of sets was increasing and the price decreasing, the BBC was devoting no more than 8 per cent of its licence revenue – under £300,000 – to its television service, and the audience – estimated at just under 20,000 – was extremely small[30]), and John, while happy to sample the studio set-up, was much more excited about moving on to Scotland to begin his next major venture in the theatre.

Arriving in the late spring of 1938, John – feeling very confident after Croydon – thrived in his new environment. Moving back and forth on a fortnightly basis between the two venues and cities, he soon started appearing far more mature, as an actor, than he had ever done before. In Adam he had a mentor who really trusted him, assigning him roles that stretched him and enabled him to develop as a serious and versatile actor. He appeared, for example, as the mercurial Konstantin in Chekhov's *The Seagull* and the suave and sharp-tongued Elyot Chase in Coward's *Private Lives*. He contributed to sober classical dramas and frothy contemporary comedies. He played good men and bad men, insiders and outcasts, extroverts and introverts. Week after week, month after month, he was given the kind of parts that tested his range as a professional performer.

The one minor setback – at least for the company as a whole – was when 'a dreadful piece' staged at the Lyceum called *An Italian Garden* was launched with a gala first night attended by the Duchess of Kent. Everyone – the actors, the director, the stage manager and the supporting staff – was nervous about the prospect of a performance before royalty, but no one was more nervous than the over-attentive Provost of Edinburgh, who began the interval by thrusting a large glass of what he assumed to be sherry into his royal guest's delicate hand. It turned out to be neat whisky. She spent the second half of the performance swaying slightly, sporting an expression that looked to the actors as if 'her smile had been fixed in plaster of paris'.[31]

John himself continued to garner praise from his director and fellow actors, and, although the critics tended to applaud the ensemble rather than single out individual performers, he was buoyed by the company's many positive reviews. Such success, however, only made him impatient to engineer his long-awaited move to the West End. 'I suppose that the first class training I was getting at Glasgow and Edinburgh should have instilled in me a greater sense of loyalty,' he later said, 'but limited recognition merely seemed to intensify my urge to get to London.'[32] The advent of the Munich crisis, in September 1938, probably contributed to this feeling of urgency; the world suddenly seemed on the brink of war and a mood of *carpe diem* arose among many young people. Just six months after John's arrival, therefore, he decided to depart, thanking Ronnie Adam profusely for the opportunity and moving back to his old digs in Ebury Street.

He acted again for Croydon Rep while studying the classified adverts in the trade papers and hoping for the arrival of more good fortune. It came late in the year via his close friend Carla Lehmann, who (as a rising star herself with a recent movie appearance now on her CV) was able to consult her growing list of contacts and put John in touch with an impresario named Bill Linnit. Part of a highly successful commercial management company called O'Bryen, Linnit and

Dunfee, Bill Linnit was currently overseeing preparations for a new West End production of Patrick Hamilton's homage to Victorian melodrama, *Gas Light*. The two leading parts had already been cast – with Dennis Arundell and Gwen Ffrangcon-Davies installed in the roles later made famous in the movie adaptation by Charles Boyer and Ingrid Bergman – and other actors were in the process of signing up to play the secondary characters, but John managed to be hired as an understudy. Although it was hardly the big break for which he had been hoping, it did nonetheless ensure that he was finally associated with a production in the West End – at the Apollo Theatre in Shaftesbury Avenue – and, even if there was no guarantee that he would actually make it on to the stage, the job came with the firm promise of a principal role once the show was taken on tour.

Gas Light opened on Tuesday 31 January 1939 to uniformly excellent reviews. James Agate in the *Sunday Times* judged it 'the best play we have had in a very long time', the *Daily Telegraph* called it 'A really thrilling evening in the theatre', and the *Daily Mirror* dubbed it a 'hair-raising, spine-tingling success'[33]. It ran throughout a very hard winter and on until the middle of May as one of the biggest hits of the year. Much to John's frustration, though not to his great surprise, none of the male members of the cast would ever show any sign of ill-health – 'They must have been unbearably fit',[34] he recalled – and so he spent much of each evening sitting alone inside his dressing room by the fire, reading books and writing letters, only venturing out every now and then to watch and listen from the wings.

The odd friend would pop backstage to visit him, and none was odder than a Wodehousian sort of character called Cyprian Waller-Bridge, 'the eccentric son of an eccentric vicar' who rather flattered John by always appearing to be hugely impressed by the fact that he actually knew an understudy. After the show was over and John was allowed out back on the street, he and his 'fan' would sometimes wander off to a nearby nightclub (owned by the husband of one of Cyprian's sisters) called The Knickerbocker, where they could get a meal and a few drinks fairly cheaply. These visits were curtailed abruptly after the occasion when John chose to dance with a 'ravishing' young hostess who, when the music stopped, smiled sweetly and then announced in a very loud and gravelly South London accent that she needed to 'go to the lavvy'; as John later put it, 'The illusion was shattered.'[35] He later took to strolling through Piccadilly and Grosvenor Place, ending up at a little coffee stall close to Victoria station, not far from his home in Ebury Street, where the local prostitutes would stop for a 'breather' between engagements. He enjoyed chatting to them and listening to their stories, and one even invited him for tea at Fuller's in Regent Street (as, she pointed out, her flat was nearby), but, as he later put it, he had second thoughts after accepting and 'funked it'.[36]

On some days, during the hour or so before he was due at the Apollo, he would simply wander around the West End, watching the crowds pour through the streets and taking in the sheer wonder of it all. Among the attractions of the time, other than *Gas Light* itself, were Rex Harrison in Coward's *Design for Living* at the Haymarket; Sybil Thorndyke in Emlyn Williams's *The Corn is Green* at the Duchess; Ralph Richardson in J.B. Priestley's *Johnson Over Jordan* at the New Theatre; Owen Nares in St John Ervine's *Robert's Wife* at the Savoy; Jack Buchanan in Clare Boothe Luce's *The Women* at the Lyric; Ivor Novello in *The Dancing Years* at Drury Lane; and John Gielgud and Edith Evans in *The Importance of Being of Earnest* at the Globe. There were so many heroes, so many spectacles, in this one very special area. Even though his own name was not up there among them all in lights, he still felt, in a very modest way, part of the scene, and it made him more eager than ever to make his way in from the wings.

Once the run at the Apollo was finally over, therefore, John was champing at the bit to step into the spotlight when the production went out on tour. Starting at Finsbury Park Empire in June, then moving on to such venues as the Savoy, the Chiswick Empire and the Chelsea Palace before setting off for the provinces and running on until the end of October in Manchester, he seized his chance enthusiastically, and won some very positive critical notices. Playing the role of the sinister husband, Mr Manningham, who appears determined to convince his young and nervous wife that she is slipping steadily into insanity, he looked coolly assured. Dominating the dark and moody setting of a gas-lit Pimlico sitting room made all the more claustrophobic by heavy curtains, fussy Victorian bric-a-brac, dusty aspidistras and frowning antimacassars, he looked a menacing figure with his slick black hair, hollow cheeks, sharply precise voice and silkily cruel demeanour. It was, without any doubt, his most accomplished performance so far; the *Guardian*, applauding what it described as a 'faultless' portrayal, remarked: 'One may praise it best by saying that Mr Le Mesurier gives one a really uncomfortable feeling in the stomach or the boots, or wherever such feelings of apprehension reside.'[37]

When the play reached the King's Theatre in Southsea late in the summer, the up-and-coming performer Sarah Churchill (daughter of Winston) took over the female lead, and introduced John to her father after her first night. The politician, having been more than a little distracted by the current parlous state of international affairs, knew nothing about the actor other than the fact that he had been rather good that evening, and John was in too great a state of excitement to do much more than nod and smile politely in his presence: 'I have to say with a certain degree of shame that I cannot remember one single word he uttered.'[38] The irony was that, had John still been called Halliley, Mr Churchill would probably have realised that he knew and admired the actor's hardworking Tory activist father, Elton, and perhaps even stayed for a longer and more relaxed kind of conversation.

When the run finally ended, John returned late one evening to his London lodgings, 'chez Titoff', in Ebury Street, and found a message waiting for him from another theatrical manager, inviting him to take over the leading role in the touring version of Robert Morley's recent West End success, *Goodness, How Sad!*, for a short forthcoming tour. Delighted to go straight from one job to another, he accepted without hesitation. The play – a light comedy – revolved around the character of an actor who has fallen on hard times in a provincial repertory company. It was not a demanding part – all that John really had to do was look debonair and sound witty, and he certainly knew how to send up life in rep – but the production promised to be very popular with audiences and pay him a good wage, while keeping his name in circulation. What he did not know when he signed up was that it would also bring him into contact with the woman who was destined to become his first wife.

Her name was June Melville, and she had just been announced as the play's director. A female director was a rarity in those male-dominated days, but then she was an exceptional woman. The daughter of Frederick and the niece of Walter, who together held a controlling influence in both the Lyceum and the Prince's as well as owning outright the Brixton Theatre (along with its resident repertory company), June was young (twenty-four years old in 1939), good-looking (with a slender figure, long dark hair and an elegantly fine-featured face reminiscent of the Hollywood star Irene Dunne) and very knowledgeable about the theatrical profession. She was also extremely strong-minded, although with perhaps a slight, and usually well-hidden, insecurity that derived from the feeling that too much had come her way via a privileged family background rather than directly through her own hard and humble efforts. An actor as well as a director and manager, she seemed bright beyond her years, very energetic and more than capable of standing up to any man.

John was dazzled by her from the very first time that they met. She struck him as beautiful, extremely glamorous – 'All the females of the Melville family seemed to be swathed in mink coats and wearing expensive jewellery. No rubbish, the real thing'[39] – and immensely charming, and he was flattered when she demonstrated not only some awareness of his recent work but also admiration for his abilities as an actor. She spoke to him so clearly and constructively, with such attention to detail, that he felt a far better actor than he had ever felt before. He wanted, as a consequence, to learn from her, and be around her, for as long as was practically possible.

In the first few weeks of their association, as he joined her and other members of the production for read-throughs and rehearsals, he simply revelled in her company, but, as plans for the tour progressed, they grew closer and eventually became lovers. Going back to his Ebury Street lodgings one evening, they 'sampled two rather disgusting bottles of I.P.A. which I had saved up for a rainy day' and then lay down together in bed.[40] For the next few weeks they were inseparable, spending each day working on the play in Brixton and each night getting to know each other better back in Ebury Street.

It was a strange and unsettling time to begin a relationship: war had only been declared the month before (on 1 September) and, understandably, people were living from one day to the next in a state of chronic insecurity. All fit and able men aged between eighteen and forty-one were now liable to be registered for conscription into the armed services 'if and when called upon'. Actual call-ups began in the autumn of 1939 with those aged from twenty to twenty-three, moving on in May the following year to include those aged up to twenty-seven and gradually extending in the months that followed to bring in older citizens (which would include John, who was twenty-eight in 1940), while a range of formal and informal roles for women was also under consideration.[41] The newspapers were full of bleak predictions, countless plans and projects were put on hold and all kinds of personal ambitions were stalled. Many young men were drifting from day to day, unsure as to when they would be abruptly uprooted and plunged into military life, and countless families were stuck in a terribly tense state of suspense.[42]

Actors, in particular, had spent the first fortnight or so of war in limbo, as the Government initially ordered all places of entertainment to be closed because it feared that large gatherings would make easy targets for German bombers. A letter published in *The Times* soon after this decision from the powerful impresario Sir Oswald Stoll epitomised the profession's anxious, and angry, reaction:

> Entertainment is necessary to the morale of the people. Crowd psychology is a potent influence. Remember 'Are we downhearted?' Remember Sir James Barrie's 'Der Tag!' Remember the film *Four Years in Germany*, initiated by the American Ambassador to Berlin. Remember the community songs and singers of soldiers and people. Remember, too, that it is not logical to close theatres and cinemas and to open churches to crowds. None can foresee where bombs will fall and whether by night or day. The people are willing to take them as they come, under ordinary precautions or intermittently extraordinary precautions. While freely acknowledging the efficiency of our system of black-outs, as such, in hiding the country from air-raiders, I submit humbly but with conviction that complete black-outs, from sunset to sunrise, are excessive; that they should be imposed only when actual air-raids are signalled; that the conversion of semi-black-outs into complete ones is quick and easy work, if top lights are at all times obscured; that, without this necessary modification, no lives were lost in theatres during the last war.[43]

The rash decision was soon reversed once politicians realised that Sir Oswald was probably right and entertainment was going to be an important source of escapism, optimism and propaganda during the difficult and dangerous times ahead. A practical consequence of the volte-face was the hurried formation of a new organisation, the Entertainments National Service Association (ENSA), designed to draw more performers to the cause of the war, but actors in general still faced a profoundly uncertain professional future.

Such uncertainty, however, made some of them more reckless,

more driven and more passionate than ever before, blocking out the fears by thinking only of the here and now, and John and June were among those who behaved in this way. They loved and lived as though tomorrow was never going to come. 'I was hooked on June's philosophy of never passing up an opportunity to have fun,' John later confirmed. 'I suppose we both felt that we should make the best of everything while we could.'[44]

They were broken up, temporarily, only by business. She remained in London at the Brixton Theatre while he set off with the other actors as the short tour went ahead, beginning in Hull in late November and zigzagging either side of the Pennines before heading back in the direction of the Midlands. While he was on the road, moving from one freezing cold and cramped little dressing room to the next, he contemplated June's distinctive appeal – she had not only 'glamour and great charm', he reflected, but also 'the wonderful knack of inspiring in me the self-confidence I had been seeking throughout my short career on the stage' – and came to the realisation that he was 'desperately in love' with her.[45] When, at the end of the year, he arrived back in London, he plucked up the courage to propose to her: 'To my astonishment, she said yes.'[46]

The wedding took place in the following spring, at 12.30 pm on Thursday 18 April 1940 at All Saints Church in Highgate.[47] The Melville family were very much in charge of the event, organising a lavish reception with 'what seemed like hundreds of guests'. Elton and Amy Halliley attended, but felt somewhat isolated among so many unfamiliar members of London's theatrical community, and were probably not much impressed by the Melvilles' rather ostentatious manner of demonstrating the extent of their wealth. John, having spent the previous night drinking at the Embassy Club with his best man, the Hon. Findlay Rea (the company manager on his recent tours), had to be guided through the occasion in a kind of daze, heavy-lidded and smiling weakly. Thanks to his recently attained status as a jobbing actor, however, he was obliged to leave the festivities at five o'clock and set off for Brixton to join the rest of the company for another two-hour performance. His bride collected him after the show for a celebratory family supper at the glamorous Moulin D'Or restaurant in Romilly Street.

There was no room in their schedule for a proper honeymoon – they were next due to appear together at the Brixton Theatre the following week in a J.B. Priestley farce entitled *Mystery at Greenfingers* (press reports noted that the newly married couple received 'a hearty reception' from the audience upon their first entrance[48]) – but they threw themselves into married life, taking a lease on a charming little house owned by Findlay Rea at 20 Smith Street, Chelsea. They hired a maid – a young Polish woman named Lenka (chosen by June's very strong-minded mother, Jane, on the grounds that, as a 'plain girl', Lenka was unlikely to be distracted from her duties by any amorous 'followers') – held some high-profile parties and enjoyed being husband and wife. They were now spending more or less all of every day together, working from morning until night at the theatre in Brixton (June usually directing and John acting) and then unwinding at various clubs and restaurants until the time came to go back home.

Soon, however, not even they could ignore the demands of the war any longer. John, who had already signed up as an air-raid warden, started patrolling the streets in and around Dolphin Square with a tin hat perched awkwardly on his head, saying things like 'Do please try your very best to remain calm' and 'Perhaps you might leave it to me' to disoriented pedestrians and elderly residents in their pyjamas, although he soon learned to assume 'a quite spurious air of command'[49]. Both he and June began helping out with some of the special shows and revues that were now being staged for the forces.[50]

As the summer progressed, they tried their best to carry on more or less as normal, retaining faith 'in our lucky star' as they maintained the repertory season. John did have to go for an Army medical, but, after being passed fit for service, he was allowed to return to work until needed, and, once again, the routine went on as before. 'I held to the clear conviction,' he would say, 'that somehow our little world was exempt from destruction.'[51] Eschewing public transport, they travelled everywhere by taxi, dined at the most sumptuous places and drank the finest wines: 'We had enough money to indulge ourselves.'[52] They kept themselves busy and they kept themselves happy.

The time that they had together, however, was clearly fast running out. It might be no more than another day, or a week, or a month, but both of them knew, deep down, that they would soon be separated. John was going to be called up for war.

CHAPTER VI

The Army Years

Your name will also go on the list!

John stopped living for the here and now in September 1940, when the here and now, for him, was blown away. It was in that month that the German bombs started to fall, and some of them landed where he lived and where he worked.

A few hours before, John had been hard at work in rehearsal with June and the rest of the company at their theatre in Coldharbour Lane. Once the session was over, he went with June out into the unseasonably bright autumn sunshine and set off in a taxi for home. As the car travelled slowly over Battersea Bridge, the barrage balloons were already riding high – a sure sign of an impending attack – and, a few minutes later, the first faint sounds of explosions broke out. Policemen and ARP wardens started swarming through the streets, ambulances and fire engines raced into view and clouds of white, grey and black smoke began to swirl up and shut out the sun. John sat clasping June's hand very tightly, staring ahead and saying nothing but knowing that they were about to be forced into the war.

His fears were confirmed when the taxi tried to turn into Smith Street, only to be halted abruptly by masses of dust-covered pedestrians and piles of bricks, timber and stones. Their house was no longer there. Part of the back wall was still standing, but, apart from a few shards of plaster sticking out near their supports and a strip of floorboard hanging down where the landing should have been, everything was buried under a mountain of rubble that now swallowed up half the road. John was in such a state of shock that he did not know what to do or say. Gazing open-mouthed at the horrible mess, he eventually heard himself ask an ARP warden, almost

absent-mindedly, what had happened to his collection of gramophone records.

'Gone, mate,' said the warden flatly as he hurried past. 'All gone.'
He had said precisely the same thing, apparently, a little earlier to
those who had enquired anxiously as to what could have happened
to John and June and the rest of the local residents.

That, then, was that: everything that the couple owned had been
lost. A land mine had dropped on their home and destroyed it.

There was more bad news to come. They were soon informed that,
shortly after they had set off in their taxi from rehearsal, an incendiary
bomb had hit the Melvilles' theatre in Brixton (which had only
recently been renamed in honour of June's late father) and
immediately set it ablaze. Several nearby churches and schools had also
been struck and destroyed during the daylight raid by a swarm of
about five hundred Nazi bombers, along with countless shops and
public houses and, of course, entire streets of ordinary homes. It was
the beginning of what would later become known as 'The Blitz' – a
period of sustained bombing over Britain in general, and especially in
London, that would last from September 1940 to May 1941, killing
an estimated 43,000 citizens and injuring a further million.[1]

John and June stood together, stunned, alone in the smoke and
commotion. It was all too much for them to absorb. Homeless,
possessionless and jobless – all within the space of a matter of hours.
After a while, when at last they could move, they wandered off, still in
a daze, to search for a chemist where both of them could buy a
toothbrush. Such tiny and isolated practical details were all that either
of them could consider; the big picture, for them, had disintegrated.
John felt utterly crushed, but June was determined to respond to the
catastrophe in her usual defiantly cavalier way. She insisted that they
go for cocktails at the Antelope pub in Eaton Terrace near Sloane
Square, followed by a full and lavish meal at the Moulin D'Or (a place
that prided itself on remaining open regardless of the disruption),
before finding a taxi and heading off for her mother's grand-looking
home at 23 View Road, Highgate. Bombs were still falling and
sparking up the sky as the vehicle ferried the couple through the chaos.
'It was like,' John would say, 'some hideous fairyland.'[2] Once safely
inside, they had some stiff drinks, talked through all that had
happened and then went up to bed, where June slipped off to sleep
and John stared at the ceiling, thinking, worrying and hoping.

A few days later, as the sense of shock began slowly to subside, it suddenly occurred to John that among the many items that had been lost thanks to the Luftwaffe were his call-up papers: 'I had in mind that I was supposed to report to a Royal Armoured Corp base at Tidworth on Salisbury Plain but for the life of me I could not remember when this appointment was due to take place.'[3] Enquiries at several local recruitment offices failed to clarify the matter, so he decided that he might as well set off 'at what I thought was about the right time'. Once, therefore, he had ensured that June had somewhere safe to stay for the foreseeable future, he went with her for one last lunch at the Moulin D'Or before, with understandable reluctance, getting into a taxi and driving away. He rolled up at Tidworth Barracks in south-east Wiltshire about four hours later – after a couple of stops for further alcoholic refreshment – with a newly purchased set of golf clubs among his personal baggage and the smell of champagne cocktails still hovering on his breath.

His unannounced arrival, looking as though he was turning up to spend a long weekend at a very nice house in the country, caused a fair amount of hilarity among the other new recruits, the majority of whom were young working-class Londoners. The mood inside, however, turned brusquely businesslike as he was issued with a service number (7918208), handed his basic battledress, denims, two pairs of boots and gaiters and then told in no uncertain terms to go off and get a haircut. What followed was ten solid weeks of gruelling training: marching and running and rolling around the grounds while being barked at by a soldier called Sergeant Bramley. This stiff-necked, frown-browed, cherry-cheeked disciplinarian would never bother even to enquire as to why one of his charges seemed to have the surname of Halliley but styled himself 'Le Mesurier', nor would he ever attempt to master the pronunciation of such a foreign-sounding name as 'Le Mesurier'. He settled instead on addressing John as 'Lee Mesure', which made him sound like a slightly exotic cowboy. After observing the alarmingly languid early efforts of this 'theatrical' character with a mounting sense of exasperation, Sergeant Bramley, who was actually quite pragmatic for someone in his position, decided that John was 'not cut out to be a corporal, let alone a sergeant', and concluded that – rather than waste too much time shouting at him to be at least a little bit less languid – it would probably be better for all concerned if they tried to make him into an officer instead.

John, unsurprisingly, welcomed this suggestion with enthusiasm, reasoning that 'the prospect of wearing warmer clothes and to be paid extra for doing so seemed eminently sensible'.[4] The fact was that Army life was turning out to be rather more tolerable than he had anticipated: true, the sweet tea was not at all to his taste, but most of the food seemed perfectly edible and, with all of the exercise, he was starting to feel fitter than he had been in years. He also enjoyed being taught how to do such things as drive a tank and operate a Bren light machine gun; these were practical tasks that seemed to have a clear and constructive purpose, so he never resented the process of strict instruction. It was only when the rules and rituals struck him as pompous or pointless that he was tempted to revert to his old passive-aggressive ways and become something of a burden to his superiors. Most of the time, however, the procedure seemed fairly appropriate and, as in rep, he liked feeling part of a lively team.

He had missed June greatly during the first couple of weeks away, but then she started visiting at weekends, staying at a nearby hotel so that, fully scented, befurred and bejewelled, she could take him and one or two of his new friends out for a very generous Sunday lunch. It was, ironically, these occasional well-meaning 'treats' that would first suggest to him that all was not well within their marriage, as it now seemed plain not only that June was drinking far too much but also that it was having an increasingly damaging effect on her personality: 'What had seemed no more than high spirits in the social whirl of London theatre not infrequently became boorish in what was now for me a more restrained environment.'[5]

While circumstances had forced John out of the bright little bubble that the two of them had once inhabited, June still seemed lost somewhere deep inside it, unable, or unwilling, to break out through the iridescent skin and face up to the bleak reality of living in a world at war. He had changed, but she had not. John had reverted to being the kind of sober and stoically purposeful Englishman who, as Winston Churchill would soon put it in Parliament, not only wants 'to be told how bad things are', but also wants 'to be told the worst', whereas June was still the sort of person who preferred to remain in denial.[6] She waved away the kind of things that worried him deeply; she cared about the kind of things that now seemed to him to be depressingly frivolous. He still loved her, but, during those visits, he found it harder and harder to like her. The more she drank and laughed and shouted, the more uncomfortable he felt in her company.

There was little time, however, to ponder such a problem. At the start of 1941, he was soon being hurried on his way to an Officer Cadet Training Unit (OCTU) called Blackdown, situated between Taunton and Wellington, to ready him for his intended wartime role.

He hated it at Blackdown, which reminded him rather too much of the bad old days at Grenham House and Sherborne, but he knew that it would be best in the long term if he kept his head down and pressed on rather than risk being sent back and returned to the ranks. Once the challenges began, therefore, he took them seriously and tried his best. He failed miserably when charged with the task of learning how to ride a motorcycle – or, as he called them, 'the mechanised two-wheeled monsters'[7] – and managed to smash one straight into a brick wall. Much to his surprise, however, he coped reasonably well with everything else, and even found the time to stage one of his old tried and tested plays from rep – *French Without Tears* – to entertain his colleagues and superiors.

If he had needed one more event to make him focus more firmly on the fight for the future, it came on Saturday 8 March 1941, when he decided to make the most of seven days' leave by driving up to London to see June in the Ford V8 that, with typical generosity, she had sent him as a present. Changing from his uniform into a sports jacket and smart new flannel trousers, he strolled over to the vehicle only to find that it now had a flat tyre. Opening the boot, he discovered that there were no tools of any kind inside, just a full bottle of Gordon's gin wrapped up in a copy of *Reynolds Weekly*. Frustrated, he got in the car and tried to start it up, but there was also something wrong with the ignition. When a mechanic at a nearby garage failed to come up with a prompt solution, John accepted defeat and telephoned June, telling her to cancel the table she had booked for that evening at the fashionable Café de Paris in Piccadilly. It turned out to have been a soberingly fortuitous late change of plan, because that very night two fifty-kilogram land mines came crashing through the Rialto roof of the Café de Paris and exploded on the dance floor. Reports would say that the police and ARP wardens who arrived soon after were confronted by a harrowing scene in the underground ballroom, where the popular bandleader Ken 'Snakehips' Johnson had been decapitated and about eighty other elegantly dressed people were still sitting, stone dead, in their seats.[8]

John did reach London the following day, but, once again, while he was shaken deeply by this news, June seemed eager to block it out and simply find somewhere else nice enough for them to dine. It was, as a consequence, an awkward and upsetting visit for him – never before had he felt so out of place in some of London's most glamorous locations – and it was almost with a sense of relief when he realised that it was time for him to return to military business.

It was not long after that he was on the move again, having been posted to the 54th Training Regiment at Perham Down, a couple of miles outside Tidworth, where he began his duties as a junior officer. A rather sullen Geordie was attached to him as his batman, waking him up at six o'clock every morning with a cup of tepid sweet tea and then pointing him in the proper direction for the parade ground. John was put in charge of ARP duty, monitoring camp security and signalling the start of the regular 'theoretical gas attacks' by setting off the alarm system. The sense of monotony that such a routine induced was interrupted every now and again by the chance to escape to London on a forty-eight-hour pass, but something usually happened to ensure that the change was not really as good as a rest.

On one occasion during April 1941, for example, he drove up to meet June for dinner at their favourite restaurant, the Moulin D'Or, only to find himself in the middle of yet another bombing raid. Although he had managed to reach Romilly Street safely enough and in good time to greet his wife and start his meal, the place was soon shaken by an explosion so loud 'that even June could not ignore' it. A land mine had hit and destroyed the nearby Shaftesbury Theatre and its adjoining buildings. Sending June off in a safe direction with the maître d', he grabbed his ever-present gas mask and tin hat and ran outside to try to do what he could to help. There in the street he saw ambulances and fire engines flying in and out of the smoke and people with bloodied faces and torn clothes desperately clawing at the wreckage in search of friends, pets and possessions. 'I did not exactly fall down in a dead faint at the sight of death and mayhem,' he would later say, 'but I did vomit at one point when trying to attach the wrong arm to the wrong body.'[9] Accompanied by the constant throb of low-flying aircraft and the coldly metallic rattle of gunfire, the bombing would go on long into the night, causing massive material damage and claiming 130 lives.[10]

After witnessing something so harrowing, it was thus a bitter sort of reprieve to be able to return to Perham Down. His unit, however, only remained there for a few more weeks before it was time for yet another move – this time to Deerbolt Camp on the outskirts of Barnard Castle in Teesdale, County Durham – to complete his evolution into an officer.

Deerbolt was a relatively modern military base with brick-built, single storey barrack blocks arranged according to squadron in neat and orderly cul-de-sacs. The ordinary rank-and-file soldiers were packed into cramped little quarters with slatted timber-based bunk beds and thick brown linoleum-covered floors, while the officers were allotted considerably more capacious and comfortable accommodation nearby. There was an above-average NAAFI (Navy Army and Air Force Institute) providing unexciting but surprisingly edible food as well as some much-needed means of recreation, and also a gymnasium that doubled at weekends as a ballroom along with a small but functional cinema (which showed the colourful Rita Hayworth and Tyrone Power movie *Blood and Sand* so often that bets started to be taken as to when and where the film would next snap and fall apart). It always seemed to be cold, wet and windy outside, but at least the camp was well enough run to allow everyone to get on with some worthwhile work.

John quite enjoyed his time at Deerbolt, partly because his Geordie batman was now slightly less sullen due to being so much closer to his native Newcastle, and partly because it was here that he made the acquaintance of a more experienced officer called Neville Crump. The large, bluff and outspoken Crump – who, with his sharp nose, broad jaw, silver temples and ruddy cheeks, looked rather like an outdoor-reared version of Maurice Chevalier – was a racehorse trainer by profession who would go on to win (among many other titles) two National Hunt trainers' championships and three Grand Nationals once his wartime duties were done. As John shared his passion for horses and racing, and was amused by his almost theatrically volatile manner (with every other word seeming to begin with an 'f' and extend for four letters in length), the two men became firm friends. They would often sneak off for drinks at the Crump family's large and well-appointed temporary home nearby at Brignall Grange (Mrs Crump being the wealthy granddaughter of the millionaire custard magnate, Sir Alfred Bird), afterwards driving on in a pony and trap to have dinner at the historic and eminently welcoming Morritt Arms at Greta Bridge.

Exploiting the widespread desire to have something else to watch in the evenings instead of yet another patched-up screening of *Blood and Sand*, John staged a play while at Deerbolt: J.B. Priestley's mysterious déjà vu drama, *I Have Been Here Before*. Not everyone liked it – Captain Crump responded simply by groaning, shouting out a word that began with 'f' and extended for four letters in length and then marching off to the bar – but the vast majority did, and the modest production ran for a week. The rest of John's time there was taken up with his obligations either as Orderly Officer (which mainly involved parrying any complaints from the men about the poor quality of the food) or Duty Officer (which entailed spending most of the night in the Adjutant's office answering the telephone). It was, on the whole, very dull and uninspiring work, but, as he feared that something terrible could happen at any moment, he was quite content to go on without the intervention of any genuine excitement.

Distraction was provided when he was dispatched on two consecutive training courses. The first was in Scarborough, where he was supposed to learn something about cookery, though the best he could manage was some weak soup and 'an indefinite stew';[11] the second in York, where he was supposed to learn something about Army book-keeping and accounts (he persuaded the Pay Sergeant to give him advance warning of all the questions – and answers – and passed with flying colours). Having completed both of these brief 'study' trips as requested, there was time for one last week on leave in London – where he joined his wife on the usual circuit of socialising – before the war really began for him in earnest. He was posted to India as a captain in the Royal Armoured Corps.

Setting off on their long and draining trek into unfamiliar territory at the start of 1943, John's unit travelled on a troopship from the Royal Navy base in Rosyth near Edinburgh, sailing down the Irish Sea and through the Bay of Biscay to Gibraltar, on into the Mediterranean, along the Suez Canal and through into the Indian Ocean. They then made their way on land via Bombay (now Mumbai) and Poona (now Pune) until they eventually reached their designated base in Ahmednagar: a distinctly underwhelming-looking camp composed of a bunch of rusty Nissen huts dotted around a dusty parade ground. It was not the kind of place that John had ever imagined being, and, although he was destined to remain there for the remainder of the war, he would never form any affinity for either the camp or the surrounding area. Bored by his regimental duties, which ranged from helping to plan tactical exercises to teaching rudimentary English to young Indian recruits, and largely neglected by the vast majority of his fellow officers, who tended to 'talk incessantly of things mechanical',[12] he went through each day feeling like something of a loner.

The situation would no doubt have seemed much better had there been an opportunity to tend to his thirst for theatre, but, as far as he could tell, any demand in camp for regular drama had long since run bone dry: '[T]he total absence of any encouragement from my brother officers . . . led to a two-year interregnum in my [acting] career. When anyone referred to entertainment, they invariably meant "leave", and "leave" was synonymous with Bombay.'[13]

Concluding that he might as well try to follow the crowd, he started visiting Bombay himself. On the first occasion he checked into the very grand Taj Mahal Hotel, where he made full use of the deep relaxing bath and the decent restaurant (he was pleased to find that the restaurant band played selections from Gilbert & Sullivan, even if it did so 'rather too frequently'[14]) and found himself feeling more homesick than ever for London. Once again electing to follow the line of least resistance, he also paid a visit to what he had been told was one of the city's most notorious brothels, at number 4 Grant Road, where he bought a drink and then paid for some time alone with 'a very beautiful Eurasian woman'. Taking him off to a room that resembled, in his eyes, 'a chalet in a Butlin's holiday camp', he sat down, looked around at the 'dreadful pictures' that decorated the walls, heard the woman telling him snappily to 'hurry up', and suddenly felt his physical urges draining away.[15] He thus made his excuses and set off back to the base in Ahmednagar, wishing that at least a few of his compatriots would soon develop an interest in staging some makeshift plays. None of them ever did.

It was ironic that John should come to feel so isolated, artistically, during the very period when the notion of entertaining the troops was receiving unprecedented political support back home in Britain. Only the previous year, the War Office had sanctioned the establishment of the Central Pool of Artistes (CPA) to boost morale among those serving their country abroad. Drawing on the best talents to be found among the whole of Britain's armed forces (rather than being limited, as the original concert parties had been, to whatever was on offer in a local division), the CPA was now sending touring units – known generically as 'Stars in Battledress' – wherever there were soldiers who needed to be entertained. Countless actors, comedians, musicians and various other types of entertainer – some amateur and some professional – were now therefore getting the chance to serve by playing their part on the wartime stage.[16] The likes of Ian Carmichael, Frankie Howerd, Benny Hill, Arthur Haynes, Bill Fraser and Eric Sykes would soon be treading the boards in France, Holland and Germany; Spike Milligan and Harry Secombe were already doing so in Italy; Arthur Lowe and Tommy Cooper were entertaining the troops in Egypt; Michael Hordern was organising plays and revues on board HMS *Illustrious* in the Mediterranean; and Terry-Thomas was touring through most of western Europe. Even elsewhere in India, Peter Sellers, among others, was acquiring invaluable experience performing in one of Ralph Reader's RAF 'Gang Shows', and Jack Hawkins was in charge of a concert party in Poona. In Ahmednagar, however, Captain John Le Mesurier was strictly limited to conventional military duties, wondering all the time to himself whether he would ever have the chance to resume his acting career.

One brief but much-needed break in the routine came when he was dispatched on an aerial photographic course that took him up to Peshawar. Travelling there from Bombay by train, the journey took him all of four days. As he had already picked up a virus and was feeling slightly feverish, the experience of being stuck in an exceptionally crowded carriage, complete with several passengers 'clinging suicidally from every nook and cranny',[17] was something of a nightmare. Squeezed between two loud and very animated Indians, John sat quietly and tried his best to re-read his well-thumbed copy of A.G. Macdonell's *England, Their England.* When that proved too great a strain on his powers of concentration, he simply did 'a lot of staring out of the window'.[18]

Changing trains at Delhi – where he somehow managed to mislay the bottom half of his pyjamas – he finally arrived in Peshawar and, once he had recovered from the ordeal of the journey, he really took to the city. 'It was as clean as a whistle,' he would recall, 'and the air was beautifully fresh.'[19] In stark contrast to the officers' mess at the camp in Ahmednagar, where there never seemed much to do except sip a cool and thick lemon-flavoured refreshment called Nimbu Pani and talk at great length about the mechanics of tanks, the equivalent setting in Peshawar boasted much more convivial and cultured company and a far better selection of drinks. John was therefore soon in a far better frame of mind. He also enjoyed the comparatively unde-manding nature of the course itself, which mainly involved attempting to identify a wide range of objects on the ground as photographed from several thousand feet up in the air, and he passed with very creditable marks.

Anxious to avoid a repeat of his recent claustrophobic train journey, he managed to arrange to fly back to Ahmednagar, even though it was in a rather decrepit Dakota plane, and then continued with his usual duties. Missing the relaxed chatter of the officers' mess at Peshawar, he tried socialising with some of the old Anglo-Indian families who lived in a degree of splendour on the east side of the town (where they munched on cucumber sandwiches, sipped Earl Grey tea and played the odd game of croquet), but he soon tired of the kind of conversation that was dominated by nostalgia for the so-called 'great days' of the British Raj. Withdrawing back into his isolated existence within the camp, he found it hard to do more than go through the motions as most of the real action went on elsewhere.

His one big adventure (relatively speaking) arrived when he was required to travel up to the North-West Frontier and take charge of a troop of light tanks that were part of an Indian mechanised cavalry regiment. It did not go very well. Finding the climate oppressively hot during the day and uncomfortably cold during the night, he found it hard to function at the top of his form. It did not help that his map-reading skills, even back in England, had always been decidedly unreliable, because one of his tasks now involved orchestrating the movements of his men over the area's wild and rugged terrain. Things went rapidly from bad to worse when he dispatched two tanks on a dubious course and then watched with a mounting sense of alarm as they undulated awkwardly over a seemingly non-existent track, eventually winding up trapped against a barrier composed of large rocks and impenetrable undergrowth. Help had to be requested urgently from HQ; once the problem had been overcome, an angry commanding officer suggested to John that it would be best for all concerned if he returned to Ahmednagar as promptly as was practically possible. Sure enough, he was soon back at the base resuming the same old boring routine.

His spirits dipped a little deeper when, at the end of 1944, he belatedly received the news that his paternal grandmother, Emma, had died, aged eighty-six, on 14 October at her home in Burnham-on-Sea. He had always been extremely fond of 'Grannie Halliley' – describing her later as 'a dear' who during his youth 'frequently gave me two-and-six or five shillings which I immediately spent on either whipped cream walnuts or ten De Reske cigarettes – in that order'[20] – and he deeply regretted the fact that he would never see her again. Another cherished link with his childhood had been lost, and now, alone abroad at thirty-two, he looked back and wondered where so many of the years had gone.

John was still serving in India a few months later when the war finally came to an end. On VE Day – 8 May 1945 – he celebrated with everyone else at the camp, raised a glass of tepid champagne, toasted the King and said a silent prayer of thanks that the whole wretched affair was well and truly over. 'Did I ever fire a shot in anger?' he would wonder to himself many years later. 'Well, I fired a shot now and then, but you couldn't say I was angry. I must say I found the whole thing very boring.'[21] After the party circuit had wound down and most of the remaining paperwork had been completed, John started to think about the prospect of being demobbed.

Before he could get his hands on his release papers, however, he had to spend a week at a transit camp about 100 miles north-east of Bombay called Deolali – a place so notorious among soldiers for its mind-numbing tedium (as well as the fact that it had previously served as a mental hospital for members of the British military) that, whenever anyone seemed to be snapping from sheer frustration, he was said to be suffering from 'a touch of the doolallys'. Forewarned about the dangers of Deolali, John decided that the wisest policy would be to find the bar, pull up a chair and simply stay there for the duration. What was ironic about this decision was the fact that, just a short distance away, a Royal Artillery concert party featuring such eager young entertainers as Sergeant Jimmy Perry (who later drew on the experience to create the sitcom *It Ain't Half Hot Mum*) was putting on its latest high-spirited show. Even at the very end of his two-year sojourn in India, John was still missing out on the kind of theatrical life that he loved.

Arriving back in England, at the docks at Southampton, on a chilly autumn morning, there was no one waiting to greet him, as no one had known for sure when he was coming. His return was thus very low-key and unemotional as he traded in his uniform for a dark brown Burton's demob suit, accepted his officer's payment – £300 – and set off for London on a train bound for Waterloo. He telephoned June from the station and they were soon reunited, going off for a long and predictably extravagant celebratory evening in the West End and then retiring to June's wartime base at her mother's house in Highgate.

For the next couple of weeks John was in the most blissful of moods. Everything that he had missed for such a long and lonely time – his wife, his family and friends, the London clubs and cafés and restaurants and, of course, the theatre – was there for him once again, and he could hardly believe his luck. Like countless others among his contemporaries, he had spent the past few years wondering whether he would ever return, and worrying as to what would (and would not) still be around if he did make it back alive. This moment, therefore, was incredibly precious, and to experience it was exhilarating.

Gradually, however, the emotion receded and a calmer sense of realism returned. John began to realise that he would not simply be able to pick up from where he had left off before his life had been so rudely interrupted. He now found himself living with June in the Melville family home, which they shared with June's mother Jane, younger sister Sheila and brother-in-law George Abel, and the atmosphere, as far as John was concerned, was not particularly warm. Abel, a Canadian-born businessman who had married Sheila in 1942, struck John as 'an abrasive fellow' who, during his new brother-in-law's prolonged absence, appeared to have assumed the role of 'the young head of the family'.[22] Perhaps sensing that John's natural diffidence and impeccable good manners would prevent him from causing a 'scene', Abel (as 'a civilian through and through') moved swiftly and treated his supposed rival ('ennobled by my captain's pips') with stunningly cruel contempt: 'After a few days, he told me in no uncertain terms to clear out and find somewhere else to live.'[23] John, just as this upstart had predicted, went quietly, preferring to keep his dignity rather than stoop to challenge Abel at such a low level, and found a suitable flat for himself and June at 28 Harrington Gardens, near Gloucester Road, in South Kensington.

John's post-war mood was further soured by a fresh set of family tensions. Although, as he would later make clear, 'The Melvilles – the genuine Melvilles – were as generous and accommodating as ever',[24] he began to feel as though he was being pressured into accepting a certain role in the family business. While he could appreciate the fact that the Melvilles had various theatrical investments that needed protecting and in some cases improving (in addition to the Lyceum, the Prince's and the Brixton, their bulging portfolio now also boasted the Palace Theatre in Watford), and June was having to devote a great deal of time and effort to managing their multiple repertory companies, the fact was that he had his own professional ambitions to pursue. He did not want to become a mere cog (even a well-oiled one) in the shiny Melville machine; the prospect of becoming more of a businessman and administrator than a performer repulsed him. He wanted to act. He was now in his mid-thirties and, having lost the best part of five precious years to the war, he was in a hurry to return to the stage and resume his proper career.

Risking the wrath of June's family, therefore, he started sending out applications and knocking on doors, hoping to find work back in the theatre or possibly now in the movies. It was a dauntingly competitive time for any performer to be hunting for jobs, as the marketplace was teeming not only with other tried and tested professionals but also with a whole new breed of younger, even hungrier entertainers who had cut their teeth with the concert parties during the war. John soon realised that he would have to spend more and more of each day touting himself out and about instead of attending to the concerns of the family firm, and such priorities provoked a certain amount of censoriousness: 'The hours I spent knocking on doors in Wardour Street were judged by the Melvilles as a wanton disregard for my true interests.'[25]

The problems he was having with the rest of the family might have been overcome had his marriage to June remained strong, but the truth was that it, too, was now in trouble. The niggling concerns about her drinking and outlook that had festered during his time away at war had been pushed aside for a while by the sheer relief that came with the peace, but now, as the novelty of being back began to wear off, such worries not only returned but also worsened. 'In the time we had been apart,' he would reflect, 'I had written to her every week and she had written to me as frequently. Yet, in those volumes of correspondence, we never once got close to anticipating a life after the war, when we could no longer rely on living dangerously as a sort of fix to keep our passion high.' Finding themselves reunited in a much more austere kind of black-and-white Britain, where rationing and red tape were part of the grim routine, it all seemed 'a cruel anti-climax'. While John's response was to seek out new challenges within his profession, June's response, as far as he could tell, was depressingly predictable: 'She drank more.'[26]

He watched with a growing sense of despair as it became increasingly evident that his wife was descending rapidly into alcoholism. Every social event now seemed to revolve around a long and hard session at the bottle. Every mood seemed to drive her to seek out some sort of intoxicating drink. Living such a high life placed an increasing strain on their finances, and John started to notice that some of her furs, jewellery and other valuables were disappearing. She also began to miss appointments and make uncharacteristic errors. On one occasion she had to leave a first night because she was hopelessly inebriated. John wanted to help but was unsure of what he should do, and frustrated by the lack of any real support. Too many of her friends and colleagues, he felt, were ignoring her illness while continuing to indulge her extravagance and accept her generosity. For a while, he tried hard not to leave her for long when he went off in search of work, but in time, as she hugged the bottle more tightly than ever, he found himself seizing on every opportunity to escape from the hellish domestic scene.

Eventually, John gave up and moved out, leaving Harrington Gardens for a bachelor apartment a short distance away around the corner in Gloucester Road. In turmoil, he felt guilty for not having done enough while remaining puzzled as to how he could really have helped.

Monitoring June's condition anxiously from a discreet distance, he tried to keep alive his career while mourning the death of his marriage. It had been over five years since they first became husband and wife, but, as he reflected on the high times they had shared, 'counting the hours in champagne cocktails',[27] he realised that they had only spent about a year of that period, in total, living together. The whole relationship now seemed strangely, bewilderingly, chimerical. Although it still did not seem right to move on, it no longer made any sense to go back. When neither he nor June could keep the news of their separation from finally reaching their respective families, June's mother travelled to Bury St Edmunds to discuss with John's parents the possibility of engineering some kind of reconciliation, but, in spite of all of their well-intended efforts, the conclusion soon dawned, even on them, that nothing could now be done. 'Our names,' John would later say, 'were already entered in that casualty list known as "war marriages".'[28]

The estranged couple would still meet up for the odd social occasion and remain on genuinely good terms, but such encounters always reminded John, unnervingly, of something June had once said: 'I shall be found dead,' she told him jokingly, 'with a cheque book in one hand and a glass in the other.'[29] The light-hearted prediction would turn out to be harrowingly close to the truth: after marrying again a few years later, this time to an Irish-born journalist, she continued helping to manage the Melville family businesses, and also directing plenty of productions, but never managed to venture very far or for very long from the bottle. Following a long and unhappy spell in hospital, she died, on 15 September 1970, at the age of fifty-four.

Back in 1946, while June carried on as normal, John concentrated on knocking on doors and asking for work. The war had robbed him, as it had so many millions of other people, of the time in which to experiment, explore and grow. He had felt young before the conflict had begun. Now, all of a sudden, he was starting to feel middle-aged. If he was still going to establish himself as an actor, he knew that he would have to do so soon.

CHAPTER VII

Hattie

The moon that lingered over London town
Poor puzzled moon, he wore a frown
How could he know we two were so in love
The whole darned world seemed upside down.

Estranged from his wife and absent from the stage, John – who was now aged thirty-four – channelled all of his thoughts and energies into the urgent task of reviving his moribund career. It remained, however, a depressingly barren period during his first few months alone. The only vaguely noteworthy engagement came towards the end of the year, at the start of December 1946, when he was hired to appear (as Uncle Noel) in a new adaptation of Richmal Crompton's popular *Just William* stories staged over the festive season at the Alexandra Theatre in Birmingham. The first half of the following year was barely any better, with just a few theatrical scraps to feed on as a guest back in rep at Croydon. Then, at last, something positive happened. He met a woman named Hattie Jacques.

Born Josephine Edwina Jaques (the additional 'c' would be added to her surname a few years later, according to her biographer, to 'recapture a little of the fashionable French derivation'[1]) on 7 February 1922 at Sandgate in Kent and brought up in Chelsea in south-west London, she had attended Godolphin and Latymer Upper School and then trained briefly as a hairdresser before spending two years during the Second World War first as a Red Cross nurse and then as, of all things, an arc welder. She then moved into a home of her own – an impressively capacious and tastefully decorated early Victorian house at 67 Eardley Crescent, Earls Court – and made her stage debut at The Players' Theatre in London. It was here that she would first come to John Le Mesurier's attention.

The Players' Theatre was an unconventional venue with an unconventional past. There had been a subscription-only Players' Theatre Club as long ago as the late 1920s in a cramped little building at 6 New Compton Street,[2] but its more recent incarnation (based initially in a third-floor eyrie in King Street, Covent Garden, relocating during the war first to a basement in Albemarle Street in Piccadilly and then, with the arrival of peacetime, to Villiers Street underneath the arches by Charing Cross station) had been the brainchild of a South African-born actor and entrepreneur named Leonard Sachs. After teaming up with fellow actor Peter Ridgeway in 1936, Sachs shaped the venue into an affectionately old-fashioned and intimate sort of music hall. Nicknamed 'The Pink Tunnel' because of the shape and colour of its auditorium, the little theatre featured sets and scenery designed by Rex Whistler and murals drawn by Felix Topolski that accentuated its distinctively quaint and characterful atmosphere (and helped to distract people from taking much notice of the fact that trains could sometimes be heard – and felt – rumbling past overhead). Sachs proceeded to hire some of the most promising young talents around, giving early opportunities to such performers as Alec Clunes, Ian Carmichael, Peter Ustinov, Patricia Hayes, Jean Anderson, Bernard Miles, Bill Owen, Clive Dunn, James Robertson Justice and Eleanor Summerfield (whom he later married). He appointed himself as a synonym-spinning, hyperbolising, gavel-banging chairman modelled on a romanticised vision of the crowd-pleasing Victorian Masters of Ceremonies, a characterisation that he would later revive when he hosted the popular BBC1 show *The Good Old Days*. Jacques had been a familiar figure there since 1944, graduating rapidly from part-time backstage duties to full-time work as a performer.

The Players' had served as her drama school. She acted there in plays, pantomimes and revues, directed some productions, wrote song lyrics and comedy sketches, choreographed a few dance routines and developed an impressive range of characterisations – including an imitation of the saucy music-hall star Marie Lloyd, a cheeky schoolgirl, a ditsy debutante, an operatic diva and a large and bossy but vulnerable Fairy Queen. She had always been known to everyone as either Josephine or Jo; it had only been since early in 1946, when she 'blacked up' for a minstrel show and someone backstage likened her to the rather large African-American *Gone With the Wind* actor Hattie McDaniels, that the sobriquet of 'Hattie' had started to stick.[3] In recent months she had been attracting a growing number of critical plaudits in the press (*The Times*, for example, praised her satirical skills as well as the way that she 'powerfully and gaily' sang her songs, while the *New Statesman* said that there was a 'don't give a darn air about her that is sheer delight'⁴), and she was a firm favourite among the Players' regular patrons.

The Players' now had some rather influential regular patrons. In the immediate post-war period, the venue – with its twice-nightly revues called 'Late Joys' – possessed the kind of cachet that attracted such famous figures as Ivor Novello, Emlyn Williams, Alfred Hitchcock (who would often relax so much there after a hard day's work that he would sit back and go to sleep), Dylan Thomas (who would often drink so much there after a hard day's work that he would slump forward and go to sleep), Jack Hawkins, James Agate, Sarah Churchill, and Sir Maurice and Lady Violet Bonham-Carter. Hattie Jacques, responding to the MC's cue – 'Your own, your very own . . .' – would come out in front of them all and captivate them with her joyous way of singing such old songs as 'I Sits Among the Cabbages and Peas' and 'She'd Never Had Her Ticket Punched Before', winning cheers and applause for her clever delivery of comic lines and her disarming mixture of power and poise. She would end her act by leaping into the air and doing the splits before skipping off into the wings. 'We want Hattie!' the crowd would shout, and she would rush back out triumphantly to perform her usual encore.

John, during this time, was struggling to get by on a range of short-term engagements, appearing in a succession of humdrum provincial productions while he waited patiently for something more challenging to arrive. On one sultry summer evening in June 1947, after going through the motions in front of a sleepy Croydon audience, his co-star, Geoffrey Hibbert, suggested that they go to the Players' – a favourite haunt of his – in order to cheer themselves up and unwind. Although they were too late to catch any of the shows, the two men decided to stay and have a few drinks while socialising with some of the regulars. This was the occasion when John Le Mesurier first met Hattie Jacques.

He was fascinated by her. She was, he would later say, 'bright and witty and vivacious and an entertainer to her fingertips', a woman who seemed to have a very appealing – and alluring – self-assurance about her voluptuous good looks. Reflecting on the often dramatic and fairly revealing outfits that she wore, John would remark: 'It was as if, knowing she was bound to be noticed, she wanted to make a real job of it.'[5] Unable to get her out of his mind, he paid another visit to the venue as soon as he possibly could in order to see her perform, and then – so enthused by what he had witnessed that he found it surprisingly easy to overcome his normal shyness – he asked her to join him for a drink. Although she hesitated, telling him sarcastically that she was not feeling particularly thirsty, she soon relented and they went on to spend what was left of the evening together (and then, back at Eardley Crescent, she cooked breakfast for him, wearing – as was her wont – a glamorous old evening dress as a house coat). A couple of days later, Hattie confided to her gay best friend, Bruce Copp, who ran the Players' restaurant and rented a room in her house: 'I've met this man who's rather special.'[6] The ever-supportive Copp accompanied her when she next saw John for an evening at the Melville-owned Lyceum ballroom; June happened to be there as well, keen to socialise with her estranged but still friendly husband, but, after watching how close he now was to Hattie, rarely diverting his gaze from her eyes, June soon slipped quietly away: 'Come on,' she muttered to Copp, 'let's leave them to get on with it.'[7]

At the end of the week, Hattie announced that she was going to come down to Chatham, where John was appearing in a production of Terence Rattigan's *The Winslow Boy* at the Empire, because she said that she wanted to find out what he was like as an actor. 'I know what she meant,' he would later reflect. 'If two performers get together, they must share a professional respect, otherwise the relationship is doomed.'[8] He was somewhat nervous about the visit, as he was already fast becoming bored by *The Winslow Boy* and he feared that his indifference would show. As it turned out, however, her presence at a thinly attended matinée performance gave him the adrenaline rush that was required and elicited the desired dramatic effect. She made it clear that she 'warmly approved' of his efforts and, from that moment on, the two actors (she always calling him 'Johnny' and he calling her 'Jo') started seeing each other regularly.

Jacques, who at the age of twenty-five was a notably sensual and flirtatious young woman, had been wary of allowing any relationship to become serious ever since an intense but intermittently long-distance wartime romance with a married US Army officer, called Major Charles Kearney, had come to a cruelly abrupt end when he returned to America and cut her out of his life (causing her so much distress and humiliation that she would always tell even her closest friends that he had died on active service).[9] The following two years had seen her satisfy her considerable sexual appetite via a breathless succession of brief and frivolous flings, but the relationship with John Le Mesurier was different. He was a more mature and reassuringly gentlemanly sort of character, quieter and calmer than most of the other men she had known, with a fine sense of humour and a kind and thoughtful nature. Crucially, at this stage in her life, he appealed to her as a true friend as well as an attentive lover.

Although his initial impression of her had suggested that she was a very confident and ebullient person (she would think nothing, for example, of raiding the wardrobe at The Players' and then, posing as some exotically haughty character, set off to the most glamorous night spot she could find to startle the wealthy clientele with her diva-like demands and striking sartorial splendour), he soon realised that, hidden beneath the surface, there was a high degree of vulnerability – not least because of her intermittent problems with her weight. She had been a promising ballet and acrobatic dancer as a child, appearing as principal dancer in all of the shows put on at her local dance school, but, when her 'puppy fat' failed to fall away as she entered adolescence, she started to be teased mercilessly by many of her peers and was reduced to tears on countless occasions. She had responded with admirable defiance, refusing to allow her identity to be defined exclusively by her weight; she fought back by projecting the kind of apparently carefree and playfully assertive persona that would intrigue so many men in her adult life. The inner sadness and self-doubt, however, would never really go away, and, once he was aware of it, John felt more protective of her than ever and was very good at reassuring her as to how much he loved, admired and respected her. He made her see how attractive she actually was, and she adored him for his attitude.

The one irony, as their relationship developed, was that, although John was ten years older and far more experienced as an actor, it was Hattie whose career now seemed to progress at a more rapid pace. A mere three months after they met, she had passed an audition for a regular role in Tommy Handley's hugely popular BBC radio show *ITMA*, playing an adenoidal schoolgirl with a spectacularly sweet tooth called Sophie Tuckshop (whose recitations of confectionery excesses were invariably followed by a giggle and the line: '. . . but I'm all right now!'). The following year she would start appearing occasionally on television and begin to receive some increasingly interesting movie offers, while still attracting high praise for her ongoing work at the Players'. John, during, the same period, struggled to gain any real momentum.

The occasional role in radio came along, but such work went straight out on the airwaves without affording him much, if any, publicity. During the autumn of 1947 he did manage to win a minor role in a relatively prominent West End production – a revival of the 1932 comedy-musical *The Dubarry* (adapted by Eric Maschwitz from the play by Paul Knelper and J.M. Welleminsky) at the Melville-managed Princes Theatre – but was given little chance to impress. The show, which had been staged by Michael Mills (the man who, as Head of Comedy at the BBC, would later be responsible for casting John Le Mesurier in *Dad's Army*), boasted a glamorous Hollywood musical star, Irene Manning, in its leading role, and some lavish sets and colourful period costumes. A long run had been predicted with some confidence. It was, indeed, initially well received, but, after a few busy weeks, it started suffering from a combination of having a leading lady who could not cope with the rigours of a West End run – 'She was very good to me,' said John, 'but not good enough for the show'[10] – and a prolonged bout of bad weather that discouraged a significant proportion of London's regular theatregoers from venturing out and about. Within a couple of months, therefore, Mills had decided to cut his losses and John was once again out of a job.

Things were no better for him when it came to his earliest efforts to make a name for himself in movies: while Jacques was crafting brief but eye-catching cameos for British-based directors of the calibre of Alberto Cavalcanti (in his big screen adaptation of *Nicholas Nickleby*) and David Lean (in his dramatisation of *Oliver Twist*), the best that Le Mesurier could manage was a handful of quickly forgotten contributions to some humble home-grown cinematic shorts.

It was almost inevitable that John should have started his big screen career making so-called 'B-movies', because the short supporting film, or 'second feature', was, in the post-war era, the closest thing that the cinema had to the theatre's tradition of rep. As in a repertory company with its routine of weekly productions, the actors and directors responsible for making B-movies had to be able to master a script as rapidly as possible, rehearse it without any delays (usually using their own clothes as 'costumes'), perform it competently in front of the cameras without the need for a second take and then move straight on to the next available project. The practice had actually been around since the late 1920s, following the passing of a protectionist law that obliged British exhibitors to screen a greater percentage of home-made films, but, after over-expansion and a subsequent slump during the 1930s and early 1940s (when a decline in quality caused many critics to dismiss the output as mere 'quota quickies'), the low-budget B-movie had only recently regained some of its old invention and momentum.[11]

One of the most notable and impressive companies that emerged in this period was Tempean Films, set up at the start of 1948 by two ambitious young men – Roy S. Baker and Monty Berman – who had first met during the war in the Eighth Army Film Unit. Once demobbed, they 'begged, borrowed and stole' to fund their first production, *A Date with a Dream*, an undemanding but commercially appealing revue-style story that starred Terry-Thomas and showcased a host of other ex-service entertainers.[12] Rarely spending more than about £20,000 per project (and sometimes as little as half of that sum), Baker and Berman would select the most popular-sounding scripts, save money on sets by only shooting in natural locations – usually either in or close enough to London to avoid any need to pay for the crew to stay overnight in a hotel – and then rush the finished products straight into national circulation in the hope that they would catch enough filmgoers in the right mood to fancy a quickie.

John Le Mesurier would soon become something of a regular for Tempean Films, often under the guidance of a young Londoner named John Gilling, a prolific freelance film maker who saved his bosses precious time and money by writing most of his scripts himself and then ordering his actors through each scene with formidably brisk efficiency.[13] Another B-movie entrepreneur whom John would encounter on a fairly regular basis during this period was a rather eccentric little character called Harry Reynolds, a businessman with a chequered show business career who now appeared keen to model himself on the old pioneering Hollywood moguls. Scheming and scrapping to make something popular on a shoestring, he would then market it loudly and proudly as the latest top quality offering from one or another of several 'posh-sounding' production companies that actually existed only inside the files of his modest London office.[14] Like the more idiosyncratic of the old repertory company managers, such figures tended to be tolerated, and in some cases warmly admired, so long as they continued – one way or another – to provide at least a few struggling actors and other crew members with a regular source of work.

Another, less fortunate, similarity to rep was the fact that there was no guarantee that one's participation in these rushed productions would ever attract the kind of attention that would lead on to offers of bigger and better projects. Most of the mainstream newspaper critics tended to ignore such modest supporting efforts, leaving only the specialist trade magazines to comment briefly on their content and quality. As Roy S. Baker would later remark: 'The main feature was always the attraction. Lots of people wouldn't even bother to see the supporting feature; they'd come in half way through just to see the feature film. The second feature was the "poor relation" of a show.'[15] It could thus be frustrating as well as exhausting to be a part of such under-appreciated endeavours, but, to those who were desperate for any chance, however slim, to shine, the supporting feature was still better than nothing.

Hungry rep-trained actors like John Le Mesurier soon found, therefore, that they had an elective affinity for companies such as these. They could more or less guarantee to be suitably cost-effective – there would be no tantrums, no rebellions and no crises, just solidly professional performances – and the companies could at least offer them some kind of a wage. John, having tried and failed on many occasions to win a role in a 'proper' full-length feature, duly began his cinematic apprenticeship by working on an uninspiring trio of these low-budget pot-boiler projects.

He made his movie debut in February 1948 in a creaky black comedy short called *Death in the Hand*, directed by the Australian Albert Barr-Smith and adapted by Douglas Cleverdon (via his own recent well-received BBC radio play) from a Max Beerbohm short story entitled 'A.V. Laider'. The drama – which was set on a crowded train – revolved around a psychic called Cosmo Vaughan (played by Esmé Percy) whose palm readings produce portentous predictions about the fate of his fellow travellers shortly before something dramatic happens to the carriage. Unusually for a supporting feature, *Death in the Hand* (which was produced by a small and, it would turn out, short-lived company called Four Star Productions) attracted a fair amount of pre-publicity, as Max Beerbohm had previously withheld his permission when film makers attempted to adapt his fictions, but the finished product proved something of an anti-climax. The cast was rather good – boasting not only the very experienced Esmé Percy and Ernest Jay but also a future Sherlock Holmes and Dr Watson double act in the form of Carleton Hobbs and Norman Shelley – but the forty-four-minute story was presented in a fast-paced and formulaic way that left the actors with little to do except keep prodding the plot along. John evidently found the experience so underwhelming that he soon not only erased it from his mind but also omitted it completely from his list of career credits.

He was much better in writer/director John Gilling's short 'psychic mystery' movie, *Escape from Broadmoor* (released by Harry Reynolds' grandly named International Motion Picture Company later the same year). In what he wrongly described as his cinematic debut,[16] John played a psychopathic murderer called Pendicost who was on the run from the police. Tall and gaunt, with slicked-back hair, hollow cheeks and a dark pair of eyes peering out from beneath the blackest of brows, he was surprisingly convincing as this coldly brutal working-class Londoner, staring at whomever he met with a glacial gaze that suggested he was studying the best way to knife them through the neck. Not for the last time, however, John was dismissive of his performance. He later dubbed it – quite unfairly – an 'inglorious' contribution to a production that was 'hilarious for all the wrong reasons', pausing only to point out the one thing that, at least for him, had gone wrong: 'My moment of truth came when I had to strike one of the [other] villains over the head with a revolver butt. I assumed, wrongly as it turned out, that it would add conviction to the scene if, instead of just appearing to deliver the deadly blow, I hit him gently. The result on screen looked as if I was swatting flies, which only goes to prove the frailty of the human cranium because, in reality, I knocked the poor man cold.'[17] The scene was one of those rare ones that ended up being cut, and, even if John remained embarrassed by what survived, the drama still did rather well at the time.

His fledgling film career then seemed to slip two steps backwards. In July 1949, he took part in another supporting feature (once again produced by Harry Reynolds, but this time under the alternative grandiose-sounding banner of The Renown Pictures Corporation) that was the latest instalment in the long-running series of quickly made comic shorts that featured the increasingly grotesque music-hall turn of 'Old Mother Riley'. Co-starring Lincolnshire-born Arthur Lucan in drag as the familiar Irish washerwoman character and his real-life wife Kitty McShane as 'her' daughter, the earlier big screen outings for the couple had involved tolerably playful little takes on politics, high society, the armed forces and big business.

Apparently running out of suitable 'big picture' themes, however, the more recent efforts had edged inexorably towards slapdash slapstick and lazy parodies of other types of B-movie fare, including the predictable ghost story and detective tale. Even the perfunctory-sounding title of this latest episode – *Old Mother Riley's New Venture* – seemed to acknowledge how tired and uninspired the series had become, and the painfully laboured plot – which saw Old Mother Riley go, via the usual 'zany' twist of fate, from being a humble washer of dishes to a luxury hotel manager who is then framed by a jewel thief and also accused of murder – served only to underline the absence of any real laughs. John appeared as the bad guy Karl, a stiff-backed floor waiter in black tie and tails who speaks in a flat Cockney accent and sends his female sidekick into the rooms of wealthy guests to steal any unusually large diamonds that they happen to have left lying about. With barely any lines to deliver, he spent most of his screen time looking shifty and vaguely constipated as his accomplice scuttled about clutching shiny chunks of glass. After disappearing for a lengthy period to allow for some unrelated comedy scenes, some aimless faux 'Oirish' nostalgia (the Old Mother Riley equivalent of Harpo Marx's obligatory musical interludes) and an egregiously caterwauling rendition of 'I'll Take You Home Again, Kathleen', his character briefly returned in order to have two custard pies thrown in his face in quick succession for no particular reason. Seemingly giving up on the attempt to bring the storyline to any meaningful resolution, the movie then promptly disintegrated into a frantic *Hellzapoppin'*-style self-referential mess.

Although John would try to console himself with the thought that at least the experience had taught him 'a thing or two about working to the camera' (and Lucan had coached him on the best technique to take a pratfall), he must have known, deep down, that far from doing anything to further his career it had probably done it some damage. As if to add insult to injury, he later discovered, as he sat and watched the finished film with Hattie in their local cinema, that the opening on-screen credits listed him incorrectly as 'John Le Meseurier'. It seemed sadly symbolic of his rapidly diminishing status.

Such setbacks were making this period, in certain ways, a peculiarly ambiguous time for him. Some aspects of his life seemed more pleasant than ever. He had, for example, just left his flat in Gloucester Road and moved in with Hattie at her sprawling house in Eardley Crescent, where he marvelled at her extraordinary skills both as an informal hostess – 'it was the sort of place that attracted poppers-in'[18] – and a homemaker – 'I often had the feeling that no practical task was beyond her'[19] – as well as watching in awe as she took so much pleasure in helping so many of their mutual friends: 'It was a bit like living with Mother Earth.'[20] He was also, however, beginning to fear that, with his career appearing to stall just as hers was starting to soar, he would soon be in danger of seeming – at least to onlookers – like something of a burden to her. 'She was well aware of my fear of not being able to keep up,' he would recall. 'She was as sensitive as I was to people calling me "Mr Jacques" or assuming, correctly, that it was she who was bringing in the best part of the family income.'[21] He was, as a consequence, in even more of a hurry than before to claw back some professional pride.

The next thing that he did, however, was seek to mark a new start in his personal life by asking June for a divorce. They had stayed in touch and remained on good terms throughout the duration of their lengthy separation, but it was now clear to all concerned that he was fully committed to Hattie. Although he was extremely chary about the prospect of another marriage after the painful failure of the first, he wanted to clean up some of the mess and move on. Not only had Hattie already established an excellent rapport with the Hallileys in Bury St Edmunds, but also John now felt as though he had been accepted by Hattie's family (especially her similarly vague and diffident older brother, Robin, with whom John often did the rounds of the Soho clubs and relaxed listening to jazz). June, who was not short of boyfriends in spite of her continuing problems with drink, responded promptly and sympathetically to the request, and the divorce proceedings duly commenced.

The hearing took place, during the summer of 1949, just around the corner from The Players' Theatre at the Law Courts in the Strand. Although neither party had remained faithful since commencing their separation, they had agreed, for appearances' sake, that John's adultery with Hattie Jacques would be cited as supplying the sole grounds for the divorce. There had been no arguments or angry scenes during the usual kind of convoluted discussions that had led them up to this point, and now the only outstanding concern related to June's possible performance as a witness. Realising that, if the case was to continue after lunch, she was more than likely to drink an unhealthy amount of alcohol during the recess, John arranged for Bruce Copp to keep a discreet eye on her until it was time for them to return. Unfortunately, when a break was indeed taken, she swiftly gave him the slip. Telling him that she urgently needed to see a friend at the nearby New Theatre, she actually headed straight to the bar and proceeded to down several double measures of malt whisky. Any embarrassment was averted, however, after one of her legal advisors poured enough black coffee down her throat to more or less sober her up. She went on to deliver her testimony in such a loud and theatrical manner that the judge praised her for the power and clarity of her performance.

A short while later, when John was away from home appearing in a production called *Playbill* at the Alexandra Theatre in Birmingham, he received a telegram from June that read: 'The cage is open, darling; you can fly away now.'[22] Once he was back in London, his unspoken plan was to carry on broadly as before; as he later recalled, 'I was more than content with our present situation.'[23] He was taken by surprise by Hattie, however, when, during the course of a casual shopping trip, she turned to him suddenly and said: 'Don't you think it's about time we got married?'[24] John, slightly dazed, stammered and mumbled and fiddled with his ear in his usual vague way and then meekly agreed: 'There was no arguing with a determined woman.'[25] The next thing they did was go off to buy each other a ring.

The couple married soon after on Thursday 10 November 1949 at Kensington Register Office.[26] Hattie wore a small violet hat, fox fur and a long brown dress with matching shoes. John wore a dark suit with a floral bow tie, and a dark overcoat with a red carnation. As they left the building, Hattie went over to the newsreel crew who were covering the event, smiled, and reprised her old *ITMA* catchphrase: 'But I'm all right now.'[27]

Elton and Amy Halliley were there to celebrate alongside Hattie's mother Mary (her RAF officer father, Robin, had died in a flying accident in 1923 when his daughter was just eighteen months old), and many other family members and friends gathered at the reception nearby to congratulate the happy couple. John and Hattie then went off for a week-long honeymoon in Hampshire at, of all places, a boarding house (called Frobisher House) at Villiers Road in Southsea run by an old friend of Hattie's called Kitty Clisby, a former masseuse at the Turkish Baths in Jermyn Street who had also worked part-time at The Players'. Boasting 'hot and cold water and gas or electric fires in all rooms', along with a 'full dinner served after theatre' in a 'coal fire lounge', the establishment's advertisement – which was often to be found in the classified pages of *The Stage* – promised its guests 'every possible comfort'.[28] The so-called 'bridal suite', however, turned out to be a modest front upstairs room with a row of perched seagulls peering in through the window. The newlyweds nonetheless enjoyed themselves there immensely.

They returned to London, threw some large and memorably lively parties at Eardley Crescent and then settled swiftly into the kind of secure and stable domestic life that both of them had always wanted. Hattie kept up her work at The Players' while increasing her involvement in radio, while John went back to searching for jobs in the film world, this time with a heightened sense of optimism.

They were happy together, they believed in each other, they supported each other, and the life that they shared felt good. With a new decade about to start, the bad wartime memories had at last started to fade and their thoughts were now fixed firmly on the future. The 1950s, both of them agreed, were going to be rather special.

CHAPTER VIII

Movie Man

It was one film after another in those days.

Just as he had hoped, the 1950s began rather well for John Le Mesurier. Although there was no rapid and dramatic surge to stardom, there was certainly the kind of reassuringly steady progress that suggested his career was finally back on track.

The destination that he most desired was the cinema. Having laboured for a fair number of years in the theatre, he now felt ready for the new technical challenge – as well as, potentially, the superior wage packet. In the short term, however, he was happy to accept whatever offers, in whatever medium, happened to come his way.

Television, for example, was now a much more appealing medium for a British actor, having been successfully relaunched after the war and given far more support from within the BBC, and John started making an effort to establish himself as a regular small screen player. Writing regularly to BBC producers and bookings managers on his best cornflower-blue headed notepaper, he alerted them to forth-coming stage appearances, 'warned' them well in advance of spells when he was likely to be available and expressed his willingness to come in for auditions or just a 'chat', and, sure enough, the odd engagement soon came his way.[1] In 1951, for example, he was given six opportunities to catch the eye in the popular children's series *Whirligig*. He also appeared as the kindly Doctor Forrest in an eight-part adaptation of Edith Nesbit's *The Railway Children*; played an aristocratic figure in a children's comedy-thriller called *Show Me a Spy!*; took part in an adaptation of an Arthur Conan Doyle Sherlock Holmes short story entitled 'The Second Stain', playing a blackmailing bounder – Eduardo Lucas – who meets with an untimely end; and participated in a nativity play called *A Time to Be Born*. Producers began to take notice of him and, as the decade progressed, he became an increasingly familiar presence on the small screen.

Radio was another context for his contributions. After passing a belated BBC audition on 26 November 1951 – during which he had impressed his judge with his 'deepish, masculine' voice pitch and 'posh' accent but also gave one reading that was considered somewhat 'dull' and 'casual'[2] – he became one of the actors regarded as 'reliable' by the Drama Department, and started averaging about five substantial roles each year. Some of these performances were broadcast again on the Corporation's Overseas Service, thus increasing his fees as well as allowing some of the many more well-travelled Le Mesuriers to hear John act for the very first time.

He also continued his domestic involvement in B-movies, working again for the tireless writer-director John Gilling in two more of his unpretentious little thrillers, *Dark Interval* (1950) and *Blind Man's Buff* (1952). He was then given a key role as a police superintendent in *The Drayton Case* (1953), the first of Edgar Lustgarten's 'Scotland Yard' series of small screen shorts in which the lugubrious Mancunian crime writer ('Have you murdered anyone?' he would enquire, sipping from a schooner of sherry. 'Perhaps you'd rather not say . . .') introduced supposedly 'true-life' tales of British suburban unpleasantness. There were similarly prominent but undemanding parts in several more fast-paced crime dramas, including *The Blue Parrot* and *Black 13* (both of which were released later the same year) and *Dangerous Cargo* (1954). He showed his versatility by playing a slightly deranged and dishevelled religious fanatic in a murder mystery called *A Time to Kill* (1955). Producers such as Roy S. Baker (who described him as 'a great actor'[3]) now regarded Le Mesurier as one of the B-movie industry's most reliable contributors, and his uncomplaining attitude, even when offered the most modest of roles, certainly endeared him to many of the busiest directors in the business. Few casting discussions, as a consequence, omitted at least a friendly mention of the man they now knew as 'Le Mez'.

The stage, however, would remain John's safety net throughout the decade, almost always providing him with something when his diary would otherwise have been left empty. In January 1952, for example, he relished the opportunity to appear as a doctor in a rather controversial little legal-themed play about the ethics of abortion called *Angry*

Dust at the New Torch Theatre, and he was applauded by a critic in
The Times for rendering the complexities of his character 'extraordinarily well'.[4] Later that year, at the New Theatre from September
to December, he took part in another thoughtful legal drama –
adapted for the stage from the Bruce Hamilton novel by actor
Raymond Massey and directed by no less a talent than Michael Powell
– called *The Hanging Judge*, portraying the Governor of Norwich Gaol
in a setting that might well have reminded him of his early days in East
Anglia haunting the courts as an articled clerk. He then attracted
plenty of praise during the summer of 1953 for his contribution to a
play called *Piccolo* at the Connaught, *The Stage* reporting that 'John Le
Mesurier is brilliant in a hard-working role'[5].

Hattie, meanwhile, continued to be the busier (and better known)
of the two, combining her popular appearances at the Players' with her
burgeoning radio career. After the premature death of Tommy
Handley in 1949 had spelled an end to her successful run in *ITMA*,
Eric Sykes wasted no time in asking her to join the cast of the new
show that he was co-writing with Sid Colin called *Educating Archie*.
Beginning in the summer of 1950, it starred (odd as it may now seem)
the ventriloquist Peter Brough and his wooden doll Archie, and
featured a supporting cast that included the teenaged Julie Andrews as
Archie's young playmate, Robert Moreton as his tutor and Max
Bygraves as an odd-job man. Jacques was given the regular role of
Moreton's girlfriend (an over-amorous woman named Agatha
Dinglebody) but was also provided with plenty of opportunities to
demonstrate her vocal versatility by playing a wide range of other
minor characters. An instant hit – the first series was extended to thirty
consecutive weeks, managed to attract an audience of 12 million
listeners and won a national newspaper's annual 'Top Variety Show'
award[6] – the programme would run until the end of the decade,
confirming Hattie Jacques in the process as one of the best-known and
most popular women currently working in radio.

While John and Hattie discussed and supported each other's
various solo ventures, they also looked out for any suitable opportunity
that would allow them to work together. During this period in the first
half of the 1950s, they did manage to collaborate on no fewer than five
separate occasions in fairly quick succession. The first – and by far the
most modest – of these projects was a peculiar shared experience
participating in the last laboured Old Mother Riley B-movie outing,

Old Mother Riley Meets the Vampire (1952), which was produced and directed by John's friend John Gilling. This time the story centred on the gin-soaked Irish washerwoman's efforts to prevent a mad scientist called Von Houson – played by guest star Bela Lugosi – from taking over the world with the assistance of an army of monstrous robots. Hattie appeared alongside Dandy Nichols in a couple of early scenes as Mrs Jenks, a regular Cockney customer at Mrs Riley's corner shop ('Got any eggs, ducks?'), while John's 'blink and you'll miss it' contribution – he ambled past Lugosi in a scene set at the docks – was, mercifully, left uncredited. Although the movie was vastly superior to the execrable *Old Mother Riley's New Venture*, it was still a dire affair. The morphine-addicted Lugosi (who only agreed to take part – under duress – after a lucrative-sounding theatrical tour of the UK collapsed before it started and left him in urgent need of funds to pay for a plane ticket back to California) wore his 'usual' pair of Count Dracula costumes – stiff and formal for outdoors, silky and shiny for indoors – and coasted through his scenes without expending any unnecessary effort ('You hat bedder lock dat yung man up somevere . . .'). Hattie, meanwhile, coped very well with a script that required her to break into a music-hall song-and-dance routine for no obvious reason; John was content, on this occasion, to spend most of his time helping out behind the scenes.

A much more interesting and mutually rewarding cinematic adventure followed a few months later, when the couple were cast in another short movie called *The Pleasure Garden*. Written and directed by the American poet, playwright and avant-garde film maker James Broughton (the bisexual former lover of *New Yorker* critic Pauline Kael), financed entirely by private subscription and shot on location in London among the ruins of the Crystal Palace Terraces, this self-styled 'movie masque' was meant to project the mood of a 'midsummer afternoon's daydream' about sexual desire frustrated by the repeated intervention of officialdom in a depressed post-war Britain. Broughton had seen, and been captivated by, Hattie at The Players' Theatre (where she came on to the stage as the Fairy Queen), and he sought to celebrate her sensuous *joie de vivre* by creating the role for her of 'Mrs Albion' – a timeless English sprite whose magical touch (once she emerges from a snack bar) awakens libidinous urges within everyone whom she encounters. John appeared as Colonel Pall K. Gargoyle, a puritanical local bureaucrat dressed in a top hat, dark sunglasses, a stiff wing collar, a black bow tie and a long black overcoat, who wishes to suppress all libidinous feelings and convert the Pleasure Garden into a cemetery. Also featured were the likes of Broughton's memorably named partner, Kermit Sheets, Lindsay Anderson, Jill Bennett, Maxine Audley, Derek Hart, Hilary Mackendrick and Gladys Spencer, as well as Players' regulars Jean Anderson and Diana Maddox.

'What is your pleasure, please?' Hattie's character can be heard asking a young female visitor at the start of the thirty-seven-minute movie. 'Your favourite, private, pleasure? Would you expect to find it in the open air, in a more or less public park? You might – if the world were a garden of love. But, in this particular garden, you are more apt to find desire locked up.' We then see a succession of 'curious strangers' (among them a repressed young daughter, a lonely war widow, a frustrated artist and an extremely camp cowboy) arrive to seek what pleasure they can find out and about in the afternoon. Memorable moments include the sight of John nailing a fig leaf over the private parts of a well-endowed statue ('Disgraceful! Distasteful!'); his startled discovery that one soon-to-be-expelled couple happens to be gay ('Oh, I see, ah, I'll have to look this up . . .'); and a brief scene in which a triumphant Hattie, having liberated almost everyone in the garden, watches as a distressed John scuttles away while being pursued by a suddenly amorous spinster ('Thank you very much indeed, madam, but no, no, no!'). The allegory ends with Hattie reciting some lines with all double entendres fully intended:

> The pleasure to go as you are and come as you please
> Twice the leisure to come together
> One at a time and two by two.

Likening his and Hattie's involvement to a labour of love, John would later say that the thrill of being able to try something so refreshingly unconventional made both of them forget all about matters relating to money: 'This was just as well because all we got was the return fare from Victoria to the location at Crystal Palace and lunch in a nearby restaurant where we were served splendid meals by an impoverished gentlewoman who wore rather bizarre hats'.[7] Released in 1953, it was shown at some prestigious festivals both in Britain and abroad; although it caused much scratching of heads among mainstream exhibitors, one of whose trade publications dismissed it as 'too pretentious' and 'a doubtful proposition',[8] it was widely praised by the broadsheet critics. *The Times* called it 'a most agreeable fantasy', adding that it was 'remarkable that the film ever got made at all' and saying that it was 'a pity there are not more like it'.[9] It was also nominated for a special award by the British Film Academy and won the Prix de Fantasie Poétique from head judge Jean Cocteau at the 1954 Cannes Film Festival.

John and Hattie went on to appear on television together (for the very welcome fee of £28 guineas each[10]) as an endearingly eccentric onscreen married couple called Mr and Mrs Mulberry in a BBC children's comedy series entitled *Happy Holidays*, which also featured their mutual friend from the Players', Clive Dunn, and was broadcast live from Lime Grove Studios during the school summer holidays of 1954. They were reunited the following year at the newly launched ITV in a series of Victorian-era plays called *The Granville Melodramas*, staged at an old music hall in Fulham that had recently been transformed into the commercial channel's first operational television studio. Hattie appeared in all seven episodes in a variety of prominent roles, John joining her in three of them.

The fifth joint Le Mesurier/Jacques project was a musical-comedy revue – *Twenty Minutes South* – that Hattie was asked to produce and direct (initially at The Players' Theatre before transferring to the St Martin's Theatre in the West End of London). Devised by Peter Greenwell, the show was a musical satire on contemporary suburban life with a cast – chosen by Hattie – that included her husband John as well as her old friends and colleagues Daphne Anderson, Donald Scott, Totti Truman Taylor, Louie Ramsay, Joan Bailey, Robin Hunter, the choreographer Dougie Squires and a young ballet dancer named Josephine Gordon. The new producer/director proved herself a shrewd and supportive organiser and advisor, and John found that he greatly enjoyed being guided along by his wife. Running from July to October 1955, the show won Hattie an encouraging amount of critical plaudits for her 'clever staging' (although some reviewers had reservations about the overall quality of the writing), and, with John relaxed and contented in a non-singing part, it was a very happy experience for the two of them to share as a working couple.[11]

This was also an eventful period personally as well as professionally for John and Hattie, because they had recently started a family. Hattie became pregnant for the first time in the summer of 1952, shortly before she was due to start work on a revue called *The Bells of St Martins*, again at the St Martin's Theatre in West Street. John thus spent the second half of the year trying to hide his mounting sense of anxiety as he watched his wife drive herself on night after night, not only as the director of the production but also as one of the main performers, taking part every evening in the kind of high-energy physical routines that involved leaping over chairs, spinning on a table, doing the splits and sliding down a playground-style chute. He was therefore hugely relieved when, after 107 performances, the show finally closed and, following the usual annual ritual of a pantomime at the Players' (which she directed without succumbing to the strong temptation to venture on to the stage), she spent the last couple of months or so of her pregnancy taking things comparatively easy.

It was all mercifully calm and straightforward during the weeks before the birth: Hattie remained in very good health, and, right up until the time when she was admitted to the Queen Elizabeth Hospital, she and John went out regularly to take in a play or a movie somewhere pleasant in the West End. Eventually, their first baby – a son they named Robin after Hattie's late father – was born very early on the morning of Monday 23 March 1953. John, as was still something of the norm in those days for the nervous first-time father, had spent most of the previous evening somewhere else – in his case in the West End, ensconced in a saloon bar drinking gin with a burly and boozy actor friend named Denis 'Den Den' Shaw. Once the call came through to confirm that all was well, however, he raced over to the hospital and was utterly enchanted by the new arrival. Three years later, their second son, called Kim after the Rudyard Kipling book, was born (a little prematurely) on Friday 12 October 1956, and the Jacques–Le Mesurier family was complete.

As parents, John and Hattie would never threaten to arrive at an equitable division of labour, because John was (or at least always made absolutely sure that he appeared to be) hopelessly inept at attempting even the most basic of practical domestic tasks. Hattie, as a consequence, returned to work soon after each birth and did her best to combine motherhood with her stage, radio, television and film work while John, in between his own acting projects, hired 'a relay of au pair girls to lighten the load' and continued to marvel, from a safe distance, at his wife's 'superhuman energy'.[12] Both of them, however, doted on their two children, even though their professional obligations placed limitations on how much leisure time they all could share. 'They spent as much time as possible with us,' Robin would confirm. 'Obviously, they were working an awful lot, but they were very good about making sure we all did plenty of things together.'[13] Hattie, predictably, was open and expressive and tactile, always ready to kneel down and play and share out the kisses and cuddles and hugs. John, equally predictably, was more reserved and gently reactive, but, like Hattie, he adored studying the evolution of each son's nascent personality. Robin, he would later reflect, was a rather shy and reticent but very observant little boy 'like me' who 'was growing into a very reasonable being'. Kim, on the other hand, would strike him as 'a funny boy' who 'seemed intent on becoming some sort of clown'.[14] John was relieved to see them develop into such distinct characters, interacting without any sign of jealousy or competitiveness.

There would always be plenty of visitors for the boys to meet and observe at their home in Eardley Crescent, including a seemingly endless procession of actors, comedians, writers and musicians (Robin would recall once being woken up at three o'clock in the morning by the sound of Spike Milligan, Peter Sellers and Michael Bentine having a jam session in the living room[15]), and, as their parents were keen to make the most of whatever gaps occurred in their busy schedules, sudden excursions would come to be almost expected. Robin would remember, for example, his father sometimes taking him and his brother off to Barnes Common for some characteristically languid Le Mesurier leisure activity: 'He'd play cricket with us a little bit, usually with one hand in his pocket and a cigarette in his mouth.'[16] There were also several trips to see the circus, which rekindled John's childhood fascination with the phenomenon even if, as Robin later admitted, the experience did not exactly impress either him or his brother: 'Dad loved the circus. That was something I never got but he adored it. I think he especially liked all of that pageantry, when all the animals were paraded around the ring, but, even though he always insisted on taking us with him, I never saw what he saw in it. And to this day, clowns really irritate me!'[17]

When neither parent could be sure of being able to devote much time to the children, they were packed off to stay for a few days with Hattie's mother, Mary, at her pretty cottage by the seaside in Margate. 'My brother and I were always really, really close to her,' Robin would say of his maternal grandmother. There was, in contrast, surprisingly little contact between the children and their paternal grandparents in Bury St Edmunds, although any perceived coolness had much more to do with disposition than design: 'We had very little to do with them,' Robin later reflected. 'They were almost like strangers – my brother and I hardly ever saw them. It was probably no more than ten times in total. They always seemed very far removed. In fact, my dad's dad seemed even more reclusive than my dad! He was very difficult to get to open up, at least as far as me and my brother were concerned. I do remember my grandmother [Amy] as being lovely – and very loving, warm and comforting – but I always found my grandfather rather severe. He wouldn't brook any nonsense, let's put it that way!'[18]

The boys simply embraced the style of life that they had been handed, accepting love and care wherever and whenever it was available, and never really noticed, let alone questioned, the unconventional nature of the arrangements. 'We just had a lot of fun,' said Robin.[19] The situation, to adult eyes, was far from ideal, and both parents were prone to pangs of guilt for their absenteeism, but there seemed no simple solution during such a hectic time in their professional lives.

John's career, in particular, was now entering a very propitious phase, not least because, early in 1955, he had finally found himself a full-time agent. Up until this point he had mainly relied on representing himself by knocking on doors, answering adverts and responding to various tips and hints to secure new engagements.[20] Although his lengthening list of personal contacts had provided him in recent times with a much better range of offers, finding work was still an unnervingly hazardous and time-consuming process. What made things worse was the fact that, even when he did win a part, his painful lack of any sound business skills meant that he was always in danger of being seriously underpaid for his efforts (he could not even be relied on to remember to bank the cheques). Hattie – who was already on the books of a well-respected agent named Felix De Wolfe – had tried to improve the situation by hiring a personal secretary to supervise John's finances and keep an eye on his diary (by a strange coincidence, the person whom she chose – a mature married woman called Joan Tollemache – turned out to be a relation of John's old inamorata from Bury St Edmunds[21]), but it came as a great relief when he finally met the man – Freddy Joachim – who was both willing and able to manage his professional life.

Joachim, by this time in his early fifties, was the son of an immigrant Jewish stockbroker who had started out working as an accountant for a theatrical agency run by Herbert de Leon before setting up a business of his own at Remo House in Regent Street. A short, stocky, well-spoken man, he came with a certain amount of 'baggage'. Apart from being dogged by an acute insecurity complex that had its roots in the fact that his parents had openly favoured the achievements of his musician brother, he was also something of a misogynist, usually refusing to represent women on the dubious grounds that they were more likely to lead 'complicated' private lives'[22] and regarded the notion of an increasingly populist 'mass media' with such suspicion that he always refused to have either a wireless or a television set inside his own house.[23] As, however, another of his clients, Denis Quilley, would recall, he must, in spite of his faults, have seemed well-suited to someone like John Le Mesurier: 'He had silvery hair and looked like a very reliable bank manager, or a businessman of a respectable nature. He was unflashy, untheatrical, charming. He was a gent – not a word you can use often about agents.'[24]

Joachim – who was currently managing the careers of eleven other actors (he always limited himself to a dozen), including Dirk Bogarde, Warren Mitchell and Eric Pohlmann – was the kind of agent who believed that if he found one decent role for his client then his work was largely done. One good high-profile role, he reasoned, would attract good notices, which would in turn attract plenty of offers of more good roles, and a successful reputation would maintain the right momentum. His first advice to John Le Mesurier, therefore, was to bide his time, wait for the right role to arrive and then make sure that he seized the moment.

John might have found such advice, at such a stage in his career, hard to take had it not been for the fact that he had just been alerted to the news that the 'right role', or at least a promising role by his current standards, was already available. He thus felt on the verge of finally breaking through from B-movies to major full-length features – which was one of the reasons why he had speeded up his search to secure an agent. An old writer friend of his named Frank Harvey had called to ask if he was interested in meeting the producer/director Roy Boulting: 'He's casting for a new film, John, and I thought you might be interested.'[25] Roy Boulting, in partnership with his twin brother, John, had already been responsible for some of the best British movies of the era – including the gritty Graham Greene crime drama *Brighton Rock* (1947), the social mobility parable *The Guinea Pig* (1948) and the political thriller *High Treason* (1951) – and the pair were known to be extremely ambitious to push far beyond their current achievements. Some of the country's most promising actors were thus being recruited into what was starting to resemble an unofficial repertory company for movies, and John was eager to be one of those enlisted. Joachim, upon hearing the news, could see the sense in pursuing such a project, so he arranged a meeting on John's behalf and a deal was soon done. John was at last going to be a 'proper' movie actor.

The project – which was based at Shepperton Studios in Surrey – was called *Josephine and Men*: a romantic comedy, written by Nigel Balchin with some assistance from Roy Boulting and Frank Harvey, starring one of John's old heroes, Jack Buchanan. Among the supporting cast were Peter Finch, Glynis Johns, Donald Sinden, William Hartnell, Ronald Squire, Sam Kydd and Thorley Walters. John, who had been cast rather belatedly in the minor role of a registrar, was rattled initially when Roy Boulting, who seemed oblivious of his new actor's track record in B-movies, treated him as though he was a total stranger to the film set, explaining everything at the most elementary level and even pointing out why there was a boom microphone hovering above his head ('This is for sound, John . . .'). He soon realised, however, that this misunderstanding was working to his advantage, as Boulting was clearly impressed by how well John responded to his instructions.[26]

The finished movie, which followed the ups and downs of a young woman whose romantic choices are determined largely by her sympathy for the underdog, received mixed reviews in the press, although the always suave and charming Jack Buchanan emerged with more than his fair share of praise,[27] but, whatever they felt about the production as a whole, the Boultings were certainly pleased with the contribution they had elicited from John. His air of strained and faintly bewildered authority was just the kind of quality they had wanted, and his performance suggested a whole range of similarly fatigued and flustered Establishment figures that would fit into various fictions. It thus did not take long for the brothers to contact Freddy Joachim and sign John up on a long-term contract, beginning with a project entitled *Private's Progress*.

Private's Progress was set to be the first in a series of playfully politicised movies planned by the Boulting Brothers (who wanted to demonstrate how to be 'extremely serious without being solemn'[28]) that satirised various facets of Britain's post-war way of life and the pillar institutions of its Establishment, including the armed forces, the law, the Foreign Office, the City of London, the trade unions and the Church of England. Set in 1942, *Private's Progress* (which would be released in March 1956) featured Ian Carmichael as Stanley Windrush, a naive, upper-middle-class Oxbridge undergraduate called up into the Army and taken under the wing of a cockney wide boy called Henry Cox (played by Richard Attenborough). Dennis Price, John's old colleague from Croydon Rep, played Windrush's uncle – a shady senior officer at the War Office called Bertram Tracepurcel – who assigns him to a 'secret operation' that is actually cravenly corrupt. Terry-Thomas – another recent graduate from B-movies – appeared as Major Hitchcock, a lazy but basically decent sort of cove who has learnt to cope with the various crises that creep towards him by passing the buck and then downing the brandy.

John was handed the part of a psychiatrist. It was another minor role (the character was not deemed significant enough in his own right to merit being given a name), but he did share a potentially memorable little scene with Stanley Windrush, interviewing him to assess his mental fitness for an officer training course, so John was determined to make the most of his limited time on screen. Responding to a suggestion by the director, John Boulting, that he should assume a slight facial twitch to imply that he was the one who really needed psychiatric help, John proceeded to give a delightfully subtle, funny and vulnerable kind of cameo performance, projecting the image not of an Establishment stereotype but rather of a real individual who is breaking slowly under the strain of trying to embody such an Establishment stereotype. Beginning coolly and calmly by inviting Windrush to engage in a quick session of word association, he is soon twitching and grimacing in bewilderment at the irritatingly prosaic illogicality that his action has unleashed:

PSYCHIATRIST: Right . . .
WINDRUSH: Wrong.
PSYCHIATRIST: No, no, no, I haven't started yet.
WINDRUSH: Ah.
PSYCHIATRIST: Beer?

WINDRUSH:	Sheba.
PSYCHIATRIST:	Coffin?
WINDRUSH:	Spitting.
PSYCHIATRIST:	No, no, no. 'Coffin'. C-O-double F-I-N.
WINDRUSH:	Oh. Um . . . Gravestone.
PSYCHIATRIST:	Mother?
WINDRUSH:	Hubbard.
PSYCHIATRIST:	Father?
WINDRUSH:	Boiled beef and carrots!

Private's Progress attracted a certain amount of criticism from some quarters – being seen to mock the armed forces was not considered, in those days, the 'done thing' – but the movie did enhance the reputations of several members of its cast. John Le Mesurier, like Terry-Thomas, would win plenty of praise from the critics for taking a relatively minor character, with very little screen time, and turning him into one of the most memorable figures in the entire film. Just as Terry-Thomas (who was barely on screen for more than ten minutes in total) had made Major Hitchcock seem so intriguingly flawed as well as funny that many viewers could not stop thinking about him, so John Le Mesurier (who himself was only on screen for a total of four minutes) personalised an impersonal figure and impressed him on people's minds (and won a very welcome positive mention in the *Sunday Times* by the influential critic Dilys Powell[29]). It was something of a problem for the movie as a whole, because the vividly distinctive nature of such supporting characters served inadvertently to highlight how weak and wooden Ian Carmichael's central role of Private Windrush actually was. For Le Mesurier and Terry-Thomas as individual actors, however, the effect served only to signal the great potential of each for serving British cinema.

John, sure enough, went straight on to contribute to many of the country's best comedy movies of the latter half of the decade, nearly always in roles that could so easily have seemed flat, underwritten and instantly forgettable had it not been for the subtle idiosyncrasies that he always smuggled on to the screen. Continuing his series of appearances with the Boulting Brothers, for example, he played an irascible golf-mad judge in *Brothers in Law* (1957) and an exasperated judge in *Happy is the Bride* (1958); in *Carlton-Browne of the F.O.* (1959), he played, by way of a modest departure, a foreign

Establishment figure – the brusque and bossy Grand Duke Alexis. He also popped up briefly in Mario Zampi's entertaining little kidnapping caper *Too Many Crooks* (1959), playing yet another tetchily perplexed magistrate – a character who proved a wonderfully subtle 'straight man' to Terry-Thomas in a courtroom scene as the bounder kept reappearing to answer multiple charges.

His most memorable – and certainly his most commercially and critically successful – movie of this period was *I'm All Right, Jack*, which was released in the summer of 1959. Another Boulting Brothers national satire, *I'm All Right, Jack* revisited the class-ridden community of characters who had previously been seen in *Private's Progress*. This time, however, instead of showing what had held them together in wartime, it focused on what was driving them apart during the peace: a series of increasingly bitter disputes between management and unions, and the growing threat to the economy (and society) posed by the phenomenon of organised strikes. It was an undeniably topical theme: in the ten years prior to 1955 in Britain, there had been an average of 1,791 strikes per year, involving 545,000 workers and at the loss of 2,073,000 days of labour; in the ten years after 1955, the average annual number would rise to 2,521, involving 1,116,000 workers and resulting in 3,889,000 days lost. A sort of 'industrial cold war' was thus breaking out all over Britain.[30] The Boultings, therefore, felt confident that they had chosen the most appropriate target for a timely comic critique.

'Both John and I felt at the time,' Roy Boulting later reflected, '[that] the idea that one particular part of society should be held guilty and responsible for the failures of society at large, and that some other area should be free of blame, was ridiculous. We felt that all areas of society shared some common blame, and this is what we had to address ourselves to.'[31] In the little Britain depicted by *I'm All Right, Jack*, therefore, the bosses were corrupt, especially the incorrigible Bertie Tracepurcel – played once again by Dennis Price – who would happily transfer his shares elsewhere and see his company go under in order to make a quick but criminal profit. The union leaders, meanwhile, were hypocritical clots, especially the archetypal 'bolshy' shop steward Fred Kite – played by Peter Sellers – who waffles on pompously but ultimately incoherently about things that will 'jeopardise' or 'reverberate back to the detriment of the workers', looks up reverentially at his library of unread books by Lenin and dreams of one day making it over to dear old Mother Russia to enjoy 'all them cornfields and bally in the evening'. Caught together in the middle, feeling impotent and confused, are supposedly insignificant little men like the drip Stanley Windrush (Ian Carmichael) and the twit Major Hitchcock (Terry-Thomas) – the former a management misfit-turned-workforce misfit and the latter a put-upon-officer-turned-put-upon-personnel manager, but both of them mere cogs in a system no less unjust now than it was before.

John reprised his psychiatrist character, only on this occasion he was given a name – Waters – and retooled as an obsessive time and motion study expert. Sharing most of his screen time with his fellow scene-stealer from *Private's Progress*, Terry-Thomas, he complements his comedy colleague with elegant precision, leaning forward and twitching and fidgeting with neurotic concern as Major Hitchcock sits back and blithely tries passing the buck:

HITCHCOCK: That's all right for the brass at Head Office – they don't actually have to deal with the workers. As personnel officer that's my job, God help me. And I can tell you they're an absolute shower! A positive shower!

WATERS: But my instructions, Major Hitchcock, are to carry out a time and motion study in every department.

HITCHCOCK: Whose bright idea was that?

WATERS: Mr Tracepurcel's. I suppose. [*Fiddles with the knot in his tie as if it was a noose*] He engaged me. But surely the men must know –

HITCHCOCK: 'Know'? Get this into your head: they know nothing other than what's in their pay-packet at the end of the week. We've got chaps here who can break out into a muck sweat merely by standing still! One thing they can't stand is being stop-watched.

WATERS: But the sole purpose of the time and motion study is to enable the men to work efficiently – well within their natural capacity.

HITCHCOCK: 'Capacity'? My dear fellow, the only capacity that's natural to these stinkers is the capacity to dodge the column!

[*Hitchcock suddenly realises that Waters is twitching wildly and looks pale and ready to faint*]

HITCHCOCK: Er, sorry old chap. [*Pats Waters on the shoulder*]
              Letting off steam like that. Had a rather punishing
              night last night. Did a spot of time and motion study
              of my own. Redhead. Rather athletic.
WATERS: [*Glowering censoriously*] Quite.
HITCHCOCK: Well, not to worry, old boy. I shall just have to think
              of a way for you to do your stuff without these rotters
              cottoning on . . .

Hitchcock's bright idea turns out to involve Waters crouching on a
roof and spying on the workforce through his old Army binoculars –
a tactic that meets with immediate failure when he spies one worker
giving him the 'V' sign before slamming the painted windows shut.

Having been bullied by Hitchcock, he is then bullied by Bertie
Tracepurcel, who advises him to quiz the gullible Windrush to elicit
the information he needs. Once Windrush has cheerfully
demonstrated how much more productive his 'brothers' could be, a
triumphant and almost twitch-free Waters reports back smugly to
Tracepurcel and the workers are duly ordered to speed up their output
– thus sparking an angry all-out strike. Nothing more is seen of poor
Waters, as the remaining action concentrates on the fate of Windrush
and Fred Kite as Major Hitchcock and others struggle to sort out some
kind of mutually face-saving solution. Once again, however, this
relatively minor character lurked in the memory long after the movie
was over.

John thus ended the decade feeling grateful to all of those
producers and directors who had helped make him such a familiar
figure in British films, and considered himself particularly indebted –
at least artistically – to the two Boulting brothers: '[They] were
demanding and difficult. After a day's work, you felt you had earned
your money. It was never very much.'[32] Pondering as to why he, of all
the many budding character actors looking to move from stage to
screen, had gone from the fringe of the film industry to somewhere
close to its centre, he concluded that, apart from the kindness
of strangers, he also owed 'a lot to my customary expression of
bewildered innocence', portraying 'a decent chap all at sea in a chaotic
world not of his own making'. Arguing that he had always felt very
much like that in real life, he wondered, with his usual self-
effacement, how much of an achievement it had really been – 'Having

sought for recognition for so long I now felt a little reticent about accepting it. Did I really deserve it, I kept asking myself?' – but he was certainly in no mood to throw it away.[33]

He was where he had always wanted to be. He had a much-loved family. He had a successful career. He now wanted to enjoy his life.

CHAPTER IX

Hancock

My dear fellow . . .

John was used to watching Hattie welcome what seemed like most of the show business world into their Eardley Crescent home throughout the 1950s, but one visitor in particular would enter into John's own life and never really leave. His name was Tony Hancock.

Theirs would be a strange and complicated relationship, beginning brightly and positively before leading the two men eventually into a much darker and problematic place, but whatever first drew them together would form a bond that was far too strong ever to be broken. Hancock, whose favourite book from childhood was A.A. Milne's *Winnie-the-Pooh*, would liken John affectionately to the character of Eeyore, the heroically philosophical sad-eyed and slow-moving donkey, and himself – rather more fancifully – to the character of Pooh, the well-meaning bear of very little brain. Eeyore was prone to bouts of passive introspection, asking himself 'Why?' or 'Wherefore?' or 'Inasmuch as which?' until either his house fell down or his tail fell off, so he would always be rather relieved whenever Pooh came along and provided him with something, and someone, else to think about for a while.[1] Hancock thought that captured his and John's personal relationship rather well. Le Mesurier, as if to confirm this Eeyorish reputation, would never volunteer anything approaching such a whimsical description; nonetheless, he seemed amused by the analogy and often acknowledged that it made a certain amount of sense. They were very different types, with very different attitudes, but they found each other interesting and tried their best to help each other out.

They would also be linked together professionally for many years on both the small and the big screen. Each was the other's ideal kind of comic foil: Le Mesurier could play the typical tall, gaunt and daunting Establishment figure who would look down on Hancock and scowl, and Hancock could play the typical tactless little upstart who would look up to Le Mesurier and splutter. In post-war Britain's ongoing comic commentary on the conflict between its haves and have-nots, its insiders and outsiders, Le Mesurier and Hancock must have seemed made for each other. Every time they shared a scene, often sitting on opposite sides of a business desk or on different levels inside a court of law, something was said and shown about the class divisions that continued to divide the country.

The pair first met in 1951, when Hancock joined Hattie in the cast of *Educating Archie* as a pompous and irascible new tutor (his catchphrase, which caught on quickly throughout the country, was 'Flippin' kids!'). The two performers struck up an immediate rapport and, like so many of Hattie's other friends and colleagues, Hancock soon started dropping by at Eardley Crescent unannounced for a few drinks and some relaxed chatter. It was on these casual occasions that he first became acquainted with John Le Mesurier.

There was nothing immediately obvious about the two of them that suggested a firm and famous friendship was destined to blossom. Le Mesurier was twelve years older (thirty-nine to Hancock's twenty-seven), came from a grander background (very much upper-middle-class to the Birmingham-born Hancock's lower-middle-class) and possessed a much more measured and equable temperament. The pair soon found, however, as they faced each other and conversed, that they did have some things in common. Both, for example, had gone through similar experiences in the services during the war (Le Mesurier in the Army, Hancock in the RAF); both were now settling into married life (Le Mesurier for two years and Hancock, to a model named Cicely Romanis, for one); both had similar tastes in literature (Stephen Leacock was one writer much admired) and music (ranging widely from classical through to jazz); both were passionate fans of cricket (Hancock was a bowler, Le Mesurier a batsman) as well as several other sports; and both loved to relax with good food, plenty of cigarettes and a generous amount of booze. They also shared similar tastes in comedy, being big admirers of such clever and subtle performers as Buster Keaton, Sid Field and Jacques Tati, preferring their humour to come from the combination of character and context rather than a lazy mixture of cartoon-like figures and crude routines.

Both men, in fact, had the knack of making each other laugh without having to be 'on' as performers. They were both great observers of ordinary human foibles, with keen eyes for the telling detail, and took great delight in recounting to each other the antics of some odd individual whom they had recently encountered on their travels. John also had such a preternatural calmness about him, and was such a good and patient listener, that Hancock felt unusually relaxed and secure in his company. 'John,' Hancock would say, 'was the kind of person you knew would one day be your best friend, perhaps not right away, but one day when you needed him.'[2] It seemed quite natural, therefore, when the pair started socialising on a regular basis, both inside the house at Eardley Crescent and, increasingly, at various venues out and about.

As neither man was of much practical use inside their respective homes – John would be more likely to carry on sitting in the dark than to get up and attempt to change a light bulb, while on one of the few occasions when Hancock did attempt to help around the house by spraying all of the furniture with some 'nice smelly stuff' that he had found, it turned out to have been a can of his wife's hair lacquer[3] – they usually faced little resistance from their families when they went out together after work in search of some harmless fun. This usually took the form of a long and unpredictable pub crawl around the streets of Soho, taking in the Colony Room in Dean Street, a legendary private drinking club run by an extraordinarily rude lesbian called Muriel Belcher, whose way of acknowledging someone – of either sex – as a welcome regular was to always address them as 'Mary', and culminating in an extended stay at the Coach and Horses in Greek Street, where they mixed on a regular basis with such legendary drinkers as the journalists Jeffrey Bernard and Sandy Fawkes, the broadcaster and writer Daniel Farson, the painter Francis Bacon and John's famously woozy old actor friend Denis 'Den Den' Shaw, before moving on to soak up some live late-night jazz.

These early times together were often extremely happy, with the pair gleefully behaving in boyish ways. They got up to such mischief as betting on late-night cat races in the living room of a friend's house, rearranging the furniture to allow for flat, hurdle and steeplechase racing sessions; playing impromptu post-pub games of cricket in dark and deserted parks and then running off after hearing the ball shatter a nearby window; and teaming up with the likes of Peter Sellers, Spike

Milligan and Harry Secombe for evenings of improvised comedy and music. They also were frequently reduced to helpless laughter by the befuddled mishaps of their friends and acquaintances, such as the slow-witted Denis Shaw. John had known 'Den Den' Shaw (who 'was built like a gorilla but instead of fur he had warts which, if anything, made him more hideous than King Kong') since shortly after the war, working with him in Croydon and elsewhere on a number of occasions and observing him in varying degrees of inebriation on or by the side of bar stools in numerous London pubs. Whenever 'Den Den' was short of cash – which was often – he would either borrow from a fast-diminishing bunch of innocents or simply pick up whatever notes he happened to find 'lying around'. John had been appearing in a play with Shaw when some money was reported as missing from the dressing-rooms, and 'Den Den,' naturally, qualified as the prime suspect. The police came in and set a trap, planting some more notes dusted with indelible blue powder that would glow under bright lights. 'Den Den' only had one line to say on stage that night, but, as the line required him to point as he stood directly under a spotlight, he was on quite long enough for the tell-tale stains to show up on his hands. The hapless 'Den Den' would also provide John with the cue to deliver one of his favourite impromptu punchlines when, one night in Great Windmill Street, he saw his tired and emotional friend being escorted up the ramp of a Black Maria. 'Hello, Denis,' said John, strolling past. 'Working?'[4]

'Den Den' ended up being banned from most of Hancock and Le Mesurier's usual watering holes, but there were plenty of other eccentrics who, largely unwittingly, entertained them during the course of their carefree carousing. Terry-Thomas joined them on the odd occasion, sparking increasingly competitive storytelling sessions that would last long into the night, and when Peter Sellers was around they would resume a playful game that involved dreaming up improbable-sounding album titles, such as *Rita Webb Sings Gershwin* or *An Evening with Arthur Mullard*. Sometimes, disguising their features somewhat with hats and scarves, they would simply stand in dimly lit bus queues and eavesdrop on the mundane conversations that went on, waiting for that one gloriously daft line that would make them snigger and hug themselves with glee.

The fast-developing friendship was unaffected when Hancock, who had never been particularly comfortable playing opposite a wooden doll, left *Educating Archie* to begin work on a radio show of his own – the hugely successful *Hancock's Half-Hour* – in 1954. Hattie was soon reunited with Hancock professionally when she started appearing (from the fourth series in 1956) as his aggressive but incompetent secretary/dogsbody called Grizelda 'Grizzly' Pugh, while John remained a trusted confidant and regular drinking companion.

The two men began their professional relationship soon after this, when Hancock explained that he wanted John to be a member of the unofficial repertory company of supporting players that he was planning to set up when he transferred his radio sitcom to the small screen.[5] John was delighted to accept the invitation, and he would go on to appear in a number of programmes alongside his friend, including seven editions of the television version of *Hancock's Half-Hour* between 1957 and 1960, and once in each of the subsequent BBC and ATV versions of *Hancock*. He was always there, primarily, to epitomise the kind of suitably sober and imposing authority figure who could be relied on to pick away at Hancock's snobbish scab – his characters would include two doctors, two colonels, an air marshal, a judge, a cruise ship captain, a National Trust officer and a politician – but the understanding that he shared with Hancock as a comic actor meant that their clashes were exceptionally sharp and subtle.

The thing that elevated most of Le Mesurier's contributions above other similar ones that were featured was that he never simply frowned or growled at Anthony Aloysius St John Hancock as though he already knew this bumptious little man as well as the viewers did at home. He always reacted as though, expecting mundane normality, he was curious, surprised and even a little amazed. He watched and listened and thought as Hancock blustered on, his eyebrow rising like a steam gauge as the realisation slowly dawned that he was in the presence of an extremely unusual, and very irritating, sort of idiot. It was this that helped to make Hancock's own performance seem so much funnier than it might have been if played against a less believably 'normal' foil who just launched robotically into a straightforwardly haughty response.

Probably the most memorable of these television collaborations was an episode of *Hancock* entitled 'The Lift'. Broadcast in June 1961, the programme followed Hancock and several other figures – including a doctor, a vicar and a secretary – as they waited to enter a lift at the BBC's Television Centre. Being his usual chippy self, Hancock had already clashed with a smug-sounding producer when Le Mesurier arrived as an officer in the RAF. 'Ah,' Hancock exclaims as the air marshal appears. 'An intrepid bird man!' The officer looks mildly perplexed as Hancock proceeds to treat him as sarcastically as possible (AIR MARSHAL: 'Trouble with the lift? Anybody pressed the button?' HANCOCK: 'Do you know, we'd never thought of that! "Anybody pressed the button?" Dear oh dear, the military mind! Of course we've pressed the button! What do you think we've been doing – trying to pull it up by the rope?') and then mocks him as he tries to take charge ('Yes, you have a go. Go on – pretend it's a rocket, you'll enjoy that!'). After everyone has crammed themselves inside (with Hancock insisting on squeezing himself in as well to push the number up from the maximum of eight to an over-heavy nine), the lift descends for a few moments until it suddenly sticks in between the fourth and third floors. Rattled by the accusation that he is solely to blame for the problem, Hancock goes on the offensive, sniping away at the others as the sense of claustrophobia starts to grow. He then aims his ire at the well-meaning air marshal as the officer is invited to take charge:

AIR MARSHAL: Yes, well, er, the way I see it is: er, we're in a
                  hole . . . and er, well, we've got to get out of it.
                  [*Furrows his brow and thinks*] So what I propose is
                  this: we hack a hole in the roof, then two of us
                  climb out, then one stands on the other's shoulders,
                  then we . . . we force open the doors on the floor
                  above. Hmmm?
HANCOCK: [*Rolling his eyes*] And that's it, is it?
AIR MARSHAL: Yes, that's it.
HANCOCK: Brilliant. Right, ladies and gentleman, if you'll all be
                  good enough to adjust your dark goggles, the Air
                  Marshal here will step forward with his oxy-
                  acetylene cutter and have us out of here in no time!
                  [*Looks at the officer with contempt*] YOU BE-
                  RIBBONED BUFFOON! This is metal – you can't
                  hack your way out of this! [*Turns to the others*] Dear
                  oh dear, they keep the bomb with blokes like him
                  on the button![6]

Having rubbished this and all other proposals to make an escape, Hancock proceeds to bore his captive audience with his views on a wide range of topics, including heavy water ('Very tricky stuff'), oxygen ('Just as well we've got it all around us. I mean, supposing you had to carry your own supply around with you – supposing when you were born they said, "There, that's your lot – drag that round with you!" You'd have to have something the size of the Albert Hall!') and over-population ('I reckon in a couple of hundred years' time you won't be able to move. We'll all be standing shoulder to shoulder all over the world, heads up fighting for breath. The tallest bloke with the biggest hooter survives!'). When they are finally rescued in the early hours of the following morning, the kindly air marshal shows pity for his tormentor by helping him out from the lift ('My dear fellow . . .'), only for Hancock to somehow contrive to get himself trapped all over again.

Appearances such as this one would remain among John's favourite memories of working on television, and he was always eager to resume his on-screen interactions with Hancock. Just as when John worked with that other vulnerable, mercurial but hugely talented comic actor, Peter Sellers, the adrenaline flowed a little more freely when he appeared alongside Tony Hancock, and the sense that he was part of something special always made him raise his game.

Two things, however, had started recently to niggle John about his friend. One was Hancock's chronic struggle to remember his lines. John was not only a rep-trained actor, well used to the discipline required for arriving fully prepared and word-perfect (known inside the profession as 'off-book'), but he was also blessed with a near-photographic memory, so lines were rarely a problem. Hancock, in contrast, had always been a notoriously 'slow study' (meaning that he found it extraordinarily hard to memorise any lines at all), and the added pressure that came when he started performing on live television only added to his problems. John had initially been rather indulgent about this 'little failing', often seeking to dismiss it as being not much worse than a bit of playful mischief: 'In a long exchange between Tony and Sid, for example, the only way of getting through it was for them to put their feet up on the kitchen table so each could read the cues off the soles of the other's shoes.'[7]

By the time of 'The Lift', however, not even John could deny that Hancock was looking seriously underprepared. After a recent minor car accident had left him too shaken to learn his script before he was next due in front of the cameras, his director had resorted to scrolling the dialogue via strategically positioned teleprompters to get his anxious star through the show, and Hancock had seized on the apparent success of this emergency tactic to argue that it should from then on be regarded as standard practice. The consequence was that, at certain moments in certain scenes, he could now clearly be seen looking past the cameras at the teleprompters instead of remaining engaged with the rest of the cast. Even then, he sometimes misread and mistimed his lines on live television, giggling like an amateur while the other, properly trained actors waited patiently for him to recover. It happened a couple of times in 'The Lift', and, although it in no way diminished the overall appeal of the episode, it still rattled someone as scrupulously professional as John Le Mesurier.

The other thing bothering John was Hancock's growing dependence on drink. Although John was already a fairly heavy drinker himself, he was careful to limit any indulgences to his leisure hours and never allowed his drinking to intrude on his duties as an actor. He also happened to have an extraordinarily high tolerance of alcohol. Even though he sometimes consumed large quantities in one sitting and rarely went for long at home without topping up his seemingly ever-present glass of gin and tonic, he never seemed to get drunk, or at least appear drunk, and, perhaps due in part to the harrowing memory of his first wife's battle with the bottle, he abhorred the sight of excessive drunkenness in others. Hancock, on the other hand, was now betraying all of the classic signs of someone who was giving in to the grip of a genuine addiction to alcohol.

Stories had been circulating for some time within the show business world about the comedian's growing reliance on booze. Success had brought with it not only a bigger wage packet but also greater expectations, and Hancock, who had always been prone to depression and self-doubt, seemed unable to cope with the pressure without reaching out for the alcohol. It was rumoured that, on a number of occasions, he had drained the best part of a bottle of brandy before going on stage, and some sources claimed that he had started drinking through the day as well as the evening as his discipline continued to decline.

John could sometimes see for himself the deleterious effect that these drinking sessions were having. His friend – previously such entertaining company when in a merely 'tipsy' state – was fast becoming a dour and pompous pub bore, subjecting whomever was present to increasingly pretentious and rambling monologues about philosophy, politics and religion, and was on some occasions liable to become aggressive, abusive and even violent. More worrying still, news was reaching John that Hancock frequently disappeared on long and solitary benders, sometimes drinking until he passed out wherever he happened to fall.[8] One of their mutual friends, Jeffrey Bernard, would recall seeing him during this period in the late 1950s at the end of an epic day of drinking in the Coach and Horses, utterly oblivious to the pathetic reality of his own condition: Hancock, he noticed, had urinated in his trousers and was barely able to speak or stand when the time came to leave the pub. Bernard, though barely in much better shape himself, realised that the star needed some assistance to get home in one piece, so he helped him outside, summoned a taxi and guided him into the back, where he promptly collapsed in a heap on the floor. Motioning Bernard to stay for a moment, Hancock fumbled through his pockets and eventually produced a creased visiting card, which he thrust into Bernard's hand and said in a beer-breathed whisper, 'If ever you need my help just call'. Bernard, suddenly puzzled, replied, 'Why on earth should I want help from you?' Hancock blinked sleepily, stifled a belch and waved him closer: 'Because,' he said, 'I think you might have a drink problem.'[9]

There was no respite when Hancock was at home. His wife, Cicely, had taken to drowning her own sorrows on a regular basis, rationalising her behaviour by saying, 'What goes down my throat does not go down his.'[10] Early in 1958, soon after the couple had left London for what both of them hoped would be a healthier new home in the country – an attractive property at Lingfield in Surrey which they christened 'MacConkey's' – they invited several of their close friends down for a house-warming party. John and Hattie were among the guests who gathered together in one of the few rooms that the couple had so far managed to furnish. 'It's okay,' Hancock announced brightly, 'the drinks will be arriving any minute.' Sure enough, a short while later, a three-wheeled van turned into the drive and pulled up at the front door. It was loaded to the roof with case upon case of vodka. Back inside, Cicely handed everyone a beer mug and Tony proceeded to fill them all up to the top: no tonic, no lemon, no ice – just a full pint of neat vodka.

John had seen it all before, and he hated it. Determined to help his friend fight his addiction, and now feeling far more knowledgeable about the subject than he had when dealing with his former wife, he tried to be around whenever he could to monitor Tony's behaviour and curtail his drinking sessions, visiting him in various private nursing homes during those periods when he was making a concerted effort to recover his mental and physical health. Such experiences made him keener than ever to help Hancock regain his focus and push on with his promising career, so when Hancock, in one of his more sober spells, looked to branch out into the movies, John was quickly on hand to offer advice and moral support.

Hancock had already made his movie debut back in 1954, in a strange little military-themed film called *Orders are Orders*, but he had only a minor role, was overshadowed by the likes of Sid James and Peter Sellers, and did not enjoy the experience at all (nor did he feel any better later on when, sneaking into a cinema to see it, his enquiry at the box office as to whether a seat was available in the circle prompted the response: 'A seat? You can have the first fifteen rows!'[11]). It was only at the end of the decade, when he felt that he had taken his celebrated sitcom as far as it could go, that he decided to make a serious bid for international recognition by starring in a movie created expressly for him by his regular writers, Ray Galton and Alan Simpson.

The new project energised him, and he worked hard on making it a success. Entitled *The Rebel*, it was envisaged – at least by him – as the vehicle that would take the familiar Hancock persona, shake off his British skin and present him as a truly universal comic misfit in the style of Chaplin's Tramp or Tati's Monsieur Hulot. The movie introduced Hancock as a quietly desperate, bowler-hatted, ordinary suburban clerk who suddenly snaps and abandons his job in order to become an artist in Paris. His method, which involves throwing various colours of paint down on to a large piece of canvas and then riding over it on a bicycle, results in nothing but colourful rubbish, but when someone else's work gets attributed mistakenly to him he is hailed as a genius and courted by all of the connoisseurs. John had only a minor role as a bespectacled and obsessive-compulsive office manager who cannot bear to see one umbrella slanting the opposite way to all of the others lined up under the hat rack, but he made sure that he remained a reassuring presence on the set, chatting to Hancock between shooting sessions and keeping him in a positive mood.

The one good scene that they shared came at the start, when the manager catches Hancock doodling during working hours and calls him in to his office:

MANAGER: This is all your work, is it?

HANCOCK: Yes, sir, it's got my name on the cover, you see.

MANAGER: Quite, yes. [*He opens up the first book and finds an ornately drawn and coloured letter 'S'*] And what's this?

HANCOCK: Let's see . . . Oh, that's an 'S'.

MANAGER: Yes. I realise it's an 'S', but what's all this . . . business?

HANCOCK: Well, it's illuminated. I sort of thought that it adds to the, er, charm of the whole thing.

MANAGER: I'm not concerned with charm! May I remind you that this is a business house and not a Benedictine monastery! How long did this rubbish take you?

HANCOCK: Only two or three hours.

MANAGER: Two or three hours? Hmmm. And do you know how long the time and motion study experiments allow for the preparation of statements of accounts?

HANCOCK: Yes, sir. Three minutes, forty-five point five seconds.

MANAGER: Exactly!

HANCOCK: [*Looks at the 'S' again*] It's pretty though, isn't it?

MANAGER: Do you think Smith, Brown, Warner & Brown are going to pay us more because we send them pretty accounts?

HANCOCK: But surely there's a place for art even in a business house?

MANAGER: The only art I'm concerned with is the art of making money!

[*He turns over the next page and finds a whole range of cartoon faces*] What on earth?!? Wha . . . What's all this?

HANCOCK: Well . . . [*Rushes round to join his boss on the other side of the desk and starts pointing at the faces*] That's Robinson . . . That's Jones . . . And that's Perkins – very good one of Perkins, isn't it? I've got his chin off very well down there, don't you think? And this is Davidson . . . That's Harris . . . [*Turns page and finds a crude and unflattering cartoon of his boss*] And . . . that's you. [*His boss gives him a bewildered look*] Well, I mean, you don't really look like that. I . . . er . . . it's a caricature. Your nose isn't really as big as all that, it's just that you take the funniest feature of a man and exaggerate it. I mean . . . that's what a . . . caricature . . .

MANAGER: This has got to stop, you know, Hancock!

When the boss asks Hancock to explain what on earth has come over him lately, Hancock reveals that he is convinced he has 'greatness' in him, but the more he talks about it the more agitated he becomes, and he starts to move menacingly towards the clearly startled office manager:

HANCOCK: I can't go on ignoring this dynamo throbbing away inside of me, don't you understand? I'm being choked! Crushed! Bogged down in a sea of triviality! I'm not a machine. I'm flesh! And blood! I can see! And hear and smell and fear! I'm vital, do you hear? You can't crush me on a monotonous, soul-destroying everyday routine for ever! Every man must find his own salvation. [*The boss gets up and starts edging away from Hancock but he keeps moving closer*] Live life as it's supposed to be lived and you're choking me [*He grabs the boss by the lapels and starts shaking him*] You're choking me, you're choking me!

MANAGER: Hancock!!!

Hancock ends up hurling his boss across the room and on to a couch. Only then, as he watches the poor man struggle to retrieve his glasses and straighten his tie, does he come to his senses and rushes over to help his boss up, apologising profusely as he guides him back to the desk and smooths him down ('Have one of your pills . . .').

It was precisely the kind of scene that Hancock had always been grateful to Galton and Simpson for writing, because it eschewed gags and slapstick in favour of a broadly believable context and two beautifully played characterisations. Once again, so many actors could have played Le Mesurier's role too simply, opting for either bland officiousness or mousy meekness, but he engages so sympathetically with Hancock, evolving as the other man evolves, that he always seems a perfectly real individual and not just a 'stiff suit with specs'. At the very end, as he is catching his breath and rearranging his ruffled clothes, he tries to seem calm while the feelings of fear and panic bounce around just beneath the surface:

I do hope you're not one of those 'Angry Young Men'. We don't want that sort of thing in United International. [*Takes another deep breath*]

Er, now, look here, why don't you, er, join the firm's tennis club and, er, sweat all of this silly nonsense out of your system?

Hancock ignores the advice and chooses existentialism instead, but it was this crucial 'straight' scene that set up the broader comedy that followed, and, as Hancock appreciated, few other character actors could have helped him make it work so well.

Shot in the summer of 1960 and released early the following year, *The Rebel* turned out to be a very amiable little comedy with several genuinely memorable funny moments. Rashly over-hyped, however, it fell short of some critics' high expectations (although an unnamed writer at *The Times* judged it a 'gratifying success'[12]), and it failed to make much of a mark on the international audience: an ill-advised title-change for the North American market, *Call Me Genius*, seemed to antagonise certain overly literal-minded US reviewers.[13] It was, nonetheless, enough of a financial success to keep Hancock a fairly attractive proposition for British investors, and he was still determined to realise his big screen ambitions.

His response to the disappointment of *The Rebel* was to take greater control over his next project. He signed a four-movie distribution deal with the Associated British Picture Corporation (ABPC) which enabled him to set up his own production company, MacConkey Films, and broke with Galton and Simpson in order to collaborate with the writer Philip Oakes on a movie called *The Punch and Judy Man*. Inspired in part by his childhood memories of growing up near the beach in Bournemouth, Hancock fashioned a fictional home town – the sleepy seaside town of Piltdown – and a character for himself, Wally Pinner, a gone-to-seed Punch and Judy entertainer. 'Here's the story, he said. 'There's this Punch and Judy man, a genuine artist in his own way, with a marriage that's going wrong and a lot of bastards on the council out to nail him . . .' It did not seem much to Oakes until, after sharing a few brandies with Hancock, he started to think that the scenario might prove a decent showcase for quirky little character studies and some memorable comic scenes, so he went ahead and worked on the screenplay.

Hancock modelled many of the supporting players on other figures whom he had encountered, including a childhood hero called The Sandman, a self-styled 'beach sculptor' who created tableaux such as 'The Death of Nelson' entirely out of sand. His art was forever at the mercy of high tides, strong winds, small children and dogs – a fate that touched Hancock as much as it amused him. He did not hesitate, when it came to casting, to ask John Le Mesurier to play The Sandman, believing that no other performer was more likely to hit the right note of pathos and still convey the comedy. Other actors enlisted included Sylvia Sims as Wally's wife, Delia; Barbara Murray as the haughty local grandee Lady Jane Caterham; Hugh Lloyd as Wally's sidekick, Edward Cox; and Mario Fabrizi as Neville the street photographer.

The movie was shot mainly on location at Bognor Regis (which Hancock had chosen because he felt it epitomised all that was risibly pretentious about traditional English seaside resorts), but some initial work was done at the ABPC studios at Elstree. Most of the cast and crew disliked using these studios, but none hated them more than John Le Mesurier: 'There was always a feeling of being watched by Big Brother which disturbed the actors,' John would recall. 'The Bureaucracy even kept a sort of Black Book into which went details of your time of arrival on the set and the number of takes you had to undergo to complete a scene. Even if you went to have a drink and a sandwich at lunch-time across the road at the Red Lion, it was like working for the Civil Service.' He could also see the negative effect such an atmosphere was having on the star of the movie: 'This really was the last sort of place for Tony to work in. He felt claustrophobic, like some kind of prisoner.'[14] Things were hardly any better, however, when the production was based in Bognor. With Hancock's marriage now falling apart (Cicely would visit regularly and there would be noisy and sometimes violent rows breaking out throughout her stay) and his drinking getting progressively heavier, with bottle after bottle of brandy and vodka being downed each day, the predominant mood on set could have been summed up by someone repeating King George V's supposed deathbed exclamation, 'Bugger Bognor!'

It did not help the situation that Hancock had chosen a talented but inexperienced twenty-nine-year-old director called Jeremy Summers to oversee the filming. Summers had mainly worked in television before joining this production, and it soon became evident that he was not yet ready to cope with a star (and boss) whose unpredictable changes of mood could play havoc with the shooting schedule. His task was made even harder by the people at ABPC – the so-called 'front office' – who constantly pestered him with ill-timed telephone calls seeking news as to what was going on. Another sign of how badly things were going came when the distinguished French photographer Henri Cartier-Bresson, who had recently arrived with plans to cover the filming from start to finish, developed his first few reels of film and found the results so depressing that he promptly packed up his equipment and left. 'Each day was an agony,' he would later say of trailing the puffy-faced and drink-dimmed comedian. 'What I was seeing was not the Hancock the world loved.'[15]

John Le Mesurier dragged himself through all of the filming feeling weighed down with worry about Hancock and increasingly pessimistic about the chances of making the movie a success. Philip Oakes would dub him 'a connoisseur of doom',[16] but, on this occasion at least, he had eminently good reasons to appear so painfully morose. Apart from the various problems on set, the weather was cold, wet and windy (Force 7 in the Channel) and there seemed to be precious little around that could provide one with some much-needed means of distraction. He regarded Bognor itself as 'pretty much a disaster area': 'The trippers had stayed away in swarms that year and the few brave regulars, who could not quite bear to break the habit of a lifetime, sat about in sad, usually damp, little groups reflecting on the irony of paying for a holiday that was best calculated to bring on depression.'[17]

One day, out of sheer desperation, he agreed to accompany Hancock to the local Butlin's holiday camp on the outskirts of the town. It did not take long before one of the redcoats bounded up and asked Hancock to make a guest appearance at one of the jolly parties they were planning for that evening, and perhaps hand out the prizes for a fancy dress competition. Hancock, in a moment of rash generosity, agreed to participate, but when the time arrived for him to set off and join the festivities he showed a marked reluctance to leave his place at the bar. He started moving only after John agreed to accompany him. The two of them then had to endure a cheesy stand-up routine from the redcoat and a procession of strangely attired holidaymakers before the moment came for Hancock to present a prize to the winner, a giggly young girl dressed as a duck – and afterwards make a break for freedom. The problem was that, as John would later put it, 'Butlin's in those days was run like a better class of concentration camp,' with a security team on patrol 'to snuff out any nasty business' and a ring of high barbed-wire fences around the compound: 'some said to keep the intruders out, others that they were there to keep the campers in'. When Hancock and Le Mesurier wandered off towards the exit they were soon pounced on by several large men in uniform and frogmarched to a small guardroom, where nobody appeared to know who they were. Only after several grudging enquiries via their huge walkie-talkies did a night duty officer turn up, confirm that the two were 'from the telly' and authorise their release. 'They're all right,' the guard muttered flatly as he jangled his big set of keys. 'It was,' John would say, 'just about the most ungracious vote of thanks we had ever received.'[18]

After that shambolic excursion Hancock went back to drinking alone in his room, while Le Mesurier sat around waiting for his next scene and willing the whole unfortunate affair to end. The curious thing was, however, that they continued to perform so well in front of the cameras. In spite of all the doom and gloom behind the scenes, there were some bright little moments being captured for the screen, and Le Mesurier was on excellent form.

Dressed in a black velvet beret, a droopy bow tie, an old dark suit and a pair of sandy suede shoes, he first appears on the beach in front of a small and chilly-looking crowd, trying to inform them about the Battle of Trafalgar while a curious little dog runs backwards and forwards threatening to either relieve itself over The Sandman's suede shoes or demolish his sculpture of Lord Nelson expiring on board the *Victory*. 'This was also the occasion', says the flustered Sandman, his eyes darting about nervously in search of the mutt, 'when the great Admiral, mortally wounded and about to breathe his last, called Captain Hardy to his side and whispered in his ear. [*He smiles weakly*] Now, some authorities have it that what he said was: "Kismet, Hardy" – which, as the classical scholars have it, means "Fate". Others believe that what he actually said was: "Kiss me, Hardy" – which of course [*chuckling shyly*] is quite another matter! Ha-ha . . . ha . . . ha-ha . . . ah . . . [*He realises that he has made no impact whatsoever, so speeds up to an abrupt conclusion*] Well, at any rate, Nelson died at 16.40 hours.'

Hancock's character, Wally Pinner, is watching his friend die another death from the promenade, and he grimaces as the lecture limps to its conclusion: 'Ooh, he's really got 'em today . . .' Once the unimpressed audience has departed, Wally comes down to offer some advice: 'Horatio's looking a bit rough today. You want to shove Lady Hamilton in there – brighten it up a bit.' The Sandman looks pained: 'Er, well, it's hardly in keeping . . .' Wally gives up: 'All right, please yourself.'

One of the best and most endearingly intimate of the subsequent scenes featured Hancock sitting back and being served tea in the Sandman's little beach hut as, rather like in real life, one man acted as confidant to the other:

SANDMAN: Now, I think you're going to like this. It's the same
            blend that we used to have at home. Darjeeling with a
            trace of souchong.
PINNER: Very nice. Well, you're pretty well set up here.
SANDMAN: Oh, yes. It's quite comfortable. Of course, it's not quite
            like a home, but, well, it has its compensations.
PINNER: You're very lucky. You want to hang on to it. [*Gets up*]
            Do you know what happened to me today?
SANDMAN: No?
PINNER: I went home to lunch – I was a little late, I'll admit that,
            but I was unavoidably detained – before I could open
            me mouth I find that I am down for the Piltdown Gala!
SANDMAN: Oh no.
PINNER: Yeah. Delia fixed it behind me back. 'Got to get in with
            a nice class of people,' she says. 'No more of these
            dreadful theatricals. You've got to get on in the world.'
SANDMAN: Milk?
PINNER: Yes, please. 'Got to make something of ourselves. No
            more of this traipsing about. Got to put down roots.'
SANDMAN: Sugar?
PINNER: Two, please. I ask you, can you imagine me stuck
            between Lady Jane Caterham and the Mayoress of
            Piltdown Bay? [*The Sandman chuckles*] It's not funny.
            It's not my idea of a night out – is it yours?
SANDMAN: Good grief, no!

[*They both sit down to drink their tea*]

PINNER: Mmm, very good.
SANDMAN: Mmm.
PINNER: Ah, you'll never get lumbered like this. You're on your
            own.
SANDMAN: [*Wistfully*] Yes . . .

PINNER: You don't know how lucky you are.

SANDMAN: Well, that's a matter of opinion. It can be rather lonely.

PINNER: Surely you don't get lonely? I'll tell you this: I'd change places with you any day of the week.

SANDMAN: Really?

PINNER: Mmm. You've got your freedom.

SANDMAN: Oh, yes . . .

PINNER: You've got nobody nagging you to 'make' something of yourself.

SANDMAN: Oh, no, certainly not.

PINNER: You made a very wise decision to stay single.

SANDMAN: [*Looking sad*] Yes, well, actually it wasn't my decision. Her lady said no.

PINNER: Oh, I see.

SANDMAN: Well, it's probably all for the best. As I understand it, marriage is a matter of give and take. Not all of us are equipped for that sort of thing. Another cup?

PINNER: No, thank you. [*Springs back up*] What am I going to do about this gala? After all, it is Delia's fault. Nobody could blame me if I turned it in.

SANDMAN: Oh, no. Nobody's going to blame you . . .

PINNER: I could simply tell them I'm not going to do it. I could tell Delia that I'm not going through with it. I could, couldn't I?

SANDMAN: Y-e-s . . . You could . . . but, you know, I can't help feeling it's really a matter for your own conscience, isn't it?

PINNER: 'Conscience.' [*Scowls bitterly to himself and heads for the door*] Thanks very much for the tea. I'll give your regards to Delia!

It is as good an example of quietly assured comic character acting as anything else on view in the British cinema of that decade. In other scenes, Hancock seemed to be forcing himself a little too hard to be charmingly Chaplinesque (e.g. the promising but overlong 'duel' he has with the young boy in the ice-cream parlour) or straining to seem 'dark' (e.g. the self-consciously tense domestic exchanges he has with his wife) but he seems to relax whenever he shares the screen with Le Mesurier and shows just how good – in spite of all the drinking and arguing that was going on behind the scenes – he still could be.

It happens again a couple of times later in the movie. In one scene, the two men bump into each other on the damp beach and the rattled Wally gets his revenge by informing the Sandman that he, too, must attend the gala event; in another the pair sit at their table with their arms folded tightly like sulking schoolboys, making each other smile and snigger by mocking the pretentiousness of the occasion. Although the overall pace and tone of the movie remained unsure, the Hancock and Le Mesurier double-act was always extraordinarily watchable.

Once released, the movie received a predictably mixed critical reception. *Monthly Film Bulletin* judged it a 'botched' effort, although it admired its determination not to seem 'wearily conventional' and found certain aspects worthy of praise: 'At some time, in someone's mind, *The Punch and Judy Man* existed as a distinctive and very engaging comedy. It hasn't come through on the screen quite like this, but one warms all the same to its performances (Hancock himself; John Le Mesurier as the sad Sandman; Barbara Murray as the desperately bored Lady Jane) and to its little, lugubrious, jokes.'[19] *The Times* was similarly keen not to damn the whole production for any of its particular flaws, describing it as a 'slight, unassuming film, but with an elusive, highly personal, quality', and suggested that it was a marked improvement on *The Rebel*.[20]

A number of other publications were considerably harsher, and, once again, the American critics were left distinctly unimpressed. John Le Mesurier, who remained very fond of the finished movie even though it had been such a strain to make, would later say that he felt its comic subtleties worked much better when it was shown eventually on the small screen: 'Tony was a creature of television. His portrayal of seedy pomposity came across so much more strongly in the intimacy of the living room where, let's face it, Mum, Dad and the family were more ready to recognise and acknowledge a part reflection of their own lives.'[21] Hancock himself, meanwhile, merely muttered dejectedly that he 'would have liked to have quit the film in the middle, but by then we'd gone too far and I had to finish it'. He said that he now wanted only to go off somewhere, possibly to France, and 'dig ditches' or 'be a beachcomber' – 'anything to get away from it'.[22]

John's friendship with Tony Hancock, which had started out so brightly, was by this stage a far more complicated affair. Booze and broken dreams were polluting the old sure and happy rapport, and the relationship would soon cause both men more anguish than either could ever have imagined. Before that bleak moment arrived, however, John would have to contend with another unexpected personal setback, this time much closer to home, that would end up breaking his heart.

CHAPTER X

Ménage à Trois

Time goes so quickly when you can't see daylight.

On paper, the 1960s should have been a richly rewarding and hugely enjoyable decade for John Le Mesurier. He had established himself as a much-admired actor in British theatre, television and cinema; he had countless interesting new offers of work pouring in; he had a kind, talented and very successful wife, and two lively and good-natured young sons, whom he adored. Then, at least in his personal life, his whole world suddenly fell apart.

It seems bitterly ironic, in retrospect, that his favourite theatrical role of this period would be that of Andrew Crocker-Harris in Terence Rattigan's play *The Browning Version* – bitterly ironic but also painfully apt. Crocker-Harris is an ageing classics teacher at a British public school who feels that he has become isolated and obsolete. Many of his students mistake his old-fashioned stiff-upper-lipped attitude and serious professional demeanour for shallowness and coldness, and his wife, Millie, is being unfaithful to him with a younger master named Frank Hunter – a fact that Crocker-Harris has been aware of, but has so far been doing his best to ignore. The title alludes to the reference within the play to Robert Browning's translation of the Greek tragedy *Agamemnon* – in which Agamemnon is murdered by his wife, aided by her lover. John would always regard Crocker-Harris as 'the best part I have ever attempted in the theatre' because, he said, 'I believe I had some understanding of a basically gentle man whose shyness was misinterpreted as hard indifference.'[1] It was also a part, sadly, that would soon return to haunt him in real life.

It is tempting to suggest that he should have seen it coming, but the problem for John during this period was that, when he was not standing up under the studio lights, he was often sitting back in the dark. His favourite idea of recreation was to while away his leisure hours in nightclubs, where he would relax by having a drink and listening to jazz. There, in the Stygian gloom of some or other Soho venue, he would let the irritations of the working day fade away as he lost himself in the music that he loved. A decent pianist himself, he was always drawn to particularly competent and creative keyboard players, but, more generally, he was dazzled by anyone who seemed to combine a good heart with great artistry. He went wherever the best musicians and singers happened to be playing: the London club scene was thriving in those days, with such appealingly intimate places as Club Eleven in Great Windmill Street, the 51 Club in Great Newport Street, the Flamingo in Wardour Street, the Mandrake Club in Meard Street and, in a basement in Oxford Street, the Humphrey Lyttelton Club all competing for custom. At the start of the 1960s, he was most often to be found inside the recently opened Ronnie Scott's in Gerrard Street, with a cigarette in one hand and a tumbler of gin or whisky in the other, his suede shoes tapping happily in time to the rhythm. He could sometimes stay there for ages in a smoky, boozy, blissful daze, chuckling at MC Scott's notoriously irreverent asides (such as 'This woman's so modest she even eats bananas sideways') and cherishing every moment of the music.

Anne Valery, the partner of the similarly inclined Robin Jacques, would claim (with perhaps a little exaggeration for dramatic effect) that John would sometimes even forget to wander back out in time when he and Hattie were meant to be co-hosting a show business party at their home in Eardley Crescent: 'John would turn up two days later and she'd say, "Where have you been?" and he'd say, "Oh, darling, I'm so sorry – very good jazz . . ." And she'd say, "But it's two days later!" And he'd say, "Time goes so quickly when you can't see daylight".'[2]

Even when he did remember to emerge for a pre-planned assignation, he often gave the impression that he had only just woken up from a long and lazy hibernation. On one occasion, he was due to meet up with some family friends at the Royal Opera House in Covent Garden on a damp and gloomy November evening. After dragging himself away from some or other club and nipping in to Bertorelli's for another quick drink, he wandered along Bow Street and entered the Opera House looking strangely puzzled. 'Darling,' he asked with a hint of a shiver, 'is it very cold for this time of year?' One of his friends replied, 'Well, no, darling, not really, but you are wearing a tropical suit . . .' He looked down at himself suspiciously and reflected on this information: 'Oh . . . yes . . .' he mumbled, still sounding rather confused. 'I see . . . I understand . . . Y-e-s . . .'[3]

Hattie, long used to her husband's legendary vagueness, was usually hugely amused by such sleepy slip-ups and harmless misdemeanours. She also relished his return from filming abroad with a fresh set of self-deprecating tales of peculiar-sounding scrapes and mistakes. On one occasion in 1962, he came back from Athens, where he had been working on a supposedly 'intense human drama' called *In the Cool of the Day* alongside Peter Finch, Jane Fonda and Angela Lansbury, and joined Hattie at home for a long and leisurely reunion dinner. He told her over several glasses of wine how much he had hated the experience, regarding his own performance – as a Persian doctor – as 'quite awful' and the whole production as 'a total disaster', and moaned a little about Finch's drunkenness (he was 'going through a bad patch') and Fonda's preciousness ('she took at least four hours with her makeup'). He then proceeded to tell her, as they started doing the washing up, how he had attempted to keep himself sane by escaping from his noisy hotel and going out to explore the Parthenon:

> It was a hot summer night and there was some kind of festival going on with people milling around in fancy clothes. One exotic creature told me she was a Greek actress. She wore a light, flowing dress which billowed out in the breeze like in one of those Victorian paintings of Eastern ladies at play, and a mask. In the full moon, I asked her to reveal her beauty. 'No,' she said, 'not until the dawn breaks.' That was several hours away but, ever the true romantic, my patience lasted until the sun came up. I then discovered that she had a small cast in her left eye and more than a hint of a moustache. Heigh ho! Until that moment, it had all been rather idyllic.[4]

Hattie laughed so much upon hearing this that she dropped and broke one of their most expensive dinner plates. 'You really shouldn't be allowed out on your own,' she exclaimed.

For all of John's eccentricities, however, the marriage to Hattie continued to seem, by show business standards, unusually warm and strong. Bruce Copp, still a close family friend, would later remark,

'There was great harmony there, always,'[5] and it was clear to all how much he not only loved but also needed her. When Hattie had to spend a brief period in hospital in 1960 to undergo minor surgery, John was left at home helpless, wandering around depressed like a man in a trance. When he visited her, looking unusually pale and gaunt, she was anxious to check that he had been eating properly. 'Yes,' he said unconvincingly, 'not too bad.' She advised him to try having some scrambled eggs. He seemed startled. 'How do I do that?' She explained: 'You put three or four eggs in a bowl, mix them up and then cook them.' John nodded doubtfully and thanked her for the advice. He returned to visit her again the following day, and Hattie asked him how he had fared. 'An absolute disaster,' groaned John. 'I put the eggs in a basin, mixed them up, put the basin on the stove and it cracked.'[6] Once out of hospital, the old domestic order was restored and life for the couple went on as normal.

They actually seemed closer than ever as a couple at the start of the 1960s. After more than a decade together as husband and wife, many of their tastes had merged to such an extent that there was little that one liked or disliked that was not echoed by the other. This happy congeniality was certainly evident when the two of them came to make their respective contributions to the popular radio programme *Desert Island Discs*. Hattie, who was featured in 1961, made the following selections:

1. Beethoven, Symphony No. 9 in D Minor (opus 125) (Robert Shaw Chorale/NBC Symphony/Toscanini)
2. 'Hello Little Girl' (Duke Ellington and his Orchestra)
3. Handel, 'Let the Bright Seraphim' (from *Samson*) (Joan Sutherland/Royal Opera House Orchestra, Covent Garden/Molinari-Pradelli)
4. Bach/Münchinger, Fugue in A minor (Stuttgart Chamber Orchestra/Münchinger)
5. 'On the Sunny Side of the Street' (Tommy Dorsey and his Orchestra)
6. 'God Rest Ye Merry, Gentlemen' (Modern Jazz Quartet)
7. 'Lord Badminton's Memoirs' (Peter Sellers)
8. 'The Red Balloon' (from *The Letter*) (Judy Garland/Gordon Jenkins Orchestra)

LUXURIES: A photograph and recording of her family.
BOOK: *The Oxford Dictionary of Quotations.*[7]

John, who took part a few years later, would come up with a very similar set of choices:

1. 'Take the "A" Train' (Duke Ellington and his Famous Orchestra)
2. 'Spring is Here' (from *Spring is Here*) (Bill Evans Trio)
3. 'Setting Fire to the Policeman' (Peter Sellers)
4. 'Come Rain or Come Shine' (from *St Louis Woman*) (Judy Garland)
5. 'Easy Living' (Bob Burns clarinet/Alan Clare Trio)
6. 'What's New?' (Annie Ross)
7. 'After You, Who?' (from *The Gay Divorcée*) (Fred Astaire)
8. Bach, Double Concerto in D Minor (BWV 1043) (David & Igor Oistrakh violins/RPO/Goossens)

LUXURY: A small distillery.
BOOK: Samuel Pepys' *Diary.*[8]

Both of them were feeling increasingly guilty about their children. The mounting demands of work meant that both now tended to leave home before the children had woken and only returned when it was time for them to go to bed. 'It was only when they started school,' John would reflect, 'that we realised, and regretted, how little we had seen of them in their formative years.'[9] The boys had started off their education at the Froebel School in Redcliffe Gardens, after which Robin was bound for Westminster Grammar and Kim a pre-prep place just off Sloane Square. Neither John nor Hattie was ever much help with their children's homework – '[We] failed dismally,' John would admit, 'as neither of us could add up or do simple subtraction, let alone cope with the mysteries of Latin, algebra or chemistry' – but both of them did what they could: '[W]hat the boys learnt from us were basic things like what was right and what wrong and hopefully how to say "please" and "thank you".'[10] The boys received further help around the house from an assortment of au pairs and some of Hattie's 'resting' gay actor friends (Hattie attracted so many gay actor friends that the phrase 'a friend of Hattie's' was, for a while, more common around the Earls Court area of London than the more widely known term 'a friend of Dorothy's').

Hattie and John not only struggled to find much free time for their two children; they were also struggling to find much free time for each other. Both of their careers were busier than ever. Hattie, for example, had started appearing regularly in the Carry On movies, beginning with *Carry On Sergeant* in 1958, and was now averaging two each year (1959's *Carry On Nurse* mildly amused John with the thought that, so many years after his brief romantic liaison at boarding school, he was finally married to 'Matron'). She had also begun her long association on television with Eric Sykes in 1960, playing his 'twin' sister in the popular BBC TV sitcom *Sykes And A . . .*, and started work on a less successful ITV sitcom called *Our House*. John, meanwhile, seemed to be everywhere, working on and off with Tony Hancock on small and big screen projects, appearing every now and again in the theatre, and making one-off contributions to a wide variety of television programmes. The last ranged from a light comic role in a 1962 episode of the Brian Rix series of farces *Dial RIX* to a dark and unsympathetic part in a 1963 Victorian-era drama entitled *The Brimstone Butterfly*, as well as a quite delightful starring role as a crooked and very randy fake vicar in a 1963 Galton and Simpson *Comedy Playhouse* instalment called 'A Clerical Error'. He also popped up in countless British and international movies, including appearances as a frosty maître d' in 1960's *School for Scoundrels*, a blackmailer in Peter Sellers's 1961 directorial debut *Mr Topaze*, a vicar in the 1962 comedy *Waltz of the Toreadors*, and a barrister in 1963's *The Pink Panther*, and commenced what would prove to be a long-running engagement as the reassuring voice of the Homepride flour commercials ('Because graded grains make finer flour').

It was while he was immersing himself in all of these projects, moving from film set to film set and country to country, and 'recharging the batteries' in the jazz clubs at night, that something happened to harm his marriage. Hattie was devoting more and more of her free time to charity, running a small bring-and-buy shop in King Street and helping several new schemes designed to raise funds on behalf of sick or handicapped children. John had encouraged her in this venture, feeling that, apart from being a morally admirable thing to do, it might also provide a welcome boost for her amour-propre. 'She wanted desperately to be liked and respected for herself, something she felt did not come easily in her own profession,' he would later say. 'She was a comedy star, yes, but always the Aunt Sally, the faintly ludicrous figure of authority to be knocked over by other people's jokes. As a charity worker, she was seen in an entirely different light. By giving her natural personality free rein, she was able to inspire love for the real Hattie and this, in turn, gave her the energy and exuberance to attempt yet more.'[11]

One of the consequences of this involvement was that Eardley Crescent became more crowded than ever, with Hattie's new charity colleagues mixing with her and John's old show business friends as people gossiped in the kitchen, crashed out in the spare rooms and helped keep the parties going in the lounge. It was not uncommon for John to return from several weeks of filming away in America, Italy, France, Germany or Spain to find his home full of strangers, relaxing on the settee, taking a bath or just following his wife around from room to room. 'I got used to the dog-like devotion lavished on Hattie by some of her friends,' he later reflected. 'Perhaps I should have been more concerned but jealousy – or, at least, the open demonstration of jealousy – is not in my character and I held firmly to the belief that Hattie was in control of her emotions. In any case, who was I, the absentee husband and father, to tell my wife how to run her life?'[12]

One of these strangers, however, started to seem, even in John's trusting eyes, rather too familiar for comfort. His name was John Schofield.

He had first appeared on the scene in 1962, when one of Hattie's main charities, the Leukaemia Research Fund, sent him to act as her driver when she was due to attend an afternoon event. Schofield was a tall, dark and handsome East Ender who described himself as an 'entrepreneur', although John would later prefer to describe him as 'a fast-talking cockney who made a living selling cars'.[13] He was married with two young children, one of whom had suffered from leukaemia and had recently passed away. Hattie was dazzled immediately by his good looks and exceptionally self-confident demeanour, and was flattered by his seemingly endless stream of compliments. Later on, after they had returned to Eardley Crescent from the charity event, they spent the rest of the evening together talking and drinking and ended up in bed. John, who was once again away filming, remained unaware of how rapidly he had been betrayed, and, over the course of the next few months, several fictitious charity events were invented in order to allow the clandestine affair to continue undetected. Once John was back at home, Schofield's sudden and increasingly regular presence was explained away by Hattie as being simply due to the fact that he had recently separated from his wife; out of pity, she was letting him visit and sometimes spend the night on the sofa as, supposedly, he 'struggled' to come to terms with his broken marriage. John, who had seen much the same sort of thing happen before, did not have much time to reflect on this story. His professional obligations meant that he soon needed to set off for another couple of weeks of filming.

In his absence, many of his and Hattie's mutual friends became concerned at the damage Schofield seemed to be doing to the marriage as she confided to some of them how 'earthy' and 'sexy' he was (his aggressive directness could hardly have contrasted more sharply with John's careful gentleness) and how she could hardly believe someone like him was so attracted to someone like her. Some of these friends grew increasingly suspicious of his motives and alarmed by her obsessive adoration of him. With John safely out of the way, however, Schofield more or less moved in, and not only tightened his hold on Hattie but also started charming the children, playing football with them, telling jokes and taking them on plenty of lively and enjoyable outings. Without realising the true nature of his relationship with their mother, the boys (who were used to having Eardley Crescent full of their parents' friends and colleagues) liked this latest visitor to their home immensely: 'He was great,' Robin would recall, 'Very different and a lot of fun.'[14] Before long, he was behaving like a second father to them and an unofficial husband to the love-struck Hattie.

The next time John returned home he was stunned to see how things had developed. Even he, for all of his vagueness and distractedness, realised now that Schofield was not just one of Hattie's many vulnerable little 'strays'. He could tell that this man was now almost certainly involved intimately with his wife, and he was greatly alarmed to see how close Schofield appeared to have become to the boys. His reaction, in such deeply distressing circumstances, seemed to confirm Tony Hancock's view of him as Eeyore, with Schofield as Tigger, the newly arrived bouncy tiger:

Eeyore walked all round Tigger one way, and then turned and
walked round him the other way.

'What did you say it was?' he asked.

'Tigger.'

'Ah!' said Eeyore.

'He's just come,' explained Piglet.

'Ah!' said Eeyore again.

He thought for a long time and then said:

'When is he going?'[15]

That was more or less how John Le Mesurier reacted to the presence
of John Schofield inside his home: he walked around him a few times,
thought to himself 'When is he going?' and then, with a heavy sigh,
tried his very best to carry on as normal. 'I could have walked out,' he
would later say, 'but, whatever my failings, I loved Hattie and the
children and I was certain – I had to be certain – that we could repair
the damage.' Rather than risk forcing any further estrangement,
therefore, John decided instead, very reluctantly, on a typically polite
but desperately uneasy compromise: 'To give us all time to think, I set
myself up apart from Hattie, keeping mostly to my own room.'[16] The
unhappy ménage à trois had thus begun.

It was an almost unbearable period for John, suddenly finding
himself little more than a lodger in his own home, forced to be a
passive and impotent spectator as Schofield slept first in one of the
spare rooms and then eventually in the same bed as his wife and played
all the time with his two young sons. Snapping back into his old
'hedgehog mode', he tried to distract himself with work, slaving away
on set and then staying for as long as possible in his dressing room, but
he could not stop thinking about all the damage that was being done
to his marriage. Sometimes, in the evenings, he sat at home, alone in
his room, often in tears, and sometimes he stayed out in clubs,
smoking and drinking too much, seemingly indifferent even to his
beloved jazz as he sat for hour after hour in the darkness. He barely ate,
rarely noticed anyone else and hardly ever bothered to read a
newspaper. He turned in on himself and his thoughts. It maddened
him to think that, at the age of fifty, he was, in effect, reverting to his
old teenage tactic of going through the motions and waiting patiently
for something positive to happen, but he simply could not think of
what else to do.

It was at this point that he found himself further burdened with a most unwelcome invitation. The producers of the popular BBC television show *This Is Your Life* contacted him to say that they were planning a programme about Hattie, and, as was the normal procedure, they wanted to acquire the covert co-operation of her spouse (who, they knew, was already conveniently in situ at the studios, filming an episode of a sitcom called *Mr Justice Duncannon*). He felt trapped: although he realised that Hattie would hardly feel comfortable finding her personal life in the spotlight during such a difficult period, and, as her cuckolded husband, he dreaded the prospect of being dragged out in front of the cameras alongside her, he did not know how to extricate both of them from the project without arousing media suspicions of marital unrest. Reluctantly, therefore, he agreed to keep the secret and, for reputation's sake, allowed the surprise tribute to go ahead. It was thus an excruciatingly embarrassing experience for both of them, and a particularly heartrending one for him, when, on 12 February 1963, Hattie became the latest subject of *This Is Your Life*.

She was surprised by the show's host, Eamonn Andrews, at the BBC Television Studio in Shepherds Bush, where she had been rehearsing the next episode of *Sykes And A . . .* 'You're kidding!' she said, looking shaken, as Andrews shouted out the title and guided her to her chair to commence the unexpected 'celebration'. The ever-affable Eric Sykes was the first guest, followed by her old Red Cross Divisional Commander, her fellow actor Shirley Eaton, her old MC from The Players' Theatre Leonard Sachs, and actor/director Bernard Miles. Andrews – managing to cite the wrong year for the date of Hattie's wedding – then called on John Le Mesurier to appear. Hattie looked distinctly uneasy as John, clearly trying his best to remain in coolly composed 'actor mode', attempted to behave like the loving and contented husband that he was supposed to be, coming out with the kind of comments that sounded carefully pre-rehearsed. He teased her about her time-keeping: 'I must confess I am rather inclined to be a bit surprised when Hattie arrives for anything, really. It's sort of a standing joke in our family. I'm one of these curious people who for some extraordinary reason find it necessary to get to appointments and rehearsals and things about half an hour too soon. There I am, wandering about like an idiot, you see, with nothing to do. [Whereas] Hattie makes every moment count.' He praised her as a homemaker:

'So many things to be done. You know, ordinary, rather dreary, mundane things like shopping lists and maybe a fuse has gone or a cupboard, for some unknown reason, might have to be turned out at the last moment . . . and off she goes, you see. She's like a whirlwind. How she manages I really wouldn't know.' The 'performance' grew more strained when Andrews asked him, with an unwitting lack of tact, 'So there's never a dull moment with Hattie?' John seemed to have to stifle a grimace before regaining his composure and replying, slowly and rather wistfully:

> I would like . . . I would like to say [*glances at her and smiles*] that I am eternally grateful to the way she runs the home. Looks after the children. Looks after me. The home comes first, I think I'm right in saying. [*She giggles nervously*] But I think that for somebody who is so busy all the time, and so much in the public eye all the time, to do all these things is very difficult, and a jolly neat trick.[17]

John then kissed her on the cheek and moved away, looking thoroughly relieved to be able to do so. A succession of other guests followed, and then, at the end, as Andrews observed that Hattie was 'essentially a family girl', her brother, mother, grandmother, two children, John and even their lively golden Labrador Blades joined her for the presentation of the famous red book. As the credits rolled, the apparently happy family stood together – John with his arm around his mother-in-law, and Hattie with hers around Robin – looking like a politely posed Victorian tableau in the *Illustrated London News*. It had all been a huge strain, but at least Hattie's public image had been protected.

The episode certainly did nothing to defuse the tense atmosphere inside the home at Eardley Crescent, and for the rest of the year it was remorselessly oppressive. Schofield now marched grandly around the house telling Hattie what to do, sometimes placing a fatherly arm around each of the children. John, who was bluntly ignored by this de facto head of the household, stayed in his room, still feeling utterly stunned by how things were evolving.

Eventually, after a few more emotionally and physically draining months, he finally decided to act rather than just react: 'I tried to bring matters to a head by announcing my departure for a week or two on what might, in happier circumstances, have been described as a holiday.'[18] He really did not want to go anywhere (he much preferred working to resting even at the best of times), but he felt he had to get away from Eardley Crescent, and his increasingly poor health suggested that he was in dire need of a rest. He chose to go to Tangier, simply because it was the first package deal that the local travel agent handed him. Booking into a smart hotel in Morocco called the Rif, he unpacked and took possession of a sun lounger near the pool – where he promptly collapsed.

The hotel doctor gave him something to alleviate the mystery illness, but John, who still had a fever and was struggling to breathe properly, was in no mood to suffer indefinitely in Morocco and insisted he wanted to go straight back home. Flights to London were routed in those days via Gibraltar, so John reasoned: '[I]f I had to die, I might as well try to do it within the Empire.'[19] Upon landing in Gibraltar, he was rushed to the King George VI Hospital, where an examination revealed that he was suffering from a collapsed lung, pneumonia, hepatitis, jaundice and 'various other minor ailments'.[20]

Hattie, who was working on another Carry On movie at Pinewood Studios, received an urgent call to come out to see him. She did so, accompanied by a far-from-happy John Schofield, but she was unable to stay for very long, so she arranged for John Bailey, an old actor friend of the family, to remain behind and keep her estranged husband company. Bailey proved himself an able 'cheerer-upper', arriving each morning bearing baskets of fruit and a selection of newspapers and glossy magazines, and stayed by the bedside to chatter brightly about a variety of theatrical matters. On one occasion he managed to make John smile by reporting that the notorious 'Den Den' Shaw had rung up the hospital in the early hours of the morning. 'I hear that my friend, John Le Mesurier, is dying,' he had slurred. 'You can speak quite freely; I'm a relative. And he owes me money.' John, still groggy, wondered aloud whose telephone 'Den Den' had used.[21]

It took more than a month before John was judged well enough to be discharged and return to England. Feeling a failure even as a holidaymaker, he arrived back in London full of trepidation as to what, if any, kind of 'homecoming' he would receive at Eardley Crescent. 'I suppose I knew in my heart of hearts that only a miracle could save the marriage,' he would say, 'but also knew that Hattie would not throw me out of the house. Being there was the only way of showing her that we still had a chance together.'[22]

It came as no great surprise, but still a disappointment, when he walked through the door to find that, if anything, things were now worse than ever: 'The atmosphere was heavy to say the least.'[23] Hattie, as expected, was her usual warm and welcoming self, but Schofield made it abundantly clear from the start that, in his view, John should 'do the decent thing and quietly disappear'.[24]

John, however, was in no state to go anywhere other than another hospital. Only a short while after his return home, his health once more declined disturbingly and he was rushed off to a Harley Street clinic for another round of tests, which this time revealed that there was a growth in his colon.[25] The news was kept private due to fears that it might damage his employment and insurance prospects, but it was decided, eventually, that some of his intestines would have to be removed, so he was moved off to St Mark's Hospital in the City Road and underwent the operation soon after. Once he was well enough to receive visitors, Hattie started coming to see him, bringing him mail and magazines as well as the good news that it would not be long before he was allowed to leave. On her third visit, however, John was concerned to see that she was wearing dark glasses. 'She said she had bumped into something and given herself a black eye,' he would recall. 'I knew better. The truth was she had been in a fight with Schofield; he was jealous of Hattie's visits to me and felt threatened.'[26]

When he was released and back at Eardley Crescent, he tried to make himself as scarce as possible, fearing that his presence would only make things worse for Hattie. He needed to see his children, and he was more worried than ever about his wife, but, still fragile from the surgery and covered in sore patches of skin caused by his latest nervous outbreak of psoriasis, he felt too weak to come up with a convincingly constructive response. He thus tried to complete his recuperation quietly and discreetly in his room, concentrating on leafing through scripts during the day but always consumed in the still watches of the night by a crushing sense of helplessness.

Thoughts of his own mortality probably weighed fairly heavily on his mind at this very lonely time. Not only had his own recent illnesses shaken him considerably after so many years of good health, but he had also recently lost several old friends, including two – Mario Fabrizi and Walter Hudd – with whom he had worked only a few months earlier on *The Punch and Judy Man*. Worse news was to come at the start of the following year, when his own father died, after a short

St Mary's Square in Bury St Edmunds: the place where John grew up – first at Number 8 (right), then at number 6 (centre, behind tree).

The young John, seated on the left of the front row, next to his sister Michelle, at Miss Underwood's school in Bury St Edmunds, circa 1919/20. *Courtesy of Jane Weare*

The young jobbing actor in repertory theatre: he was 'incredibly good-looking,' said one female contemporary. 'People pined away for him!'

Sherborne public school: John resented it 'for rejecting anything that did not conform to the image of manhood as portrayed in the ripping yarns of a scouting manual'.

John with first wife, June Melville, on their wedding day, 18 April 1940, at All Saints, Highgate: they spent most of their marriage, he would say, 'counting the hours in champagne cocktails'. *Topfoto*

John as a psychopathic killer in his second 'B' movie, *Escape from Broadmoor* (1948), which he dismissed as 'hilarious for all the wrong reasons'.

Welcome to slapstick: accepting a custard pie in *Old Mother Riley's New Venture* (1949).

Being suitably censorious, as the bureaucrat determined to stamp out any form of free expression, in the 'art' movie *The Pleasure Garden* (1953).

John as the twitchy psychiatrist in his Boulting Brothers breakthrough, *Private's Progress* (1956).

'I don't wish to alarm you, but...': John (with Hattie Jacques lurking behind him) in an episode of *Hancock's Half Hour* (1959). *Rex Features*

The Punch and Judy Man (1963): the on-screen rapport between Le Mesurier and Hancock survived the off-screen tensions. *The Kobal Collection*

Happy Holidays: John and Hattie share some leisure time with their two young sons, Robin and Kim. *Rex Features*

John, playing the 'dear old stick' Colonel Maynard, with Sid James in a 1966 episode of the sitcom *George and the Dragon*. *Rex Features*

Left to right: JLM, Ronnie Barker, Peggy Mount, Harry Secombe, Richard Todd, Bill Fraser, Jimmy Hanley and John Standing raising money for Army Charities, March 1969. *Mirrorpix*

As a jobbing actor, John had to appear in what he termed 'a lot of crap'. Here he is in 1972 trying to restrain Peter Wyngarde from doing too much in an episode of the action-adventure-moustache show *Jason King*. *Rex Features*

Derek Taylor, John's close friend and fellow English gentleman. *Getty Images*

Filming *Jabberwocky* (1977). John and his friend Max Wall drank Guinness throughout each evening and then rose at 'the usual unearthly hour of the morning to jump through the hoops'. *The Kobal Collection*

John – cigarette, as ever, in hand - with Kenneth More in 1978 on the set of *The Spaceman and King Arthur* at Alnwick Castle, Northumberland - not too far from where John was stationed during the war. *Mirrorpix*

We are the boys who will make you watch again: Sergeant Wilson ('Would you mind awfully...?') issues some 'orders' to the platoon in an episode of *Dad's Army*.
© *BBC Photographic Library*

Cheers! The cast (with, second from right, Hamish Roughead standing in for John Laurie and, far right, John Bardon for James Beck) relax in 1975 during the run of their stage show. *Mirrorpix*

The 1976 Christmas special: Mainwaring launches yet another unwise operation as Wilson starts to worry. *Mirrorpix*

The cast (along with Jimmy Perry) socialise at the Variety Club in March 1971. The on-screen dynamics continued off-screen, with the laid-back Le Mesurier happy to leave Lowe to huff and puff. *Rex Features*

John on location with John Laurie. He once asked the proud old thespian who, in his opinion, ranked first in all the portrayals of Hamlet. *'Me, laddie!'* barked Laurie. *'ME!'* *The Kobal Collection*

John, still in poor health, posing for a publicity still to mark the very last episode of *Dad's Army* in 1977: 'This was the final roll-call, the "Last Post," as it were'. *Mirrorpix*

Appearing in Peter Sellers' swansong *The Fiendish Plot of Dr Fu Manchu* (1980). John himself hoped to 'go out in harness,' leaving colleagues saying: 'He wasn't a bad old nuisance. Now he's off to get in a muddle in another place!' *Warner Bros/BFI*

'I'm more than somewhat fond of you...' John with his third wife, Joan, in 1970, reunited at their Ramsgate home after the trauma of the Hancock Affair. *Rex Features*

'He was the kindest man in the world': Joan Le Mesurier with step-son Kim (left) and son David (right) after John's memorial service at St Paul's Church on 16 February 1984. *Topfoto*

illness, at the age of eighty-three in Bury St Edmunds. Elton Halliley had retired from his role as secretary to the National Society of Conservative and Unionist Agents back in 1947 (his many years of service were celebrated in a special event at the Royal Pavilion in Brighton, where he was presented with a 'quite lovely illuminated album' bound in blue leather, and again soon after in another special ceremony thrown by the Conservative Party grandee Douglas Hacking in London), and had been awarded the OBE in the New Year's Honours List of 1952 for his services to politics.[27] After he had done his best to hide his disappointment that his son had chosen not to follow in his (and his father's) own footsteps as both a solicitor and a political organiser, his growing pride in John's subsequent achievements as an actor had been made plain enough, in the Halliley family's usual low-key way, to have touched his son, and their relationship throughout his retirement had been warmer than ever before. His loss, therefore, was another painful blow that was hard for John to take. The funeral and cremation took place in Cambridge; he went there on his own, and then returned to London in the most fatalistic of moods.

It was not long after this that a profoundly careworn John (although by no means reconciled emotionally to the prospect of divorce) gave in to the inevitable and, with a heavy heart, started pondering – very hesitantly – the prospect of moving out of Eardley Crescent. The thought of suddenly being on his own at the age of fifty-two filled him with a mixture of fear and sadness, but he knew that, sooner or later, such a day would have to come.

When he had played the cuckolded Andrew Crocker-Harris on stage in *The Browning Version*, the play saw his wife's affair come to an abrupt end when the man who had taken his place suddenly sympathised with him and stepped aside. Though Crocker-Harris admits that he has been wounded by the betrayal, he nonetheless refuses to blame his unfaithful wife: both she and he are victims of the marriage, he says, each unable to give the other the kind of support that they need, and it is this fact that has turned whatever love they once had to hatred. In John's own life, in contrast, John Schofield remained utterly unrepentant, and seemed set to stay on for good at Eardley Crescent, with the besotted Hattie more than happy to walk one step behind him and help fund his various new business schemes. She was nothing like Crocker-Harris's callous wife, but, nonetheless, it now appeared that she simply wanted, and desired, her lover much more than she wanted her husband.

John was heartbroken. There was still plenty of work jotted down in his diary, of course, and a good amount of money was continuing to come in, but none of that seemed to matter any more. He seemed to have been robbed of his personal life, and he wandered through each day feeling thoroughly empty and aimless. 'I kept up the pretence of all's well in the rush of everyday business,' he would say. 'But in the evenings when I let down the defences, I could shake with the panic of knowing what was happening to me.'[28]

Apart from the desperately vague hope that Hattie would eventually take him back, there was only one other thing that was keeping him going. It was the thought of a young woman he had first met some months before. He called her 'my little friend', and he had never needed someone like her so badly in all of his life.

CHAPTER XI

Joan

I'm more than somewhat fond of you.

The woman whom John Le Mesurier called his 'little friend' was Joan Malin. She came into his life soon after his marriage had started to fall apart, and she would still be there when it was finally deemed to be over.

Born in Oldham in Lancashire, but brought up in Ramsgate in Kent by her fairground-working parents, Joan Malin had been married to the budding actor Mark Eden,[1] with whom she had a son, for six years from 1953 to 1959, before separating and moving to London.[2] 'I didn't really have any specific ambitions at all at that time, apart from just keeping my head above water,' she would later reflect. 'I certainly wasn't looking for a rich husband. Not by a long chalk. I wasn't even looking for a proper romance during that period. I was just a bit restless. Several of my friends had gone to London before me and kept telling me I should follow them there and live a bit, so in the end I did.'[3] She had been working as a secretary by day and a barmaid by night when, early in 1963, she met John Le Mesurier at the Establishment Club. She was thirty-one. He, not quite fifty-one, was nineteen years her senior.

The initial attraction had been for the venue, not the man. The Establishment Club – opened in 1961 by Peter Cook in partnership with one of his fellow Cambridge graduates, Nicholas Luard – was located on the site of an old strip club at 18 Greek Street in the heart of Soho, and was currently being managed by Hattie and John's mutual friend, Bruce Copp. With 7,000 members on its books and a waiting list of more than 5,000, it was one of London's most fashionable night spots, offering satirical comedy upstairs and live jazz downstairs. Regular visitors, apart from John Le Mesurier, included most of

Peter Cook's comic contemporaries as well as actors Terence Stamp, Michael Caine and Peter O'Toole, musicians Paul McCartney, John Barry and Lionel Bart, theatre critic Kenneth Tynan, louche Labour politician Tom Driberg and fashion designer Mary Quant. Jeffrey Bernard was regularly thrown out. The club had recently hosted the controversial American stand-up Lenny Bruce and the reinvigorated British comic Frankie Howerd, as well as an impressive array of jazz pianists, guitarists and singers. Every night, as the seemingly ever-present David Frost used to say, promised to be 'super'.

Joan had gone there, very excitedly, as one of the guests of a rather flamboyant gay actor and choreographer called Johnny Heawood. 'Who's in tonight?' he enquired as Bruce Copp greeted them at the bar. 'John Le Mesurier's watching the show,' Copp replied, pointing upstairs, 'but he'll be out any minute now.' Heawood was startled when Joan asked him who John Le Mesurier was. 'You'll know his face when you see him,' he assured her.

When John did wander out, he noticed Heawood – with whom he had appeared in *The Pleasure Garden* ten years before – and went over to say hello. Heawood introduced him to his guests and John suggested that they all join him down in the basement for the next performance by the Dudley Moore Trio. Moore – another friend – came over to John shortly before he was due to begin his set and asked if he or anyone else at the table happened to have any requests. Joan asked for the wistful 1939 Bob Haggart/Johnny Burke instrumental 'What's New?' John raised his eyebrows: 'How does a slip of a girl like you know an old song like that?' Joan explained that, apart from the fact that it happened to be her all-time favourite, she adored so much of the music of that era, and had a particular affection for classic torch songs and ballads. John, clearly intrigued, smiled and said: 'Perhaps when someone special comes to Ronnie Scott's Club, you might like to come with me, my little friend.'[4]

They were clearly enjoying being in each other's company, chatting and smiling during the breaks between the performances. John would later say that he had found her a 'very attractive' young woman who was 'open and vivacious and could make me laugh easily'.[5] Joan would remark that she had found him 'a gentle, fatherly man who, in spite of his biting humour, had an air of sadness about him'.[6] She relished the novelty of the experience, and he stopped mulling over all of his worries and just enjoyed himself for a few idle hours.

Bruce Copp, who rarely seemed to miss anything remotely interesting that went on inside the club, certainly noticed the effect that Joan was having on John, and he was delighted to see his friend smile and relax for what felt like the first time in months. Knowing that Hattie was still besotted with her new lover, Copp wanted to see John start having a little fun of his own, and so, behind the scenes, he proceeded to plan some matchmaking, arranging for Johnny Heawood to bring Joan to a supper party that was being held the following week at Eardley Crescent. Hattie, the hostess, had been tipped off by Copp, so she watched discreetly from a distance as John, sitting quietly on his own as far away as possible from a noisy and ebullient-looking John Schofield, was pleasantly surprised by Joan's arrival. 'Hello, my little friend,' he said, breaking into a nervous smile. The two were soon laughing and gossiping, and Hattie, like Copp, hoped that something good would come of the fledgling relationship.

The pair did start meeting up socially after that evening at Eardley Crescent, but neither appeared quite sure as to what they were actually doing. Joan found John charming and funny and kind, and, while she was not looking for the friendship to become intimate, she was touched by how sad and vulnerable he seemed. 'His sadness was really overwhelming at times,' she would say. 'His heart was broken, really broken, by Hattie. He really loved her.'[7] John, on the other hand, felt an immediate and strong physical attraction to Joan, but was still so confused and depressed about the sudden collapse of his marriage that, by his own admission, he was not always the best of company during their dates. It was often unclear even to both of them, therefore, whether their first few meetings were primarily casual, romantic or therapeutic. 'Joan was wonderfully patient and tolerant,' he would say, 'even when, on occasion, my nerves split down the middle and I was reduced to crying into my hands.'[8]

Bruce Copp, ever eager to move things along, gave Joan a moon-lighting job at the Establishment, serving drinks at the busy ground-floor bar, thus making it easier for John to see her informally and discreetly on a fairly regular basis. It worked, but only up to a point. John would saunter in, spend more time than usual at the bar and then go upstairs and downstairs to soak up the comedy and music before returning for another drink or two with Joan. He still, however, went home each night to Eardley Crescent, shutting himself straight away inside his increasingly cluttered and cramped little room.

It was at this point that Hattie and John Schofield made the rash decision to try to push Joan into beginning an affair with John. Seeking her out at one of their regular parties, they explained how things had developed, how unfortunate it all was, and how much better it would be for all concerned if John soon moved out and found himself someone else to love. A short while later on his own, Schofield chose to be far more brusquely direct: '[He] told me bluntly that John was mine for the taking,' Joan would recall. 'He even told me that I should have a very comfortable life if I married John, and ended up by saying that it would make them both very happy if I took John off their hands.' This clumsy and tactless move backfired badly, making Joan more determined than ever not to be dragged any deeper into this unhappy romantic imbroglio. She told Schofield that she found his suggestion offensive and tasteless, and insisted that John was, and would remain, a friend 'and no more than that'. The only thing that Schofield's intervention had thus achieved was to make Joan dislike him intensely: 'I wished that Hattie would come to her senses and get rid of him.'[9]

Things went on more or less as before, except that Schofield was angrier than ever about the situation and Joan was even more sympathetic towards John. She could see that Hattie was a kind person whose heart had lured her into a cruel context, but she could also see that the egotistical Schofield was capable of some startlingly callous acts, and she worried about the effect that it was all having on John. He simply did not seem made for loud rows and angry confrontations. His impeccable manners seemed to render him motionless and mute.

The demands of work, however, meant that John was seldom in situ at Eardley Crescent during this period. In the months that followed his first few dates with Joan, he had to fly off to European locations in the Veneto and Rome, Athens, Crete and Paris, and to various studio sets in and around Los Angeles, as well as spend weeks on end shooting at Pinewood, Shepperton and Borehamwood. His hectic schedule helped distract him from his domestic problems, but it also disrupted his attempts to develop his relationship with Joan. Month after month, he would appear, take her out for several successive evenings and then set off to start work on another project. The mutual interest was there and was growing, but the momentum was always being interrupted.

'It was a strange courtship,' Joan would reflect. 'We were such an ill-matched pair, but we found a great deal of common ground in our friendship and he made me laugh a lot, in spite of his being almost permanently depressed.'[10] He always had stories to tell her, and he was always genuinely interested to hear her talk about her own work and life. Even though Joan remained unsure as to where precisely the relationship would, and should, be heading, she was therefore already craving more of his company. As she would say:

> I loved his reliability and good manners, and I basked in the respect that being in his company brought when he took me out to dinner or to the bar. I enjoyed the cards he was always sending, which were funny and descriptive. In short, he was becoming a part of my life and his fondness for me was giving me a confidence in myself that I had never experienced until then.[11]

John, however, remained almost paralysed by his own internal confusions. 'Often during our evenings together he would arrive in tears or break down later,' Joan would later recall. 'I could usually cheer him up temporarily but his situation was at stalemate.'[12] He was still unable to contemplate ending his marriage to Hattie, in spite of the fact that he could see she was obsessed with someone else, but he was also desperate to keep seeing Joan, even though he appreciated that, as she was so much younger than him and apparently unattached, there was always the danger that she would meet and fall in love with another man. He was torn, and he knew it, but he was struggling to find a solution. Writing to Joan from his room at Eardley Crescent late in 1963, he said: 'Whatever happens I cannot lose you entirely, you mean more to me than anyone. I am going to try and get things sorted out so that I can be a better person for you and others.'[13]

He saw as much of Joan as he could over the course of the next few months, as his longing for her grew stronger and stronger. He had only slept with one woman since Hattie had shut him out, and that had merely been a relatively meaningless one-night stand when, some months before while filming outside London, a young woman from the production company invited herself into his room, proceeded to take a shower and then led him into bed.[14] Although he had enjoyed rediscovering 'that old feeling of intimacy' and was now eager to experience it again with Joan, he remained unsure as to how she really felt about him, and was wary of doing or saying anything that might threaten to scare her away. The dates remained tensely chaste, therefore, while John (who bought her an electric blanket partly in the hope that it would dissuade her from seeking out the warmth of someone else's body) tried his best to wait patiently for any sign that Joan might be similarly inclined to change the nature of their relationship.

The couple finally did become lovers during the summer of 1964. John was filming *Those Magnificent Men in Their Flying Machines* on location in Felixstowe, while Joan was on holiday at her family's home in Ramsgate. One evening, after a long day in front of the cameras, he turned up at Joan's door unexpectedly, looking tired and terribly sad. More stories had reached him about John Schofield's carefree excursions with Hattie and the two children, and he was struggling to control his emotions. Eager for some distraction, he invited Joan and one of her female friends out to a local late-night drinking club. It did not take long, once they had arrived, before he was recognised by a fan who came over and asked for an autograph. As he signed his name and chatted politely, Joan, after spending so many months by his side, suddenly found herself looking at him in a different light: 'For the first time it struck me how attractive he was, with his broad shoulders and fine, aristocratic features. At that moment he looked round and caught my eye. A little dart of desire hit me in the stomach.'[15]

On the way back, after they had dropped her friend off at her digs in the nearby London Road, John put his hand on Joan's shoulder: 'He had often done this before, but this time it was different. He kissed me for the first time, and it was so exciting that we ended up making love in the car in a cul-de-sac round the corner from London Road. Nothing was said between us and later, when he left me at the door, I was in a state of total confusion.'[16]

The sudden change in their relationship signally failed to force all of the other problems to fade abruptly away. John took her to Bury St Edmunds to meet his now-widowed mother, and Joan was happy to bring him down to meet her own family in Ramsgate, but no big decisions were taken and no dramatic announcements were made. Nothing much changed, for example, in either's living arrangements: John still wanted to be near his sons, and Joan still wanted to preserve her own space. 'I wasn't in love with John,' she later explained. 'I enjoyed having sex with him – in fact, sex with John was more abandoned and uninhibited than with anyone I'd ever known – but I wanted my life to continue just as it was.'[17] John himself tended to avoid using the word 'love' on those occasions when he tried to speak to Joan about how he felt, preferring instead to stress how 'fond' he was of her: 'Love,' he explained, 'is an overused word that shouldn't be bandied about.'[18] He did attempt to propose to her one evening at a restaurant in Churton Street known (rather aptly, considering the anguished nature of so many of his past conversations there) as Grumbles, but his phrasing was so excruciatingly tentative and vague – 'I'm sure you don't want to take me on . . .' he mumbled – that Joan was able to change the subject swiftly without causing him any pain. 'I let the whole thing pass over my head,' she would say, 'because, no, I didn't want to take him on.'[19] The couple therefore went on more or less as before, meeting up for dates at their usual favourite places, except that they now also met up, whenever they could, to make love.

It was an undeniably awkward situation – not least because John was a fifty-two-year-old man who could not bring his girlfriend home for the night. Joan suggested that he start looking for a bachelor flat, arguing that he might just discover that he enjoyed the sense of independence it would bring him, but he remained unconvinced. 'It was a vain hope,' she would reflect. 'When it came to looking after himself, he was one of the most helpless people I have ever met. He didn't know one end of a tin opener from the other. I felt deep down that he was my responsibility, or would be before long, but though I cared for him I was still trying to hang on to my independence.'[20]

In time, however, the warmth John felt for Joan finally gave him enough strength to move out of the home that he had shared so awkwardly with Hattie and find a place of his own: three floors up in a horseshoe-shaped block of flats called Barons Keep in Barons Court, off Gliddon Road in West Kensington. Joan was based not too far away in St George's Square, Pimlico, and so, after work, she went over with the intention of helping him unpack and start to settle. 'Dear John,' she later recalled, 'the flat was in a hopeless muddle – he had put everything in the wrong place. It touched me to see his helplessness; I knew then I would have to care for him.'[21] She rearranged his furniture, sorted through his other possessions and made up his bed, and then he took her off for a long and fairly boozy dinner at a restaurant – much beloved by his favoured show business circle – called Tratoo in Abingdon Road off Kensington High Street.

It was there, on that night, that John proposed to Joan again, but this time – by his standards – far more clearly and directly. As Joan later recalled, 'He said "Would you please, please, come and live with me?"'[22] On this occasion, she accepted without hesitation.

By the start of 1965, therefore, they were living together openly in Barons Court as a 'proper' couple. A bigger flat soon became available next door, at number 56, with large bright rooms and a balcony, so they made the short move and settled in there. They were soon joined by two somewhat neurotic pet cats – one a Siamese and the other a Burmese Rex – and started being visited by plenty of their mutual friends (who particularly liked the fact that the building boasted a private 'drinking club' on the ground floor). Hattie, meanwhile, was pleased to assist her estranged husband by arranging for accounts to be opened at two of his favourite department stores, Derry & Toms and Barkers, as well as at his regular wine merchant, Norton & Langridge, thus ensuring that all John needed to do was to pick up a telephone to keep himself well-stocked with most of his so-called 'essentials'. Joan, after some discussion, gave up her day job at Gibbs Pepsodent for the foreseeable future and stayed at home to look after the apartment as well as, of course, to look after John.

He was, she would say, 'a darling to live with. He gave me the freedom to be myself and never tried to change me in any way.'[23] John put all of his money into a joint account, handed over his cheque book to Joan and stopped bothering to look at his bank statements. 'He simply wanted to get on with his work,' she later recalled, 'and leave all those tasks to me.'[24] John, indeed, seemed more positive than he had been for years. After all of the anguish that had dogged him for so long, he was ready for a new start. He was well aware of Joan's lingering uncertainties – apart from the age difference and his two failed marriages, he reflected, what was on offer 'was my unreal world of film and theatre where the pressures of insecurity, not to mention the demands of a fractured ego, could be too great to sustain'[25] – but he was determined to make this partnership work for her as well as for him.

It helped that the news of their engagement had been received so well not only by their mutual friends, but also, most importantly for John, by his two sons. Robin – then aged twelve – wrote to both of them:

Dear Daddy and Joan,

I am really so glad that you are getting married, because I love you very much. I hope you are very happy together, I know that Kim and I will like it a lot.

All my love,
Robin.[26]

His younger brother's letter read:

Dear Daddy and Joan,

I hope you both have a happy marriage, it's a lovely idea.
I love you both a lot.
Kim.[27]

Joan's own young son, eight-year-old David, was similarly supportive. Although he seemed content to remain for the time being in the more familiar environment of Ramsgate, where he attended school and was cared for by his maternal grandparents, it was made clear that he was welcome to visit and stay at Barons Court whenever he wished.

The other person who responded promptly to the announcement of the engagement was Hattie. Her own note to John mixed regret with relief when reflecting on the imminent end of the whole sorry saga that they had shared:

Dear Johnny,

Thank you for telling me your news. I do feel I would like to tell you that truly and sincerely I wish for your happiness, for your peace of mind and everything to be good in your future marriage. Joan is a lovely person who I know understands and loves you and is so much better for you than I could ever have been. We have all been through a pretty wretched time but out of it all I'm sure will come great happiness for all of us.
God bless and my love,
Jo.[28]

Happy that good will appeared to have arrived in place of so much tension and ill-feeling, John was eager to move on and marry Joan as soon as was practically possible, and so, while Joan divorced Mark

Eden (on similarly friendly terms) on the grounds of his desertion, the couple arranged for Hattie to take proceedings against them – thus ensuring that she would be cast by the media in the role of the victim and escape any negative publicity. 'It was all very amicable,' Joan would say, 'although it entailed a visit from a private detective, who had to look into our bedroom to ensure that we really were living in sin. He kept clearing his throat in embarrassment when he asked us personal questions, much to our amusement.'[29] Once this somewhat farcical ritual had been completed, the relevant paperwork was processed and the respective actions went ahead.

Hattie Jacques divorced John and Joan divorced Mark Eden on the same day: Friday 27 May 1965. It was arranged between the respective sets of solicitors that Hattie's case was heard first, and Joan was allowed to stand at the back of the courtroom while the divorce was being granted. Although the formal procedure dictated that the two women, as 'antagonists', could not acknowledge each other in any way, Hattie smiled and blew Joan a quick kiss as she left the room. Once the second divorce was completed, everyone went back to Eardley Crescent, where, over several glasses of good vintage champagne, they toasted each other's futures. 'We all launched off into what seemed like "happy-ever-afters,"' Joan would reflect. 'Hattie had her chap. I had John. Yes, it was all hope for the future.'[30] The late edition of that day's *Evening Standard*, however, would feature a picture of Joan captioned 'The other woman', and the following morning the newspapers were full of reports branding John as an adulterer and Joan a marriage breaker.[31] 'I wish the press,' Joan would later say, 'could have seen us all celebrating.'[32]

A subsequent court order, issued on 3 August 1965, instructed that 'the Respondent do pay to the children Robin Mark Le Mesurier Halliley and Kim Charles Le Mesurier Halliley as from the date hereof all monies payable for their school fees and one half of the monies necessary for their purchasing school uniforms and sports clothing until they shall respectively attain the age of 18 years and further order Petitioner's costs'. The decree absolute was issued in the High Court on 31 August 1965, confirming John as 'guilty of adultery'. Hattie would later say of her former husband:

> John was and still is a gentle and very lovely man. We are still great friends . . . it doesn't matter how civilised people are about dissolving

a marriage, it's still a wretched business. John and I are the greatest of friends and still I love him and I think he loves me. There were never any recriminations. I wouldn't have been able to stand that, bad feelings between the parents of children. He's a lovely person, so sweet . . .[33]

Hattie soon received a predictably long-winded letter from her solicitor that ended with the studied remark: 'You are, of course, as you will appreciate, now free to re-marry should you so desire.'[34] She certainly did want to marry John Schofield (and ideally as soon as possible), but, although his name now started appearing in the telephone book with the given address of 67 Eardley Crescent, she was destined to wait in vain for his proposal.

She continued to help support him financially during the next few years. It appears that, after a while, he started to row with her, flirt (or worse) with some of her friends and sometimes, it has been alleged, treat her violently.[35] In 1966, when she was in Rome filming *The Bobo* with Peter Sellers and Britt Ekland, Schofield visited her on the set and (as she later confided to Joan in a long and tearful long-distance telephone call) they ended up having a huge row because she suspected him of having an affair. Bruce Copp saw her soon after she arrived back in England: 'She was wearing dark glasses and a scarf over her head, and her face was all bruised. She had a black eye and a bruise [on her cheek] and a contusion [under her left eye] that actually left a permanent scar.'[36]

The following year, when she was in hospital being treated for a kidney complaint, he turned up to announce coldly that he was leaving her immediately for a woman he described as 'an Italian heiress'.[37] Throwing a medallion that she had given him (three fingers moulded together in gold and inscribed 'I Love You') on to her bed, he simply turned around and walked straight out of her life. The desertion would break her heart, and many of her friends felt that she never fully recovered from the hurt.

John and Joan, meanwhile, pushed straight ahead with their own plans. 'In stark reversal to the happy-go-lucky way in which my relationship with Hattie developed over the years,' John later reflected, 'I was now much more inclined to speed things along, to have confirmed by public acclamation, as it were, the happiness that I felt and, by so doing, somehow increasing the chances of it lasting.'[38] News of their engagement, therefore, was promptly made public and they were married on the morning of Wednesday 2 March 1966 at Fulham Town Hall, with John smart in a sober dark suit and Joan resplendent in a fashionably cut light blue dress. Bruce Copp, the triumphant matchmaker, was present as John's best man, and the other guests were the writer-performer Marty Feldman and his wife Loretta, and a good friend of Joan's called Sheila Newton along with her own husband, Tom. Neither Hattie nor the children were present, but she sent a touching letter to the couple, while the boys provided a picture of John and Joan as a pair of goldfish swimming happily around in a bowl with two smaller fish, named 'Robin' and 'Kim', following them blowing heart-shaped bubbles. After the ceremony was over, the couple and several of their friends moved on for a long celebratory late lunch at Tratoo, and then John and Joan returned to Barons Court where several more bottles of champagne were opened.

There was no chance of them embarking immediately on a proper honeymoon, because John was already booked to make several guest appearances in an ITV sitcom – a spin-off from the popular soap opera *Coronation Street* – called *Pardon the Expression*. Early the following morning, therefore, he and Joan caught a train for the Granada studios in Manchester, where he began working with the star of the show, Arthur Lowe, and she visited some of her many Lancastrian relations. It was hardly the most romantic of starts to a marriage, but both of them remained in the happiest of moods.

It seemed as though the bad times were finally over. John's career was looking impressively stable and successful, he was enjoying plenty of respect and affection from both the public and his peers (David Niven, with whom he appeared in the 1965 comedy *Where the Spies Are*, had said recently that working with John was 'like meeting an old chum in a club'[39]) and, best of all as far as he was concerned, he now had Joan. She made him feel alive again after four long years of being locked tightly inside a terrible dream. Everywhere they went, when he introduced her to other people, he would never describe her simply as his wife; he would always make a point of calling her 'my friend who is also my wife'.[40]

That was why he now looked to the future with such a renewed sense of confidence and optimism: because he was set to share it with the 'little friend' that he so adored. What actually happened next, therefore, would shock him to the core.

CHAPTER XII

The Sad Affair

Are there any of us so pure, so free from sin in our own personal wives – lives! – that we can dispassionately – nay! objectively – nay! . . . dispassionately – judge another?

One of the first things that Joan had known about John was how good and close a friend he was of Tony Hancock. No matter how difficult and unreliable the comedian had proven himself to be, John never faltered in his faith. On stage and off, in failure as well as success, he had always been one of the few people upon whom Hancock knew that he could always rely.

They had continued to work together occasionally since the difficult days of *The Punch and Judy Man*. Both, for example, had made brief contributions to the movies *Those Magnificent Men in Their Flying Machines* (1965) and *The Wrong Box* (1966), as well as sharing the odd scene on the small screen. They had been in more regular contact in their private lives, Tony consoling John over the collapse of his marriage and John providing support for Tony as he continued to battle against alcoholism.

Joan had thus become used, very early on in her relationship with John, to this special attentiveness towards Hancock. Time and again, John would return from visiting his friend in whatever nursing home the comedian was currently languishing and would be moved to tears as he related the latest experience. 'He was sitting dejectedly in the garden,' he recounted on one of these occasions, 'trying to make a fucking coffee table in order to please his therapist.'[1] Although she was very impressed by John's loyalty and sensitivity, she was far from impressed, during these unusually emotional reports, by what she heard about Tony Hancock as a man, developing a mental image of 'an intense, self-centred hypochondriac, lacking the humour in real life that he so brilliantly displayed on the screen'. The more she heard, in fact, the more she hoped that John would keep this troubled character to himself: 'To be honest, I wasn't too keen to meet him.'[2]

By the late autumn of 1964, however, John had felt that a meeting between his best male friend and the woman whom he hoped one day to marry was long overdue, so he arranged to take Joan to see Hancock at the comedian's house in Lingfield. Bracing herself for a difficult few hours in the company of a desperately melancholic individual, Joan was pleasantly surprised when the front door of MacConkeys was opened by a 'laughing expansive man' who greeted his two guests warmly with 'a great welcoming hug'.[3] The rest of the day flew by, with Hancock fussing over Joan, laughing at her funny remarks and asking her plenty of questions about herself, her life and her interests. As they all relaxed that evening over dinner at the local pub, he nodded at Joan and said to John, 'You've got to keep this one, Johnny.'[4]

The couple met up with Hancock again a couple of times soon after, first backstage at a theatre where he was appearing in cabaret, and then when he was hosting an edition of the televised *Sunday Night at the London Palladium*. The comedian had by this time left his long-suffering wife, Cicely, and the five-year on-off affair that he was having with his publicist, Freda 'Freddie' Ross, was currently undergoing one of its 'off' periods, so he now resembled far more closely the kind of sad and troubled figure that Joan had first imagined. Seeing him in his dressing room, slumped in an armchair, wrapped up in a fluffy white towelling bathrobe, his shaking hands slipping out from under the sleeves, she could not stop herself from exclaiming, 'Well, if this is what show business does, I'd rather be a lavatory attendant.'[5] Hancock responded with just a brief, rueful-sounding laugh.

Joan would not encounter him again for about a year. She merely heard a succession of disturbing reports from John about his friend's professional travails, chaotic private life and ongoing battle with the bottle. Hancock had, for example, collapsed while working on a Disney movie in America and was quietly dropped from the production; Cicely divorced him, citing his adultery with Freddie Ross (who, in turn, would soon make an attempt at suicide); plans to reunite him with Sid James on a new project fell through; an offer of the starring role in a stage musical came to naught; he married Freddie, moved into a flat in London overlooking the Edgware Road and started rowing with her again more or less immediately; he went down to Lingfield to see Cicely and ended up fighting again with her; he then returned to Freddie in London; he was admitted to a London nursing home for treatment of his alcoholism while the press were informed that he was suffering from 'nervous exhaustion'; and he was then admitted to yet another nursing home. It was all desperately bewildering for those who were there to witness this hugely talented man's sad decline, and no one found it harder to take than John, who confided to Joan and a few other trusted friends that he feared Hancock 'was drinking away his career'.[6]

It was during the summer of 1966, a few months after John and Joan had married, that, one Sunday evening, a dramatic telephone call came suddenly from Hancock begging John urgently for help. He had parted from Freddie, and had shut himself away with just a single upright chair, a bed and a mound of empty bottles. He had, he explained, gone for days without opening the door or picking up the telephone, but now, with the prospect of a high-profile solo concert at the Royal Festival Hall (scheduled for 22 September, with an edited version set to be broadcast the following month on BBC2) plunging him into a state of panic, he desperately needed company and support. John unhesitatingly rushed off to collect his friend and brought him back to stay with him and Joan in Barons Court.

As Hancock came bounding through the door of the flat, a broad and almost manic grin on his face, Joan was shocked to see how ill and gaunt he now looked, but she was happy 'to have the chance of mothering him'.[7] He remained there for just over a week, sleeping on the couch and wandering around wearing John's dressing gown. He did not eat much, but he drank a little and talked a great deal, seeming to relax in the company of people he trusted. With John usually spending the evenings learning his lines, Hancock would sit in the kitchen with Joan, chatting about a wide range of topics, leaping up whenever she rose and following her around, rather as some men used to do with Hattie, 'like an amiable bloodhound'.[8] The following Monday morning, after John had left early to begin work on his latest movie at Borehamwood, Hancock, in a rare moment of honesty and self-awareness, sat in the kitchen with Joan and asked her, 'Do you know that I'm an alcoholic?' She replied that she had always suspected he was. He went on to explain that his agent had arranged for him to go into a nursing home in Highgate to dry

out before commencing a week-long run at the Bournemouth Winter
Gardens, where the aim was to rehearse some material intended for
the big event at the Festival Hall. Seeing how nervous he was, she
agreed to accompany him in his car to the clinic, and she sat with him
in the waiting room sipping tea and munching on biscuits. 'How
romantic,' he said with a wry smile, 'our first meal alone together.'[9]
Just before he was taken inside for the treatment to begin, he made
Joan promise that she and John would visit him that night. The two
of them did so, but were told that Hancock was currently under
sedation and unable to see anyone, so they returned home and spent
the remainder of the evening talking about the man who was now
very much their mutual friend.

Once Hancock was out of the clinic he went straight down to
Bournemouth to prepare for his show. The following week, John
was told that he was needed in Paris to shoot some location shots
for his latest movie, so Joan saw him off at the airport and then went
back to Barons Court. She was making plans to spend a short period
away in Ramsgate with her son and parents when the telephone
rang. It was Hancock, asking if he could come back to stay for a few
days with her. Joan tried to explain that, as John was away, she was
about to take a break, but he persisted. 'Look,' he said, 'I'll be out
all day. I'm rehearsing for this show and it's scaring the shit out of
me. I'm sure John won't mind.'[10] Joan relented and told him that
he could visit.

She was hosting a small dinner party that evening for a few friends.
When Hancock arrived, he charmed all of her guests and then, when
they had left, he charmed her. After sharing another bottle of wine, they
started to look at each other intently, sensing that, unless they were
careful, something dramatic could well be about to happen. Eventually,
Hancock decided to make a move, kissing her passionately. 'I'm John's
best friend and I'm in love with his wife,' he exclaimed. 'What are we
going to do?' Joan simply said, 'Let's sleep on it.'[11]

Who seduced whom? 'It was mutual,' Joan would say. 'Well, he
made the first pass. And I told him to stop because I knew I was falling
for him and just couldn't fight him. But he became so romantic,
saying he wanted to marry me, give me babies, move to the country . . .
all of those things.'[12] The two of them woke up the following morning
convinced that, sudden as it was, they were now firmly in the grip of
'a grand passion': 'In one single night,' Joan would later reflect, 'Tony

had become the centre of my life and his happiness was my first priority.'[13]

The world, for them, seemed to stand still and silent during those next few days. The doors stayed shut, the telephone was left off the hook, and the couple remained in bed, finding out all they could about each other. It was the most intense kind of reverie.

Reality rudely intruded one morning when a postcard arrived from John. 'Here I am in Paris, France,' it read cheerfully. 'Can't wait to get home to my little friend and wife.'[14] Both Hancock and Joan suddenly seemed to wake up and take in the enormity of what had just happened. Joan said that she simply could not bear to hurt John after all he had been through with Hattie, and so the affair, if it was to continue, would have to remain a secret. Hancock, however, refused to agree: 'It wouldn't be honest,' he insisted. 'It would make John more unhappy in the long run.' He suggested that he should take responsibility and talk to John face to face, but this only made Joan even more agitated and she begged him for more time in which to think.

She decided to call a close female friend for advice, perhaps hoping that rational intervention would shame her into doing the decent thing, but, when the friend came to see them at the flat, she too was soon charmed by Hancock and ended up urging Joan to make a clean break of it and go off with her lover. Joan, however, was still wracked by doubts: 'I kept thinking about John's gentleness and his love for Tony. I felt as if I were about to commit a murder.'[15] Hancock simply refused to relent, and telephoned his mother, explaining what had happened; he then handed the telephone to Joan, so that his mother could tell her to choose her son. The pressure on her was, in both senses of the word, remorseless.

Joan would later claim, rather generously, that, in her opinion, Hancock was so impatiently manipulative mainly because of his desperation to drive away his own great sense of guilt: 'Tony was as horrified at the thought of hurting John as I was; yet he was equally horrified at the thought of losing me. By convincing others, he was trying to convince himself that he was right. He pulled out every stop and in the end John's fate was sealed.'[16]

Joan said that she needed to be alone when she talked to John, so Hancock moved out the day before he was due to fly back from France. Taking another female friend with her for emotional support, she met John at Heathrow and, after he had handed the two women gifts of perfume, they went off to a restaurant for dinner. It did not take long, predictably, before John asked Joan if she had heard from Hancock. Trying hard to seem casual, she mentioned his rehearsals for the imminent show at the Festival Hall and then quickly changed the subject. The conversation continued for a while until, unable to bear the strain of trying to seem 'normal' any longer, Joan complained of feeling tired. Cutting the evening short, John took her home to Barons Court. Once inside, she broke down immediately and told him what had happened. 'Even then,' she would later reveal, 'he didn't get angry – it would have been so much easier if he had. He just walked up and down hugging himself, and then he wept.'[17] Once the tears had subsided, she gave him a sleeping pill and got him into bed, and then prepared herself for a long and painful night alone with her thoughts. The following morning, she arranged for a mutual friend to come over to comfort John, and then she left the flat and set off to see Hancock.

He had installed himself in the opulent Maharajah Suite at the Mayfair Hotel. While he waited anxiously for Joan to unburden herself of the truth, he had started drinking (and, with the craven crassness of an addict, had called his estranged wife to inform her: 'I have found someone younger and prettier than you'[18]). By the time Joan arrived, he was very drunk, in tears and on the phone to, of all people, John. 'You've got to go back to Johnny,' he shouted over at her and sobbed. 'I can't bear it – you've got to go back to him.'[19] When Joan hugged him, however, he hugged her back, and, quite predictably, the telephone was put back down. Such brief and isolated contrition was typical of Hancock in this sort of state: it slid out of him like the dregs at the bottom of a bottle, merely leaving more space to be filled by a fresh draught of self-serving thoughts.

Back at Barons Court, John – who had ended the call from Hancock by doing his best to console Joan – was still in a profound state of shock. 'There was nothing I could say or do,' he would later reflect, 'because nothing made sense to me.'[20] As the days went by and some of the shock subsided, he tried hard to rationalise how his 'little friend' had behaved: 'I think she felt, rightly or wrongly, that Tony needed her more than I did, that she could be a steadying influence on him – even that she might eventually stop him drinking. She also felt that if he could regain his professional confidence, then all would be well.' John, however, had lived through such a scenario himself during the latter part of his own first marriage, so he could not help but feel that Joan was bound to end up being similarly, and very cruelly, disabused: '[L]ike all alcoholics, Tony was really two people. He was the life and soul of the party, the funny man who inspired love and affection, the generous friend who sought approval and desperately wanted to be liked. And he was the drunken braggart whose black moods of self-loathing almost always ended in violence and abuse directed at those who loved him most.'[21]

In the immediate future, however, there was no time for much reflection. Hancock was obsessed with his big date at the Royal Festival Hall and Joan was desperate to get him into the right frame of mind to make the most of such a major opportunity. Dogged by fears that the event would prove a disaster, he fussed over every detail, rehearsing with far greater effort and care than he had invested in a performance in years. When the moment came, however, he failed to do anything to discourage suspicions that his career was already in terminal decline. Appearing emaciated, grey, strained and sluggish right from the start, he subjected those who were present to a selection of 'highlights' from his past, including painfully pedestrian new versions of overfamiliar routines (which he performed by peering into the wings at his cue cards), as well as several clumsy attempts at 'fresh' comedy and a set of knowingly incompetent impressions (of Robert Newton, Charles Laughton and George Arliss) that even he had to admit were now so dated as to bemuse anyone under the age of thirty. With his once-expressive face now stiff and slow, and his fine comic timing no longer truly sharp, his worst impersonation of all that night was of the great Tony Hancock in his prime.

The friendly audience – who had been obliged to sit patiently through an overlong session of supporting entertainments – responded warmly to his efforts, but, when a recording of the show was screened the following month on BBC2, the shambolic state of the performance was exposed for all to see. Even Joan would later acknowledge that much of the applause on the night had been down to 'pure nostalgia, a thank-you for his past glories'.[22]

Relieved that at least the ordeal was over, Hancock and Joan left London as soon as possible to spend some time relaxing together in a modest little bungalow at Broadstairs on the coast in Kent. John, meanwhile, was trying hard to cope on his own in Barons Court.

'[T]he risk of sinking into a slough of self-pity was very strong,' he would say. 'Particularly at the end of the day when I sat alone in the flat we had so recently shared and drank far too much. So I forced myself to get out and meet people.'[23]

One of those who listened to him patiently and tried to offer moral support during this extraordinarily difficult time was, ironically, Joan's own former husband, Mark Eden, who later explained: 'I remember him saying [of Hancock], "He's my best friend. And I brought him to my house. And he walked off with my wife. That's the bit I find very difficult to accept".'[24] It was rare, however, for John even to hint at how he was really feeling, let alone unburden himself of any of his innermost thoughts. Slipping back into 'hedgehog mode', he usually preferred to go off alone and lose himself in the darkness of the nightclubs. Ronnie Scott's, which had recently been relocated to Frith Street, became virtually his second home as he sought to distract himself with jazz: 'Listening to artists like Bill Evans, Oscar Peterson or Alan Clare always made life seem that little bit brighter.'[25]

He also looked to immerse himself in work. It was unfortunate, however, that at this time the British film industry was beginning to lose much of the energy and invention that had driven it on through the first half of the 1960s, and there seemed to be fewer good roles on offer for subtle character actors such as John. He felt ill-suited to the commercially popular Carry On movies – 'For me the best humour requires a light touch but the Carry On team could never resist going at it with a sledgehammer. I put down this heavy approach to the director because all the actors concerned were good in their own right'[26] – and most of the other comedies around struck him as frustratingly inferior to the kind of substantial satires staged by the Boulting Brothers in the 1950s. There were still plenty of big international comic 'romps' being planned, in the style of the commercially successful *It's a Mad, Mad, Mad, Mad World* or *The Great Race*, but the prospect of flying off somewhere to play a minor (and probably stereotypical) character who would only merit a few minutes on the screen no longer appealed to him even as a light-hearted and well-remunerated distraction. He was, in truth, bored of being asked to play English hotel managers or Persian doctors or Egyptian diplomats or Eastern European apparatchiks, and knew that his declining enthusiasm was beginning to show on the screen.

He was hopeless, for example, with most accents – not only foreign ones but also any British ones that differed noticeably from his own. Although he had been capable of a decent enough Cockney during his early years in B-movies, even that dialect had deteriorated in recent years and he no longer seemed to have the appetite for most of the vocal challenges that came his way. In *Carlton-Browne of the F.O.*, for example, he had played the part of the Grand Duke – a man who was supposed to hail from the Pacific island colony of Gallardia – with an accent that made the character sound like an angry Welshman trying to do an impression of Jimmy Cagney. In *Those Magnificent Men in Their Flying Machines*, he had portrayed – mercifully briefly – a French painter with all the conviction of an English actor who was still waiting for a string of onions to be draped around his neck before springing into action with a nasal 'Hor-he-hor'. The nadir had arguably been his risibly woeful stab at Italian in the otherwise quite entertaining Eric Sykes vehicle *Village of Daughters* in 1962. From his first appearance as a local priest called Don Calogero, his accent had gone on a peculiar little *passeggiata* through Spain, Mexico, Sweden, India, Israel, Cardiff and West Kensington, sounding so hypnotically unconvincing that it actually ended up being strangely endearing.

He did have, however, some talents that were seldom being put to any use in worthwhile movies. His subtlety as a dramatic actor, in particular, was by this stage seriously under-appreciated and largely left untapped. His genuinely excellent performance (as an urbane but quietly sinister British official) in the 1964 Disney adventure *The Moon-Spinners*, for example, would have fitted very neatly into the kind of sophisticated suspense movies still being made by Alfred Hitchcock, and he would surely have relished the chance to play a more complicated – and far better written – kind of character for one of the very best British-based directors (it would have been particularly interesting to have seen him in one of Joseph Losey's collaborations with Harold Pinter, as he had excelled in a 1965 BBC1 adaptation of Pinter's *Tea Party*), but such opportunities were few and far between. Although his skills as an actor had the genuine respect of plenty of his contemporaries, including the likes of Peter Sellers, Alec Guinness, David Niven, Terry-Thomas, Kenneth More, Carol Reed and Noël Coward, the current cinema rarely provided him with anything more challenging than the occasional eye-catching cameo.

John thus made it known to his agent Freddy Joachim that, at least for the near future, he was more interested in the small screen than he was in the big: 'The television offers that came my way,' he would later say, 'were altogether more satisfying than anything I was likely to encounter in the now almost moribund movie industry.'[27] This seems, in truth, to have been a case of him making the most of a fairly bleak situation, because most of the offers that he was receiving from television programme makers were not in any serious sense 'exciting' either. There were a few one-off supporting appearances in plays (including editions of *Armchair Mystery Theatre* and *Play of the Week*) and adventure series (such as *Adam Adamant* and *The Avengers*), and some minor recurring roles in a number of prospective sitcoms, but nothing that seemed likely to offer him a seriously rewarding new challenge.

The project that Joachim eventually found for him was a new ITV sitcom, written by Vince Powell and Harry Driver, entitled *George and the Dragon*. This show teamed him with the cackling Carry On star Sid James, who had been seeking another small screen comedy vehicle for some time, and the foghorn-voiced Peggy Mount, who was already well-known for playing a succession of big-boned bellowing battleaxes. John was given the supporting part of Colonel Maynard, a wealthy but somewhat eccentric old soldier who is now largely content to potter about in his capacious home, Greystone Lodge, and treat himself to the odd tumbler or two of brandy.

'We didn't actually write the role specifically with John in mind,' Vince Powell would recall. 'Alan Tarrant, who was Head of Entertainment at ATV at the time, was the one responsible for casting him, but Harry and I were delighted to get him. We'd worked with him a few months before on *Pardon the Expression*, and of course had seen him in many, many, films over the years, so we knew how talented he was. He never forced things. That was important. We didn't want the Colonel to be a broad sort of music-hall "turn" – we wanted him to be a believable character, and John was so good at bringing that type to life.'[28]

Sid James appeared as the Colonel's chauffeur and handyman, George Russell – an improbable but incorrigible flirt whose inability to keep his hands off any attractive young woman has so far driven no fewer than sixteen cooks and housekeepers to flee from his clutches and hurriedly quit their post – and Keith Marsh provided comic support as Ralph, the not-so-great unwashed and unshaven gardener. Exasperated by George's inability to control his lustful urges ('I've thought about putting bromide in his cocoa!'), the Colonel is pleasantly surprised when the next woman to arrive is an infinitely more formidable middle-aged widow called Gabrielle Dragon (Peggy Mount).

Each episode saw George and Ms Dragon locked together in a dogged battle for supremacy within the Colonel's chaotic household while Ralph the unturned worm switched his allegiances back and forth however it best suited him in the latest awkward situation. The Colonel himself – later described by Le Mesurier as 'a dear old stick'[29] – was often little more than an amused or bemused onlooker as the action unfolded ('If anybody wants me, ah, I'll be moving about outside, er, somewhere else . . .'[30]). Thanks, however, to some engagingly wry lines as well as John's subtly eye-catching little physical tics – the shy little sideways lick of the lips, the delicate finger-tipped stroke of the forehead, the comforting rub behind the left ear and the sudden arching of the eyebrows – he made the most of his relatively brief scenes on the screen. In one early outing, for example, he mixed anger and absent-mindedness with elegant comic finesse as he launched into a pompous diatribe about supposedly impartial broadsheet newspapers daring to single out particular politicians on their front covers:

COLONEL: I'm going to protest. It's high time somebody took a stand. It's an imposition, and they'll be having cartoons next! Anyway, I'm going to write a letter. [*He sits down at his typewriter*]

GABRIELLE: Colonel . . .

COLONEL: Er, don't interrupt me flow, do you mind?

GABRIELLE: But Colonel . . .

COLONEL: What is it?

GABRIELLE: [*Gesturing at his typewriter*] Wouldn't you be better with some paper in it?

COLONEL: Damn machines! [*Gets up to retrieve a few sheets*] Oh dear, oh dear!

GABRIELLE: Er, Colonel, any more coffee?

COLONEL: Yes, I think there is a cup left if you fancy it.

GABRIELLE: No, no, not for me. Do you need any more? Have you had sufficient?

COLONEL: Oh, ah, yes, yes, I have, thank you very much.

GABRIELLE: Kidneys all right?

COLONEL: Yes . . . you see, it's the fruit sauce, you see . . . it flushes them out, you see . . .

GABRIELLE: I was referring to your grilled ones on toast!

COLONEL: Oh! Yes, yes. They're fine, thank you very much, dear. You keep it up – they're very good indeed![31]

The sitcom (which was filmed at John's old stamping ground at Borehamwood Studios) was hard work to make – each episode was rehearsed and then shot back-to-back and the schedule was unusually gruelling – but that suited John at a time when he was desperate for any diversion that would take him away from the pain in his private life. He was pleased, therefore, when the show – which ran from November to December 1966 – proved itself to be a major ratings success (with an average of 5.5m viewers per week[32]) and another run was soon commissioned.

The filming of the second series, which would reach the screen in October 1967, came close to being abandoned after the first few episodes, because Sid James suffered a massive heart attack in May that almost killed him. After being rushed to hospital, he spent three weeks in an oxygen tent, and was obliged to convalesce for more than three months before returning to complete the series. John considered him a friend (they had bonded mainly due to their mutual love of horse racing), but he – like Peggy Mount – was privately concerned to see James return to work sooner than had been expected, fearing that the need to overcome his gambling losses was making him take too many risks with his health. James, however, was very much the senior partner of the trio as far as the producers were concerned, and what he wanted to happen usually did. He came back, therefore, looking terribly pale and gasping for breath, and, in spite of the anxiety that his frail condition caused the rest of the cast, the filming was duly resumed.

The modest highlight of this second set of programmes, as far as the contribution of John Le Mesurier was concerned, would be the episode entitled 'The Old Flame', which saw Colonel Maynard prepare himself to marry his childhood sweetheart, Priscilla (played by Sonia Dresdel). Once the initial excitement of the reunion has worn off and the realisation dawns that, after decades spent apart, they have precious little still in common (HE: 'Would you like a cigarette?' SHE: 'I haven't smoked in years – I think it's a filthy habit'; SHE: 'Do you still play tennis?' HE: 'No, not any more, I've got a bit of a dodgy disc, y'know . . .'), he is somewhat taken aback to find that his staff have already formed their own firm opinion on the matter of the marriage:

GABRIELLE: We have a very serious complaint.
COLONEL: Oh lord, it's not gyppy tummy, is it? There's a lot of it about . . .
GABRIELLE: No, Colonel. It has to do with your intended!
COLONEL: Well, er, what about her?
GABRIELLE: Well, if you don't mind my saying so, I think she is an unpleasant, overbearing, loudmouthed snob!

[*He ponders this for a moment before breaking out in a shy smile*]

COLONEL: I couldn't agree with you more!
GEORGE: What did you say, Colonel?
COLONEL: I agree with everything you say. You see, she's not the sort of 'Little Dimples' that I knew, y'know? She's changed completely. She frightens the life out of me![33]

The show – though already settling far too readily for the predictably formulaic – once again proved extremely popular with the public, and would return for two more peak-time series (both averaging, like the first, about 5.5m viewers each week[34]). John never would be the centre of attention for very long, but he continued to steal the odd scene and seize every opportunity to elicit some unforced laughter. 'He was brilliant,' scriptwriter Vince Powell would say. 'You could always rely on him to really act rather than just deliver some comic material. The viewers could watch him and say, "I know someone like that!" He made it seem easy but he was a very clever performer, and I know that the other actors really appreciated what he did.'[35] He was arguably at his best in the opening episode of the fourth and final series, which saw Colonel Maynard trying to be seen to support the Government's current 'Backing Britain' campaign while attempting to smuggle his favourite 'foreign' products past Ms Dragon by hiding them inside his umbrella:

GABRIELLE: Oh, Colonel!
COLONEL: Ah, er, there you are, Miss Dragon. Er . . . still at it?
GABRIELLE: Just finished, Colonel.
COLONEL: Oh, yes, ah, ha-ha-ha! Well . . . I'm home.
GABRIELLE: Yes, Colonel, so you are.
COLONEL: Yes . . . well . . . I think, er, if nobody minds, I'll, ah,
                just take my umbrella up to my room.
GABRIELLE: Oh – whatever for?
COLONEL: What? Oh. That's a . . . very interesting question.
GABRIELLE: Well, it's a very strange thing to do, Colonel.
COLONEL: Yes, well, ah . . . ha-ha . . . d'you think it would be less
                strange if I were to take it into the lounge?
GABRIELLE: Well . . . not quite as strange as taking it up to the
                bedroom.
COLONEL: A-ha! Good! Thank you very much.

[*He sets off sheepishly then glances back anxiously over his shoulder.*]

COLONEL: D-Did you say something, Miss Dragon?
GABRIELLE: Not a word, Colonel.
COLONEL: Good.
GABRIELLE: Colonel?
COLONEL: Yes?
GABRIELLE: Why have you got bottles in your umbrella?
COLONEL: Oh, dear oh dear oh dear! Y'see, it's no good, y'see, it's
                no good at all – you're far too clever for me!
GABRIELLE: Colonel! I am absolutely disgusted with you, I really am!
COLONEL: Well, you see, the fact is, y'see, I rather fancied a drink,
                my dear.
GABRIELLE: But . . . didn't you enjoy the parsnip wine?
COLONEL: No, look here: I don't want to offend you in any way,
                but, you see, you can't really compare parsnip wine with
                brandy, though, can you, eh? [*He sets back off again*]
GABRIELLE: Colonel . . .
COLONEL: Hmm, yes, my dear?
GABRIELLE: You've forgotten your bottles.
COLONEL: Oh, no, no, I couldn't possibly take them back now,
                you see. Fair dos, a fair cop, the game's the game and all
                of that kind of thing. And, after all, we are trying to
                back Britain, aren't we?

GABRIELLE: Ahhh!
COLONEL: Yes . . . it would have been a damned sight easier with
             diamonds![36]

John would remain grateful to *George and the Dragon*. Apart from providing him with plenty of priceless exposure over the course of a hectic two-year period, it helped him to hold on to his sanity while the saga of his wife's affair with Hancock dragged inexorably on.

Everything he had heard about how that relationship had been developing disturbed him deeply. The couple, he knew, had barely spent any time together in the bungalow at Broadstairs before Hancock started drinking heavily again, and Joan had been shaken by his violent and abusive rages. The face would change, the eyes went dead and the words he snarled were, if anything, even more hurtful than the bruises he caused. He insulted her, he insulted her parents and even her nine-year-old son, David, of whom he seemed to be getting increasingly jealous. Joan later said: 'He vied for attention like a child himself.'[37] Any well-meaning attempt to keep him away from the bottle merely increased the degree of danger that she faced, and on one occasion he became so enraged by her obstructive efforts that he hurled empty glasses against the walls and tried to smash an iron coffee table straight through the French windows. It did not take long before he drank himself into a coma and had to be rushed back to his drying-out clinic in Highgate, where he was kept under deep sedation and administered vitamin injections and electric shock therapy.

Joan often turned to John at such harrowing times, visiting him at Barons Court where she would sit down and pour out her heart to him as he listened sympathetically: 'My poor darling,' he would say softly, 'how awful for you.'[38] In spite of his own sadness and pain, he always did his best to reassure her that things would soon be better before watching her walk back out through the door. 'I was steadfastly in love,' she would explain, 'and John steadfastly loved us both.'[39] Indeed, on one, slightly calmer occasion John even persuaded her to take him back with her to see Hancock in his flat: 'And they were both so polite and sat there and talked. Tony was mortified, ashamed really of what he'd done, and when John left he said, "Why did you do that?" and I said, "He wanted to see you. He misses you".'[40]

By November 1966, Hancock's health had improved sufficiently for him to make a brief guest appearance on a television show hosted by his old friend Harry Secombe. With his confidence buoyed by the experience, he then accepted a lucrative two-week engagement to star in cabaret at a hotel in Hong Kong. Back in London in December, when the lease of his Knightsbridge apartment expired, he and Joan moved into a service flat in Dolphin Square while more suitable accommodation was prepared for them at 22 Abbot's House, St Mary Abbot's Terrace, not far from John in Barons Court. The precarious period of stability was, however, short-lived. Joan went off to spend a family Christmas with her son and parents in Ramsgate (where, somewhat awkwardly, they were joined for some of the festivities by John), whereupon Hancock, left to his own devices, slipped back into his old bad habits. Once again, the drinking soon had a dramatic effect on his health.

When Joan returned at the start of the New Year and saw how poor a condition he was in, she acted quickly to arrange medical treatment, but the prescribed combination of the anti-psychotic drug Largactil and a high dosage of barbiturates caused a bad reaction, leaving Hancock unable to sleep and plagued by a series of wild hallucinations. Within days he had suffered a fit caused by a liver attack; after being treated with a plurentavite injection, he was warned by a specialist that, if he continued to drink, it would probably be no more than three months before he was dead.

Shaken to the core, Hancock wrote his will and moved with Joan into their new apartment in a belated bid to lead more of a 'normal' life. Drinking tea incessantly while attempting to write a satirical screenplay on the predictably grand subject of religion, he also joined Joan for outings to art galleries, the theatre and the cinema, started eating better and seemed content to spend his evenings with his feet up watching *Come Dancing* on television. By March 1967, he felt sufficiently healthy and stable to begin negotiations with the commercial channel ABC to make a new comedy series, and started attending script conferences the following month. Every day, he would go to work, call Joan to reassure her that he was behaving himself and return home at the same time every evening. Then, one day, he came back three hours late, with tears rolling down his cheeks, begging forgiveness: 'I've let you down,' he said, promising her that it was an isolated incident. She said that she believed him – even though she had her doubts – and stood by him, but, soon after, the drinking started all over again.

His moods returned to the old mercurial pattern, and so, when he suggested a romantic weekend away in Paris, she was too relieved to see him in good spirits to do anything other than go along with the suggestion. It was a grave mistake. Even Hancock's first wife, Cicely, had made a point of seeking Joan out to warn her, 'If you go to Paris, be careful, because he always drinks a lot there. And don't let him near the brandy. He turns into a killer on the stuff.'[41] Joan soon found out for herself. They arrived in Paris, he started drinking, he went near the brandy, and, very rapidly, he turned into a 'black, evil, stranger'.[42] There were arguments, fights and bitter confrontations. It never stopped; it just got worse and worse. They returned to England at the end of the weekend battered and bruised and beaten.

Hancock was put straight on a 'tapering-off' cure, with Joan feeding him two ounces of alcohol diluted with water every day while he shook with delirium tremens, and, in time, he was able to return to work. His ABC series – an awkward hybrid of sitcom and variety called *Hancock's* which featured him as a nightclub proprietor introducing a succession of middle-of-the-road musical guests – went ahead in June, but, after a couple of relatively incident-free weeks, the drinking intervened yet again and his performances deteriorated rapidly. The show was shunned by most critics, and it signally failed to attract anything close to the large audience that was tuning in regularly to see John in *George and the Dragon*. Hancock followed this sad débâcle with a disastrous week at Batley Variety Club (which ended up being curtailed due to his unprofessional behaviour) and a month in cabaret in Hong Kong. When he returned, in August, he read through all of the bad reviews and started drinking more heavily than ever before.

He went missing for four days on two separate occasions during what remained of the summer. After the first, he reappeared at his flat with bloodshot eyes and a face darkened with stubble, his tie hanging on back-to-front and his trousers slipping down below his hips, his body stinking of alcohol, smoke, sweat and urine. After the second, he turned up in an even worse state, and responded to the sight of Joan by grabbing at her and shouting obscenities. It was all too much for her: she went into their bedroom and swallowed several sleeping pills in a desperate bid to block out everything that was happening. When, a few hours later, she began to slip back into semi-consciousness, she found herself on the floor and Hancock attempting to force himself on her. She fought him off, made her way back to the bed and swallowed whatever other pills she could find. The two of them were discovered, unconscious in separate rooms, some time later by their housekeeper, and they were taken away in separate ambulances.

Another, half-hearted, attempt at reconciliation would follow, but far too much damage had already been done. 'I think you should go right away from me for your own good,' Hancock ended up saying to her, during a cold but unusually sober moment, 'because there's some part of me that is capable of harming you, even killing you.'[43] Joan realised regretfully that he was right: the man she loved was no longer there. He had been replaced by a tragic little monster. 'It was over,' she admitted of the relationship. 'I had lost him.'[44] Exhausted, dejected and now reluctantly resigned to her fate, she turned to the person most likely to comfort her without any threat of criticism or complaint: her husband.

Joan went home to John in October 1967. She had been away for just over a year.

He welcomed her back, she would say, 'lovingly and warmly, as if I had been on some heroic mission'.[45] Everything about the reception was thoroughly positive and scrupulously tactful: 'No word of recrimination passed his lips and no questions were asked. He simply wanted the past year erased from our minds. He believed that if we didn't talk about them and bring them to the surface, the memories would evaporate and disappear.'[46] Joan was in no state of mind to believe that real happiness and peace could be retrieved so simply and easily, but she went along with the spirit of denial because she could not think of what else to do.

Although the memories remained fixed all too firmly in her mind – 'Tony was with me constantly, though I heard nothing from him, not a word, and I made no contact'[47] – she worked hard at reviving her marriage, 'determined to make it up to John for the wrongs of the past year'.[48] It was a struggle at first – 'I was very melancholy for a while because it was all so quiet and I didn't know what to do with myself, apart from looking after John'[49] – but she soon busied herself by redecorating the flat, moving the furniture around as if to symbolise her search for a new start. She updated John's book-keeping, replenished his dwindling stock of luxuries and generally did what she could to make him feel comfortable, cared for and loved. Not everyone among their old set of mutual friends had forgiven her for how she had behaved, so they mixed with fewer people and spent more time as a couple on their own, going out to restaurants, theatres and clubs or staying in for quiet and relaxing evenings at home. Slowly but surely, it seemed, a calm and reassuring routine was being restored, but it was hard for Joan to avoid glimpsing some reference to Hancock either on television or in the press. In October, for example, she came across a report that said the comedian had flown off to Australia for some appearances in cabaret, and, after someone had laced his tomato juice with vodka at a pre-show party, a painfully shambolic performance ended abruptly and prematurely after he had fallen off the stage. The news upset her greatly, but she tried to keep her thoughts focused on John and continued redecorating the house.

John was away at Shepperton Studios during much of November and early December, working rather reluctantly on a clumsily 'fashionable' movie called *Salt and Pepper* (which co-starred Sammy Davis Jr and Peter Lawford as a pair of 'hip' spies in Swinging London), so Joan went to stay in Ramsgate to start planning Christmas festivities for the whole family. One Sunday, however, her son, David, told her he had recently overheard his grandparents discussing the fact that Hancock had telephoned them, and they had told him that their daughter was now back with John and he should leave them alone to repair their marriage in peace. Although Joan knew how fond her parents were of John, and how pleased and relieved they had been when she moved back in with him, she was excited to think that Hancock had tried to get in touch. That evening, she saw him on television, being interviewed on *The Eamonn Andrews Show*, looking surprisingly healthy and back on form, and she was entranced all over again. 'All his past sins were forgiven,' she would say, 'and I wanted nothing more than to run out of the house and go to him. No warning bells rang, common sense fled. I just wanted to see him.'[50]

She had already made plans to return to London the following day, but her parents, sensing the effect that seeing him on the screen had probably had, were anxious about what she might be considering. 'Forget him, old love,' said her father after the programme was over. 'Think of John. He's been through enough, because of Tony.'[51] She nodded in agreement and went to bed.

The next morning, however, she called Hancock from a telephone box in town. Thrilled to hear her voice again, he arranged to meet her when she arrived in London at Victoria station. A couple of hours later, she stepped off the train and he embraced her. 'I felt like a junkie,' she would say, 'having my first fix after a long period of self-control and denial.'[52] They went straight to his flat, where they talked through the night. He asked her to come back for good, but she insisted that they had already had their chance and 'muffed' it, and, besides, she could not bear to hurt John all over again. He seemed, albeit reluctantly, to agree. It was then, however, that Joan relented to some extent, promising to spend every available moment of her free time with him as long as John did not start getting suspicious. Hancock was delighted: 'I'm going to prove myself worthy by not letting you down again,' he declared. 'And one day you're going to marry me.' Joan – 'totally lacking any shadow of guilt and feeling complete again' – kissed him and then set off home to see John.[53]

From this moment on she started to live the biggest lie of her life, staying with her husband while slipping away to see her lover. 'Most of the time John was working,' she later recalled, 'and when he was at home it was possible at some point during the day to use the excuse of shopping or visiting friends.'[54] Even when Hancock revealed that he was seeing another woman – on a strictly platonic basis, he insisted, during those times when he would otherwise be left on his own – Joan continued sneaking off to be with him, persuading herself that it would have been 'unfair' of her to have resented him for maintaining any other, supposedly lesser, relationship: 'After all, John and I had made love since I had returned to him.'[55] The trysts, therefore, went on, and the telling little clues started to creep out into view, but, as far as they knew – or wanted to know – they carried on undiscovered.

How much John really knew about the resumed affair, however, remains unclear. Joan would later remark, in a manner that perhaps sounded rather more cold and condescending than she might have intended, that 'the man I was married to . . . had the ability to stick his head firmly in the sand and keep it there until the danger had passed,' mainly because 'he never asked a question if he didn't want to know the answer'.[56] John himself would merely confess that, in his heart of hearts, he had doubted that either Joan or Hancock 'believed that their separation would be permanent', but he had tried to give his wife the space – and the trust – required for her 'to recover her sense of domestic balance' while he, in an effort to behave 'tolerably well', did his best to ignore any suspicious signs.[57]

There was some respite to all of the intrigue and anxiety over Christmas, when Hancock went home to see his mother in Bournemouth and Joan went with John, as had long been planned, to stay with her family in Ramsgate. It turned out to be a strain for everyone involved, with Hancock catching pneumonia and John and Joan going through the motions even though both of them knew that there was 'something forced about the jollity'.[58]

Early in the New Year, however, Hancock received an invitation to make a new television series, and his mood suddenly improved. The offer came from a broadcaster – ATN7 – in Australia, where he still enjoyed a large and loyal following thanks to the many repeat showings of his old BBC work, and the idea was for him to film a thirteen-episode sitcom there called *Hancock Down Under*.[59] Joan tried to talk him out of it, fearing that, finding himself alone for several months in another country, he would soon grow restless and depressed, but he was adamant that it was not only a good idea but also the best chance of reviving his ailing career. In preparation for the project, he told her, he was going to dry out completely – and this time for good. She in turn promised him that, if he did indeed manage to stay sober for one entire year, she would agree to leave John and marry him.

He broke his vow more or less immediately, falling into a coma in his flat after downing a bottle of brandy in a mere five minutes, but, after urgent medical attention and yet another injection of vitamins, he regained his health and somehow managed to convince Joan that he could now be trusted to stay dry. He appeared to keep his word, and for the next few weeks his relationship with Joan was intensely close and loving as they made the most of what time together they had left. When, one day in March 1968, the time came for them to part, they made plans to write to each other regularly, with Joan sending her letters to wherever he was based in Australia and Hancock contacting her via a special Post Office box number she had set up back in Ramsgate.

Boasting to the sceptical British press that 'My best is yet to come,'[60] he boarded the plane in a buoyant mood. Before he set foot on Australian soil, however, he had started drinking again. By the time he had completed a short stay in Melbourne, where he worked with his head writer on the new show's scripts, his resistance to alcohol had collapsed completely. His daily routine, it seems, now took the form whereby he started the day with a 'hair of the dog' steadier, followed soon after by some pills washed down by another alcoholic drink, followed a little later by a tranquilliser to counteract the drink, followed by a stimulant mixed with a slug of vodka to counteract the tranquilliser. It was the kind of woozily illogical sequence typical of heavy drinkers under pressure to keep functioning, and it proved predictably counter-productive. Rehearsals went ahead in Sydney during April, but the drink had its usual negative effect on both his memory and his comic timing, and, when the pilot episode was recorded in the middle of the month, the result was a depressing mess. ATN7's anxious executives responded promptly by destroying the tape of the show and booking Hancock into a private hospital, where he would spend his forty-fourth birthday, on 12 May 1968, doped up and docile inside its detoxification clinic.

Throughout this troubled time he kept in contact with Joan on an almost daily basis by letter and telephone. He did not mention the fact that he was drinking. He mentioned the country, the weather, the people, the cricket, the scripts, the rehearsals, the crew, the shows – everything but the drinking. The thing that he talked about most of all was his love for Joan. He said how much he missed her, thought about her and longed to see her again once this current project was completed. 'His letters,' she would recall, 'were almost shy, with no passion or eroticism in them – he had a fear of sounding sentimental – but they were full of love all the same.'[61]

John, while all of this was going on, was in mourning for his beloved mother, Amy, who had died on 6 April, aged ninety, in hospital at Bury St Edmunds after suffering from a combination of bronchial pneumonia and cerebral arteriosclerosis.[62] Attending the funeral in Suffolk alone, and in no mood to become embroiled in an unseemly family squabble with his sister Michelle (with whom relations remained coolly distant and quietly tense[63]) over any issues relating to inheritance, he limited himself to accepting two of his mother's eighteenth-century Lowestoft armorial china porter mugs, each one bearing the Le Mesurier crest, along with an antique silver salver and a serving bell, and then travelled straight back to London. Grateful to have at least some of his thoughts distracted by the ongoing demands of work, he threw himself into finishing filming *George and the Dragon* at Borehamwood before moving straight on to start a new international movie project with Fred Astaire – entitled

Midas Run – that would take him off to locations in various parts of southern Italy. Joan, as a consequence, was left relatively free to concentrate on her long-distance relationship with her lover.

Once Hancock had been released from the clinic, ATN7 lodged him temporarily in the home of the company doctor before arranging for him to move into an apartment that he would share with the family of his director, Eddie Joffe. From this point on he made a sincere effort to fight his addiction to drink, learn his lines and generally get into the right physical shape and state of mind to complete his obligations. He managed to film the first three episodes of the series fairly competently, and continued to write home to Joan. He was increasingly worried, he told her, about his imminent divorce from his wife, Freddie, because, apart from the inevitable bad publicity and legal and financial complications, he suspected that Joan would be cited in the case. What exacerbated his anxiety at this time was the fact that a postal strike had just broken out in Australia, and he was therefore unable to be sure not only of what Joan was receiving from him, but also of what, if anything, he should be expecting from her. There was always the telephone, of course, but his increasingly hectic shooting schedule, combined with the seven and three-quarter hour time difference between Britain and Australia (as well as the need to call at a time least likely to lead to the 'wrong' person answering at the other end), meant that the usual lines of communication had suddenly broken down.

A further problem arose during that month when, as expected, the British media started covering the build-up to Hancock's divorce case. Joan, also as expected, was named in the legal papers as 'the other woman' and, soon after, two reporters from the *Sunday Express* arrived at her door in search of an 'exclusive' account.[64] Relieved that John was away working in Rome at the time, she tried to bluff her way out of the story by claiming that any relationship she might have had with Tony Hancock was now over for good, and that she was now very happy to be back with her loyal and loving husband. Unfortunately, Hancock got to see the subsequent report in Australia, and Joan's apparently dismissive comments, along with the lack of any recent letters, convinced him, in his currently stressed and slightly paranoid state, that he had been abandoned. The following month, Freddie Hancock was duly granted a decree nisi in the London Divorce Court on Friday 21 June on the grounds of cruelty and adultery (thus prompting another wave of negative publicity). Reflecting on his fate within his lonely room in the Sydney suburbs, the comedian sank even deeper into his depression.

It was straight after this that two (undated) letters from Hancock finally reached Joan, who happened to be visiting her parents in Ramsgate. On a single day, she received one of them via her box number – a very loving note telling her, 'All will be well, just hold on to the fact that we will be together in time'; the other, clearly the more recent of the two and enclosed inside a separate letter sent to her mother, declared, 'I loved you more than I thought possible, but now I realise that you never shared this feeling. . . . In a few weeks our relationship will be dead, cold and unremembered.'[65]

Immensely distressed, Joan was anxious to contact him to explain what had actually happened. She wanted to call him immediately from Ramsgate, but there was always someone else around when she went to use the telephone, so she decided to wait until she returned to London the following day. Ironically, soon after she had left, Hancock's mother – who had just been in touch with her son and heard how upset he had been by all of the newspaper reports – tried to reach Joan at her parents' home, but Joan's own mother had rebuffed her, saying that the marriage was now solid and Hancock should stop seeking to wreck it. Meanwhile, back in London, Joan called Australia repeatedly, but Hancock was always out of reach either in rehearsal or travelling from one place to another. Before she could try again, John arrived back from Rome, full of news and stories and gossip. She felt obliged to accompany him on an evening out at one of their favourite local restaurants, followed by a visit to a jazz club, and the couple did not get back to Barons Court until the early hours of the morning.

Later on, while Joan was in a deep sleep, the telephone rang. John answered it. The caller was an agent named Peter Campbell, a colleague of Freddy Joachim. John mumbled something quietly and put the receiver back down. The telephone rang again, and again, and again. 'Who the hell keeps ringing this early?' groaned Joan, still half asleep.

John was sitting on the edge of the bed, his shoulders slumped, his face straight and pale. 'Are you properly awake?' he asked softly. 'Of course I am,' she muttered, 'with all the bloody phone calls.' He moved closer to her: 'Then sit up, I have something to tell you. It was on the news this morning from Australia . . .'[66]

She did not want to hear any more. She put her hands over her ears and shouted, 'Don't tell me. Don't say it.'[67] She knew what he was going to say. Tony Hancock was dead.

John did eventually explain what he had been told. Hancock had finished his day's work at the studio and retired to his room to work on his latest script. Early the following morning, on Tuesday 25 June, he had been found slumped in a chair by a table, with an empty bottle of vodka by his side. He had taken pills. Many pills. He had washed them down with what was believed to have been his first alcoholic drink for several weeks. He had left two messages, one to his director and the other to his mother, scribbled on the blank back of his script. One of the lines had read: 'Things seemed to go too wrong too many times.'[68]

By her own admission, Joan was 'demented with grief'.[69] She raged at Hancock: 'You stupid bastard,' she screamed. 'You rotten coward!' Then she turned on John, blaming him insanely 'for being alive, for winning'.[70] Finally the whole truth came tumbling out: how she had really felt about Hancock; how she had carried on seeing him in secret; how she had agreed to marry him if he stayed sober. John, who had never witnessed such a show of intense and complex emotions before, called for a doctor, who came over and sedated her. She spent the rest of the day alternating between crying and sleeping. Hattie Jacques – who had also been alerted to the sad news – rang in the evening, begging Joan not to vent her anguish on John: 'He loves you so much,' she said, 'try not to hurt him.'[71] It was far too late, however, for that. John was now reeling from so many unexpected blows he could barely control himself, let alone care for his heartbroken wife. After struggling on for a few draining days (made even worse by a severe outbreak of psoriasis), he decided that it would be best for her to get away from London for a while to rest and reflect, so he arranged for her to stay with one of her cousins in Marbella.

Other details of Hancock's final hours would begin to circulate during her absence, including the fact that his last telephone call the night before he died had been to his first wife, Cicely, pleading with her to take him back. Cicely, who by this time was herself a helpless alcoholic (she would die, from a fall, at the start of the following year), had turned him down flat, and some would go on to speculate that it was this rejection, combined with the guilt that he felt for having driven her to drink, that had sent him over the edge.[72] As far as Joan was concerned, however, it had been her supposed 'abandonment' of him that had broken him, and the thought of it produced a pain that she feared would never fade away.

The time she spent in Spain did nonetheless have a positive effect on her. When she travelled back home to London, though still in a seriously fragile frame of mind, she was able to see things more rationally. It was only now that she could begin to understand how badly John was suffering, too, trying to deal during this *annus horribilis* not only with the deception but also the loss. Whatever else she felt, therefore, she knew that she owed him, at the very least, some kindness and compassion. He, in turn, was just relieved to have her back looking a little more like her old healthy self: 'Her nerves were much steadier and she was more self-possessed.'[73] He took her out to dinner on her first night back, and, very gently and tentatively, they started to have some conversations about what each of them had been doing during the other's absence. 'He never asked me if I loved him,' Joan would later recall. 'For John that would have been very presumptuous. But over dinner I did tell him I loved him, and of course it was true, but not in the way I loved Tony. Never again would I love anyone like that.'[74]

John only heard her say 'I love you'. That was enough for him. She was back in his life, and he was grateful.

Not only would he always refuse to blame his 'little friend' for any of the horribly painful things that had happened; he would also defend her against anyone else who attempted to criticise her on his behalf. On one occasion, for example, a few months later, the two of them were relaxing in a club when a well-known character actor, clearly the worse for drink, came over and called Joan a 'tart and a trollop for hurting lovely John with that bastard Tony Hancock'. John was outraged: 'How dare you speak to my wife in that way?' he roared. 'What do you know of others' feelings, you insensitive little turd. If I ever hear you speak to my wife or any other woman in that manner, I'll knock your teeth down your throat!'[75] When they got home, he began to shake and had to drink a large glass of brandy. Joan said how proud she was of him, but he dismissed the comments shyly, saying that any man would have done the same.

It was this fundamental, unforced and very moving human decency that drew Joan back into her marriage and made her realise how lucky she was to be with someone like John. 'Heaven knows why he wanted me,' she would reflect, 'but he did.'[76] It would not be long, therefore, before the two of them were busy planning their life together as a couple all over again, moving into a new second house – in Ramsgate – and relishing the chance to make a fresh start.

The first thing they did, however, was catch up on what had been happening in John's acting career. Apart from the various movies he had been making, he wanted Joan's opinion of a new television series he had just completed. After all of the unhappiness that both of them had gone through, he hoped that, at the very least, it might just lead to a little laughter. This show was called *Dad's Army*.

CHAPTER XIII

The *Dad's Army* Years

We are the boys who will make you think again.

The offer of a role in *Dad's Army* had reached John a few months after his wife resumed her clandestine affair with Tony Hancock. The first episode would reach the screen just over a month after Hancock's suicide. The show, therefore, came into his life at a profoundly bad time, but it would soon lift his career to a higher level and bring him more happiness and contentment than he had ever dared to expect.

Dad's Army was the brainchild of Jimmy Perry, an actor and budding writer, and David Croft, a BBC producer/director who had a proven track record for shaping such comedy shows (including *Hugh and I* and *Beggar My Neighbour*). Set in the fictitious south-east seaside town of Walmington-on-Sea, it was an affectionate but surprisingly accurate comedy about Britain's wartime volunteers, who were either too young or too old for active service, known collectively as the Home Guard.[1] The main characters would include a middle-class bank manager-turned-captain named George Mainwaring and an upper-class chief clerk-turned-sergeant called Arthur Wilson, along with Jack Jones the elderly butcher and lance corporal. The rank and file included undertaker James Frazer, retired gentlemen's tailor Charles Godfrey, spiv Joe Walker and a teenage boy called Frank Pike, as well as greengrocer and ARP warden Bill Hodges, while representing all things comically spiritual were the Rev. Timothy Farthing and his verger, Maurice Yeatman.

As the core of the comedy was to be rooted in the deeply class-conscious relationship between the pompous but insecure self-appointed leader Mainwaring and his self-effacing but effortlessly urbane second-in-command Wilson, particular care went into choosing the right pair of actors to play them. The casting of Captain Mainwaring proved to be quite a complicated affair. It was offered initially to John's old colleague from *Private's Progress*, Thorley Walters, but he turned it down immediately: 'He thanked me very much for asking,' David Croft would later recall, 'but he said that he couldn't think why I'd thought of him. But he would have been very good.'[2] An attempt was made to enlist the versatile comic actor Jon Pertwee, who toyed with the idea before belatedly dropping out of contention in favour of a Broadway play. It was only then that Jimmy Perry's preferred choice, Arthur Lowe, finally got his chance.

Something similar happened with the role of Arthur Wilson. John had not been at the top of the list of candidates. Jimmy Perry's original suggestion had been the portly and bespectacled Robert Dorning, who had already established an excellent on-screen rapport with Arthur Lowe as his boss in the ITV sitcom *Pardon the Expression*, but Michael Mills, the BBC's Head of Comedy, was adamant that the role was tailor-made for John Le Mesurier because, as Mills put it, 'he suffers so well'.[3]

John, however, was not, by this stage in his career, an easy actor to hire. His agent, Freddy Joachim, remained a firm believer in the principle that good performers receive offers rather than request them and then sit back and ponder their options at leisure, so he was always urging John to appear somewhat aloof to any prospective employers. 'Don't ever be easy to get,' Joachim kept telling him. 'Give yourself a little rarity value.'[4] John was also coming to the end of his fourth and final series of *George and the Dragon*, and was not looking to go straight into another television sitcom.

When the sample script arrived, therefore, John treated it with a certain amount of caution. On reading it, he doubted that it had the potential to become much more than a 'minor situation comedy', but he was intrigued by the news that he was wanted for the role of the sergeant rather than the captain – 'casting directors usually saw me as officer material'.[5] He read the script again, and liked it a little more. Perry, he felt, 'knew how to turn a funny line', and Croft, he noted, was 'a theatre man who had brought to television a reputation for cool, calm organisation'. 'Promising,' he thought to himself, 'all promising.'[6] He informed Joachim that he had only one real reservation about the proposal: the fee. It was, he complained, far below what was usually offered by a second-rate film production company, and significantly less than he had been receiving from the BBC's commercial competitor for his supporting role in *George and the Dragon*, so he felt he was entitled to hold out for considerably more. Joachim, who would probably have preferred to keep his client available for much more lucrative movie projects anyway, duly proceeded to haggle at length on John's behalf.

While these negotiations were going on, efforts were made to assemble the rest of the cast. David Croft had wanted Jack Haig, an old favourite from his time as a producer at Tyne Tees Television in the 1950s, to play Lance Corporal Jones, but he turned the part down in order to concentrate on a lucrative new vehicle for his well-established and popular children's character, Wacky Jacky. The obvious alternative, as far as Croft was concerned, was John Le Mesurier's old friend Clive Dunn, who, although he was a mere forty-eight years of age, knew how to portray elderly comic characters. Apart from his long involvement with the Players' Theatre, he had appeared in everything from Windmill revues to children's sitcoms, and had first made his name on television as Old Johnson, the aptly named eighty-three-year-old waiter and Boer War veteran in Granada's *Bootsie and Snudge* (1960–3), the popular follow-up to *The Army Game*. Like Croft (both of whose parents had been actors), he came from an established show business family, and the two men had known and liked each other for years (Dunn's mother, in fact, had once had an affair with Croft's father[7]).

Putting their friendship to one side, however, Dunn did not jump at the offer when Croft first made his approach: he had just started work on *The World of Beachcomber*, BBC2's fine adaptation of J.B. Morton's much-admired newspaper columns, and, as he would put it, he 'wasn't particularly hungry'.[8] A former prisoner-of-war – he spent four harrowing years in a German labour camp in Liezen, Austria – he would also have been forgiven for regarding the subject-matter with suspicion, but, in fact, he found it quite appealing. The reason for his reluctance had more to do with the well-known high casualty rate of new situation comedies: 'The ups and downs of the profession had made me cautious.'[9] While not turning down the part of Lance Corporal Jones outright, therefore, he asked for – and received – more time in which to weigh up his options.

Getting on with other business, Croft chose Arnold Ridley (a real war hero who had twice been invalided out of the Army – the first time following the Battle of the Somme, and then again in 1940 following the evacuation from Dunkirk – and had also written a number of popular plays, including *The Ghost Train* in 1925) as the sweet-natured and somewhat incontinent Private Godfrey. 'He'd worked for me before,' Croft would recall. 'He'd been very good, very funny, and he was a lovely, gentle character. He looked right, sounded right. I was a bit worried about him because I think he was already seventy-two when I first interviewed him for the part. I'd said, "I don't think I can save you from having to run about a bit now and then. Are you up for it?" And he'd said, "Oh, yes, I think I'll manage." As it turned out, of course, he couldn't, but we got an enormous amount of capital out of helping him onto the van and things like that, you know. So he turned out to be a very successful character.'[10]

Casting Dumfries-born John Laurie as Private Frazer was another of Michael Mills' suggestions. Laurie – at seventy-one – was a hugely experienced actor who had played all of the great Shakespearean roles at the Old Vic and Stratford (John had first seen him back in 1933 in that open-air performance of *A Midsummer Night's Dream* at the Botanical Gardens in London), and also appeared in a wide range of movies, including two directed by Alfred Hitchcock – *Juno and the Paycock* (1930) and *The 39 Steps* (1935) – three by Laurence Olivier – *Henry V* (1944), *Hamlet* (1948) and *Richard III* (1954) – and four by Michael Powell (the most notable of which was *The Life and Death of Colonel Blimp*, in which he played the ever-loyal Murdoch). He had been working intermittently on television since the mid-1930s, but it had only been since the start of the 1960s that he had begun appearing on a relatively regular basis in a wide variety of dramatic and comic roles. He was far from impressed, upon reading the first script of *Dad's Army*, by what at that stage was still a seriously underwritten character (who was described simply as a 'Scotsman'), but he had a policy of never refusing offers of work, and so, without the slightest trace of enthusiasm, he agreed to take part in a show whose lifetime he confidently expected to last no longer than six half-hour episodes.

James Beck was a far more willing recruit to play the amiably shifty Private Walker. Jimmy Perry had actually created the part for himself, but had been advised by David Croft to stay on the other side of the camera ('I felt that, as one of the writers, he would be needed in the production box to see how things were going. I also felt, I suppose, that it wasn't going to make for a particularly happy cast if one of the writers gave himself a role – the other actors would've been inclined to say that he'd written the best lines for himself'), so Beck became the beneficiary of the change of plan. The thirty-nine-year-old actor from Islington had been working hard over the course of the past few years at establishing himself on television. By 1968, viewers would have glimpsed him at some time or other in the odd episode of such popular police drama series as *Z Cars*, *Dixon of Dock Green* and *Softly Softly* – usually playing a character on the right side of the law – or in a one-off role in a sit-com such as *Here's Harry*, but few could have put a name to the face. The prospect of a major role in a new show such as *Dad's Army*, therefore, was precisely the kind of opportunity that Beck had been waiting for. Playing a spiv actually represented something of a departure for an actor who had grown used to being cast as various kinds of law enforcers, but, remembering Sid Field's memorable wartime comic wide boy figure of 'Slasher Green', he knew the type had great potential. 'He was obviously a talented actor,' David Croft would later remark. 'He just came to me, in fact, in an audition. I had used him before, and I fancied him very much for that particular part. There weren't any other real competitors for it – except Jimmy, of course, and we'd already ruled him out – so casting Walker turned out to be one of the easiest ones of the lot.'[11]

Ian Lavender had David Croft's wife, the agent Ann Callender, to thank for the part of the platoon's youngest member, the naive Private Pike. Lavender – a twenty-two-year-old, Birmingham-born actor whose fledgling career up to this point consisted simply of two years in drama school at Bristol's Old Vic followed by a six-month season playing juvenile leads at Canterbury's Marlowe Theatre – had recently become one of Callender's clients. Early in 1968, just before he was due to make his television debut in a one-off ITV/Rediffusion drama called *Flowers at My Feet*, she urged her husband to watch him. 'So I did,' recalled Croft, 'and I was most impressed. He played a young juvenile delightfully.'[12] Croft checked that none of his superiors was concerned about any potential conflict of interest and then went ahead and hired the actor for the part.

Once Pike had been picked, Croft turned his attention to the supporting players. Janet Davies, a bright, reliable performer whom Croft had used in a recent episode of *Beggar My Neighbour*, was hired as Frank's widowed mother (and Sergeant Wilson's clandestine lover), Mrs Mavis Pike, and several seasoned professionals – including Colin

Bean, Richard Jacques, Hugh Hastings, George Hancock, Richard Hancock, Richard Kitteridge, Vernon Drake, Hugh Cecil, Frank Godfrey, Jimmy Mac, David Seaforth and Desmond Cullum-Jones – were engaged (at six guineas each per episode) to make up the platoon's back row. (It would not be until later on in the show's run that Frank Williams – best known to viewers in those days for his long-running role as the dithering Captain Pocket in *The Army Game* – was brought on board as the fussy and epicene Rev. Timothy Farthing, and Edward Sinclair – yet another Croft original – was invited to play the part of the permanently gurning Maurice Yeatman.)

Only one more key character needed to be cast for the pilot episode: the nasty, nosey, noisy ARP warden Hodges. David Croft thought almost immediately of Bill Pertwee. Pertwee, in real life, could not have been less like the loud and loutish character Croft and Perry had created to darken Mainwaring's moods, but he was quite capable of investing such a role with a degree of comic vulnerability that would lift it far above the realm of caricature. Like his cousin, Jon, Bill Pertwee came to television after learning his craft both in Variety – first as a colleague of Beryl Reid, later in partnership with his wife, Marion – and radio – as a valued and versatile contributor to both *Beyond Our Ken* (1958–64) and *Round the Horne* (1965–7). After catching the eye in a series of *The Norman Vaughan Show* on BBC1 in 1966, he found himself increasingly in demand not only for comic cameos but also as a warm-up man for various television shows, and he started to think more seriously about pursuing work in the medium 'to add another string to one's bow, as it were'.[13] In 1968, just as he was preparing for a season of performances at Bognor Regis, he heard from David Croft.

Even though the air-raid warden was not, at that stage, conceived of as a regular character, Croft knew that Pertwee could be relied on not only to turn in the kind of spirited performance he required to test the role's comic potential, but also to inject some welcome energy and good humour into a company of tough and occasionally testy old professionals. 'I booked Bill because he was good, of course, but I also booked him in order to keep everyone else happy and sweet. He was always very bubbly, very well-liked by everyone, and he's marvellous fun.'[14]

This left Croft to concentrate on his two outstanding casting problems: John Le Mesurier and Clive Dunn. Both of them, frustratingly, still seemed reluctant to commit. Dunn, in fact, had called his friend John and told him: 'I'll do it if you do it.'[15] John's reply had been: 'Yes, but . . .' He suggested that they 'hung out a little' in the hope that the money might improve.[16] Dunn agreed, and delayed making a decision.

Unbeknown to him, however, David Croft had already taken the precaution of enlisting a standby for the part of Jones, an inexperienced but very promising twenty-eight-year-old actor by the name of David Jason – 'I'd used him fairly recently in an episode of *Beggar My Neighbour* and he'd been marvellous,' recalled Croft.[17] Jason had just started work on the ITV/Rediffusion teatime sketch show *Do Not Adjust Your Set* (1967–9), his first real television breakthrough – but was quite prepared to commit himself to a high-profile David Croft comedy. Late in February 1968, therefore, Croft – who was now growing impatient – spotted Dunn in the BBC canteen, and took the opportunity to ask him if he had reached a decision yet about joining the cast; an embarrassed Dunn stalled again, and then slipped quietly away 'hoping that John would [soon] make up his mind and that David would not resent the delay'.[18] Dunn's agent, Michael Grade, a close friend of the BBC's then Head of Variety, Bill Cotton, spoke to him on an informal basis in order to ensure that the Corporation realised that his client really was predisposed to join the show. As David Jason would later recall: 'I went to the BBC and read for the part at 11 a.m.; soon after, my agent received the message that I had the part; by 3 p.m., I was out of work! Over the lunch period Bill Cotton had persuaded Clive to take the part, and hadn't informed the producer. The rest is history!'[19]

John, as soon as Freddy Joachim had negotiated a considerably better deal (£262 10s per episode), followed suit. Both men received and signed their contracts on 29 February 1968 (although John's fee was set at a sum £52 10 shillings higher than Dunn's – and, indeed, Arthur Lowe's[20]), and the cast of *Dad's Army* was at last complete. It was time for the team to meet up and start work.

The atmosphere, according to Jimmy Perry, was 'very tense'[21] on the chilly morning at the end of March 1968 when the cast first came together. In those days, before the construction of the BBC's own custom-made rehearsal rooms in North Acton, programmes were prepared in a wide variety of unlikely-looking venues secreted among London's least alluring nooks and crannies. In the case of *Dad's Army*, the site for the initial read-through was a stale-smelling back room of the Feathers public house in Chiswick. Here, seated side-by-side around a large mud-coloured table, were the actors whose task it was to bring the inhabitants of Walmington-on-Sea to life. 'I looked at that motley crew,' remembered Perry, 'and I thought to myself: "This is either going to be my biggest success or my biggest failure – it all depends how they get on".'[22]

John already knew most of them, to varying degrees. Apart from his good friend Clive Dunn, he had worked before with Arthur Lowe (fleetingly on the set of two movies – *The Day They Robbed the Bank of England* in 1960 and *Go to Blazes* in 1962 – and, more recently and meaningfully, in four episodes of *Pardon the Expression*, playing his boss Sir Charles Dobson) as well as John Laurie (very briefly in a low-budget 1961 movie called *Don't Bother to Knock* and again in the 1967 Charlie Drake vehicle *Mister Ten Per Cent*). He had acted in a couple of Arnold Ridley's plays during his time in rep, and had encountered all of the others socially apart from the young newcomer Ian Lavender. He, therefore, was one of the most relaxed as the various members of the cast were introduced to each other and the opening session commenced.

David Croft took any signs of nervy uncertainty in his stride – he was used to the awkwardness of these occasions – but the less experienced Jimmy Perry could not help scrutinising every look, every nuance, every mild little moan and overloud laugh for portents of good days or bad days to come. His spirits sagged when John Laurie turned to him and said in a voice of casual menace, 'I hope this is going to work, laddie, but to my mind it's a ridiculous idea!', but later, during a coffee break, they were revived when Bill Pertwee came over and assured him that the show was 'going to be a winner'.[23] He remained, nonetheless, oversensitive and apprehensive; this had been his big idea, his personal project, and now it was set to be tested.

Preparations had certainly been thorough. David Croft was determined to make the programme seem as true to its period as was humanly possible. Any line that sounded too 'modern', such as 'I couldn't care less', was swiftly removed from the script; the services of E.V.H. Emmett, the voice of the old Gaumont-British newsreels from the 1930s and 40s, were secured to supply some suitably evocative scene-setting narration; two talented and meticulous set designers, Alan Hunter-Craig and Paul Joel, were brought in to create a range of believably 1940s-style surroundings; Sandra Exelby, an accomplished BBC make-up specialist, developed a variety of period hairstyles and wigs; George Ward, the costume designer, searched far and wide for genuine Home Guard brassards, badges, boots, uniforms, respirators and weapons, ordering what other outfits were needed from Berman's, a London costumier (he made a point of having Captain Mainwaring's uniform made from a slightly superior material in order to reflect the higher salary he would, as a bank manager, have received); someone even managed to find an old pair of round-rimmed spectacles for Arthur Lowe to wear. John (whose experience with *George and the Dragon* had been a far more casual and sometimes careless affair) and the other actors could not help but be impressed by the exceptional attention to detail.

'It had to look right,' Croft would later confirm, 'and, of course, people had to be able to really believe in the characters.'[24] Both he and Perry had worked hard to provide each major character with a plausible past. Jack Jones, for example, had been given a long and elaborate military career (which went all the way from Khartoum, through the Sudan, on to the North-West Frontier, back under General Kitchener for the battle of Omdurman, the Frontier again, then on to the Boer War and the Great War in France) to lend credence to his regular rambling anecdotes – and each actor was encouraged to draw on any memories which might help them to add the odd distinguishing detail. John Laurie, for example, remembered his time as a member of the Home Guard in Paddington – 'totally uncomical, an excess of dullness' – and found an easy affinity with Frazer's strained tolerance of 'a lot of useless blather'.[25] John, meanwhile, had the memory of many well-bred military Le Mesuriers on which he could draw, as well as his own experiences of going through the motions – very nicely and politely – during the Second World War.

Filming (which brought with it an additional payment of £151 per main actor[26]) took place between 1 and 6 April 1968 at the old East Anglian market town of Thetford – a location that, much to John's approval, was not too far away from his childhood home of Bury St Edmunds, as well as his favourite racecourse in Newmarket. He and Clive Dunn travelled there together by car, Arthur Lowe came by train and the remainder of the cast and crew arrived by coach. Every external scene for the whole of the first series had to be filmed during that single (unseasonably chilly) week, and so the pace was unrelenting.

After Thetford came the rehearsals: at 10.30 on the morning of Monday 8 April, the cast, along with Croft and Perry, reassembled at St Nicholas Church Hall, Bennett Street, Chiswick, to begin work on the pilot episode, which by this time had been given the title 'The Man and the Hour'. Some of the actors seemed well-advanced in their characterisations. Arthur Lowe, for example, was quietly confident that both his look (a compressed Clement Attlee) and manner (proud, pompous and pushy) would work rather well; Ian Lavender, whose prematurely greying hair would be disguised on screen by a combination of colour spray and Brylcreem, had decided to give Pike a long claret and sky blue Aston Villa scarf (hastily replaced, in the opening credits sequence, by a pale blue towel because the wardrobe van had left Thetford early), a mildly quavering vocal manner and a childishly inquisitive expression – but one or two, it seemed, were still in need of some advice. Bill Pertwee, for example, kept being urged by David Croft to make Hodges even louder and more obnoxious, delivering each line in the music-hall style of 'on top of a shout'; while Jimmy Perry continued to be astonished by John Le Mesurier's unorthodox methods of assimilation:

> Talk about casual! The previous week, on the first day of filming at Thetford, John was sitting there very nonchalantly in the lounge of the hotel, and he'd said to me: 'Oh, James: how do you want me to play this part?' Well, that was a laugh for a start! As far as I knew, John Le Mesurier only had one performance. Anyway, I said to him: 'Look, John, it's all yours on a plate – just do it as you feel.' So he said, 'Yes, oh, all right, old boy,' and then he lit a cigarette and said, 'Who are you going to bet on in the 2.30 today?' Make no mistake, he was very, very, good, but, really, that man just swanned through life.[27]

Gradually, however, John warmed to the role by warming the role up, moving away from the kind of stiff and stuffy figures he sometimes portrayed on the screen and resolving instead to model Arthur Wilson on none other than John Le Mesurier: 'I thought, why not just be myself, use an extension of my own personality and behave rather as I had done in the army? So, I always left a button or two undone, and had the sleeve of my battle dress blouse slightly turned up. I spoke softly, issued commands as if they were invitations (the sort not likely to be accepted) and generally assumed a benign air of helplessness.'[28]

During this period the cast and crew received a very important visitor: Huw Wheldon, BBC Television's current Controller of Programmes and its next Managing Director. Wheldon was still very much a programme maker at heart, and nothing gave him greater pleasure than seeing genuine talent succeed, but a few months before – as he himself would later freely admit – he had been 'one of a small group of programme executives who became distinguished for recognising that a script by David Croft and Jimmy Perry called *Dad's Army* would not work'.[29] Out of respect for David Croft, however, Wheldon had gone along with the decision to commission a series of six episodes, and he had reacted positively to the news that the leading roles had been given to Lowe and Le Mesurier: 'This pleased me,' he acknowledged, 'but it did not change my mind. I knew it would fail.'[30]

A few months later, he heard that rehearsals had begun, so he decided to drop in on the proceedings unannounced in order to see how the programme was developing:

> They were doing a five-minute sequence and I could not make head nor tail of it. I could not follow the action. Suddenly I realised that I had done the casting wrongly in my own mind. I had taken it for granted that John Le Mesurier, elegant, intelligent, sardonic and rather weary, was the officer; and that Arthur Lowe, brisk, belligerent and bustling, was the sergeant. But [it was actually] the other way round. Lowe was Captain Mainwaring and Le Mesurier was Sergeant Wilson. I was delighted. It was the first note of unpredictability in a series that has been fresh and unpredictable and creative ever since.[31]

The show had found another ally – and, in the weeks to come, it would need every one of them.

The pilot episode was recorded (in black and white) on the evening of Monday 15 April in the relatively capacious Studio 4, Television Centre, before an audience of approximately 320 people. It seemed to go fairly well (as did the subsequent five episodes, which were rehearsed and recorded in sequence over the course of the following few weeks). Only John Le Mesurier, among the cast, still appeared doubtful about how well the programme was progressing, but then the ever-Eeyorish John was not only naturally doubtful about most things

('I worry about every new series, every new play. I worry whether people will tire of my face, even whether the car will start . . .'[32]), but had also suffered so many low blows in his personal life during the past few months that he was now in a more or less constant state of apprehension as he waited for the next 'fresh hell' to arrive. 'I remember seeing him one day in the bar at Television Centre,' recalled his writer friend Barry Took:

> He was sitting there, having a drink, wearing this wartime outfit. I said to him, 'What are you up to?' And he said, 'Oh, it's a new series we're doing for the BBC. About the Home Guard. It's a disaster, my dear boy, I really can't tell you, oh, it's absolutely appalling, it can't possibly work, no, no, my dear boy, it's an absolute disaster!' And I looked at him and thought, 'I bet it isn't!' But that was Le Mez, that was his attitude – always thinking that the worst could happen.[33]

It was not long, however, before several other people associated with the programme began feeling less than sanguine about its prospects. Some executives had wondered, upon first hearing about the show, whether it might end up being accused of 'making mock of Britain's Finest Hour'. Although most such doubts had diminished as the project progressed, there was still some anxiety about what was, after all, the first British sitcom set during wartime.[34] Early in May, Paul Fox, the Controller of BBC1, viewed a tape of the pilot episode. Being mindful of such concerns, he objected both to the opening title sequence, which featured actual shots of refugees fleeing the German army in France and Belgium, and to the closing credits, which also featured a montage of authentic war scenes. His opinion was that such footage, in a comedy programme, carried too great and unnecessary a risk of causing offence on the grounds of tastelessness, and so, after much internal debate, a new animated sequence (featuring swastika-headed arrows approaching Britain) was created for the start and shots of the cast were inserted at the end.

There was still one more ordeal to endure before the show was finally able to go on air, and that was the preview. 'Oh dear,' sighed Jimmy Perry. 'Oh dear!'[35] The pilot episode was previewed on three consecutive evenings at Television Centre. David Croft would later recall what happened:

We showed it to about three different audiences of about 150 people, and they were stopped from talking to each other. It was a Swedish lady [Kathryn Ernst], I think, who ran the sessions, and she had distributed questionnaires for them to answer and tick off and so on. She wouldn't let anyone discuss it until they had written all of their opinions down, and then it was thrown open to discussion. Well, they didn't like it. They didn't like it at all. People said things like: 'Why do we still have to have these things about the war?' and, 'Don't the authors know the war's over?' and, 'We've seen quite enough of this!' I think the best comment we got was, 'I quite liked it,' from one sleepy gentleman.[36]

Jimmy Perry, who attended each session alongside his co-writer, could only suffer in silence. 'You kept hearing the same thing,' he said. '"Rubbish!" "Don't like it!" you know, and this went on for three nights, and I was dying!'[37] Eventually, the results were collated and a report was sent directly to David Croft: 'It was not a good report – if people had heard about it there probably wouldn't have been a second series – so I'm afraid I suppressed the evidence and we went ahead just the same.'[38]

The show was finally deemed ready for airing, with the first episode – entitled 'The Man and the Hour' – reaching the screen on Wednesday 31 July 1968 at 8.20 pm on BBC1. John watched it at home alone in Barons Court. Having gone through weeks of constant anguish since the death of Tony Hancock, and still anxious about his grieving wife's troubled state of mind, he poured himself a stiff drink, sat back and hoped that the next thirty minutes would turn out to be the kind of pleasant surprise that would help to lift his sagging spirits.

The programme began with a brief prologue set in the present day, with a very elderly George Mainwaring launching Walmington-on-Sea's 'I'm Backing Britain' campaign by reminiscing proudly about the last war: 'It was the darkest hour in our history: the odds were absurdly against us, but, young and old, we stood there, defiant, determined to survive, to recover and, finally, to win! The news was desperate, but our spirits were always high . . .' The picture then dissolved, the credits ran, Bud Flanagan sang Jimmy Perry's cleverly redolent theme song ('Who do you think you are kidding, Mr Hitler/If you think we're on the run?'), and the E.V.H. Emmett-narrated 'newsreel' transported the audience back to May 1940, when Walmington-on-Sea's branch of the Home Guard was in the process of being formed. The sound of an 'all-clear' siren is heard, accompanied by an establishing shot of the brightly polished front door of the town's Swallow Bank, and then, inside, the camera catches sight of Mainwaring, standing by the window, smiling triumphantly to himself as the enemy planes depart. 'Ah!' he barks. 'Going home, are they?' The story, at last, has begun.

No time, from this point on, is wasted, and everything flows smoothly along. One by one, each theme, each character, each connection, is introduced and established with rare speed and ease. Mainwaring, for example, sparks off the class struggle almost immediately by boasting to Wilson that he held a commission and had served in the last war, thus prompting his assistant to start searching furtively for sore nerves to niggle:

WILSON: Somewhere in the Orkneys, wasn't it, sir?
MAINWARING: I was a commissioned officer, Wilson, and I served
               in France. During the whole of 1919!
WILSON: Yes, but the war ended in 1918, I thought, sir.
MAINWARING: Well, somebody had to clear up the mess!
WILSON: Oh, yes, of course.
MAINWARING: Where were you during the war?
WILSON: Oh, Mons, Gallipoli, Passchendaele – I was a
               Sergeant in the RA, sir.
MAINWARING: Oh, never mind that![39]

Wilson, in turn, sparks off the war of dispositions by issuing a decidedly limp introduction to the first group of volunteers:

WILSON: Would you, er, would you mind stepping this way,
               please?
MAINWARING: Wilson! Come here, come here! I intend to mould
               those men out there into an aggressive fighting unit.
               I'm going to lead them, command them, inspire
               them, to be ruthless killers. And I'm not going to get
               very far if you're going to invite them to 'step this
               way', am I? 'Quick March' is the order!

Frazer soon underlines his impudence:

MAINWARING:	I imagine you've not had any previous Army experience?
FRAZER:	No. None at all.
MAINWARING:	No. We can usually tell, can't we, sergeant?
WILSON:	Yes, we can, sir.
MAINWARING:	Once a soldier, always a soldier.
FRAZER:	I'm a sailor. Chief Petty Officer, *Rrr*oyal Navy, retired.
MAINWARING:	Sign there.

Godfrey's old Edwardian good manners come next (MAINWARING: 'Will you just sign there, will you?' GODFREY: 'Oh, I'd love to!'), followed by Walker's winking roguishness (MAINWARING: 'Any previous military experience?' WALKER: 'I got a girlfriend in the ATS!') and Jones' reckless enthusiasm (MAINWARING: 'When did you leave the Army?' JONES: '1915, sir. I was invalided out, sir. The old minces – I couldn't quite make the focus, you see, sir.' MAINWARING: 'Presumably that's why you've signed the table').

There is just time for the fuse to be lit under the feud between the captain – 'Are you out of your mind? Do you realise that history is taking place in there?' – and the warden – 'In five minutes' time an ARP lecture is taking place in this 'all!' – before the arrival of the first parade, the first lecture, and the first 'uniforms' (armbands) and 'weapons' (pouches of pepper). The episode closes with another speech from the round little man:

> Well, we're making progress. A short time ago, we were just an undisciplined mob. Now, we can deal with tanks. We can kill with pikes, we can make them all sneeze with our pepper – and, after all, even the Hun is a very poor fighter with his head buried in a handkerchief! But remember, men, we have one invaluable weapon on our side: we have an unbreakable spirit to win! A bulldog tenacity that will help us to hang on while there's breath left in our bodies.
>
> You don't get that with gestapos and jackboots! You get that by being British! So come on, Adolf: we're ready for you!

The credits rolled to the sound of the Band of the Coldstream Guards, and then it was all over: the end of the beginning.

An estimated audience of 7,171,000 had watched the programme[40] – an encouraging start for a brand new situation comedy – but, as John and his colleagues realised more keenly than anyone else, before the show could build on this promising foundation it would first have to survive the snap reactions of the television critics. Back in 1968, during an era before preview screenings and advance copies on video or DVD, such reviewers had to watch a programme 'live' and come up with a response as quickly as a theatre critic, dictating their copy over the telephone to their respective newspapers no later than an hour before midnight. It was therefore not surprising, given the circumstances, that one or two experienced critics responded to the debut edition of *Dad's Army* in precisely the same way as they would have covered any other new situation comedy; namely, with caution.

The normally admirably astute Nancy Banks-Smith, for example, told readers of the *Sun* that the show seemed merely 'a nice little thing' – pointing out that the phrase was 'much used by women to describe someone who's no competition' – but she did concede that 'John Le Mesurier turns in a performance which is almost better than necessary. Nearly persuading you to keep a wary eye on the nice little thing. In case.'[41] Sean Day-Lewis, writing in the *Daily Telegraph*, was similarly circumspect, praising Croft and Perry's 'real gift for satire', but criticising the 'tendency to go for laughs at all costs, even if they punctured the atmosphere',[42] while Michael Billington of *The Times* felt that the show seemed 'afraid of making too much fun of a hallowed wartime institution', although he also acknowledged that Arthur Lowe's 'true, touching performance' was one that he would 'return to with pleasure'.[43]

What was surprising was the number of critics who were prepared, after viewing just one episode, to predict that the series would be a success. 'Who could resist', declared Mary Malone in the *Daily Mirror*, 'the sight of little home guard commander, Mainwaring, harnessing his raggle-taggle fireside fighters into a force bent on the fight to a finish in the true Dunkirk spirit? This make-do-and-improvise war effort is funny and human and nostalgic. This war I'll watch.'[44] The *Sunday Telegraph*'s Philip Purser praised the programme similarly for 'the brimming possibilities' of its subject-matter, the 'nice period style' and 'a set of characterisations that have been maturing over a dozen years and in some of the greatest cellars in comedy',[45] while playwright Tom Stoppard said in the *Observer* that the show was 'liable to bring a smile and a tear to every lover of England and Ealing'.[46] The most positive – and prescient – critic of all, on this particular occasion, was Ron Boyle, who wrote in the *Daily Express*:

> I cannot say I cracked a rib, split my sides, or even raised a good hearty belly-laugh – but some instinct is telling me that the BBC is about to come up with a classic comedy series. . . . The trouble here with the opening episode was that it had to set a stage for better things to come. I mean – ask anybody under the age of 30 about the LDV and they would probably guess it was some Iron Curtain secret police or a new ingredient that adds magic to soap powder.
>
> But now everything is established. The time is shortly after Dunkirk. Britain is ready to fight in her own backyard. Dustbin lid for a shield and broom handle for bayonet. Young viewers are going to treat it as a marvellous send-up. On a par with Batman and Adam Adamant. And then dad is going to clip everybody round the ear and tell them the Local Defence Volunteers really did exist – and so did the spirit of lets-get-at-them which now raises chuckles, but at the time was so deadly serious. The more I think of it I don't see how this series can fail . . .
>
> As the fuss pot commander of the local pitchfork brigade, Arthur Lowe immediately scores. A pair of John Lennon spectacles, a toothbrush moustache, a high wing collar and we can forget all about Swindley . . . and begin to find a soft spot in our TV hearts for Mainwaring, the scourge of the Nazis.
>
> The script mercifully avoided all the tempting cliché traps. Already I am ready to root for doleful Sergeant Wilson from the bank, Lance Corporal Jones, the doddering old local butcher, Joe Walker, the black marketeer, and all the rest of this motley gang. Give it a week or two and I'll tell you whether this is really comedy's finest half-hour. All I say now is that the possibilities are tremendous.[47]

No new situation comedy had ever received a more welcoming review from a national newspaper critic. The BBC was quite entitled to consider *Dad's Army* an immediate critical success.

John, who would later confess that he had feared that 'a comedy about the Home Guard would be riveting only to those who had been in the Home Guard or one of the other branches of civil defence', was pleasantly surprised by the initial reaction. He wanted, nonetheless, to wait until the whole series had been seen before accepting that it was indeed a bona fide 'hit'.[48] He still feared, in his depressed state, that it would struggle to find and hold on to a large enough following.

Such doubts, however, were soon dispelled. The BBC was so enthusiastic about the programme that it commissioned a second series before the second episode had even been broadcast, and the remainder of the run was warmly received.

John's characterisation of Sergeant Wilson grew more interesting as the series progressed. Wilson's discreet amusement at Mainwaring's efforts to prove his superiority to him, both at the bank and on the parade ground, had been evident immediately.[49] In subsequent episodes, Wilson's connections with other inhabitants of Walmington-on-Sea also started to be explored. His suspiciously close relationship with Mrs Pike – and, as a consequence, with her son Frank (who calls him 'Uncle') – began to emerge as the most comically intriguing aspect of his personal life, balancing his occasional tendency to seem rather smug with a welcome degree of vulnerability. He knows that, although he can tease his superior officer all he likes, he is himself only one slip-up away from complete humiliation: every time the naive but unnervingly garrulous young Pike opens his mouth to speak to Mainwaring, 'Uncle Arthur' seems to wince with worry about how to stop his private life from wrecking his public reputation. In episode three, for example, it only takes the arrival of Pike with a message from his mother to make Wilson wobble as he realises how compromised he could be now that he is subject to orders not only from Mainwaring but also from Mrs Pike:

MAINWARING: Pike! I told you yesterday: no mufflers on parade! You don't see Grenadier Guards wearing mufflers, do you, sergeant?

WILSON: Well, I never really thought to look, sir.

MAINWARING: Of course you don't!

PIKE: Well, I got a note from me mum, sir.

MAINWARING: Note? I'm not interested in notes! You're in the Army now, Pike!

WILSON: [*Sheepishly*] Sir, I think perhaps you ought to read it.

MAINWARING:	Oh! Very well! [*Reads out loud*] 'Frank is starting with his chest again. He ought to be in bed. If he can't wear his muffler he's to come home or he will catch his death.' [*Turns to Wilson*] We can't have him wearing that thing on parade! It makes the whole platoon look ludicrous!
WILSON:	Well, perhaps he could wear it on patrol, sir? [*Turns to Pike*] What time do you go on?
PIKE:	Ten till twelve, sir.
WILSON:	It'll be dark by then, sir.
MAINWARING:	Oh, very well.
PIKE:	[*Whispering to Wilson as he moves past*] Thank you![50]

By the arrival of the sixth and final episode, on 11 September, the various interactions within the show's richly comic ensemble had become a firm highlight of the viewing week for an audience that had risen to an impressive 9,746,500 viewers.[51] As the final shots of the actors ('You have been watching . . .') marked the end of the series, few if any of the doubters could still have questioned how successful the series had proven itself to be. 'I'm very sorry', wrote one reviewer, 'to see the last (for the time being) of *Dad's Army*. It was that rare article, an excellent idea splendidly carried out. You can't say more for any programme than that.'[52] The sentiment turned out to be a common one, as the critics queued up to celebrate all of the episodes that they had seen. On 16 September, five days after the run had ended, Keith Smith, BBC TV's Chief Publicity Officer, sent another batch of clippings to David Croft, along with the following note:

> More newspaper reviews for you. Just for the record there has been no comedy series in the last twelve months which has attracted anywhere near the number of reviews *Dad's Army* has. Nor has any comedy series received this kind of universal praise.[53]

John Le Mesurier finally allowed himself to accept what he and his colleagues had achieved, and, for the first time in such a long, long time, he felt like celebrating. At the age of fifty-six, he had found – almost stumbled upon – the role of his life. The closing of the series coincided with the return of his wife from her recuperative stay in Spain, and he could hardly wait to share the good news with her. 'He was full of it,' Joan would recall. 'Over dinner on my first night [back] he spoke of nothing else. His eyes were soft with an inner contentment and he talked about the cast and the work. After all that he had put up with over the previous two years nobody deserved it more.'[54]

It was not long before the show was also having a positive effect on Joan. As she would later recall:

> I was still very fragile then – so many people who loved John now hated me for what had happened. I felt I was a pariah. But when I started meeting the other actors and their wives, they were all so lovely to me. Nothing about it – the affair and everything – was ever said or mentioned. They just accepted me. And it soon felt like I was part of a big family. We really did all get along famously. All the wives used to go up to the studio every Friday for the recording, we'd all sit together, then we'd all go out together with the cast for dinner, drink too much, and have a wonderful evening.[55]

It was just the kind of experience that she and John had needed: a warm and stable environment in which they could get used to being together again while feeling connected to a new community. It stopped them dwelling on the recent past; it eased them back to life in the here and now.

They bought their second home soon after this – a large Victorian terrace house in Ramsgate that boasted fine views from the upper windows of Sandwich Bay and Deal – and resumed a marriage that had been disrupted so dramatically. Joan threw herself into the project of redecorating the property, and John went back to work with a renewed sense of contentment.

It was the start of a long and extremely happy period for him, both personally and professionally, and *Dad's Army* would run throughout this time like the strongest and most central connecting thread. The first five-year period of its existence was one of uninterrupted progress: the audience kept getting larger (rising from an average of around 8.2 million in 1968 to around 16.3 million by the end of 1972[56]) and the applause kept getting louder. David Croft won a BAFTA award in 1971 for Best Light Entertainment Production and Direction,[57] Jimmy Perry won an Ivor Novello award in the same year for the best theme from any film, television or stage show, and both of them won Writers' Guild of Great Britain awards (in 1969, 1970 and 1971) for

Best Comedy Script. The entire cast, meanwhile, was honoured in 1971 by the Variety Club.

The show seemed to be everywhere. On television, it featured not only in its regular slot, but also in 'guest spots' on BBC1's annual *Christmas Night with the Stars*,[58] a special BBC2 Noël Coward tribute called *The Coward Revue*,[59] a one-off *Royal Television Gala Performance*[60] and an edition of *The Morecambe & Wise Show*: 'Do you think this is wise?' asked Eric. 'No,' answered Arthur Lowe, 'this is Wise – the one with the short, fat, hairy legs!'[61] It appeared in comic strips (being featured each week from 1970 in *Look In* magazine) and in the marketplace (there were colouring, dot-to-dot and 'activity' books, a board game, a bubble bath, a set of sweet cigarette cards, a souvenir magazine and a series of annuals[62]) and was seen in an increasing number of countries overseas, beginning in 1970 with New Zealand, Australia, Holland, Belgium, Sweden, Spain, Malta, Finland, Sri Lanka and Tanzania.[63]

The individual members of the cast seemed to be everywhere, too: Arthur Lowe, for example, provided voiceovers for Spam, Lyons Pie Mix and Gold Blend coffee commercials, acted in a succession of Lindsay Anderson movies, stole the show as a drunkenly anarchic butler in Peter Medak's satirical farce, *The Ruling Class* (1971), co-starred with Ian Lavender and Bill Pertwee in the BBC Radio 2 sitcom *Parsley Sidings*,[64] and selected his favourite recordings for BBC Radio 4's *Desert Island Discs*.[65] Clive Dunn outdid them all during 1971 alone in terms of prime-time ubiquity by appearing as the subject of *Desert Island Discs*, *This Is Your Life* and his own BBC1 special, *An Hour with Clive Dunn*, as well as spending three weeks at number one in the charts with his novelty single 'Grandad'.[66]

John Le Mesurier was very nearly as difficult to miss: he appeared in several movies (including *The Italian Job* and *The Magic Christian* in 1969 and *On a Clear Day You Can See Forever* in 1970), made guest appearances in numerous other television shows (including an episode of *Sykes* in 1972 that reunited him briefly with Hattie Jacques[67]) and radio series (among them the two Richard Briers vehicles *Doctor in the House* and *Brothers In Law*). He also found the time to film a quirky little motorsport short, *The Culcheth Job*, with the popular British rally driver Brian Culcheth.[68] As an in-demand advertising artiste, he publicised BOAC Airlines on Australian TV, as well as continuing to supply the reassuring voice behind not only the Homepride flour commercials but also (with Arthur the sure-pawed cat) the Kattomeat ads. In addition to all of this, like Lowe and Dunn, he was given his own edition of *Desert Island Discs*.[69]

The growing popularity of *Dad's Army* among the very young as well as the adult population would also lead to additional links with children's television – most notably in the form of Arthur Lowe's involvement as narrator of the *Mr Men* cartoons[70] and John's assumption of the same role for another animated series called *Bod*, as well as appearances by both men on *Jackanory* and *Blue Peter*.[71] The success seemed to be infectious.

The consistently high quality of the *Dad's Army* shows was certainly impressive. The characterisations, for example, gradually grew richer and more distinctive. Mainwaring became bolder, but also more vulnerable; Wilson was a little less submissive, and, in his own sly way, slightly more sardonic; Frazer, now securely ensconced as the town's undertaker, grew even spikier, as well as – thanks to his candle-lit tales of the countless terrible ways to die on and around the gloomy Isle of Barra – spookier; Godfrey was frailer than ever, as well as – once his rifle had been replaced with a first-aid kit – more sleepily pacific; Walker's rough diamond seemed to have received a furtive little polish; and Jones was still Jones, only more so. A more prominent role for the remorselessly crude (but newly promoted) Chief ARP Warden Hodges ensured that Mainwaring's social pretensions would from now on be under fire not only from above but also from below, and his patience on parade was strained even further by the introduction of two more irregular irritants: the vicar and the verger.

One of the most interesting of the early episodes, as far as John's character was concerned, came towards the end of the second series, in March 1969, with 'Sgt Wilson's Little Secret'. It begins badly enough for Wilson when, after Pike produces yet another admonitory note from his mother (warning that she will not tolerate her son being ordered to do anything that might 'set off his chest again'), Mainwaring declares that someone must tell this mollycoddling woman to mind her own business:

MAINWARING: As you're friendly with her, I think you ought to do
                it. You are friendly with her, aren't you?
WILSON: [*Looking awkward*] Yes, I am, sir. Yes, we go to the
                cinema, together, every now and then. And
                sometimes she asks me back for a meal, y'know . . .
                That sort of thing.

MAINWARING:	What sort of thing?
WILSON:	Well, whatever she happens to be cooking at the time.
MAINWARING:	Oh, I see.
WILSON:	She's got my ration book at the moment, sir, you see. It makes it a lot easier, do you see?
MAINWARING:	Yes, yes, I'm quite sure it does. But the point is you've got to have a talk with her!
WILSON:	Yes, right, sir.[72]

Back home, Mrs Pike tells Frank that she has been asked to take in a little boy as an evacuee, and remarks that it will be 'funny being a mother again after all these years'. Wilson – who is on his way in for tea – overhears the latter part of their conversation from outside the door and, jumping to completely the wrong conclusion, comes over all faint. Later that evening, feeling hopelessly compromised, he forces himself to 'confess' to his astonished superior officer:

MAINWARING:	Are you in some sort of trouble?
WILSON:	Er, well, it's not me, you see, sir. It's not me, it's, er . . . Mrs Pike.
MAINWARING:	How do you mean?
WILSON:	Well, she's, um, er, she's, er . . .
MAINWARING:	Now look, Wilson, I'm not only your commanding officer. I'm also your friend. And I don't want you to feel any hesitation in confiding in me. Now, what's all this about Mrs Pike?
WILSON:	Well, you see, sir, she's, er . . . [*Looks up at the ceiling, glances to either side, swallows hard and then forces a slim grin*] going to have a baby.
MAINWARING:	Really? Oh, that is good news! I believe her husband will be delighted. [*The penny drops*] Wait a minute! She's a widow, isn't she?
WILSON:	Y-yes, that's right.
MAINWARING:	Then how on earth can she be having a baby?

[*Wilson fidgets. Mainwaring bridles. The awful truth dawns.*]

| MAINWARING: | I thought you said you only went round there for meals! |

WILSON:	[*Rubbing his face in shame*] I did tell you, didn't I, sir, that she's got my ration book.
MAINWARING:	Yes. She's got something else, now, hasn't she! [*He leaps up and starts pacing around the office*] I can hardly believe my ears! I've come to the conclusion I don't know you, Wilson. You're a cad, that's what you are! How long have you known her?
WILSON:	Er, quite a few years now, sir.
MAINWARING:	Well, why on earth haven't you asked her to marry you?
WILSON:	I don't know, sir, it's just one of those things I just haven't been able to get around to, somehow, sir.
MAINWARING:	Well, you'd better get around to it, hadn't you? Quickly! You can't go about behaving like Errol Flynn!

Suitably chastened, Wilson heads off and, very reluctantly, pops the question to Mrs Pike. The frantic wedding preparations that follow are brought to a premature close, however, when she turns up with the newly arrived young evacuee – 'little Arthur' – and thus hands Wilson an excuse to wriggle out of his unwelcome commitment.

'A. Wilson (Manager)?' (broadcast as part of the fourth series in December 1970) was another episode – dramatically very audacious in its own quiet way – that had the benefit of a beautifully judged script and some superbly sensitive character acting. One morning in the bank, Mainwaring receives two telephone calls. The first is from head office, informing him that Wilson has been made manager of the nearby Eastgate branch of the bank; the second is from Area HQ, informing him that Wilson's commission has come through.

While he is still reeling from these two unexpected blows, the telephone rings again – this time it is the vicar. 'What are you going to tell me about Wilson?' snaps Mainwaring. 'That he's been made Archbishop of Canterbury?' When Wilson finally, belatedly, glides in to begin work, Mainwaring is positively apoplectic:

MAINWARING:	Judas!
WILSON:	I beg your pardon?
MAINWARING:	Judas!
WILSON:	I'm awfully sorry but I don't quite follow you.

| MAINWARING: | You follow me all right, Wilson – you've been following me for years, waiting to step into my shoes![73] |

Suddenly, all of the resentment that has long been simmering within Mainwaring comes rushing to the boil:

MAINWARING:	Just because you went to some tuppenny-ha'penny public school!
WILSON:	Yes, well, I wouldn't call Meadowbridge that.
MAINWARING:	Meadowbridge! You know where I went, don't you? [*Bitterly*] Eastbourne Grammar!
WILSON:	Well, what's wrong with that?
MAINWARING:	Oh, don't be so patronising about it! I had to fight like hell to go there – and I had to fight even harder to stay there!
WILSON:	Well, that's all to your credit.
MAINWARING:	You never fought for anything in your life! Brought up by a nanny, father something in the City – all you had to do is just sit back and let everything come to you!
WILSON:	Yes, well, it wasn't quite as simple as all that.
MAINWARING:	I've been the manager of this bank for over ten years now. I ought to have gone on to better things years ago. Yet every time I've gone for an interview for a promotion it's always been the same thing: 'What school did you go to?' And as soon as I told them, that was that!
WILSON:	Well, I'm sure that didn't really influence them!

Things proceed to fall apart. Mainwaring grows increasingly spiteful, Wilson increasingly smug: 'Ambition's turned his head,' complains a tearful Mrs Pike. As the day of their separation arrives, the two men, like some old warring, soon-to-be-divorced couple, seem intent on saying all of those things that are normally best left unsaid:

| MAINWARING: | Why are you going now? It's only Wednesday. You don't take up your position in Eastgate until Monday. |

WILSON:	Yes, well, I know, but they've been having a lot of difficulty over there, sir, you see. The manager's been called up, and Mr West from the head office is going to stay on in Eastgate in order to show me the ropes.
MAINWARING:	Mr West of head office, eh? We are honoured! Why are you travelling in uniform?
WILSON:	[*Casually*] Well, I don't know, just sort of, kind of handy, you know.
MAINWARING:	Rubbish! You're travelling in uniform so that you can parade up and down the platform looking for salutes!
WILSON:	[*Suddenly sounding rattled*] And why not? You did!
MAINWARING:	How do you mean?
WILSON:	The day you got your new uniform, I followed you.
MAINWARING:	You followed me?
WILSON:	Yes, I did! And I watched you go up and down the high street three times looking for a serviceman to salute you, and in the end you had to make do with a sea scout!
MAINWARING:	Say what you have to say and go.
WILSON:	[*Calming down again*] Well, I've just come to say goodbye, sir. I wondered if you'd like to come up to the station and see me off.
MAINWARING:	I certainly would not! Our relationship ends here and now.
WILSON:	Oh, really, sir! After all we've been through together, for heaven's sake, can't we let bygones be bygones?
MAINWARING:	Don't try to soft soap me!

Wilson reaches out to shake Mainwaring's hand, but Mainwaring fails to respond. They salute each other in silence, and then Wilson departs. Mainwaring, however, cannot resist shouting out after him: 'And if I did look for salutes, at least I did them properly – that salute you just gave me was rotten!'

Wilson's independence turns out to be brutally brief. On his very first morning as manager, just after he has settled down behind his very own imposing desk inside his very own impressive office, the air-raid siren sounds and he leaves to enter the shelter. Later, when he returns, he finds that the first bomb to have been dropped on Eastgate has landed on his very own bank. Searching through the ruins, he comes across the portion of the door that bore his name. He picks it up, reads the plate, 'A. Wilson, Manager', thinks to himself for a moment, then tosses it aside and moves on.

Mainwaring sounds contrite when he hears the news from head office: 'At nine o'clock the poor chap was manager of a bank and at five past he had no bank to manage.' He calls Wilson into his office: 'It's most unfortunate,' he tells him. 'Yes, it is,' says Wilson. 'Most unfortunate.' Mainwaring is clearly sorry, but not that sorry: 'No – don't sit down,' he says coolly. 'I'm rather busy.' He hands his sergeant back his stripes – 'Get 'em sewn on by tonight. That's all.' Wilson, once he is back on the outside of Mainwaring's office, looks up wistfully at the name on Mainwaring's door, sighs softly to himself, and then goes off to serve, once again, in Mainwaring's platoon.

What this and several other episodes dared to make explicit was what would normally remain implicit: namely, that *Dad's Army*, like any other great situation comedy, told tales about trapped relationships. Just as Hancock will never shake off Sid and Harold Steptoe will never extricate himself from Albert, neither Mainwaring nor Wilson will ever be free of the other, nor will either ever escape from the prosaic constraints of Walmington-on-Sea.

Mainwaring and Wilson were very easy characters to believe in. Whenever Mainwaring put down the telephone, grimaced, then summoned up the sickliest of grins and said, 'Just chatting to the little woman,' and whenever Wilson responded to Mrs Pike's audible enquiry, 'Will you be around later, Arthur, for your usual?' by wrapping a hand over his eyes and whispering, 'Oh, Mavis!' nothing more needed to be said, or shown, because one already knew. Just by watching these two men each week, listening to their stories, following their exchanges, studying their asides, it was possible, without even trying, to compile brief biographies of both of them in one's mind:

George Mainwaring: Born in Eastbourne in 1885. His father was either – depending on whose account one chooses to believe – a well-regarded member of the Master Tailors' Guild who ran a high-class gentleman's outfitters on the Parade, or the beleaguered proprietor of a modest little side-street draper's shop.

George's childhood was one long struggle, but he did manage to win a scholarship to his local grammar school, where he took a cold bath every morning, buried his nose in books, and did all that he could to cultivate a clear brain and a sharp eye. After school, he joined the Eastbourne branch of Swallow Bank, slowly and methodically working his way up from office boy to Assistant Chief Clerk. When the Great War broke out in 1914, he volunteered at once – only to be turned down on account of his poor eyesight; four years later, following several more unsuccessful attempts to join up, he was commissioned as a 2nd Lieutenant in the Pioneer Corps, and arrived in France just in time to clear up the mess, but too late to qualify for any medals. Shortly after returning to civilian life, he met and married Elizabeth, a nervous, big-boned, sensitive-nosed, reclusive vegetarian from a relatively well-connected family in Clagthorpe. The couple's childless but 'almost blissful' marriage received a welcome boost in the early 1930s when George was promoted to the position of manager at the Walmington-on-Sea branch of the bank; he proceeded to immerse himself in his work, while she hid herself away inside their modest little home at 23 Lime Crescent. In 1940, just when George seemed to have resigned himself to a life of quiet desperation, fate intervened, and he seized his chance to answer his country's call with his own special brand of bulldog tenacity.[74]

Arthur Wilson: Born in a large, rambling country house in Gloucestershire in 1887. His father was something in the City, his great-uncle was something in the House of Lords. His childhood, thanks to an excellent and attentive nanny, was idyllic, and his education, at the medium-sized Meadowbridge public school, was also perfectly pleasant. After failing the exam to enter the Indian Civil Service, he began his working life in the City, where he soon acquired a reputation for romance rather than banking. He served in the Army from 1915 to 1918, securing a commission as a captain, and was in an excellent position to witness at first hand all of the great wartime British disasters. Shortly after returning to civilian life, he met and married one of Mrs Cochrane's Young Ladies; she left him soon after the birth of their only daughter, who would grow up to serve in the WRENS. In the early 1930s, while working at the Weston-super-Mare branch of Swallow Bank, he encountered an attractive young widow, Mrs Mavis Pike; when promotion to Chief Clerk took Wilson to work under George Mainwaring at Walmington-on-Sea, Mrs Pike, along with her young son, Frank, chose to follow him. In 1940, just when Arthur was waiting patiently for more good fortune to land in his well-tailored lap, Mainwaring intervened, and he resigned himself to at least a year or two of quiet desperation.[75]

One reason why these two characters were so credible was the fact that they seemed to believe in each other. It was obvious, from the way that Mainwaring studied Wilson and Wilson studied Mainwaring, that each man was the other's most devoted critic, biographer and social anthropologist. Mainwaring, for example, would analyse Wilson's appearance and demeanour, itemising his faults – the overlong hair ('You're not a violin player, you know!'), the unfastened collar and cuffs, the 'dozy' level of alertness, and the fact that his right hand had sometimes been known to come to rest on his hip ('It only needs a couple of inches more and you could be taken for one of those nancy boys!'). He would then exclaim: 'Why must you give yourself airs all the time? Why don't you behave normally, like me?' Wilson, in turn, would make a mental note of each of Mainwaring's many insecurities; then, when the time seemed right, he would smile, give a knowing little look, and offer words of supposed comfort ('Your face doesn't look nearly so round and moonlike') or commiseration ('How awfully embarrassing for you, sir'). Whenever the two of them were together it was the relationship – rather than merely the men – that one watched.

'It is no coincidence,' wrote one critic at the time, 'that each role [is] interpreted by a man who knows what real acting is, and not by some clumsy egomaniac.'[76] It was quite correct: as actors, the two men shared the same high standards, even though, as individuals, they had so little else in common.

Lowe and Le Mesurier were, in many ways, as unlikely a couple as George Mainwaring and Arthur Wilson. Lowe's background was northern working-class (born in Hayfield, Derbyshire, in 1915 – the only son of Arthur, a railwayman, and Mary Ford – brought up in Levenshulme, South Manchester, and educated at Alma Park Central grammar school); Le Mesurier's was southern upper-middle-class.

Lowe's route to success was long, indirect and arduous. A spell as a stagehand at Manchester's Palace of Varieties and a period, while serving in the Middle East as a sergeant-major in the Army, spent performing in plays and revues for the troops, was followed after the war by his professional stage debut in Manchester rep and years of hard toil in the provinces. There was the odd small role in British movies before a West End debut in 1950, and finally, from the early 1960s, regular work in television.[77] John, by comparison, seemed to have practically ambled his way to fame.

The two men differed from each other markedly in terms both of taste and of temperament. Lowe was a dapper little man of hard habits and fixed routines, whereas Le Mesurier was something of a suede-shoed libertine. Lowe lived in Little Venice with his actress wife Joan Cooper, and the two of them spent most of their leisure time either fine-dining or relaxing on board their lovingly restored Victorian steam yacht *Amazon* (which rarely left the security of the jetty); the twice-divorced Le Mesurier still preferred to unwind by losing himself in the shadowy nightclubs of Soho. Lowe was relatively easy to ruffle: he dreaded, when 'off-duty', hearing someone shout out at him, 'How's Mr Swindley, then?' or 'Ow yer goin' on, Captain? All right?' – he would stiffen up and say, 'My name is Arthur Lowe.'[78] On one occasion, when assorted members of the cast had joined him and his wife on board *Amazon* for an informal lunch party, he startled his guests by suddenly shouting, 'Weigh anchor!', moving the boat out a mere 100 yards on the river, and then promptly dropping the anchor straight back down again, simply because he had spotted a 'snotty-nosed kid' staring over at them from the bank – 'We don't want to have our lunch with that sort of thing going on,' he explained.[79]

Le Mesurier, in contrast, was rarely ruffled by anything. Even after enduring all of the torrid trials and tribulations of the past few years, he still appeared to relish all that was odd or unexpected in life, wandering into out-of-the-way bars in the hope of encountering some woozy little eccentric, travelling miles for the chance to hear an expletive-speaking parrot and reacting with calm good manners when an attractive female fan demanded one evening that he take her straight out into a ditch and make love to her. 'Well, my dear, I'd like to oblige you,' he told her, 'but it's rather late and dark, and I really can't see myself clambering about at this time of night looking for a ditch. Perhaps we ought to do it by daylight.'[80]

There were times during the making of *Dad's Army* when Lowe seemed to regard Le Mesurier's extracurricular adventures with the same strange mixture of censoriousness and envy that Mainwaring reserved for those of Wilson. On one occasion, when the team was due to assemble for another fortnight of location shooting, John (having grown bored of his own car and abandoned it, on a whim, beneath the Hammersmith flyover) arranged for Bill Pertwee to give him a lift down to Thetford. Setting off from London on a Friday, John persuaded Pertwee to take a detour to Newmarket in order to visit the national stud and converse with an interesting assortment of trainers and jockeys; he then proposed another detour, this time to his beloved Bury St Edmunds, where he and Pertwee toured the local pubs and eventually spent what was left of the night at the Angel Hotel. The two men finally completed their journey – which would normally have taken no more than four hours – when they drove into Thetford on Sunday evening. Lowe, noticing their belated arrival at the hotel, came over and asked what kind of trip they had experienced. 'Fine,' said John, smiling sweetly, 'it took two days.' Lowe merely looked at his colleague, muttered 'Extraordinary,' and walked away.[81]

Things were no different during make-up sessions, in which Lowe would sometimes find himself temporarily unattended while one woman was busy giving John a manicure, another was brushing his hair and a third was fetching him a sandwich. As Ian Lavender would later recall:

> John could get those women to do anything for him. I mean, I actually saw him persuade – no, 'persuade' is the wrong word – I saw him charm a make-up girl into taking the watch off his wrist, winding it up and then putting it back on again! 'Oh,' he'd say, 'it's far too much trouble, could you possibly do it for me, my dear?' And she'd do it, as if it was the most natural thing in the world for her to do![82]

There was, for Lowe, only one meaningful way in which to react to such a scene: an arch of an eyebrow, a quick puff of the cheeks, and another mumbled 'Extraordinary'.

In spite of all their differences, however, the two men genuinely liked, admired and trusted each other. When they acted together, they shared a rare and special rapport. 'So well attuned were we,' John would later remark with affection, 'that often an exchanged glance between us was enough to make a point in the script. One critic was kind enough to say that we did not really need dialogue – it was quite evident what we were thinking simply by studying our expressions.'[83] It was true: Lowe – a sublime bridler – could sum up a dozen lines of text simply by sitting up and inhaling sharply as if he had just been scalded by a piping hot baby potato, as could Le Mesurier merely by sliding the tip of his tongue along his thin-lipped, lopsided smile. No word, when it was used, was ever wasted: Lowe, for example, managed, by varying his intonation, to make 'Wilson' sound not only like a name but also, whenever the situation called for it, a question, an accusation, a cry for help or a threat, whereas Le Mesurier never uttered a single 'Yes, sir?' without having first marinated it in sarcasm. There were no false notes: each actor drew not only on his own disposition but also on his own wit to bring his character smartly into life.

How much of their real-life selves actually was there in their on-screen alter egos? The answer has to be that there was more and more as the show continued on its run and the writers took note of their strengths (and toyed affectionately with one or two of their weaknesses). Lowe, perversely, used to solemnly insist that 'there was nothing of my own personality in Mainwaring'[84] – a claim that, as David Croft would confirm, caused many a jaw to drop. 'Arthur was enormously like Mainwaring. No doubt about it at all. And Jimmy and I took all kinds of things from his own personality and wrote them into the part. Somehow, he never seemed to notice.'[85] No one – not even his closest friends and family – ever denied that Lowe was indeed a somewhat pompous little man. 'He was very conscious of his position,' Ian Lavender would recall. 'He saw himself as the senior man on the set, the leader of the cast as well as the captain of the platoon.'[86]

John, on the other hand, was perfectly well aware of the similarities between himself and Arthur Wilson, and was amused when Perry and Croft went on to add extra little details, such as the handsome Sergeant's vanity about his hair (John was quite a connoisseur of shampoos and conditioners and always cared about the quality of his coiffure) and his charming 'way with the ladies'. As Jimmy Perry would later remark:

You've either got it or you ain't, and, boy oh boy, John had it. The first time he'd meet a woman he'd search out for something nice to say about her, like, 'I must say that dress really does suit you awfully well,' or 'What a very pretty name,' or 'That belt you're wearing, it's lovely, and it makes your waist look absolutely tiny' – so we started having Wilson do the same thing, much to Mainwaring's annoyance![87]

Although Lowe and Le Mesurier differed in their responses to questions of attribution, they were close in their views as to what made these on-screen individuals tick. They saw the flaws but also respected the virtues, and made sure that they conveyed the full complexity of the personalities.

Lowe described Mainwaring as, above all else, 'a very brave little chap': 'When he says "He who holds Walmington-on-Sea holds England," he means it. It's bloody ludicrous, but he means it . . . and all the other Captain Mainwarings in the Home Guard meant it too. That's part of the appeal of the series. There's truth in it all the way through.'[88] Mainwaring has wed himself to the war effort. It has become his grand passion, his one true vocation, and he simply cannot understand why the grip it has on others is often so much looser than the one it has on him:

I mean, fancy men not wanting to come on parade! It's the highlight of my day! Do you know, once I'm having my tea, I can feel the excitement mounting inside of me. I put on my uniform, and I march down here to the parade, and I feel a warm glow of pride in what we're doing and what we've achieved. We're doing something for England![89]

He is the kind of Englishman who takes a particularly great sense of pride from the thought that St George was so much smaller than his dragon. Even when a bomb lands on his bank, and all of the windows have been smashed, and the door of his office is jammed, and part of his wall is missing, and water has started dripping down from the ceiling on to his desk, Mainwaring merely puts up his umbrella and refuses to budge:

'You see that chair? Well, that's my chair; the Manager's chair. This is my desk; the Manager's desk. My office; the Manager's office. I wasn't made Manager overnight, you know, it was a long, hard struggle: office boy, clerk, Assistant Chief Clerk, Chief Clerk, Assistant Manager and, finally, Manager. It's taken me twenty-five years to get this office, and there's no red-necked, beer-swilling foreigner going to throw me out of it![90]

What he knows – or rather, what he thinks he knows – of the outside world could be scribbled down in stark black and white on the back of a postage stamp. He is not too keen on the French ('They're never very much good after lunch, you know'), exasperated by the Italians ('a shambles'), suspicious of the Russians (although he acknowledges that 'they can't be all that bad otherwise they wouldn't be on our side'), quietly contemptuous of the Americans ('a few extras,' he calls them, 'a second eleven, as it were') and, of course, he detests the Germans ('a nation of unthinking automatons' who do not respect the laws of cricket). He knows what he loves, however, and what he loves is England – his very own green and pleasant, proper, prudent, not too posh, not too common, hat-tipping, hard-working, game-playing vision of England – and he is prepared to give his all in order to defend it. 'I have to be a hard man,' he insists, 'otherwise we'd all be under the Nazi jackboot by now!'

Wilson, Mainwaring believes, is a soft man. 'You worry me,' he moans. 'You'd do anything rather than face up to your responsibilities. You've never really grown up, have you? You're not a middle-aged Chief Clerk at all – you're a sort of Peter Pan!' Nothing seems more great an obstacle to Mainwaring's dream of creating a 'well-oiled fighting machine' than his sergeant's obdurate over-politeness:

MAINWARING: Wheel them in.
WILSON: All right sir. [*Goes to doorway*] Would you, er, would you kindly, er, step this way, please?
MAINWARING: Oh, Wilson! Bark it out! Bark it out!
WILSON: Right. [*Raises his voice*] Would you kindly step this way, please!

John played Wilson like a thorn that had found a side:

It seemed to me that Arthur [Lowe], on screen, identified a central, but rarely performed, character in the British class system – the product of the lower middle class – essentially conservative, fiercely patriotic and strong on the old values – but a natural opponent of idle aristocrats as much as of upstart workers. Naturally, Captain Mainwaring disapproved of Sergeant Wilson, whose accent and manners suggested a comfortable background, one that had evidently removed any sense of ambition or daring. Indications of sloppiness or excessive caution ('Do you think that's wise?') were met by explosions of indignation and a frenzy of activity signalling another usually hopeless adventure for the Walmington Home Guard.[91]

Mainwaring knows that, in spite of all of his huffing and puffing, he will almost certainly remain stuck on the same rung of the social ladder. Wilson, in contrast, despite his chronic reluctance to huff and puff, will continue to rise blithely from one rung to the next, acquiring along the way such privileges as membership of the exclusive golf club ('I've been trying for years to get in there!' Mainwaring protests), lunching on hard-to-find smoked salmon ('I had snoek fishcake at the British Restaurant!' moans Mainwaring) and inheriting an eye-catching aristocratic title. The only thing stopping Mainwaring from becoming a revolutionary, Wilson realises, is the fact that he is such a snob:

MAINWARING: Things'll be very different after the war, you mark
                my words! The common man will come into his
                own. This country will be run by professionals:
                doctors, lawyers . . . bank managers . . .
WILSON: You mean people like you?
MAINWARING: All right, yes: people like me.
WILSON: [*Smiling mischievously*] You mean 'common'?
MAINWARING: Now watch it, Wilson!
WILSON: I didn't know you were a socialist, sir.
MAINWARING: How dare you! You take that back!
WILSON: But you just said that, after the war, the country was
                going to be run by common men like you.
MAINWARING: I said nothing about 'common men'! I said 'the
                common man'! People who've got somewhere by
                their own efforts – not because their father had a
                title. Their day's over!
WILSON: [*Sarcastically*] Well! I wonder what will happen to
                them?
MAINWARING: Ha! They'll go to work – that's what'll happen to
                them! We shall have true democracy.
WILSON: Well, supposing they don't want to go to work?
MAINWARING: Well, they won't have any say in the matter![92]

Wilson's aristocratic matter-of-factness, his disinclination to shake his imagination out of its slumbers (save for those occasions when someone likens his looks to those of the dashing Jack Buchanan – 'Do you really think so?'), stands in stark contract to Mainwaring's wild idealism ('We are in the front line every minute of our lives here!'). It is not that Wilson is incapable of authentic thoughts and emotions; it is just that, as a somewhat enervated pragmatist, he is not prepared to rehearse them:

INSTRUCTOR:	Right! Now, I'm a Gestapo officer. Now you, Sergeant –
WILSON:	Mmmm? Yes?
INSTRUCTOR:	What are you doing in France?
WILSON:	I'm not in France.
INSTRUCTOR:	Oh yes you are! You got there by parachute. I've captured you, and now I'm interrogating you.
WILSON:	Oh, I see. Well: 'Bonjour.'
INSTRUCTOR:	You're not supposed to tell me anything! Now: What are you doing in France?
WILSON:	I don't know.
INSTRUCTOR:	You're trying to blow up a munitions factory.
WILSON:	[*Sounding bored*] All right: I was trying to blow up a munitions factory.
INSTRUCTOR:	So! You admit it!
WILSON:	Oh, really! This is too absurd!
INSTRUCTOR:	I'll show you how absurd it is! [*Gets hold of Wilson's hand*] I'm putting matches underneath your fingernails! I'm setting light to them! They're burning down! Now they've reached your fingers! You're in agony! How do you like that?
WILSON:	Well, to be absolutely honest, it isn't really bothering me very much![93]

It takes a great deal to rouse Wilson from his well-bred placidity (even the persistent Mrs Pike, who continues to harbour hopes of a proper marriage proposal, has to make do with the loan of his ration book), but bad manners will always rattle him:

WILSON:	Oh, now, really, sir!
MAINWARING:	What's the matter?

WILSON:	Well, I really must protest, sir. Just because you're the officer you don't have to take the hammock! I mean, you just strut over there, put your hand out and say, 'I'm taking that!' I mean, it's just the sort of behaviour I cannot stand!
MAINWARING:	[*Sounding shaken*] Well, I'm very sorry, Wilson. Perhaps it was a little unthinking of me. A little undemocratic. But you know I'm the last person in the world to take advantage of my position.
WILSON:	[*Warily*] Oh, really, sir?
MAINWARING:	We shall take it in turns, of course.
WILSON:	Thank you.
MAINWARING:	But I shall use it first.[94]

Wilson, unlike Mainwaring, is clearly unsuited to times of war – his class has conditioned him to shilly-shally, whereas Mainwaring's has conditioned him to scrap – but, at the right moment, in the right circumstances, he is quite capable of confounding his critics. 'When the occasion demands,' he assures his sceptical captain with one of his wry little smiles, 'I can bawl and shout – just like you.' The Germans, from a distance, fail to fire his fiercest feelings – while he acknowledges the fact that some of them have 'rather an abrupt manner', their uniforms strike him as 'awfully smart' ('They really do something for one, don't you think?') and he cannot stop himself from observing that they seem 'awfully well-disciplined' – but he finds more than enough to motivate him in the contemplation of his own heartfelt English idyll:

Every day, I walk up the high street to work, and, as I pass those little shops, a nice, friendly, warm atmosphere seems to come wafting out – I mean, even from that dreadful fellow Hodges' greengrocer's – and then I stroll on a little bit further and I pass Frazer's funeral parlour, and then before I cross the road to come to the bank there's Jones' butcher shop – white tiles all gleaming and shining, and old Jones standing there with his straw hat on and wearing his striped apron, and giving me a cheery wave – and do you know, sir, it sort of, I don't know, it sort of sets me up for the day. I feel it's my time, you see.[95]

It made for a strange relationship, this marriage of the right stuff and the real thing, but, somehow, it worked. Each man knows, in his heart of hearts, that he needs the other. Wilson knows that, if Mainwaring was not there to push him, he might very well stagnate, whereas Mainwaring knows that, if Wilson was not there for him to push against, he might very well fall flat on his face ('They recognise authority when they see it. Er, you'd better come with me'). When one of them comes up with the answer, the other comes up with the questions; when one orders Pike to prime the grenades, the other persuades him to load them with dummy detonators; when one praises his platoon for having guts, the other prays that he will never get to see any. It is, in the circumstances, a most appropriate partnership: unorthodox, edgy, amateurish, improbably effective and very, very English.

Although this association with Arthur Lowe was the crucial on-screen partnership, John revelled behind the scenes in the company of the entire troupe. He was particularly close to Clive Dunn ('He makes me laugh'[96]), James Beck ('He was clever and as sharp as a whip'[97]) and Bill Pertwee ('A good man to have around'[98]), all three of whom shared his enjoyment of music and alcohol, but he enjoyed spending time with the whole ensemble of his fellow actors. Although there was never much time for socialising before or after the recording sessions, the annual fortnight at Thetford, when the exterior scenes for the next series were filmed, brought everyone together and bonded them increasingly strongly as a team.

This location shooting always revolved around a cluster of tried and trusted routines and rituals. The Bell Hotel, a former coaching inn situated in the heart of the old part of the town, served as the base for the principal members of the cast, while the smaller Anchor Hotel, just across the river, accommodated the remainder of the team. Saturday saw the arrival of the production crew, along with several caravans full of costumes and equipment, and the actors followed, via various routes and diverse modes of transport, on Sunday.

The initial sights and sounds remained, year in, year out, much the same. David Croft and his production manager, Harold Snoad, could be seen attending to details both minor and major; Jimmy Perry could be heard reassuring people that his battered old medicine chest contained everything from throat sprays to senna pods; Arnold Ridley would be double-checking that his room overlooked the quiet river rather than the noisy courtyard; John Laurie and Ian Lavender would be chatting in the reception area; James Beck would be asking someone to spare him a cigarette; John Le Mesurier, Clive Dunn and Bill Pertwee would be busy exchanging short jokes and tall stories; Arthur Lowe would be enquiring anxiously if the local corner shop still stocked his precious cork-tipped Craven 'A's; and Frank Williams and Edward Sinclair would be bustling about in a manner strongly reminiscent of the vicar and the verger. Keys were collected, rooms explored, bags unpacked, and then, in the evening, old friendships were rekindled.

Each morning began with Arthur Lowe's notoriously detailed analysis of the breakfast menu. 'I see you have kippers,' he would say to the worried-looking waitress. 'Tell me, are they boil-in-the bag or are they' – at which point his left hand would essay a friskily undulating motion – 'real swim-about kippers?'[99] He would also ask if the cold ham was tender – really tender – and note that, while he was perfectly happy to have his coffee strong, he preferred to take his tea weak – and that meant depositing only one tea bag in his pot rather than the two that the tea-boy always seemed intent upon giving him. The other actors, who grew to relish this regular performance, were by this stage already finishing off their own meals and starting to study the day's itinerary and discuss their forthcoming scenes. John, in spite of having stayed up most of the night telling stories and sipping spirits, would appear well-prepared for the day's work, whereas James Beck, because he had stayed up most of the night in the company of 'Le Mez', would appear somewhat the worse for wear. A production assistant would eventually appear and announce that the coach was due to leave for the latest location in five minutes, whereupon the cast and crew would rise and make their way out of the hotel.

Lowe, more often than not, would be the last to leave, and, when he did finally emerge, it was not uncommon for him to discover that the coach had departed without him. 'These early morning starts play havoc with my lavatorial arrangements,'[100] he would grumble to Jimmy Perry, who usually found himself having to wait behind in order to chauffeur the dilatory actor to the next site. Perry once bought him some packets of All-Bran, which, after some initial resistance – 'I'm not touching that muck! It's like eating the stuffing of a mattress!' – alleviated the problem considerably. 'You know,' Lowe would sigh, sounding like some cheap advertisement, 'All-Bran has totally changed my life!'[101]

The daily shooting schedule – like all shooting schedules – involved lengthy periods of inactivity punctuated by brief but intensive bursts of action. Most of the cast would while away the idle time by sitting back in their chairs and reading. Arnold Ridley would lose himself in the theatrical and sporting columns of the *Daily Telegraph*, while John Laurie and his fast-learning protégé, Ian Lavender, would compete with each other to see who would be first to complete the *Times* crossword; John would either chain-smoke as he studied the *Sporting Life* or pace up and down looking vaguely fretful (a habit that David Croft sometimes found sufficiently distracting to send him off to the nearest pub until his services were next required). Arthur Lowe's focus, however, rarely seemed to be far away from food: elevenses, for example, called for at least a couple of rounds of sandwiches (usually bacon and sausage, but sometimes ham if it was 'genuine Wiltshire' and not that 'packeted muck'[102]), which would then be followed by a full traditional English lunch and afternoon tea. Dinner, inevitably, was a topic that Lowe first began to ponder well before the end of the afternoon, but then again, as Ian Lavender would confirm, this was one meal that everyone came to cherish:

It was like a family gathering. There was the crew, the cast, the extras – who, incidentally, were never called, or treated like, 'extras'; they were always referred to as the 'extra-specials', and were made to feel part of the team – and we'd all come back to the hotel and join up for this evening ritual. It actually really did serve an important purpose, because it gave us all the chance to talk. I remember asking David Croft why filming always took a fortnight even though, essentially, everything could probably have been wrapped up neatly enough in eight or nine days, and he said: 'You haven't seen each other for nine months. These two weeks aren't just about filming; they're also about all of you sitting around before, during and after dinner and talking, getting rid of all of your stories from last year – what you've been doing, what jobs, where you've been, what happened to so-and-so, all of that – so that by the time we get to rehearsals you haven't got anything left to talk about and I've got your undivided attention.' And, of course, it worked. A very canny man, David, very canny indeed.[103]

Although the combined age of the main cast was, at the start of the 1970s, 523,[104] there were plenty of lively pranks and antics during the fortnight. At the mildest end of the spectrum, the show's two septuagenarians, Arnold Ridley and John Laurie, often seemed to be locked in a private one-upmanship competition. The sight, for example, of Ridley settling into his special sturdy chair to rest his legs between takes was usually the cue for the ever-mischievous Laurie – who was only one year younger – to leap up and stagger past with some weighty piece of equipment, or break out into a gentle little jog, or stride briskly back and forth while 'assuring' his semi-recumbent colleague, 'You just take it easy there, son!'[105]

Towards the other end of the scale, a more farcical incident occurred back at the hotel one night when Bill Pertwee decided to surprise John, who was having a nightcap in his room with James Beck and a crusty old real-life Army colleague, by bursting in stark naked except for a pair of black boots and his white ARP helmet. When Beck retaliated by locking Pertwee out of his own room across the hall, he had to creep off and hide quietly in a broom cupboard until John ('When will you learn to behave yourself, Billy?') took pity on him and called the night porter for a spare pass key.[106] One of John's own little party pieces was to draw on his old 'Old Mother Riley' training and perform impromptu pratfalls in the hotel bar – an action that not only always provoked a pleasingly wide variety of reactions, but also prompted one of the attractive young make-up women to rush over, fall to her knees and cradle his head in her lap.

The final daily ritual was the viewing of the rushes at the Palace – a little cinema in Thetford. Each evening at 10.30 pm, the cast and crew would arrive outside the building and wait for the 'late' doors to open. Once inside, everyone would settle down and watch a few cartoons while the local projectionist spooled up the latest reel of newly processed film – sent down by train from London – and readied it for screening. When the sequences were shown, Bill Pertwee would later recall, they were often accompanied by such teasing remarks as, 'Look at the warden, over-acting again,' 'How many more faces is he going to pull?' or 'so and so could have done better then'. 'A funny sequence would be greeted with spasmodic applause or laughter. Arthur Lowe would generally fall asleep but wake up at just the right moment to make a cryptic remark. We would then return to our respective hotels for a night-cap or two.'[107]

When the fortnight finally came to an end, everyone paused to thank the local people for their patience and hospitality, before packing up, checking out and returning, a little reluctantly, to London (John usually heading there via another detour to the races at Newmarket). The next time that they all would meet was at rehearsal, when the pace was considerably brisker and the mood rather more businesslike.

Rehearsals, however, were not without their own problems. 'One of our big worries,' Jimmy Perry later acknowledged, 'was Arthur Lowe. Although when it came to the recording in the studio he was magnificent, it was a struggle to get him to learn his lines during rehearsals.'[108] It hardly helped that an unrepentant Lowe made a point of declining to take his script home with him – 'Oh, I'm not having that rubbish in the house!'[109] – and never seemed aware of the chaos that he was causing. David Croft, who was left to clear away – or cover up – the mess, probably had most cause, most often, to feel exasperated:

> He never got any better. A lot of those hesitations that you see on the screen are actually Arthur thinking to himself, 'What the hell am I supposed to say next?' Sometimes, of course, that sort of thing helps an actor, because it means that the thought process has to be there – you know, if an actor knows the part inside out they can be inclined to push the line in too quickly, whereas if there's a slight hesitation, although it's only a fraction of a second, it's an important fraction. So sometimes it worked to our advantage. On the other hand, he did paraphrase some very good lines; we didn't get quite what we wanted and there was no hope of doing a retake once the line had gone. So it could be very frustrating.
>
> John Le Mesurier was quite different from Arthur in that respect. He had a photographic memory – he used to say, 'Don't tell me, don't tell me, it's on top of page 82,' and he could 'see' the picture, see the page. And he was always in rehearsal a quarter of an hour before we started, and he always knew his part. Quite extraordinary.
>
> Arthur just wouldn't take away his script. He always kept it in a desk in the rehearsal room. I think his problem was that during his days in repertory he'd had a more or less photographic memory and later on it had begun to fail him. So he didn't realise that he needed to actually get down and study the part. John Le Mesurier would call me and say, 'Can't you get him to learn the bloody thing?' So I started sending him two copies of the script.

I told him, 'You can leave one in the rehearsal room and perhaps you'd like to place the other one under your pillow in the hope that some of it will percolate through the feathers during the night!' But all he did was go up to Jimmy and say, 'David seems to be in a foul mood these days. What do you think caused it?'[110]

Croft forgave him, just as John and everyone else forgave him, because of the innumerable occasions when he did everything right. He was able to make an unfunny line seem funny, or a funny line seem even funnier, with a sublime piece of timing, a sly arch of an eyebrow, a sudden gasp of indignation, or some other smart little technical trick that only the finest kind of comedy actor could execute without the slightest sign of effort. He was good – exceptionally good – and that made up for everything.

John, without such routine mishaps, was equally impressive, and he shone throughout the rest of the run with some of the most intelligent, understated and enduringly amusing character acting ever seen in a popular sitcom. There were several splendid episodes in which he could 'show off' Wilson: in 'Room At the Bottom' from the third series, Mainwaring finds himself temporarily demoted to the rank of private and placed under the command of his sergeant; in 'Getting the Bird' from the fifth series, Wilson's relationship with a mystery young woman provokes plenty of gossip; and in 'The Honourable Man' from the sixth series, Wilson, much to Mainwaring's horror, inherits a title and promptly 'moves up a place' in the social hierarchy. The vast majority of the shows, however, were ensemble productions, making the most of all of the characters, and some of John's most impressive contributions came in these multi-faceted fictions.

In a cleverly claustrophobic episode entitled 'Something Nasty in the Vault', Wilson and Mainwaring are forced to sit together in the strong room of the bank, cradling an unexploded bomb, while the rest of the platoon, and Hodges, race around trying very hard not to panic (in an unusually tender moment, Wilson gets Mainwaring to scratch his itchy nose). Another episode, called 'Keep Young and Beautiful', saw all of the part-time soldiers, apart from Pike, searching for ways to disguise the signs of their advancing years. Frazer, Godfrey and Jones appeared semi-embalmed, Mainwaring sported charcoal eyebrows and a limp brown wig and Wilson winced from the discomfort of wearing a 'gentleman's abdominal support': 'You're a rum cove,' the captain moans to his sergeant. 'You wear that uniform like a sack of porridge, but in some ways you're as vain as a peacock!'

In 'Gorilla Warfare', the platoon sets off on an exercise in which they have to escort Mainwaring, in the guise of a very important secret agent, to a clandestine destination: Wilson unnerves his excited superior officer more or less immediately by rolling up with a suitcase full of his personal comforts:

MAINWARING: Now look here, Wilson. As my sergeant, you're
               supposed to set an example of toughness. You're
               supposed to . . . [*sniffs*] Are you wearing scent?
WILSON: Scent?
MAINWARING: Yes. Scent!
WILSON: No, it's just a little bit of eau de cologne I put on
               after I shave.
MAINWARING: You put scent on after you shave? I've never heard
               of such a thing!

Another episode, 'Ring Dem Bells', allowed John to share with Wilson his enduring affection for one of the actor idols of his youth, as he and the rest of the men are recruited to appear in an Army training film. 'Oooh, he isn't half like Jack Buchanan, innee,' exclaims the costume lady, much to Mainwaring's irritation, as she sizes Wilson up for his outfit. 'He'll make a lovely officer!'

Arguably the most memorable 'team' episode of all was 'The Deadly Attachment', which marked the start of the third series in 1973. It had everything: the confrontation with the German U-boat captain ('Face to face with the enemy at last, eh?'), the pertinent contribution from Pike ('Hitler is a twerp'), followed by the sudden threat from the angry Nazi ('Your name will also go on the list – vot is it?') and Mainwaring's swift intervention ('Don't tell him, Pike!'). Godfrey is caught dozing, Frazer caught moaning, Hodges is held hostage, Walker takes fastidious orders for fish and chips, and the grenade is dangled down Jones's trousers. 'It was originally going to be down Arthur's trousers,' David Croft would recall, 'but, of course, he wasn't having any of it. He said he'd have it inside his tunic, but not down his trousers. So we handed that part of the business to Clive Dunn. It was much better that way, of course, and I think Arthur was a little jealous.'[111]

There was also, of course, Wilson's very English brand of aggression: 'Now, listen to me, you German fellows! Would you mind getting up against the wall and putting your hands up, please?'

It was a particularly good example of the ways in which the character of Wilson often linked all of the other figures together, acting as a confidant to some, such as Pike ('Uncle Arthur! It's not fair my name going on the list! I was only joking!'), a mediator to others, such as Frazer ('Maybe you'll tell us just what we're gonnae do now!'), and a pillar of strength to the likes of Jones ('I did do well, didn't I, Mr Wilson, didn't I do well?') as well as a combination of assistant, analyst, diplomatic advisor and artful irritant to Captain Mainwaring. He also contrived a way to save the day, on this occasion, by choosing not to do certain 'hasty' things that he deemed to be 'awfully tricky' and 'very, very, dangerous'.

The audience feedback for such shows was consistently high, and, as it moved on through the 1970s, the success of *Dad's Army* never seemed to slide.[112] Not only did the programme itself keep coming back for series after series (and a radio version was introduced[113]), but also a movie was made in 1971, followed by a stage revue four years later. Both of these spin-offs underlined just how large a following the programme, and its cast, had acquired.

The movie was not such an enjoyable experience for the actors, because, thanks to some predictable meddling by the American backers (Columbia Pictures) and a new director (Norman Cohen), the production never seemed particularly sure of what it was trying to create. John, one of the members of the cast most at home on a movie set, was distinctly unimpressed, complaining that the screenplay was 'little more than three half hour episodes joined together',[114] but it was actually rather less coherent than that. Croft and Perry's original script had been 'opened out' by Cohen, who had looked to replace the intimacy of the television show with something more 'cinematic' while trying to keep hold of the regular small screen audience.

It was filmed at a breathless pace within a mere six weeks at Shepperton Studios and on location at Chobham in Surrey, Seaford in Sussex and Chalfont St Giles. In one sequence, John, Arthur Lowe and John Laurie had to accompany a white horse on a raft as it drifted down the river: the erratic movements of the hidden tow lines that were meant to be controlling the raft unbalanced the horse, causing it to slip and fall on John Laurie, badly bruising his ribs. It had been a fairly harrowing day, and, as John Le Mesurier would later reflect, it was not over yet:

> As sun set at about seven o'clock, some clever publicity fellow thought it would be splendid if he could get a long shot of several of the platoon on the horse's back. We climbed on to this dear creature, someone shouted, 'Action!' and the horse, being tired after a long day, sank a few inches into the muddy banks of the Thames. She then reared up and threw us off. I landed in John Laurie's lap, which momentarily winded him. My wrist-watch disappeared into the Thames. Naturally, I put in for an over-extravagant sum in compensation. But next morning, someone had to go and retrieve it from the river. I could have killed him.[115]

Filming finally came to an end with the completion of a few minor inserts. Arthur Lowe, who was always very prudish when it came to any degree of disrobing, congratulated himself on keeping his trousers up for the duration (John had been left to lead the men in their underwear for Perry's 'passage of time' montage, while Lowe provided the rather smug voiceover: 'Jerry will never catch us with our trousers down!'), and everyone else congratulated themselves simply for having reached the end of an exhausting but somewhat unrewarding month and a half. The reception, however, was fairly positive, and the production would end up being deemed an overall success: it had been inexpensive to make, it performed well at the domestic box office,[116] and it would go on to age much better than the majority of other big screen sitcoms of the era.

The stage revue, which arrived in 1975, proved an altogether more enjoyable experience for those who took part. The original cast, by this time, had lost Jimmy Beck – he died in 1973, at the premature age of forty-four, from a combination of heart failure, renal failure and pancreatitis[117] – so John Bardon was selected to replace him as Walker.[118] John Laurie, meanwhile – fearing that, at the age of seventy-eight, the daily slog might prove too much of a strain – had passed on the project, and Hamish Roughead, a suitably mature Scottish actor, was chosen to play the part of Frazer.[119] The troupe tried the production out, first of all, on a short provincial tour that began at the Forum Theatre in Billingham, and it was reassuringly well received.

John, true to form, had not been sanguine about the enterprise: 'Why do we have to go to this Billingham place, Billy?' he had moaned to Bill Pertwee as they headed up to Cleveland. 'It's miles from anywhere, we shall all probably get lost.'[120] He also made his way from place to place in his usual absent-minded manner. Frank Williams would later recall:

> John once said to me, 'What do you do about your dirty washing?' I said, 'Well, John, I find a laundry that will do it during the week, and I take it in and then collect it at the end of the week.' So I said, 'What do you do?' He said, 'Er, well, I just sort of leave it around in my room and, er, somehow, some kind person always does it for me.' And that was so typical of John – being helpless and having people come to his rescue![121]

The West End opening, on Thursday 2 October, was a hugely successful affair. Most of the actors were allowed at least one party piece: John, for example, gave a rendition of 'A Nightingale Sang in Berkeley Square' ('I didn't, of course, actually sing,' he would explain in his usual self-deprecating manner; 'it was a sort of half singing, half talking version, rather in the manner of a poor man's Rex Harrison'[122]) that was not only distinctive but also rather moving. 'It was another example of John being charmingly eccentric,' Ian Lavender would recall, 'with that odd delivery, finding it all slightly amusing and off-centre, and laughing when he came to sing, or say, "And, ha-ha, a nightingale sang in Berkeley Square!" And, of course, it was delightful – a real highlight of the stage show.'[123] John was subsequently both surprised and very flattered when some of his own favourite performers, including the jazz singer Annie Ross, went backstage to congratulate him on his interpretation of such a classic song.

He also shone alongside Arthur Lowe when the two of them appeared as Flanagan and Allen to sing the popular old song 'Home Town'. John had struggled initially to master the very basic choreography required for the routine – indeed, when David Croft suffered a heart attack shortly after the show had opened, he attributed it, perhaps only partly in jest, to 'the extreme difficulty of teaching John Le Mesurier to cross the stage on the same foot as the rest of the cast during "Home Town"'[124] – but, once the curtains came up and the audience was present, he was able to deliver his usual assured performance, and the number always elicited heartfelt applause.

The show as a whole was treated very kindly by the critics (*The Stage* singling John out for his 'remarkably subtle portrait'[125]) and the box office was so busy that one reporter suggested that, but for the venerable ages of many members of the cast, the revue could have 'run for years and perhaps become as much of a tourist attraction as *The Mousetrap*'.[126] After five very well-attended months in the West End, the production went on tour, from March to September 1976, before the team reassembled to make more television programmes.

A one-off special followed that Christmas, and then, in 1977, came the ninth and final series. No one had really wanted the show to end, but at that point it seemed, reluctantly, the right thing to do. 'We realised that, well, none of them was getting any younger,' Jimmy Perry would say. 'One day it just sort of hits you like that. They were the kind of tough old pros who wanted to go on till they dropped, but [David and I] knew that we'd have to finish it. "Leave the audience wanting more" – that was the motto.'[127]

The mood on the set for that valedictory series – which was recorded during the summer – was quietly but sincerely emotional. John, who had set off to start work on the show 'with an aching sense of sadness', would liken the experience to that of 'an old boys' reunion, made all the more poignant by the knowledge that this was the final roll-call, the "last Post" as it were'.[128] When the shows were screened in the autumn of 1977, an average of 10.5 million tuned in each week to see them – a remarkable testimony to the programme's continuing commitment to the highest possible quality.[129] The final episode – 'Never Too Old' – was a real labour of love. Croft and Perry had wanted it to be funny but moving; to do justice to the show, the characters and the actors, and honour the spirit of the real-life Home Guard, and to come to an elegant end rather than an awkward halt. Thrillingly, it managed to do all of those things, within thirty minutes of consummate situation comedy, with wit, good taste and compassion.

It went out on the evening of 13 November – Remembrance Sunday – and opened with an unexpected admission from Jones: 'I have fallen in love, Captain Mainwaring. With a woman.' Mainwaring is shaken by this news – 'I can't be expected to face a Nazi invasion with a woolly-headed corporal!' – and even more shaken when he is told that the woman in question is none other than Walmington-on-Sea's most flirtatious widow, Mrs Fox (whose relationship with the old soldier had previously been described by Jones as 'purely teutonic').

Once Mainwaring has established that this is not a passing fancy –
'Oh, no,' says Jones, 'it's definitely not a passing fancy – I've fancied
her for seventeen years!' – and sat patiently through the butcher's bout
of self-doubt – 'Does she love me for myself, or does she love me for
my meat?' – he concludes that the union might actually work. 'After
all,' he confides to Wilson, 'they're both the same class.' Mrs Fox
(played by Pamela Cundell with just the right air of innocent menace)
persuades a distinctly ill-at-ease Mainwaring to act as her father (MRS
FOX: 'You wouldn't give me away, would you?' MAINWARING:
'Wouldn't I?'), and Jones asks Wilson to serve as best man, after which
the wedding ceremony goes ahead (MRS FOX: 'Mr Mainwaring – I
think I'm going to cry.' MAINWARING: 'Oh, do try not to'). Then,
at the reception, Mainwaring offers the newly married couple a toast:
'I wish you both the very best of luck, and may you be as happy as I
have been with my own dear wife, who unfortunately can't be with us
this afternoon.'

The atmosphere in the studio was made all the more special for the
cast by the fact that the two writers had arranged for as many wives
and partners as possible who had Equity cards – such as Arthur Lowe's
wife, Joan Cooper (who played Dolly Godfrey), and Arnold Ridley's
wife, Althea Parker (who played an unnamed wedding guest) – to join
the performers in front of the camera for the scene set at the reception.
'David [Croft] tends to hide a lot of his feelings,' Ian Lavender would
later observe, 'but, deep down, he's a sentimental old bugger.'[130] Croft
acknowledged: 'It was a very emotional evening. The production
gallery was unusually quiet throughout the recording, and, as the end
drew near, there were plenty of people with lumps in their throats.'[131]

The on-screen wedding celebrations are brought to a sudden halt
after a call from GHQ. Reports of barges moving around the North
Sea coast lead to the platoon being placed on immediate standby, and
Jones finds himself spending the night at the end of a cold pier with
Pike instead of inside a warm hotel with his wife. While the two men
stand on patrol, however, they are joined by Mainwaring, Wilson,
Frazer and Godfrey, who have brought along a dusty bottle of
champagne with which to drink their friend's health. Hodges,
inevitably, arrives to disturb the mood, pausing only to point out that
the invasion alert was a false alarm, and to mock the men who are still
standing guard ('What good would you be against real soldiers?
They'd walk straight through you!'), before departing back into the

darkness. The champagne is then poured into mugs (or, in Godfrey's case, a medicine glass), the men begin to drink, and the final few beautifully judged minutes are allowed to unfold:

PIKE: Mr Mainwaring? Warden wasn't right, was he, when he said the Nazis would walk straight through us?

MAINWARING: Of course he wasn't right!

JONES: I know one thing – they're not walking straight through me!

FRAZER: Nor me. I'll be beside you, Jonesie.

MAINWARING: We'll all be beside you, Jonesie. We'll stick together – you can rely on that. If anybody tries to take our homes or our freedom away from us they'll find out what we can do. We'll fight. And we're not alone – there are thousands of us all over England.

FRAZER: And Scotland.

MAINWARING: And Scotland. All over Great Britain, in fact. Men who'll stand together when their country needs them.

WILSON: Excuse me, sir – don't you think it might be a nice idea if we were to pay our tribute to them?

MAINWARING: For once, Wilson, I agree with you. [*Raises mug*] To Britain's Home Guard!

ALL: [*Turning to face the camera*] To Britain's Home Guard![132]

The studio audience applauded, the closing credits rolled, and then, after nine years, nine series, eighty episodes and forty-eight hours and ten minutes of great acting, fine writing and glorious television, it was all over. An estimated 12,524,000 people had watched an era come to an end.[133] The BBC's own internal audience report was full of praise for the show and tinged with sadness at its passing: 'It was felt that all the characters had been beautifully portrayed . . . The production, too, was highly praised for bringing out a convincing sense of period and for paying great attention to detail. Altogether, it was generally agreed that the programme had always been magnificent, that the cast could not have been better chosen and it was sad to see the series come to an end.'[134]

The critics, too, lined up to pay tribute to what the *Guardian*'s Peter Fiddick described as 'one of the jewels of TV comedy':

> It is bound to be remembered for sentiment and nostalgia, and it's made the most of those, but that makes it all the more necessary to record, as the absolutely final credits roll, that it has given us finer farces, straighter faces, richer characterisation, and a deal more social observation, than most of the more pretentious dramas, and always kept us guessing which would turn up next. . . . It will be missed.[135]

The BBC, Bill Pertwee would later recall, had failed to arrange a farewell celebration in time to mark the final studio recording: 'We'd all put our best bib and tuckers on, you know, thinking someone was probably going to surprise us with a bit of a party, but they just handed us the usual black dusting bags for our stuff, turned off the lights and we all trudged off to the bar for a drink.'[136] A tabloid newspaper,[137] sensing an opportunity to embarrass the Corporation, arranged for each member of the *Dad's Army* cast to receive a special medal 'For services to television entertainment', followed, on the night the final episode was transmitted, by a valedictory (and much-photographed) dinner at London's Café Royal. 'It was quite a jolly evening,' recalled Clive Dunn,[138] with a considerable amount of wine being consumed, although John Le Mesurier, who was off alcohol at the time and was therefore limited to sipping orange juice or mineral water, would later confess that the 'only way I had of getting myself into the spirit' of the occasion was by smoking what he described, euphemistically, as 'extra strong cigarettes'.[139] There were some memorable after-dinner speeches, which, Dunn later pointed out, 'were not repeated in full, because some of the remarks we made were not necessarily conducive to selling more newspapers'.[140]

'It was a good evening,' David Croft would confirm. 'A very funny evening. John Laurie got very abusive, as he was wont to do, but amusingly so, and I remember that Arthur's wife, Joan, who was inclined to get rather merry, got up to make a speech. She'd been going about three or four minutes when, all of a sudden, she slipped under the table – just like that – and Arthur, of course, took no notice and just carried on as if nothing had happened!'[141] Bill Pertwee thanked the hosts for their generosity, and then Arthur Lowe rose to second the sentiment, although he rather spoiled the effect by adding that, in spite of this, there was 'no way' he would allow 'such a rubbishy newspaper' as theirs inside his house.[142] 'This is a sad occasion for all of us,' Lowe went on to declare. 'I've never wanted the show to stop, but some of us' – he said, looking round at the others – 'are getting on a bit.'[143]

John Le Mesurier (who was still puffing out some powerful cannabis clouds) reminisced about the filming, said nice things about his colleagues and observed that 'being in *Dad's Army* was like belonging to a gentleman's club';[144] Clive Dunn joked that 'Having a final dinner like this is a bit like going to your own funeral';[145] Ian Lavender remarked that he looked on the day when he was chosen for the part of Private Pike as 'the luckiest day of my life';[146] Arnold Ridley got unsteadily to his feet, smiled his usual crinkly smile, said 'Thank you very much',[147] and then sat straight back down again; and John Laurie, Clive Dunn would recall, 'stood up and said in his wildest Scottish brogue that, although a lot of remarks had been made about the series and the participants, no one had so far mentioned that "Actors are a load of ***ts!" Silence reigned for all of five seconds, and then the assembly fell apart.'[148]

Another function followed a short while later, when the team was summoned by the BBC's Board of Governors to an 'official' farewell luncheon party – a 'rather formal occasion', sighed John, 'which none of us enjoyed over much'.[149] Lowe, Le Mesurier and Laurie contributed one last cameo appearance, in character, to the 1977 Christmas edition of another bona fide and much-loved national institution, *The Morecambe & Wise Show*.[150] Then the year came to an end, the reality sank in, and the cast and crew of *Dad's Army*, with some reluctance, 'stood down'.

John, in later years, would always try to play down the extent to which his long association with the show had elevated him to an unexpectedly lofty level of fame. Indeed, he loved to recount the occasion when someone saw him in a pub and whispered to a friend, 'Oh, look, there's Sergeant Wilson from *The Army Game*,' and he took even greater pleasure in recalling when another 'fan' came up to him at a charity fete and exclaimed, 'I know who you are: Daphne du Maurier!'[151] Deep down inside, however, he knew that the popularity of the programme had made him into a bona fide and very warmly regarded national treasure. He was immensely grateful, and, in his own quiet way, rather proud. As a professional actor, however, his first thought, once the show was over and all of the fond farewells had been said, took the form of a very sobering practical question: 'How does one follow that?'

CHAPTER XIV

Do You Think That's Wise?

Most sensible people give up working at sixty-five or even younger.
But what would I do with myself?

John Le Mesurier almost missed out on the opportunity to ask himself 'How does one follow that?' At one stage, it looked as though he would not be well enough to finish *Dad's Army*, let alone follow it with something – anything – else.

In the autumn of 1976, after completing the run of the *Dad's Army* stage show and finishing filming the Terry Gilliam movie *Jabberwocky*, as well as finalising plans to move into a newly purchased detached property a short distance away from his and Joan's current house in Ramsgate, he had taken on a fresh set of commitments that together represented a punishing schedule for a man of sixty-four years of age. Apart from recording a *Dad's Army* Christmas special, he flew to Amsterdam with Arthur Lowe to make another television appearance, and then set off to Salisbury in Rhodesia (now Harare, Zimbabwe) for a season starring in the J.B. Priestley play *An Inspector Calls*. After struggling to cope with the humid climate – the theatre was always stiflingly hot, and his costume consisted of a thick three-piece worsted suit covered by a heavy overcoat ('It was like carrying around one's personal Turkish bath'[1]) – he returned to England early in 1977. More or less immediately, he accepted an offer to travel to Australia (where he and *Dad's Army* were hugely popular) to appear in a new production of Molière's *The Miser*. He just had enough time to film a one-off play for BBC1 – David Mercer's satire *Flint* – before jetting off to Perth. Once again, however, the heat proved a problem. Just under three weeks after his arrival, he collapsed during rehearsal and was rushed straight to hospital.

Joan, who had been planning to join him once the play was up and running, heard the news from John's agent and wanted to fly over immediately, but was advised to stay where she was and wait patiently for him to return. As usual, his attitude was: if he was going to be ill, then he wanted to be ill back in England. She was thus extremely shocked, when he arrived at Heathrow two days later, to find him in a wheelchair, looking thin, frail and ashen-faced: 'He seemed to have aged ten years in the few weeks he had been away and I was hard pressed to hold back the tears.'[2] The Australian doctor, rather oddly, had diagnosed depression and prescribed anti-depressants without giving him a thorough examination, and Joan suspected that he had confused the effects of her husband's condition with its causes. Giving the physician the benefit of the doubt, she let John take his first dose the following day – only to see him fall promptly into a semi-conscious state. She decided to flush the rest of the pills down the lavatory and made plans to get a trustworthy second opinion as soon as was practically possible.

Once they were home in Ramsgate, she duly rang the family doctor, who came over immediately, examined John carefully and diagnosed a serious problem with his liver. The next day, John was admitted to Ramsgate Hospital, where a consultant confirmed that he was suffering from cirrhosis of the liver.

John, after watching not only his first wife, June, but also his friends, Tony Hancock and Jimmy Beck, succumb so rapidly and dramatically to the lure of the booze, was stunned by the news. 'The curious thing was,' he would say, 'I had never thought of myself as a heavy drinker. I liked to drink, yes. Sometimes I drank too much, sometimes not at all. But apparently it was the cumulative effect over the years that had done the damage. I was told I must never drink alcohol again.'[3]

He spent the next few months resting at home, profoundly depressed. Joan studied health food books and tried to persuade John to eat his way back to good health via bowls of raw fruit and plates of green salad, but he would have nothing to do with such 'unpleasant' things. Determined to stay positive, she called in a neuropath, who examined John and then confided to Joan that, unless he changed his diet dramatically, he would probably die quite soon. The neuropath prescribed raw fruit and filtered water for a month before progressing to raw vegetables and salads, with not even tea or coffee, let alone alcohol, for liquid refreshment. John reluctantly obeyed. When he was next examined at the local hospital, the specialist was pleasantly surprised to find that his liver – though still in a seriously poor condition – had shrunk back to more or less its proper size and actually appeared to be mending.

John was judged to be out of danger, but he was still startlingly thin and weak, with his sad eyes sunken deep into his craggy face and his skin looking a pale shade of yellow. He improved, very slowly, over time, but he missed his alcohol greatly. Pubs and clubs had been his favourite social places, and few things gave him more pleasure than idle conversation with a large glass of vodka or scotch close at hand. Hattie Jacques sent down a crate of non-alcoholic wine, but, although he appreciated the gesture, he complained that it tasted like watery grape juice. He did try, on those days when he felt a little stronger, to venture down the road to his local pub to reconnect with the regulars, but it felt strange to sit there nursing a glass of warm lemonade, and he soon shuffled back home again to suffer in isolation.

The only thing that roused him during this period (aside from the offer of a cameo role, as Marley's Ghost, in a forthcoming BBC1 adaptation of *A Christmas Carol*, which he filmed with sadly little need for any pale and 'spectral' make-up) was the news that he was needed for another series of *Dad's Army*. Neither David Croft nor Jimmy Perry was aware of how ill he had been (and still was), so they had included him in their plans as usual without giving the matter a second thought. It was, Joan would later admit, a mistake for him to sign up. He looked terrible and, if anything, he would seem even worse once placed under the harsh studio lights, which emphasised his sunken eyes and waxy pallor. So great, however, was his love for the show, and so strong his affection for his fellow members of the cast, he could not resist the chance to take part, and so he went ahead with the project.

John tried desperately hard to improve his health in the months that followed, but he was still clearly in a very poor physical state when, in June 1977, the call came to join the rest of the *Dad's Army* team in Thetford for another fortnight of filming. He knew that he was not really well enough to work, but he also knew that this would almost certainly be the show's final series and he simply could not bear to miss it. His colleagues, meanwhile, had been forewarned by Joan about the fragility of his condition, but, when he arrived, they still found it hard to hide their distress at how frail and emaciated their old friend had become. 'He was pathetic,' David Croft would recall:

> He looked so ill. I remember one day in particular, when the weather had turned rather cold, being so concerned about him that I ordered all the lights to be arranged around him in a sort of six-foot square area and then turning them all on to warm him up a bit. He was in such a bad way. It was very hard, very sad. And when we went on to do the last episode in the studio I remember thinking, 'Well, that's the last we shall see of John Le Mesurier.'[4]

He somehow made it through all six episodes of the closing series, and still managed to shine every now and again with his wonderfully light but precise technique. Once the recordings were over and the farewell parties had finished, however, he was left alone to deal with those in the media who suspected that he was about to expire.

It was an intensely worrying time for him professionally as well as personally, because he was now considered to be a bad risk by the insurance companies, and the job offers were drying up rapidly. It was thus not long – and certainly much sooner than most onlookers suspected – before John's financial situation was also a cause for concern. 'People always thought that John was incredibly rich,' Joan would reflect, 'because his face appeared in so many films over the years. But what they didn't understand was that he often worked for just one day or two days in cameo roles which actually paid very little, so although he had a face that was recognised all over the world, he certainly didn't have a hefty regular income.'[5] Anxious about his declining funds, therefore, John decided, very reluctantly, to sell his Barons Court flat. Although he (much more so than Joan) liked spending his leisure time in London, he resigned himself to 'resting' indefinitely in Ramsgate. 'I feel very lonely without you all some-times,' he wrote to Arthur Lowe, 'and am sad not to be busy, as you are. But the slightest physical exertion puffs me out . . . Mind you, if we were all called on location to Thetford tomorrow, I'd be there!'[6]

One of the few bright spots in his life at this time was his fast-blossoming friendship with Derek Taylor. A former journalist from Liverpool who had made his name in the 1960s first as the publicist of The Beatles (as well as the Beach Boys and The Byrds) and then as head of The Beatles' increasingly chaotic Apple press office, he had more recently been active as a music executive, rising swiftly up the hierarchy at Warner Brothers in America to become Director of Special Projects. He had first met John in 1975, when he was overseeing the production of the soundtrack album of the *Dad's Army* stage show, and the two of them soon recognised each other as kindred spirits. Not only was Taylor a masterful PR man with a wonderfully light touch – it was he who, quite casually, decided to dub the Brian Wilson song 'Good Vibrations' a 'pocket symphony' – he was also a charmingly easygoing bon vivant: not for nothing was his era at Apple dubbed 'the longest cocktail party'.[7] Like Le Mesurier, he was a dapper, irreverent, intelligent English gentleman (looking rather like a more languid, longer-haired version of Ronald Colman) with a sharp eye, a dry wit and a good heart.

He had so enjoyed his initial encounter with John, even though so much else was going on at the time in the studio, that, when they next met, he brought John a very carefully chosen gift: the collected works of Stephen Leacock. 'How kind of you, dear fellow,' John exclaimed, genuinely touched. Taylor pointed out two pieces in particular ('My Financial Career' and 'The Awful Fate of Melpomenus Jones') that he hoped that John would appreciate, and was delighted when John replied by recalling how, many years before, his father had often read to him those very stories. 'Clearly,' Taylor would reflect, 'we had connected.'[8]

The two men kept in touch, meeting every now and again and sending each other playful little notes and cards. On one occasion, for example, John wrote to Derek from a miserable little production booth off Dean Street in Soho where he had gone to record his latest batch of voiceovers: 'I was due to do a Cadbury commercial but at the last moment it was cancelled because the product became inedible and in fact tasted like an ageing turd. . . . So it's back to the drawing board or the labs again so that the commodity can be made more enchanting. I laugh about these things sometimes but not always.' There would also be tart little remarks from John about other actors ('Given to wearing Anderson and Shepherd suits, full of charm and haughtiness, he is convinced he is thirteenth or fourteenth in line to the throne') as well as many delightfully whimsical observations about peculiar encounters ('At 3am the bell rang and there was someone breathing heavily through the letterbox saying that he had met me in Tregunter Road, Earls Court, in 1950 and had something he wanted to show me.

We called the police and sent him merrily on his way'). Taylor, in turn, shared snippets with John about The Beatles, the Monty Python troupe and the vicissitudes of the music business, the media and existence in general.

'They were two of a kind, they really were,' Joan would say. 'They loved the same things, the same books, the same music, the same kind of humour . . . everything. They fitted together beautifully.'[9] Taylor himself later remarked admiringly of his friend that it was John's peculiar ambivalence, his ability to seem both happy and sad at the same time, that struck such a chord: he clearly knew that life could be bloody and cruel, said Taylor, 'but like those bad films among the good in which he appeared . . . there was always the shining Le Mesurier moment when things didn't seem quite so ghastly after all'.[9]

As the relationship developed, Taylor came up with the idea of John recording an album all of his own. 'Tentatively,' he would recall, 'moving with the speed and determination of elderly snails, we built the structure, grain by grain.'[11] The pair of Leacock readings seemed to suggest themselves immediately, and a couple of fine Noël Coward compositions ('The Boy Actor' and 'I Wonder What Happened to Him') were soon added. Two of John's favourite jazz performers, singer Annie Ross and pianist Alan Clare, were invited to contribute, Clare accompanying Ross for renditions of his own 'That Tune' and the Simon and Garfunkel song 'So Long, Frank Lloyd Wright', and playing solo on 'John O'Groats' and John and Joan's old favourite 'What's New?' In addition to a sublime reprise of his stage version of 'A Nightingale Sang in Berkeley Square', Taylor also persuaded John to sing a suitably witty number by Cole Porter entitled 'Thank You So Much, Mrs Lowsborough – Goodby'. The record was completed by John reading a passage suggested by Joan from Laurie Lee's memoir *Cider With Rosie*, as well as a delightfully odd little letter addressed to 'John Le Mesurier' – it had actually been sent years before to quite a different John Le Mesurier – and the well-known 'Indian Prayer' about remembering the dead while remaining engaged with the living. 'It is an album for everyone,' Taylor promised in his sleeve notes. 'It will make you very happy and at times it will make you sad but not for long, for most of all it connects.'[12]

Released late in the autumn of 1976, during a period when the UK album charts were dominated by a mixture of disco, 'soft rock' and Abba, the record was never going to trouble the Top 40, but most of those who did hear it were charmed by its elegant and very English idiosyncrasies. 'It got some good reviews in record journals,' John would later acknowledge in his usual understated style, 'but did not increase my bank balance by much.'[13] He was actually, in private, very proud of this labour of love – indeed, working on the project had, in Joan's opinion, given him 'more pleasure than anything he had ever done before'[14] – and it certainly cemented his friendship with Derek Taylor. They met often from this point on (Taylor had recently returned to England and was now based in Sudbury, Suffolk, not far from the area where John grew up) and became even keener correspondents than before; when John fell ill, Taylor's wry little missives helped lift his flagging spirits. 'Derek's letters were a joy,' Joan later remarked. 'John would read them over and over again and when the family came to stay, Derek's letters were obligatory after-dinner entertainment.'[15]

Staying positive, however, remained a struggle for John. Even when he began to feel well enough to resume his acting career, the opportunities to go out to work were still depressingly thin on the ground. The agent Freddy Joachim had by this time retired,[16] and John was now being represented by Peter Campbell, a former actor (under the name of Peter Marden[17]) based in offices at Berkeley House in Hay Hill, West London. Campbell, to his credit, was trying his best to spark his client's career back into life, but, with all of the rumours still circulating about the delicate state of John's health, the few offers that trickled in were distinctly underwhelming. Apart from the odd voiceover for radio and television commercials (and a pleasant but very low-paid project recording a double album of Bible stories for children[18]), the least-worst offers that arrived obliged John to take part in such dire attempts at low-budget cinematic 'sauce' as *Rosie Dixon – Night Nurse* (1978). It was hugely frustrating for him as a performer, as he was now looking for quality rather than quantity as he tried to ease himself back into regular employment.

He started to toy with the idea of writing his memoirs, which he planned to call *A Jobbing Actor*, but, as Joan would later recall, the prospect of reminiscing about himself had never held any real appeal:

> He seldom volunteered things about his past or his family, so it wasn't even as if I could help him to remember that much! He'd taken me to meet his mother once, soon after we'd got together, and she was a

rather shy and polite and very charming lady, but apart from that he didn't talk much about either of his parents, or his sister or his childhood, or much about anything else that had happened long ago, really.[19]

Intriguing little bits and pieces of Le Mesurier family lore had tended to land in his lap quite by accident over the course of the years. Vincent Price, for example, once told him on a film set that he had rescued a colourful totem pole, with the Le Mesurier name displayed above its base, from a Los Angeles curiosity shop and was now using it as an ornament in the garden of his Hollywood mansion (it turned out that it had been carved by members of a Cree-speaking community in honour of John's Uncle Cecil after he had settled among them in British Columbia[20]) but he had never had the time nor the inclination to reach out for and explore any detailed genealogical records. He was not quite a closed book – more the kind of man who preferred to move on and leave past pages unmarked and unthumbed – but he was certainly ill-suited to penning the kind of comprehensive and candid autobiography that was fast becoming the fashion. Although he did start to put some lighter things down on paper, he continued to wait impatiently for the arrival of a worthwhile distraction.

As if to add insult to injury during this barren period of his professional life, John's regular press cuttings service ensured that he was swamped on a daily basis, from the latter part of 1978 through to the autumn of 1979, with every newspaper report about another, completely unrelated John Le Mesurier. His namesake was the managing director of a discount carpet company who had recently acquired notoriety as a co-defendant, alongside former Liberal party leader Jeremy Thorpe and two other men, in the forthcoming 'Trial of the Century' at the Old Bailey for conspiracy to murder Thorpe's alleged lover, Norman Scott.[21] 'I'm paying for all of this crap and the man's a total stranger!' moaned John every time another hefty batch of unwanted clippings crashed through his letterbox and landed loudly on the mat.[22] It felt for a while as though he was no longer even the most famous John Le Mesurier.

What made the poverty of the projects even more galling was the realisation that, before his illness, he had probably been in the most impressive form of his acting career. Apart from his many years of success as one of the stars of *Dad's Army*, he had also won great critical acclaim early on in the decade for his performance in a 'serious' dramatic production.

The name of the play – written by Dennis Potter – was *Traitor*. Based, very loosely, on the real-life case of Cambridge spy Kim Philby, the fiction focuses on a drunken former KGB double agent named Adrian Harris who has defected to Russia (as Philby had done back in 1963) and is now residing in a sordid little Moscow flat as a group of western journalists arrive to interview him. Puzzled by his claim to still love the England that he has betrayed, and offended by his refusal to show any repentance for the deaths that his treachery has caused, the visitors probe him mercilessly in the vain hope of eliciting a scintilla of contrition.

The director, Alan Bridges, had worked with John before and had faith in his ability to portray the tired and troubled defector, but he had to struggle to convince some among the BBC hierarchy that a man they had come to pigeonhole as a 'comedy actor' was right for the dramatic role (for which he would be paid the then-large sum of £800[23]). In the end, Bridges had to threaten to drop out in order to get his way.[24] Dennis Potter agreed with Bridges: already a great admirer of John as a performer, Potter could also see that he could cope with a character who hailed from the same generation and the same class, and exhibited the same sort of slyly dissident attitude. John was certainly no communist (he was still enough of his father's son to be, by disposition, a fairly old-fashioned Tory[25]), but he had no sympathy for the prejudices associated with the upper classes, hated the humbug and hypocrisy of the political elites and was naturally resistant to routine regimentation. Like Potter, he was cynical about 'flags and drums and pomp and circumstance' as emblems of 'Englishness', preferring instead a notion of national character that is 'slightly melancholy, slightly rueful, and in many important ways extraordinarily gentle'.[26]

John was also quick to understand Potter's more general (but perhaps quasi-autobiographical) interest in Adrian Harris as a compromised human being, agreeing with the playwright when he said: 'I think a feeling of betrayal is almost part of our metabolism. I mean, we have at one stage our ideals, and then you go into jobs, you compromise, you get sick because you can't think too personally about exactly what it is you are tramping underfoot, and you write, buy food, occupy a big house, take a big mortgage, all the things I'm doing.'[27]

John had worried, upon first reading the script, that there were 'too many words', and came close to passing on the project, but Joan simply refused to see him let such a great opportunity slip away:

> I always used to read the scripts that they sent him. He used to say, 'What do you think?' and most of the time I'd just say, 'Well, it's bread and butter, isn't it?' And he'd nod and say 'Yes.' But when *Traitor* came through the door, I said immediately after reading it, 'Gosh, this one is something! You've got to do this one!' But he didn't want to do it at all. He worried himself into a right old state. He came out with so many excuses – 'Oh, it's all so ephemeral, these things all get forgotten so quickly, it's not worth it . . . Oh dear oh dear, the speeches are all a page and a half long, it's so much work . . . I doubt I'd be accepted in such a role these days . . . I don't think I can learn all of those lines . . .' – so I teased him, I said, 'Okay, go on then, keep on raising your eyebrows in light comedies and don't let anyone know if you can act in anything else or not. It's up to you, darling.' This sort of thing went on between us for ages. But I wouldn't let up. I'd keep saying, 'Can I just quote you this bit?' And he'd say, 'No! I don't want to hear it!' I practically knew the whole damned thing by heart before he really started on it! And then eventually he gave in and said, 'Oh, go on then, I'll bloody well do it!'[28]

With this predictable period of procrastination now over, the thought of the role proved irresistible, and, with a good deal of encouragement from Joan, he threw himself into his preparations for the production. Contrary to the image that he liked to project of being a fairly lazy actor, he was actually very detailed and disciplined about how he prepared for each performance, so he found it frustrating, initially, that there was barely any reliable information, at that time, on Kim Philby and his activities. It did not take long, however, before he started to lose himself in the lines, concentrating on building up a sense of Adrian Harris as a distinct individual and feeling increasingly familiar with his world. As Joan explained:

> We went down to Ramsgate and spent about three weeks alone together doing nothing but just going through the part and constantly hearing the words, because John was always terribly proud about going into the first day of rehearsal properly 'off-book' without the script.

But this time, even after all of that preparation, he was still so nervous he asked me to go in with him on the first day, to sit at the back and give him some moral support.[29]

The rehearsals were held over a sixteen-day period between the middle of April and the start of May. By the time of the recording (from 9 to 11 May), he was ready, word perfect and fully absorbed in the complex personality of the edgy, evasive, vulnerable but still defiant double agent.

The play – broadcast, as an edition of BBC1's *Play for Today* drama strand, on 14 October 1971 – begins with Harris sitting alone in his cold and cramped high-rise apartment, rearranging the books, cigarettes, pencils, pens and nibs on his desk in an obsessive-compulsive fashion as the dull sound of routine construction work drones on incessantly outside. Crumpled inside his creased grey suit, and cradling a half-empty bottle of whisky, he looks up at a small picture of the fair and deep-meadowed English countryside that is hanging on the otherwise bare and grubby wall, and, as he sips his Scotch, he grimaces as he reminisces about a simpler, if not kinder, time. When his daydreams are interrupted by the ring of the door bell, he tries to pour his drink back into the bottle and gets up, anxiously, to meet the waiting journalists: 'Come in, "gentlemen", if that is the curious appellation you even more curiously prefer.' As they sit down and attempt to introduce themselves, he wastes no time in underlining the obvious contempt that he feels for all of his guests: 'I don't give a damn who you are. You all have the same sort of employers, after all. You could be called Nelly Dean for all I care. I'm sure that you will agree, upon reflection, that your particular private claims to individuality will have precious little consequence when your sub-editors get their dirty little paws on what will no doubt be your dirty little copy, so, you see, your names don't matter to me.' He then, without any sign of enthusiasm, invites them to ask him questions – 'brief and to the point'.

One of them asks him if his 'journey of duplicity' from Eton, Oxford and the Foreign Office to a 'sparse little room' in Moscow has made him happy. 'Happy?' he sneers:

Happy? Well, what's that got to do with it? What's this room got to do with it? I mean, if it had expensive furniture and fitted carpets and stuff I suppose that you would think my 'duplicity', as you call it, would be that much more worthwhile. You see, you all come from countries that judge a man by his material possessions rather than his mind. You're all so corrupted by this vulgar heresy of sales that you cannot help but judge what I have done in terms of the furniture in this miserable little room. And I'll tell you this: if I have to end up in a bare cell, without any colour or light, I would still have been right. And I would still do what I have done all over again.[30]

He goes on to rail against the 'cant and claptrap' of the country of his youth, driven by the 'horse dung and sicked-up bile of politicians' and the 'festering hypocrisies of the English ruling families'; denounces the preening shallowness of his privileged upbringing: 'I went straight from my prep school to Eton, from Eton to Oxford, from Oxford to the Brigade of Guards, from the Guards to the Foreign Office – all the way from a nursery with a wooden rocking horse in it to a nursery with a rocking horse in it!'; and dismisses the caring pretensions of the supposedly liberal establishment: 'They're no more aware of the poverty and the filth and the stunted opportunities or the true nature of the lives of most of their fellow citizens than they are of the landscape on Mars!' His identity as an 'English communist', he continues to insist, has never troubled his conscience.

When he hears the word 'traitor', however, he looks mortally wounded. 'Traitor?' he says, his voice quavering a little. 'To my class? Yes. To my country? No. Not to England.' He gets up, glass in hand, and walks over to gaze at the gently idyllic picture on his wall. 'It's hardly socialist realism, is it?' one of the journalists mutters sarcastically. Harris, however, though rattled and the worse for drink, continues to stare ahead and insist that he still loves England – his England – regardless of what his critics might think, and in spite of the English lives that his actions have cost. His England, he says, softening, is still suggested by the richness of the picture on display:

All soft, damp light and gentle colours suddenly leaping into brilliance – or slowly fading into a river haze or a dark overhanging hedgerow . . . the water mill, and the cricket field, and gentle faces . . . lemonade in the haystack . . . rooks coagulating on the tall bare trees like premature blobs of night . . .

It is only the 'other' England that he claims to have betrayed: the cruel and class-ridden one that he can still picture in his mind 'painted in blood and tears and sweat and slime and shit'. He is, by this stage, too drunk and distressed to continue coherently, and the journalists, visibly disgusted at his pathetic state, soon decide to put on their coats and prepare to go. 'I saw,' he mumbles as they leave, 'what people lived like.'

The play closes with a flashback to the start, but this time, as the journalists make their way up the stairs to the apartment, we see Harris inside, not just touching things in a pointlessly fussy way but checking to see if the telephone is tapped and then finding a surveillance bug hidden beneath a table. 'Ah, they don't trust me,' he mutters to himself, his sad mouth twisted up into a faint wry smile. Then the door bell rings and he tries to pour his drink back into the bottle. 'Remember the microphone,' he thinks to himself as he rises, anxiously, to open the door, 'and be careful – and for God's sake remember the microphone.'

John would describe the role of Adrian Harris as 'the best part I ever had on TV',[31] and his performance – which was utterly compelling throughout – attracted uniformly positive and admiring reviews. Nancy Banks-Smith, writing in the *Guardian*, said of him: 'Cursed with so Hamlet-like a face, he seems to have been coerced into comedy. This, his Hamlet, was worth waiting for.'[32] John Lawrence, in *The Stage*, was more complimentary about John than he was about the play, applauding him for doing so well in what was 'an extremely difficult job . . . It is to his credit that one's attention was retained to the extent that it was'[33], while a critic in *The Times* praised him for making 'vividly real' a 'superbly persuasive portrait' via 'one of the best performances [he] has ever given'.[34]

The performance won him the year's Best Actor BAFTA, which he received in a ceremony at the Royal Albert Hall in March 1971. A very proud Joan was there to see him walk up to receive the award from Annette Crosbie, while Hattie Jacques watched at home with Robin and Kim, all three of them sitting in front of the television with tears in their eyes.

It was a great personal triumph for John. Although it would not stop him from being far too widely underrated and often taken for granted (even by some who really should have known better), it did prove, to those with an open mind, that he was capable of powerful and true dramatic performances as well as the most subtle kinds of character comedy.

David Croft, his *Dad's Army* director, would later remark somewhat surprisingly that, although he always considered him a 'dear man',[35] he 'never rated John very highly as an actor', arguing that he lacked versatility and was best understood as a mere 'behaviourist'.[36] The normally sharply astute Croft was in this instance surely wrong: not only did his own beautifully crafted sitcom demonstrate how technically clever John could really be, but also such plays as *Traitor*, though admittedly few and far between, revealed how much wider his range might have been if only he had been given more opportunity and encouragement.

It did not help that John, modest to a fault, was always so happy to dismiss his own talent. 'He never thought much of his work,' his old colleague Richard Briers would confirm, 'I thought he was marvellous!'[37] and, as Annette Crosbie reflected, 'He probably made it all look too easy . . . He didn't take himself, or the job of acting, so seriously as to persuade any producer or director that he or she was as essential as they liked to think.'[38] If he was guilty of anything in reality, however, it was never of an absence of ability; it had much more to do with a gradual diminution of ambition.

When the roles were genuinely rich and well-written, as was the case with Adrian Harris and Arthur Wilson, then he was inspired to push himself and produce some truly peerless performances. When, however, the roles were small, simplistic and underwritten, he invested more than the script deserved without always straining to reach the summit of his own high standards.

He had been far more innocently assiduous back in his days toiling away in rep, and then on into the 1950s during the first phase of his movie career. As that decade had progressed, however, a certain fatigue did creep in as he was asked to play yet another minor figure stranded on the fringes of the plot. In 1957, for example, the BBC producer Stuart Burge wrote to him apologetically about a forthcoming role (as Prosecuting Counsel in a TV play entitled *The Lafarge Affair*), explaining: 'You will see that the script gives very little idea of character, but, as in all such parts, it is dependent upon what the actor can contribute himself.'[39] The message, throughout the many years that followed, tended to be the same: turn this cliché into a real individual without taking any credit for the invention. His reliability continued to be exploited far too often by lazy writers and directors who knew they could leave him to warm up the raw role and turn the bland into the believable without any kind of catalyst, but he continued to be open to projects as good and demanding as *Traitor*, and, in the second half of the 1970s, he was deeply disappointed by the dearth of good-quality scripts.

Adaptations of Chekhov – including some of his darkly ironic short stories as well as his classic plays – would surely have suited John beautifully at this stage in his career, not only because of his cleverness, restraint and discipline as an actor but also because he himself had lived such a Chekhovian life. Twice cuckolded without losing either his dignity or his compassion, but cut to the quick all the same, he would surely have found precisely the right tone for the gently melancholic Chekhovian context, playing characters balanced so finely between the tragic and comic. When, for example, a wife says of the kind husband whom she has betrayed, 'That man crushes me with his magnanimity,'[40] it is not too hard to think of John. The poignant one-act play *Swan Song*, in which an elderly actor wakes up in his dressing room in an almost empty theatre and reflects on his life within the profession, would certainly have given him a worthwhile challenge, while the role of the ailing retired judge Peter Sorin in *The Seagull* or the sardonic but skint Count Shabelsky in *Ivanov* might well have inspired, *mutatis mutandis*, a memorably mature portrayal.

Instead of being asked to work with such rich material, however, the majority of the invitations that now came his way involved him doing little more than looking stern or bemused in isolated episodes of second-rate sitcoms or raising his eyebrows in comic 'sex romps'. Indeed, the first movie offer that he received after *Traitor* was a minor role in Val Guest's cheap and cheerless *Au Pair Girls*, a cheesy nosegay of pendulous breasts, drooping bottoms and flaccid jokes accompanied by the sound of clinky-clank guitars, patty-pat bongos and dozy saxophones, which obliged John to stroke a prostrate young woman's bare chest: a task that he executed with all the enthusiasm of someone searching for something edible on a tray of soggy canapés.

There were no bitter complaints from him about all of this, let alone any noisy tantrums. He never did do such things. He was normally so even-tempered and polite that, even when he did allow himself a rare moment of rudeness, his 'victim' invariably failed to recognise it for what it really was. On one such occasion, for example, a tiresome pipe-smoking minor television director interrupted a cosy night out in a club that John was enjoying with Joan by slapping him hard on the back and inviting himself to sit down with them at their table. Rolling his eyes, John leaned over to his wife and, still glaring at their unwelcome guest, groaned loudly, 'This man bores for England, you know, and I believe he's carried boredom abroad to Australia, isn't that right?' The man merely responded by exclaiming cheerfully, 'You are a card, John!', slapping him once again on the back and insisting on buying him a drink. John, raising an eyebrow wearily, accepted and returned to being polite.[41]

He remained, however, in his own discreet way, deeply devoted to the profession that had lured him away from the law almost half a century before. As Joan would say:

> While it's true that he'd never burned with ambition, he did care
> about acting. He really did. I remember once when we were on a tour
> abroad – we were just out shopping somewhere one afternoon – and
> this woman came up to him and said, 'Oh, I saw you in rep in 1938,
> in this very dramatic play, and your performance that night was one of
> the most wonderful I've ever seen!' And John was so thrilled to think
> she'd kept that memory of him as an actor. That sort of thing really
> meant something to him. And he wanted to do more things that
> would have that kind of effect on people, even though, typically, he
> always worried that they wouldn't.[42]

He coped on the set, whenever the project in question failed to excite him, by being a slyly stubborn performer. Once he had rehearsed a scene, working out his delivery and movements to his total satisfaction, he would not welcome the suggestion of any additional changes. If a request came from the production gallery to take another step forward or to the side before saying a line or moving a prop, John – rather than get embroiled in an argument – would simply claim, very sweetly, not to understand what was being proposed. 'I'm awfully sorry,' he would say, with a slight chuckle and a quick rub of an earlobe, 'but I don't quite see what you mean . . .' If another attempt was made, he would soften the hands and bat it straight back, very elegantly and charmingly, with another profession of complete incompetence – 'Oh dear, I really am very stupid, you know . . .' – and then do the scene exactly as he had planned.[43]

He was nonetheless rather disappointed, in private, by the apparent reluctance to consider him for some of the 'meatier' roles that some of his contemporaries were still getting on a regular basis. He did not crave to play King Lear, but he did long for something a little more engaging than yet another single day's work on set trying to make the most of a peripheral role as an interchangeable official.

A further reminder of his real range arrived when another impressive dramatic performance – filmed shortly before his decline in health – finally reached the screen at the start of 1978 under the banner of BBC1's *Play of the Month*. His portrayal in *Flint* of a rebellious clergyman (sporting a black leather jacket with 'Jesus Rules OK?' emblazoned on the back in big silver studs) with a weakness for motorbikes and young women once again received several very favourable reviews, but, once again, it failed to lead to a discernible increase in the number of above-average projects that were sent on via his agent. It was mainly for this reason that, towards the end of the year, he agreed, somewhat reluctantly, to travel to the Far East to star in a series of 'after-dinner' performances of Alan Ayckbourn's *Bedroom Farce*, beginning at the Hilton Playhouse in Hong Kong before moving on to similar Hilton-owned venues in Singapore and Kuala Lumpur. It was utterly uninspiring, but at least it was work – well-paid work – and, mercifully, it promised to take him away from what was threatening to be an extremely cold winter, enabling him to further improve his health in a far more clement climate.

He had, by this stage, started drinking alcohol again. After about a year and a half of imbibing nothing stronger than lemonade (which he had tried to supplement with the odd smoke of cannabis until concluding that such a substance, although much inhaled during his many marathon jazz club sessions, was not really 'my bag'[44]), he had succumbed to temptation and started having a furtive sip of beer at his local pub. Joan had found out via her and John's mutual friend Annie Ross, who in turn had been tipped off by an anxious Peter Campbell (in whom John had confided but then sworn to secrecy). Joan called in the family doctor once again to remind John of the harm that he was doing to his liver, and, following this severe admonition, he seemed to resume his alcohol-free routine. A few months later, however, he started returning from his daily trip to the local pub smelling of extra-strong mints, and an exasperated Joan tried to make him see the error of his ways: 'I nagged, pleaded and wept.'[45]

Eventually, out of desperation, she organised an informal family 'intervention', and had those who cared most about him urge him to stay on the wagon for good. He listened patiently to everyone's argument, but responded by defending, very politely, his own position: 'In all seriousness, my darling, I would rather have five years of living my way and having a drink from time to time with chums than ten years like this.'[46] He promised to drink nothing but beer, and only in moderation, but stressed that he was incapable of giving up alcohol completely. Joan, resigning herself reluctantly to their shared fate, feared that she would now have to watch her husband deteriorate at a distressingly rapid rate, but, improbably enough, the opposite seemed to happen: 'The funny thing was that as soon as beer was back on his diet, he started to put on weight [and] the colour came back to his face.' It was a strangely illogical way for such a crisis to have been averted, even in the short term, but both of them were far too relieved to feel like questioning how it had happened. 'We were closer then than ever,' Joan later reflected, 'and happier. His illness had been a sharp reminder of the impermanence of things.'[47]

Joan was thus delighted to accompany John when he embarked on his tour of the Far East, relishing the chance to shake off some of their recent worries in an unfamiliar environment. The Asian luxury hotel 'supper club scene' was quite a burgeoning phenomenon at the time – apart from John's company, musical acts such as the New Seekers and Sandie Shaw were currently working there in cabaret and several other well-known British actors and comedians, including Derek Jacobi, Timothy West, Isla Blair, Derek Nimmo, Ronnie Corbett, Miriam Karlin, Alfred Marks and Dave Allen, were performing to enthusiastic audiences at various other venues – and it certainly made a change from the old provincial theatre circuit back at home.

John coasted through his shows, relaxed with Joan at the race tracks, restaurants and nightclubs, took in some of the traditional tourist sights and rather enjoyed the vague unreality of the whole experience. He was brought back down to earth with a bump, however, when he returned home in March 1979 to find that, if anything, things had grown worse than ever during his absence: 'The post was full of bills, but not much in the way of suggestions for paying them.'[48]

He was greatly relieved, therefore, when Peter Campbell proceeded to prove himself far more active and 'hands-on' than his previous agent (who was notorious for turning down precious offers of work on the assumption that something better would sooner or later turn up[49]) had ever been. Freddy Joachim, John would say, had ended up making him feel a little too taken for granted, to the point where he suspected that he was considered 'a Second XI client'. 'On the very rare occasions he took me out to lunch,' John reflected, 'it was never the Ivy, always the cafeteria at Bourne and Hollingsworth.'[50] Campbell, on the other hand, visited John regularly, listened to his concerns and made a genuine effort to alleviate his financial anxieties.

Two projects that he had arranged were already 'in the can': one a decent cameo role in an edition of Michael Palin and Terry Jones's fine BBC2 comedy series *Ripping Yarns* (which was due to be broadcast in the autumn) and the other a very well-remunerated supporting part in the colourful Disney-produced comic fantasy *The Spaceman and King Arthur* (which was set for a summer release). Campbell moved promptly to add some radio plays, including a quirky one called *The Kamikaze Ground Staff Reunion Dinner* for BBC Radio 3, and – playing the role of The Wise Old Bird – *The Hitchhiker's Guide to the Galaxy* for BBC Radio 4. He also secured an above-average ITV comedy-drama called *An Honourable Retirement* (in which John played a retired civil servant and amateur angler given to fantasising about his supposed exploits as a spy) and some lucrative voiceovers, as well as some well-paid work in Val Guest's next movie, *The Shillingbury Blowers*, and a planned Peter Sellers project entitled *The Fiendish Plot of Dr Fu Manchu*.

With his career apparently back on track and his finances suitably boosted, John found it easier to enjoy, in his own inimitable way, his personal life at home. Joan, by her own admission, had by this time become a 'gardening fanatic', buying a greenhouse and turning a large part of the land over to a wide range of plants and vegetables. John's involvement in the enterprise was limited to watching her from the comfort of his peacock chair on the patio, shouting out occasionally such encouraging questions as, 'Do you really like doing this?' but he did enjoy the sense that they were 'sharing' a leisure experience.[51] They also went shopping together on a fairly regular basis, although Joan was bemused by the way in which this particular activity turned her normally vague and lackadaisical husband into such a lively and decisive operator:

He knew exactly what he wanted, and the speed with which he
entered and left the premises was nothing short of mercurial. 'I'll have
this jacket,' he would say to the assistant, picking the most expensive
cashmere from the rack. He never asked the price. In the shoe
department he gave the same performance. 'These shoes in my size?'
he would say, and somehow they always seemed to fit. He would then
rush off to the nearest bar, leaving me to pay and wait for the goods to
be wrapped.[52]

Inside their home he remained as impractical as ever, relying on
Joan to do all of the cooking, cleaning and DIY, responding to each of
her efforts with an awestruck expression and the usual grateful
exclamation, 'How very kind of you, you've just saved my life.'[53] His
children had always harboured the suspicion that he sometimes
exaggerated his helplessness in order to avoid any onerous-sounding
household chores; Robin, indeed, would say that his father 'should
have got a BAFTA for portraying vague'.[54] Joan sometimes felt the
same – 'I know he did it on purpose, it was subtle and funny, an in
joke'[55] – but there was no real doubt that, left to his own devices, he
would have struggled to look after himself, let alone anyone else. He
did try, on one rare occasion when Joan succumbed to influenza and
was bedridden for a few days, to venture into the kitchen, but the
experiment came to an abrupt halt after he informed her that he had
made her some tea by heating the leaves inside the electric kettle and
left a 'boil in the bag' curry to cook on the top shelf of the oven.

Although Joan remained, in many ways, a 'modern' woman with an
indomitably strong streak of individuality, she had long since
reconciled herself to fulfilling some of John's very traditional
expectations about the responsibilities of a wife. His agent, Peter
Campbell, had once suggested that she consider a career of her own as
a theatrical agent, but the idea was nipped swiftly in the bud by her
highly alarmed husband. 'Peter suggested I went in with him working
at his agency,' Joan would recall, 'and I would have liked to have done
that, but John didn't want me to. He was very against it – not in a
domineering way, because he wasn't ever like that, but he just said,
"Oh, dear! There'll be calls in the middle of the night from actors,
begging to be reassured or consoled or something awful like that.
Please don't take all of that on because I'm enough trouble on my
own!" So that was that.' She knew that he was never going to change:

'He needed someone to look after him, but I was never under any illusions about that, and I didn't resent it. After all, he was such a lovely man.'[56]

Theirs had always been a marriage of opposites – Joan was active and volatile, John passive and pacific – but, having somehow survived their terrible early crisis (or, as John would always prefer to call it, the time 'when you were AWOL, darling'[57]), they had settled into a relationship that, while remaining somewhat unconventional, really worked. Both of them had been guilty over the years of the odd one-night stand or brief little fling or flirtation – Joan because her grand affair with Tony Hancock had left her with 'a taste for passion and drama' and John because women were often attracted to him. As Joan would put it, 'He was so polite that he really didn't like to refuse anyone. John would never go lusting after anyone. But women really, really liked him. We'd go to parties and he'd immediately be surrounded by women, listening to his every word, trying to hold his hand and all of that. There'd always be plenty of offers!'[58] Neither of them, however, had ever considered these so-called 'adventures' to have been anything other than harmless 'passing fancies'.[59] John agreed with Joan when she reflected that, if they could overcome the trauma caused by her time away with Hancock, 'we could weather just about anything',[60] and both of them were now very happy and relaxed within the marriage. One of the cards that he often left for her around the house ended with the remark, 'Just to know you are about somewhere in my life is to me enough,' and he really meant it.[61]

Apart from relaxing with Joan, John also met up whenever possible with his two sons, Robin and Kim (who by this time was answering – to anyone other than his father, mother and stepmother – to the name of Jake). Both of them had left school as soon as they could and were now pursuing careers as professional musicians, Robin as a guitarist and Jake as a drummer and part-time roadie. As Robin would later explain:

We'd both been given free rein by our parents to do what we wanted to do and neither of us had been interested in following them into the theatre. But one of the things my father did once say to me was that he'd have preferred to have earned a living playing the piano instead of acting, which I always found quite intriguing. And one great thing that he did was to introduce me to Ronnie Scott's as soon as I was old enough to go, and I met some wonderful people there. I met Oscar Peterson, for example, through him, and many other great musicians, and it was all quite an inspiration growing up.[62]

Robin had graduated from an initial spell with his own rock band, Reign, to spend three years hidden in a furry costume as one of Mike Batt's Wombles, before signing a solo publishing deal with Riva Records, relocating to America and becoming a much-respected member of Rod Stewart's touring band. His younger brother Jake, meanwhile, was still seeking a means to establish himself better in the business, but was acquiring plenty of worthwhile experience working for a wide range of more experienced performers. John, as a devout admirer of all dedicated 'jobbing musicians', took a sincere interest in following his two sons' careers, and was always pleased to find out more at first hand as to how each was faring.

In 1978, Robin had collaborated very happily with John on an album inspired by a children's book called *The Velveteen Rabbit* – 'I read the story,' Robin explained, 'thought it had possibilities and then asked Pa if he'd come on it too'[63] – and the memory of the shared experience was something that both men would always treasure. Jake, too, made the most of his visits to see John down in Ramsgate, where they could catch up on each other's activities, and was always pleased to act as a sounding-board when his father was pondering whether or not to participate in a possible project. 'We get on wonderfully well,' John said of his relationship with both of his sons. 'I've always treated the boys as friends. Occasionally they come to me for advice.'[64] He would add with a shy sense of pride that, like him, they were the kind of people 'who are not motivated by eagerness for fame. We just want satisfying work – and survival.'[65]

Other regular visitors to the house in Ramsgate included Derek Taylor, Peter Campbell, Annie Ross and Mark Eden, as well as Joan and Mark's own son, David. John would often take great pleasure in entertaining all of them after dinner by singing Noël Coward songs, reciting prose and poetry or, his favourite party piece, reading aloud excerpts from *Married to Wilfred* by Mabel Pickles (a memoir about her life with the first in a long line of self-admiring 'professional Yorkshiremen' broadcasters that John found so entertaining he rarely got through more than a couple of pages without collapsing into a fit of laughter). 'It was definitely a case of laughing at them, not with them,' Joan would recall fondly. 'It was just so wonderfully corny, it always made John hoot!'[66] One po-faced passage by Mrs Pickles that never failed to do the trick was the following account of the arrival of bedtime on their honeymoon night:

> My very special pink satin nightgown, lace-trimmed, had enchanted me in the shop. Now I would much rather have been in sweater and brogues and tweed skirt, striding with Wilfred over the sand dunes. Beneath the wall-light above our heads Wilfred's hair looked a startling red against the blue of his poplin pyjamas. We gazed unhappily at each other. Before I realised what I was saying, I blurted out: 'I wish we were at home around the piano, singing "Lily of Laguna".' 'So do I,' admitted Wilfred.[67]

John also enjoyed the company of the people he encountered during his twice-daily trips to the pub (where he eagerly gleaned all of the local gossip). The local rag-and-bone man, bearing the unforgettable name of Turd Cox, was a particular favourite, bringing a smile to John's face whenever they met out in the street: 'Morning, John!' 'Good morning, Turd!'[68] When his stepson, David, joined him inside the pub, John would relish playing a private little game that involved matching each new customer to his or her drink of choice. Joan would recall: 'As people came in and went past to buy a drink, John would look at them discreetly and then whisper to David things like, "That one will be . . . a brown ale, and the other one's . . . a sweet sherry." And quite often he got it right. He and David would always play little games like that, and really get the giggles. They got on very, very well.'[69] Even when John found himself at home alone, he could always keep himself entertained for hours on end either by reading and listening to music, or just by sitting back and watching the antics of his and Joan's two pet cats, Maime and Nicodemus.

There was never a time, however, when John could afford to pass on a well-paid project, so play continued to be interrupted by work. Apart from his movie, radio and television projects, he was also lured back to the West End stage in the spring of 1980 when the director Michael Blakemore cast him in one of the starring roles, alongside Constance Cummings, in a high-profile revival of the 1920s Noël Coward play *Hay Fever*.[70]

The last time John had appeared in a production of this classic comedy of manners (about a bohemian family whose theatrical excesses torment a group of unsuspecting visitors) had been back in his days in rep, when he had been assigned one of the younger roles, but now, at the age of sixty-eight, he was going to take the leading part of David Bliss, a self-absorbed novelist co-existing awkwardly with his fading thespian wife Judith and their two spoilt children. He was anxious about the challenge, regarding the play, with its abrupt changes of mood and tempo, as Coward's 'trickiest', but, when the production opened at the Lyric, Hammersmith, on 23 April, he was sufficiently in control of the material to appear calm and composed in his role, and the critics were quick to applaud his efforts. His co-star Constance Cummings, however, was deemed by some to be miscast as a *monstre théâtrale* like Judith, and the production as a whole failed to excite many of the reviewers. It did nonetheless attract full houses during its run, and then, with Glynis Johns replacing Cummings, went out on a fairly lengthy provincial tour.

At the start of the new decade, therefore, John's prospects seemed rather positive. His health was better than it had been for some time, his home life was happy and his career was keeping him busy. He might not have followed *Dad's Army* with anything of similarly high quality, but at least, as a self-styled 'jobbing actor', he was still very much in demand, and still very much beloved by the British public. What he hoped to do next was simply, and humbly, to keep on going for as long as he possibly could.

CHAPTER XV

Conking Out

I'm fed up of it now.

The year 1980 turned out, in some ways, to be a troubling one for John Le Mesurier. His own career muddled on, but intimations of mortality would never leave him alone. Apart from the depressing knowledge that both Terry-Thomas and Kenneth More were losing their long and painful battles against Parkinson's disease, and David Niven was beginning to show the effects of a form of motor neurone disorder that would soon be diagnosed as amyotrophic lateral sclerosis (also known as Lou Gehrig's disease), he was further shaken when several other old friends passed away. In June, for example, his *Dad's Army* comrade John Laurie died of emphysema, and in July Peter Sellers suffered a fatal heart attack. The loss that he would feel most keenly of all, however, occurred on Monday 6 October, with the premature death, aged just fifty-eight, of his former wife Hattie Jacques.

It was their youngest son, Jake, who called him early that morning with the news that she had slipped away during the night. She had been in poor health for some time, with her burgeoning weight placing a growing strain on her heart, and had also been dogged by ulcerated legs and serious breathing problems exacerbated by her incessant smoking. John – who was staying in London at the time (in a rented flat in Shepherds Bush) while *Hay Fever* continued its run – was stunned: he had last seen her just a couple of days earlier, when he had visited Eardley Crescent. She had seemed much like her old ebullient self, so it took a while for the facts to sink in. It was not long, however, before the telephone started to ring with requests for his public response, so he had to recover his composure quickly, organise help for Jake and Robin, contact other friends and family members, and then deal with the waiting media. 'We have lost a very remarkable lady,' John told reporters. 'I feel very shocked and full of grief. She had a wealth of talent which was often underestimated. Some people are dim-witted at times. They see a large lady and can't see further. She always showed tremendous generosity and kindness to other people and was a great giver of thought and help.'[1]

The funeral took place at the Putney Vale Crematorium in Chiswick, south-west London. John, accompanied by Joan, attended alongside Robin and Jake and many more of Hattie's close family and friends. Before entering the building, he encountered a small group of onlookers who were sitting outside beneath a tree. Joan later recalled:

> One of them said, 'We're very sorry to hear about Hattie. We've come all the way from Fulham – we all just wanted to be here to pay our respects.' John said, 'Oh, how kind,' in his gentlemanly way. And he said, 'Look, I'm sure we could possibly find room at the back of the church if you'd like to come in and stand there.' And this woman said, 'No, no, it's your private grief and we wouldn't want to intrude.' And then as we came out, the same ladies were still there, and one of them said to John, 'I don't suppose you could give us a lift back to Fulham, could you?' And John absolutely roared with laughter.[2]

Although, as things turned out, there was not enough room in any of the cars for him to comply with their request, John reflected that, if Hattie had still been around, she would somehow have managed to find a happy solution. She always did.

A 'joyous' memorial service followed soon after, at which John paid generous tribute to his former wife for being 'a giver' rather than a 'taker': 'She had an aura of kindness around her.'[3] Then, over the Christmas period, he honoured Hattie's memory, and her indefatigably festive spirit, by hosting a suitably lavish party at her old home for all of her usual guests. Greatly touched by the fact that, shortly before her death, and sensing that she might not be around to distribute them herself, she had already bought and labelled presents for him and their sons and many of her friends, he made sure that the festivities were as elaborate and extravagant as she would have wanted. Once the party was over, however, he was left to reminisce alone about the woman – not the public Hattie but the private Jo – whom he had lost but never really stopped loving.

He wrote a letter to Derek Taylor at the start of 1981: 'I am so glad last year is over and done with,' he said, 'so many of my loved ones disappeared, and it was a sod from a professional point of view.'[4] Taylor, who was himself grieving deeply over the murder of his own close friend John Lennon, could only concur, but he tried to strike a positive note by ending his reply with a line taken from the prayer that John had recorded for his album: 'Such an unhappy year in so many ways but for now, while we live, let our thoughts be for the living.'[5]

It came as something of a merciful relief, after coping with too many sad moments of mourning, that John was kept very busy for much of 1981 with his career, not only touring with *Hay Fever* but also working on a number of other projects for radio, television and movies. He played the ageing Bilbo Baggins, for example, in a BBC Radio 4 adaptation of J.R.R. Tolkien's *The Lord of the Rings* trilogy. 'It's a bit too fey for me,' he confided to Derek Taylor. 'But I have friends like Michael Hordern, Ian Holm and Robert Stephens in it – they don't understand it either.'[6] He also appeared as the family priest Father Mowbray in an episode of Granada TV's extremely well-received production of Evelyn Waugh's *Brideshead Revisited*, and he took part in a short film, featuring several dramatised poems by Sir John Betjeman, entitled *Late Flowering Love* – John played Colonel Hunter Dunn in a segment inspired by 'A Subaltern's Love-Song'. The most pleasantly sentimental engagement of the year, however, arrived during the summer when he was reunited with his old comedy sparring partner Arthur Lowe for a BBC Radio 2 spin-off of *Dad's Army* called *It Sticks Out Half a Mile*.

Conceived by the show's two writers, Harold Snoad and Michael Knowles, as a 'sequel' to the TV sitcom, the pilot episode of *It Sticks Out Half a Mile* was set three years after the war had ended, in 1948. It began with George Mainwaring – now retired ('early, of course') from managing the bank and back in Britain after a brief spell abroad as a supervisor at a cuckoo clock company in Switzerland – deciding to renovate a decrepit seaside pier in the quaint little south-east English town of Frambourne (just up the coast from Walmington-on-Sea), only to find when applying for a bank loan that the manager of the local branch is none other than his former chief cashier and Home Guard Sergeant Arthur Wilson.

John greatly enjoyed working with Arthur Lowe again, and the feeling was mutual. Picking up from where they had left off as

Mainwaring and Wilson, the two talented character actors seemed to rejuvenate each other, interacting so smartly that they made even the more banal parts of their dialogue sound funny and, once again, endearingly real. The opening scene in Swallow Bank set the tone well:

WILSON:	Er, come in, Mr Mainwaring.
MAINWARING:	Good Lord! Wilson – it *is* you!
WILSON:	Ha ha, yes. I'd have to agree with you there.
MAINWARING:	What are you doing here, Wilson? At this branch? In this office? I mean, where's the manager?
WILSON:	Well, actually, you're looking at him.
MAINWARING:	You? You're the manager?
WILSON:	Yes, that's right.
MAINWARING:	Standing in because of illness I suppose?
WILSON:	No, no, no, no, no. I've been manager here for exactly a year today as a matter of fact.
MAINWARING:	Good Lord!
WILSON:	Yes. Well, why don't you sit down before you fall down?
MAINWARING:	Thank you.
WILSON:	Yes, it's awfully good to see you again. While I was at Bexhill I heard that you'd left Walmington-on-Sea and gone abroad.
MAINWARING:	Yes. That's right.
WILSON:	Well, whatever made you decide to do that?
MAINWARING:	Well, after you left, I began to realise that banking didn't mean quite the same for me any more.
WILSON:	Oh, what a lovely thing to say! I'm really quite touched!
MAINWARING:	You've no need to be. My decision had absolutely nothing to do with your leaving.
WILSON:	Oh, really?
MAINWARING:	Oh, good heavens, no! It was just that, after having been in the front line of this country's defences, suddenly being just a bank manager again seemed rather tame somehow.
WILSON:	Oh, I see.[7]

The edginess of the old relationship was promptly restored before the plot proceeded any further:

WILSON: Anything you tell me is in the strictest confidence.
                 After all, I am a bank manager.
MAINWARING: Not to me you're not! To me, you'll always be
                 Sergeant Wilson.
WILSON: Ah, yes. But you must remember that time changes
                 lots of things. Now, how can I help you, er, Mr
                 Mainwaring? Or perhaps, as we went through so
                 much together in the Home Guard days, I could
                 call you by your first name?
MAINWARING: My first name?
WILSON: Yes. You know . . . George.
MAINWARING: I know what it is, thank you!
WILSON: And you could call me Arthur. What do you say?
MAINWARING: Well, somehow I don't think that would be very
                 businesslike.

Having persuaded Wilson, eventually, to allow him to realise his dream of restoring the pier, Mainwaring, as he signs the papers at Frambourne Council HQ, is clearly also looking forward to restoring what he regards as the proper status quo:

MAINWARING: Well, Wilson . . . er, Arthur . . . We made it –
                 Frambourne Pier is mine! All mine.
WILSON: Well, it will be, in twenty years, when you've paid
                 off the loan.
MAINWARING: Oh, don't worry – the bank will get its money back.
                 Have I ever let you down?
WILSON: Well . . . I distinctly remember several, er . . .
MAINWARING: Yes, all right, all right . . .

Both Le Mesurier and Lowe considered the completed recording to be a success, and agreed to return when the writers had enough episodes to turn the pilot show into a series. John spent that Christmas with Joan in California as the guests of his son, Robin, who was appearing at a number of major venues there with Rod Stewart. It was a strikingly unconventional way for him to spend the festive season, but, as Robin would later recall, the experience proved a special one for the two men, as adult friends as well as father and son, to bond more closely than ever: 'Dad and Joanie came to San Francisco and saw us play there, then they came and stayed with us in Los Angeles and took in another show. The great thing was then that I could do it for him. I could get him the tickets, have him come to the concert and have a good time. It was wonderful, a really great time, having him there on my turf, so to speak.'[8] Joan Le Mesurier confirmed that, although the rock music left his ears ringing temporarily, the visit 'did John the world of good':

> I tried to leave him and Robin alone when they had a chance to just relax together, and I think that John got the chance to get a few things off his chest while he was there – things like his guilt at not being around so much during the early years, and talk a bit about Hattie and share the sense of loss that really only they could know – and he was really very proud of Robin and what he had achieved purely through his own efforts.[9]

John returned to Britain at the start of the following year feeling refreshed and eager to link up again with Arthur Lowe. There was even talk of adapting the show for television if the radio ratings proved strong, so hopes were high. The plans for an extended reunion, however, were thwarted abruptly and cruelly when Arthur Lowe died, on 15 April 1982 at the age of sixty-six, shortly after suffering a stroke in his dressing room at the Alexandra Theatre in Birmingham. Shocked and saddened by this latest loss, John joined the other surviving members of *Dad's Army* in paying a proper public tribute to their old colleague and commanding officer. With reluctance, the existing recording of the pilot episode, still not broadcast, was put back discreetly on the shelf.

The air of nostalgia, however, continued to hover over John's career during the rest of the year. He collaborated with Clive Dunn on a novelty song – written by Joan's son David Malin – called 'There Ain't Much Change from a Pound These Days' which was released as a single. As Joan would recall:

> That came about from an idea of John's. It was one of those phrases that he kept hearing crusty old majors and other characters saying in

pubs: 'There's not much change from a pound these days!' So David, who by that time had started his own career as a musician, thought it would be fun to write a song about it. And John and Clive liked it and recorded it. I think it enjoyed the dubious distinction of being one of the lowest-selling records of the year, but they all really enjoyed doing it, and that was the main thing.[10]

Recording it felt like a nice little 'family affair', and John relished the chance to relax and reminisce with his old friend. During their conversations, he reminded Dunn of the time when his young daughter, having grown bored while attending a matinee, had announced very loudly: 'I'm fed up of it now. I want to go home.'[11] He laughed and said how he and Joan now used the phrase whenever either of them sensed that tedium was setting in.

Another brief but enjoyable reunion occurred a little later in the year, when he made a guest appearance in an episode (entitled 'Carnival Time') of the popular David Croft and Jimmy Perry BBC1 sitcom *Hi-de-Hi!* Playing Hugo Buxton, the haughty Provost of Jeffrey Fairbrother's alma mater, King's College, Cambridge, he arrived at Maplins holiday camp to persuade the doggedly donnish entertainments manager to return to academia as the Chair of his old faculty. It was merely a cameo role that afforded John little to do apart from reacting silently to the chaos that unfurled in front of his eyes, but he gelled well in those brief scenes that he shared with the similarly artful Simon Cadell as the hapless Fairbrother.

After watching the so-called entertainers set fire to their own carnival float and crash into a swimming pool, Buxton barks: 'I can't think of one logical reason for you to stay here a second longer in this mad house!' Fairbrother, however, though soaked and supposedly humbled, is unexpectedly defiant: 'You see these people, Hugo? They're real, they're alive and they are my friends. They devote their waking hours to making people happy and I am proud to be one of them!' Buxton scowls and, just before spinning around and flouncing off back to his college, shouts: 'Oh, round spherical objects!'[12]

The remainder of 1982 saw John meander through several episodes of a critically panned Thames TV detective spoof called *Bognor* and Channel 4's bewilderingly uneven supernatural comedy series (starring Andrew Sachs as an erroneously deceased pools winner) entitled *Dead Ernest*. It was all fairly well-paid work and he was grateful for it, but it failed to really engage him. He was far more enthusiastic about the unexpected revival of *It Sticks Out Half a Mile*, which had been encouraged by the suggestion from Arthur Lowe's widow, Joan Cooper, to rewrite it for a new cast: 'Arthur thought it had so much potential,' she said.[13] John was now reunited with two more of his old *Dad's Army* colleagues, Ian Lavender and Bill Pertwee, and a new pilot episode – featuring this time Arthur Wilson as the bank manager and Pike and Hodges as the duo intent on renovating Frambourne pier – was recorded in September. A full series was swiftly commissioned by the BBC, and, in addition to the pilot, twelve more episodes were recorded over February and March of the following year.

John sounded on fine form in this new but still very familiar fiction. The first scene that he shared with Ian Lavender as Frank Pike, for example, when Wilson's nosey secretary Miss Perkins brings the young man into his office, drew deftly on memories of the former sitcom to set up the current plot as swiftly as possible:

PIKE: Hello, Uncle Arthur.
WILSON: [*Trying to remain businesslike*] Good morning, Mr Pike.
             Well, it must be ages since we last met. When was it now?
PIKE: Last night.
WILSON: Ah, yes, er, well, thank you, Miss Perkins, that'll be all.
PERKINS: Yes, sir. [*She leaves the room*]
WILSON: What on earth are you doing here, Frank?
PIKE: I made an appointment.
WILSON: Ah yes, I know that, but I still don't understand. I mean,
             I had supper with you and Mavis, er, your mother,
             yesterday at your home, and you didn't say then you'd
             made an appointment to see me this morning.
PIKE: I didn't want Mum to know! And I didn't get a chance to
             tell you after supper 'cos Mum sent me to bed early. Ooh,
             by the way, I found your pyjama bottoms on the
             bathroom towel rail this morning. What were they doing
             in our house?
WILSON: Ah. Um, they'll be the ones your mother very kindly
             laundered for me. I expect she was airing them.
PIKE: Oh. Why weren't they in the airing cupboard then?
WILSON: Well, ah, it was probably full.

PIKE:	No, it wasn't, 'cos I got a clean pair of pants out this morning and it was practically empty. Anyway, they were all creased.
WILSON:	Your pants?
PIKE:	No, your pyjama bottoms.
WILSON:	Well, perhaps she hasn't ironed them yet!
PIKE:	She always irons them before she airs them.
WILSON:	Well, ah, oh, I don't know, anyway, I'm a very busy man, Frank, I can't sit here all the morning talking about bottoms and pants! Now, why did you want to see me?
PIKE:	I want to talk to you about money.[14]

Once Pike has shocked Wilson with the news that he not only wants a loan but also intends to invest it all in the pier, he cranks up the pressure by threatening to tell his mother some gossip he has heard about what Wilson got up to when he first arrived in Frambourne:

WILSON:	Er, now, look, Frank. On reflection, perhaps you do deserve a chance to try your hand at something new. So I'll give you a loan – but for goodness sake don't let me down!
PIKE:	Oh, don't worry, Uncle Arthur, I won't! And thank you very much! I'm sorry about the blackmail bit, but at least it proves I'm not that stupid.
WILSON:	[*Sadly*] Yes. It does indeed.

The next step, before the story moved on, was to reintroduce Wilson to the 'frightfully common' ex-ARP warden Bert Hodges:

HODGES:	Long time no see, eh, Mr Wilson?
WILSON:	Yes, ha ha, er, yes, it is, mmm.
HODGES:	You haven't changed much.
WILSON:	No, ah, nor have you.
HODGES:	I can just imagine what you said when you found out that I was Frank's partner!
WILSON:	Can you really?
HODGES:	Yeah: 'Not that awful greengrocer!'
WILSON:	Well, I, er . . .
PIKE:	Isn't that funny, Uncle Arthur – that's just what you said!
WILSON:	Frank! Just be quiet, please!

Hodges promises success ('You know what you get from little acorns?') while Wilson predicts setbacks ('Yes – big nuts!'), and the 'seaside saga of post-war pier perpetuation' rolls on. Some of the subsequent episodes (which were broadcast later in the year) would fall rather flat, certainly by the very high standards of *Dad's Army*, but the unforced rapport between Le Mesurier, Lavender and Pertwee kept the series sufficiently entertaining to justify it as a spin-off, and it was certainly an enjoyable show for the three of them to make. 'It was like one last get-together,' Bill Pertwee would say, 'one last party with great friends.'[15]

By this time, however, John – now aged seventy – was visibly tiring, and, as the new year began, his appetite for fresh challenges seemed to atrophy quite rapidly. In March 1983, he managed to deliver a very decent performance in the four-part London Weekend Television adaptation of Piers Paul Read's novel *A Married Man*, a drama about an unsettled barrister who turns to politics, directed by John Howard Davies and starring Anthony Hopkins but, although he charmed cast and crew alike with his usual dry wit – 'He was a dear man and a good friend,' Davies would recall, 'who had the remarkable ability to make me laugh every time I met him'[16] – the project left him drained. He went on to record voiceovers for a couple of short films – a bizarre sci-fi musical called *Facelift* and the charming Eric Morecambe vehicle *The Passionate Pilgrim* – but seemed to lack the energy to take on any of the acting offers that were still coming in. Perhaps, having seen more of his old friends die over recent months, he was becoming more anxious about his own mortality, but he started to suffer from the kind of nightmares that made him wake up in a fearful sweat. Early one summer morning, for example, he turned to Joan and, white-faced and trembling, proceeded to tell her about a vivid dream in which Arthur Lowe had appeared and said cheerfully, 'Come on, Johnny, we're all waiting for you. Don't tell Joanie.'[17]

About three weeks later, on Tuesday 5 July, John fell ill and began to haemorrhage. Joan rushed off to call for an ambulance, and John was taken straight to the local hospital. Although the consultant managed to stop the bleeding, he warned that the problem could quite conceivably happen again in the near future. Robin Le Mesurier, fortunately, was able to visit his father soon after the initial treatment:

I was on tour again at the time in Europe, I think at that stage we were in Lyon, and I suddenly got an impacted wisdom tooth, and, although I had to get back on tour as soon as possible, I knew Dad was sick, so I came back to England to have surgery and I went down to see him for a couple of days. That was pretty hard, to see your dad in a hospital bed, waning, like that. But at least I was there and got to see him.[18]

After spending a week recuperating, John was discharged and sent home to subsist on a salt-free diet with instructions to rest as much as possible. Joan was desperate to remain optimistic: '[I] believed that the haemorrhage had been a warning, that all he had to do was to stop drinking, which this time he did, and that everything would be all right.'[19]

She did all that she could to help him recover, and he appreciated how caring she was. 'We were closer than ever after that scare,' she would say. 'I went everywhere with him, not that he could go very far – a short walk along the cliffs was all that he could manage.' She alerted Robin and Jake about their father's condition, and Robin – who was back on tour again with Rod Stewart – kept in touch via telephone, while Jake – who was still living in London at Eardley Crescent – came down to see his father as often as he could. John wrote to Derek Taylor about those above-average days when he was able to get to the local pub for a glass of bitter lemon: 'People are very kind and thoughtful,' he said, 'and tell me how pleased they are to see me "about again" and then proceed to give me a blow by blow account of their own ailments. All of which is not too riveting but "well meant," as my mother used to say.'[20]

It was only about a month, however, before it all happened again. Early one morning in August, John started haemorrhaging and, on this occasion, Joan's former husband and John's good friend Mark Eden was there. They called an ambulance and John was soon back in hospital receiving emergency attention. Joan, who was now unable to avoid the fact that her husband was terminally ill, sat outside the ward, put her head in her hands and surrendered to the deepest despair. The consultant emerged eventually to announce that it would be sensible to move John to King's College Hospital in London as soon as possible, so Joan, Mark and their son David got in a car and followed the ambulance as quickly as they could.

Once in London at the hospital, Joan was allowed to see John at his bedside. The bleeding had stopped, and he was descending into a deep coma. The doctor told her that, although John was unconscious, and would remain so for at least forty-eight hours, he might still be able to hear her. She took hold of his hand very gently, bent over him and whispered in his ear: 'If you can hear me, John, squeeze my hand.' His fingers tightened around hers. 'Now, John,' she said, more firmly, 'you are in London, in the best hospital in Europe. You are out of danger and all you have to do is relax and rest.'[21] He opened his mouth and said very softly, 'National Health?' Joan answered in the positive. 'Thank God,' he mumbled, and slipped off to sleep.

He remained in hospital for two weeks. Derek Taylor wrote a letter in the hope of cheering him up, promising to bring round some 'really fabulous people' to sit by his bedside, including 'Diamante the armless pianist and Rovera the dog woman who was brought up by corgis in Norfolk before going into the business'.[22] It raised a rare smile from John, but he spent most of his time curled up in traditional 'hedgehog mode', just waiting for the pain and discomfort to fade away.

After being discharged at the start of September, he spent the next two months doing very little except rest at home in his red leather armchair, while Joan tried her best to keep him interested in food despite the rigidity of his salt-free diet. He resumed writing his memoirs, but, sensing that there was not much time left, the tone was unavoidably elegiac:

> If I could have one last wish, I think it would be to go out in harness, so to speak. To make my exit while waiting in the wings to make an entrance, and for the assembled company to say 'Well, he wasn't a bad old nuisance. Now he's off to get into a muddle in another place!' Better still, to conk out in the dressing room after giving a good performance with the laughter and applause of an audience ringing in my ears.[23]

He never would finish the book properly – not just because of his declining health but also because of his doubts that enough people would be interested in reading it. As Joan would reflect, he remained the most modest of men, never believing that he was anything special: 'He was always slightly surprised when people wanted his autograph, and always answered each fan letter personally. He said it was nice of them to bother, though he couldn't for the life of him understand why people wanted a piece of paper with his name on it'.[24]

Friends continued to cheer him – and Joan – up with their frequent calls, letters and visits, but, as the weeks went by, John began to tire more easily and spent an increasing amount of time asleep upstairs in bed. There were still days when he seemed sharp and bright, but there were others when he withdrew deep into himself, too frustrated by his fatigue to talk. On one particularly gloomy Sunday, when he was bothered during lunch by a fly that kept buzzing by him, Joan tried to lighten the mood by telling him about an article she had read in some newspaper claiming that the best way to swat a fly was to confuse it by striking it from two separate directions at once. She then rolled up two old papers and demonstrated the theory by flattening the fly that was still pestering him. 'That's the only good thing that's happened all fucking day,' he muttered.[25]

Early in November, he started haemorrhaging again, and was taken by ambulance back to Ramsgate hospital. Too ill to be moved to a private room, he remained in the main ward, where Joan – who went home each day only to sleep and wash – did what she could to assist the overworked nursing staff and waited patiently for those moments when John was awake and alert. The doctors had warned her that death from liver failure could be 'awful', and she felt there was nothing left to do except 'pray that he would make a good end', but she maintained a brave face for him to see. 'I still talked to him as if he were suffering from a passing illness that simply had to be endured,' she later recalled. 'John didn't want to know the true nature of his illness.'[26] No matter how much pain he was experiencing, however, he remained impeccably well-mannered, always thanking the nurses for whatever they did and apologising for causing them any trouble.

One Saturday afternoon, the old television set at the end of the ward was tuned to a channel that was showing *Where the Spies Are*, the 1965 movie in which John had appeared with David Niven. There the two of them were pictured, tall, tanned and well-tailored in a succession of colourful and exotic locations, so full of life and mischief. Watching it eighteen years on, just a few months after Niven's own sad death, summoned up so many memories for Joan (who had only recently started dating John when the filming commenced), making it even harder to cope with what was now happening to her frail husband: '[I]t was painful and eerie to see John on the screen looking so handsome and healthy, while in reality he was lying in that ghastly ward so close to death.'[27]

Mark Eden came to see him one morning. John, by this time, was clearly extremely weak, but, as Eden took his hand, he smiled and said, 'Hello, my dear fellow, I see you've grown a beard.' Eden explained that he had done so because he was about to play the part of the professor in a new production of *Educating Rita* and thought it might make him look more intelligent. 'And has it?' said John with a twinkle in his eye. It would be the last little joke that he would make. Once his friend had gone, he went back to being silent and still.

Later the same day, as the ever-attentive Joan was sitting by his bedside, he turned to her suddenly, sighed and said softly, 'Darling, I'm fed up of it now and I think I would like to die.' He then held her hand tightly and added, 'It's all been rather lovely.'[28] He said nothing more, but Joan leaned forward and whispered a tearful 'thank you' into his ear for sharing his life with her and told him: 'It's all waiting for you, darling. Let go now and be happy.'[29] Within an hour, he had slipped into a coma from which he would never wake, and doctors pronounced him dead at 7.45 am the following morning (from a ruptured oesophageal varix – a varicose vein in the gullet – a common complication of cirrhosis of the liver). The date was Tuesday 15 November 1983, and his age was seventy-one.

That evening, back at the house in Ramsgate, Joan was comforted by family and friends, and everyone reflected with great warmth on the good man that they had lost. There was no need for much discussion as to how to announce his passing, as he had left careful instructions for them all to follow: 'I want you to promise me that you will put in the Obituary column of *The Times*, that I didn't fall asleep in God's garden, or pass through the vale, or any such nonsense, I simply conked out.'[30] It was, everyone agreed, funny, unfussy and so 'very John', and it had just the right effect. He had left one last smile behind.

Epilogue

What is going to become of us all?

———————

What will survive of us is love.

John Le Mesurier was cremated, and his ashes were buried in St George's churchyard in Ramsgate. The vicar in residence at the time forbade the family from using the expression 'Conked Out' (or his other favoured phrase: 'Snuffed It'), so his gravestone bears the following epigraph:

JOHN LE MESURIER

Beloved Actor
Born 5th April 1912
Died 15th November 1983

'Resting'

The media coverage of his death was widespread and unusually warm. Several old programmes and movies were shown to mark his memory, many former colleagues came forward to record their tributes and the obituaries were as affectionate as they were respectful. *The Times* was typical when it praised him for his 'gentle, irreverent humour' and remarked of his career: 'He was one of those dependable character actors whose name seldom appeared above the title but who could lend distinction to the smallest part.'[1] The *Guardian* was probably the most movingly astute when it declared:

The character he cumulatively created will be remembered when others more famous are forgotten not just for the skill of his playing but because he somehow embodied a symbolic British reaction to the whirlpool of the modern world – endlessly perplexed by the dizzying and incoherent pattern of events but doing his courteous best to ensure that resentment never showed.[2]

The small and private family funeral took place in Ramsgate on Monday 21 November 1983, and a memorial service (described as 'a celebration of the life rather than a mourning of the loss'[3]) was held at the Actors' Church, St Paul's, Covent Garden, at noon on Monday 16 February 1984. Among those present at the latter event were Joan and her son, David Malin (along with his wife, Susie, and their young daughter Emma), and John's sons Robin and Jake; Hattie's brother, Robin Jacques; Bruce Copp; Peter Campbell; Jimmy Perry, David Croft, Ian Lavender and Frank Williams, as well as the widows of Arthur Lowe and Arnold Ridley; Derek Nimmo, Freddie Jones, David Warner, Joan Sims, Wendy Richard, Annie Ross, George Melly, Max Wall, Bill Shine, Robert Beatty, T.P. McKenna and Ned Sherrin; and, somewhat ironically given John's 'difficult' days at public school, a representative of the Old Shirburnian Society. It was a carefully planned but unusually informal and light-hearted affair, Joan later recalled, because 'John would have hated tears at his last gathering.'[4] The music was chosen from his favourite movie, Jacques Tati's *Monsieur Hulot's Holiday*, and the main addresses were given by Bill Pertwee and Mark Eden.

Pertwee recalled with fondness the halcyon days of *Dad's Army*, with many funny stories about the detours they used to take on the way to Thetford for filming – such as the time when, forced to share a double-bedded hotel room in Newmarket after stopping for a late-night curry, he woke in the early hours of the morning to find John sitting up in bed writing. 'What are you doing at this hour, John?' he whispered. 'I'm trying to put lyrics to those dreadful noises you're making, dear boy,' John replied[5] – as well as the experiences that they had shared on set. He also underlined the deep respect with which John had always been held throughout the acting profession. Eden read out a witty and touching tribute to John that Derek Taylor had written, drawing on the countless letters that they used to exchange, which ended with the following heartfelt remarks:

He achieved more than he knew. He had become not just a good man, but a great one, and it has been reflected these last days in a torrent of obituary quite without precedent for anyone other than a knight of the theatre or a world star. 'No wonder,' the *Guardian* leader said, 'that so many whose lives were very different from his own came to be so enormously fond of him.' We, his friends, who knew and loved him in our ways, offer his dear family our thanks for sharing such a man with us in such generous measure.[6]

John himself was also heard when his poignant recording of 'An Indian Prayer', from his album *What is Going to Become of Us All?*, was played to everyone present:

> When I am dead
> Cry for me a little.
> Think of me sometimes.
> But not too much.
>
> Think of me now and again
> As I was in life,
> At some moment it is pleasant to recall.
> But not for long.
>
> Leave me in peace,
> And I shall leave you in peace.
> And while you live
> Let your thoughts be with the living.[7]

When the service was over, there were hugs and kisses on the steps outside as the cameras flashed and the questions were shouted, and then Joan and many friends and family went off to toast John's memory and share more stories that made everyone sigh and laugh. 'Strange how a man who so seldom smiled and who had such a sad face,' Joan reflected, 'could conjure up so much laughter.'[8]

It seemed odd to them all after this to have to get on with a life that now lacked 'Le Mez'. There were no more sweet-natured cards and whimsical letters, no more socialising to a background of jazz and no more calls promising 'playtime'.

John's elder son, Robin, continued to add to his international reputation as a guitarist, touring and recording from the home in Los Angeles that he shared with his second wife, Jules. Apart from his work with Rod Stewart, he also collaborated with the likes of Ronnie Wood, Bernie Taupin and the venerable French rock star Johnny Hallyday. When asked about the kind of things that he now recalled most vividly about his father, he stressed that they were 'only good things', and added: 'Whenever my dad had something to say, which wasn't really that very often, because he wasn't that gregarious or outspoken, but, when he did say something, the entire room would go quiet and they'd all listen to what he had to say. And he always had that amazing dry wit. His humour, especially, is something I'll never forget.'[9]

Robin's younger brother, Jake, however, met with a tragic fate: although one friend who knew him throughout his adult life would describe him as 'a very gentle guy with a lovely, dry sense of humour' who was 'strikingly handsome and women adored him',[10] Jake became distracted from the pursuit of his own promising musical career (which had seen him work with the likes of Yazz, The Orb and The Dream Academy) by his addiction to heroin. He started disappearing from view for long periods at a time, suffered from bouts of deep depression and, in spite of attempts by his brother and stepmother to help him break the habit, died a terribly premature death, aged just thirty-four, on 6 October 1991 – eleven years to the day after the death of his mother, Hattie Jacques. He was found alone in a squalid flat with a needle in his arm and a large quantity of heroin in his body.[11]

John's widow, Joan, moved out of the house that they had shared, fearing that she would end up as 'the curator of a museum',[12] and spent seven happy years abroad in Sitges, a small Catalan coastal city about twenty miles south-west of Barcelona in Spain, before returning to Britain and her parents' old home in Ramsgate. She completed John's memoir, *A Jobbing Actor*, wrote one memoir of her own, called *Lady Don't Fall Backwards*, which focused on her affair with Tony Hancock, and then another, called *Dear John*, that celebrated the memory of her husband.

She continued to take great pleasure in being the senior member of the extended Le Mesurier family, linked to so many lives united by all the warm memories of Le Mez, and she never stopped being grateful for the blessings that he left. 'It was a really, really good marriage,' she reflected. 'I was terribly lucky, because it wasn't one that I'd deliberately sought out – you know, a man much older than me, out of my sphere and my class, and he did need an awful lot of looking after – but it just happened, and it was all so worth it. He was the kindest man in the world.'[13]

John, meanwhile, has remained visible via the regular reruns of *Dad's Army*, a show that continues to entertain not only those who watched it when John was alive but also by those who were born long after he had gone. His performances can also be seen today in countless classic movies that are now preserved and widely available for collection on DVD ('How very kind of you, you've just saved my life'). It is, indeed, remarkably easy these days to find something that allows us, once again, to relive one of those 'shining Le Mesurier moments' that can always help to make us smile and keep us sane.

He received no formal recognition from his country by the way of honours – unlike so many of his illustrious Le Mesurier forebears, who gathered most of their gongs from their efforts for the extant British Empire, and a fair few of the Hallileys, who got the nod for their services to law or politics. John, as a 'mere' entertainer, would always remain overlooked – and, apart from his well-deserved BAFTA for *Traitor*, no other awards were forthcoming from within the world of show business. It mattered little to him – he always said that he did not believe in prizes – but, nonetheless, he deserved much more than he received. Subtlety always risks being either overlooked or under-appreciated, and John's subtlety as a character actor meant that he was often unfortunate enough to suffer from both of these misjudgements. Studied carefully, however, his lightness of touch remains a special lesson in how to make such roles seem real. As for the wonderful scenes that he, as Wilson, shared with Arthur Lowe, as Mainwaring: they continue to seem as relevant, as well as funny, as they did when they were first broadcast. If ever another 'Greetings from Earth' capsule is shot up into space, clips of Wilson and Mainwaring certainly ought to be included on any disk bearing the label 'Meet the English'. John Le Mesurier will surely always be there with us, in our mind's eye, whenever we find ourselves trapped in the company of the pompous and the pushy, with that sly little smile at such people's routine delusions of grandeur. No matter how many supercilious officials, sanctimonious politicians, smug celebrities and shamelessly talent-free fame seekers we have to endure, just the thought of this good and gentle man ought to be enough to remind us that it is not impossible for decent, honest and admirable people to 'show off', as he put it, in the public realm without ever seeming shallow or spoilt. Apart from the elegance of his acting, therefore, his legacy is the fine example that he set as an endearing individual.

Some said that he just played himself. That is unfair – there was far more to his talent than that – but, even if it had been true, John Le Mesurier, as roles go, was certainly a high-class act.

He always said that the most important words in the English language were 'please' and 'thank you'. If he was still with us today, the great temptation would be to request of this most modest of men, for all of the years that we have been watching him, 'Please, let us say, "Thank you".'

Credits

Every effort has been made to assemble a list of performances that is as comprehensive as possible (although, given the intensity of the repertory season and the gaps in the archival records, the theatrical section has been left as a selective survey). Any unintentional omissions or inaccuracies will be corrected in a future edition.

Legend:
* = billed as 'John Halliley'
HS = BBC Home Service
LP = BBC Light Programme
Third = BBC Third Programme
GOS = BBC General Overseas Service
# = available commercially in DVD format in one or more regions
† = an episode guide to *Dad's Army* can be found in my book on the show

STAGE (selective)

January 1935	*While Parents Sleep*	Palladium Theatre, Edinburgh*
February 1935	*Dangerous Corner*	Palladium Theatre, Edinburgh*
March 1935	*Cavalcade*	Palladium Theatre, Edinburgh*
July 1935	*Up in Mabel's Room*	Coliseum, Oldham
September 1935	*Mary, Mary, Quite Contrary*	Sheffield Repertory Theatre*
November 1935	*Twelfth Night*	Sheffield Repertory Theatre*
September 1936	*Peace in Our Time*	Croydon Repertory Theatre*
October 1936	*Dusty Ermine*	Croydon Repertory Theatre*
October 1936	*The Apple Cart*	Croydon Repertory Theatre*
November 1936	*Bees on the Boat Deck*	Croydon Repertory Theatre*
November 1936	*Ah! Wilderness*	Croydon Repertory Theatre*
November 1936	*The Constant Nymph*	Croydon Repertory Theatre*
December 1936	*Charley's Aunt*	Croydon Repertory Theatre*
January 1937	*Charley's Aunt*	Croydon Repertory Theatre*

September 1937	*Love on the Dole*	Croydon Repertory Theatre
July 1938	*Payment Deferred*	The Royal, Glasgow
July 1938	*The Romantic Young Lady*	Lyceum, Edinburgh
July 1938	*The Romantic Young Lady*	The Royal, Glasgow
August 1938	*Petticoat Influence*	The Royal, Glasgow
August 1938	*Husband to a Famous Woman*	Lyceum, Edinburgh
August 1938	*Husband to a Famous Woman*	The Royal, Glasgow
September 1938	*The Moon in the Yellow River*	The Royal, Glasgow
October 1938	*Private Lives*	Lyceum, Edinburgh
January–May 1939	*Gas Light*	Apollo, London
May 1939	*Gas Light*	Finsbury Park Empire, London
May–June 1939	*Gas Light*	Savoy, London
June 1939	*Gas Light*	Chiswick Empire
June 1939	*Gas Light*	Chelsea Palace
July 1939	*Gas Light*	Grand, Blackpool
October 1939	*Gas Light*	Prince's Theatre, Manchester
November–December 1939	*Goodness, How Sad!*	(tour)
January 1940	*Journey's End*	Palace Court Theatre, Bournemouth
January–February 1940	*French Without Tears*	Grand, Blackpool
March 1940	*The Man in Half Moon Street*	Brixton Theatre, London
May 1940	*Mystery at Greenfingers*	Brixton Theatre
May 1940	*The First Mrs Fraser*	BrixtonTheatre
December 1941	*French Without Tears*	ENSA
December 1946	*Just William*	Alexandra, Birmingham
June 1947	*The Winslow Boy*	Empire, Chatham
October–November 1947	*The Dubarry*	Princes Theatre, London
23 May 1949	*The Linden Tree*	Alexandra, Birmingham
June 1949	*Love in Idleness*	Alexandra, Birmingham
August 1949	*Playbill*	Alexandra, Birmingham
December 1949–January 1950	*Queen of Hearts*	Alexandra, Birmingham
14 August 1950	*The Smooth-Faced Gentleman*	Alexandra, Birmingham
1951	*Traveller's Joy*	New Theatre, Bromley
January 1952	*Angry Dust*	New Torch Theatre, London
September–December 1952	*The Hanging Judge*	New Theatre, London
July–August 1953	*Piccolo*	Connaught, London (Worthing rep)
October 1953	*The Snow Was Black*	The New Watergate, London
March 1954	*Here Comes April*	Connaught, London
June 1955	*Twenty Minutes South*	Players' Theatre, London
July–October 1955	*Twenty Minutes South*	St Martin's Theatre, London
February 1956	*Coroner's Verdict*	Richmond Theatre

June 1956	*Malice Domestic*	New Lindsey Theatre
19 November 1961	Army Benevolent Fund Gala	Victoria Palace, London
23 July 1962	The *Daily Express* Starlight Dance	Lyceum, London
13 June 1965	*Homage to T.S. Eliot*	London Fringe Theatre
20 September 1970	Poetry Reading	Little Medway Theatre, Kent
31 December 1973	The Television Arts Ball	Royal Albert Hall, London
September 1975	*Dad's Army*	Forum Theatre, Billingham
2 October 1975		
February 1976	*Dad's Army*	Shaftesbury, London
8 August 1976	*One of Us*	Aldwych, London
Autumn 1976	*An Inspector Calls*	Salisbury, Rhodesia
August 1977	In Concert	New Fair Oak Theatre, Rogate
January–March 1979	*Bedroom Farce*	Hilton Playhouse, Hong Kong, Singapore and Kuala Lumpur
23 April–31 May 1980	*Hay Fever*	Lyric, Hammersmith, London
July–September 1980	*Hay Fever*	Provincial tour
August 1981	*Hay Fever*	Yvonne Arnaud Theatre, Guildford
September–October 1981	*Hay Fever*	Ashcroft Theatre, Croydon
October 1981	*Hay Fever*	Alexandra Theatre, Birmingham

RADIO

29 November 1946 *Just William* (LP)

2 March 1947 *Escape or Die* (HS)

14 April 1947 *Mutiny in the Navy* (Third)

17 August 1947 *Alexander the Corrector* (HS)

29 August 1951 *Trafalgar Square* (HS)

9 September 1951 *The Trial of Sir Walter Raleigh* (HS)

23 October 1951 *Focus on General Elections* (HS)

28 October 1951 *Alcock and Brown* (GOS)

22 November 1951 *Lord Delamere* (GOS)

8 February 1952 *I Was a Communist* (GOS)

19 February 1952 *Dr Arnold of Rugby* (HS)

12 May 1952 *Edward Gibbon Wakefield* (GOS)

26 June 1952 *At the Sign of the Maid's Head* (HS)

18 July 1952 *Portrait of Sir Edward Coke* (HS)

16 June 1953 *The World My Parish* (HS)

9 September 1953 *Elizabethan Theatre* (GOS)

20 May 1954 *Rodney Stone* (HS)

1 September 1954 *Brigadier Gerard* (LP)

31 March 1957 *Abu Hassan* (Third)

1 April 1957 *Abu Hassan* (Third)

25 June 1968 *Doctor in the House* (BBC Radio 4)

31 January 1969 *Late Night Extra* (BBC Radios 1/2)

9 June 1970 *Brothers In Law* (BBC Radio 4)

16 June 1970 *Brothers In Law* (BBC Radio 4)

12 March 1971 *Today* (BBC Radio 4)

27 July 1971 *Brothers In Law* (BBC Radio 4)

12 July 1971 *Open House* (BBC Radio 2)

17 May 1972 *Sounds Familiar* (BBC Radio 2)

3 July 1972 *Brothers In Law* (BBC Radio 4)

17 Feb 1973 *Desert Island Discs* (BBC Radio 4)

28 January–10 June 1974 *Dad's Army* series 1 (BBC Radio 4)

25 December 1974 *Dad's Army* special (BBC Radio 4)

11 February–24 June 1975 *Dad's Army* series 2 (BBC Radio 4)

16 March–7 September 1976 *Dad's Army* series 3 (BBC Radio 4)

16 December 1979 *The Kamikaze Ground Staff Reunion Dinner* (BBC Radio 3)

24 January 1980 *Hitchhiker's Guide to the Galaxy* (BBC Radio 4)

3 December 1980–7 January 1981 *Stiff Upper Lip, Jeeves* (BBC Radio 4)

8 March–30 April 1981 *The Lord of the Rings* (BBC Radio 4)

24 October 1982 *The Flower Case* (BBC Radio 3)

9 December 1982 *The Dog it was That Died* (BBC Radio 3)

13 November 1983–15 January 1984 *It Sticks Out Half A Mile* (BBC Radio 2) (nine episodes)

21 August–2 October 1984 *It Sticks Out Half A Mile* (BBC Radio 2) (four episodes)

TELEVISION

17 April 1938 *The Marvellous History of St Bernard* (BBC TV)

18 December 1938 *Richard of Bordeaux* (BBC TV)

14–17 June 1946 *They Flew Through Sand* (BBC TV)

17 February–28 April 1951 *Whirligig* (BBC TV) (six episodes)

20 February–17 July 1951 *The Railway Children* (BBC TV) (six episodes)

31 July–8 November 1951 *Show Me A Spy!* (BBC TV) (four episodes)

1 December 1951 *Sherlock Holmes* (BBC TV)

24 December 1951 *A Time To Be Born* (BBC TV)

25–27 December 1952 *1066 and All That* (BBC TV) (two episodes)

4 December 1953 *Teleclub5* (BBC TV)

10 July–18 September 1954 *Happy Holidays* (BBC TV) (six episodes)

29 March 1955 *The Unguarded Hour* (BBC TV)

27 June 1955 *Douglas Fairbanks Presents* (ITV)

30 November–13 December 1955 *The Granville Melodramas* (ITV) (three episodes)

21 January 1956 *Douglas Fairbanks Presents* (ITV)

11 April 1956 *Douglas Fairbanks Presents* (ITV)

3 July 1956 *Crown Theatre Presents* (ITV)

9 July 1956 *Douglas Fairbanks Presents* (ITV)

25 August 1956 *Saturday Playhouse* (ITV)

12 October 1956 *Assignment Foreign Legion* (ITV)

24 November 1956 *Errol Flynn Theatre* (ITV)

16 December 1956 *Fireside Theatre* (ITV)

28 January 1957 *Douglas Fairbanks Presents* (ITV)

28 March 1957 *Television Playhouse* (ITV)

16 July 1957 *The Gay Cavalier* (ITV)

9 September 1957 *Douglas Fairbanks Presents* (ITV)

10 September 1957 *Assignment Foreign Legion* (ITV)

2 December 1957 *Hancock's Half-Hour*, 'The Lawyer' (BBC TV) #

15 December 1957 *The Lafarge Affair* (BBC TV)

15 February 1958 *Sword of Freedom* (ITV)

7 March 1958 *Television Playhouse* (ITV)

3 April 1958 *Douglas Fairbanks Presents* (ITV)

16 January 1959 *Hancock's Half-Hour*, 'The New Nose' (BBC TV) #

20 January 1959 *Play of the Week* (ITV)

30 January 1959 *Hancock's Half-Hour*, 'The Horror Serial' (BBC TV)

7 March 1959 *William Tell* (ITV)

27 March 1959 *Hancock's Half-Hour*, 'The Servants' (BBC TV)

19 April 1959 *Errol Flynn Theatre* (ITV)

9 October 1959 *Hancock's Half-Hour*, 'Lord Byron Lived Here' (BBC TV) #

11 October 1959 *Interpol Calling* (ITV)

30 October 1959 *Hancock's Half-Hour*, 'The Cruise' (BBC TV) #

10 November 1959 *The Enormous Shadow* (ITV)

18 January 1960 *Saber of London* (ITV)

4 March 1960 *Hancock's Half-Hour*, 'The Cold' (BBC TV) #

7 April 1960 *Somerset Maugham Stories* (ITV)

5 June 1960 *Play Gems* (ITV)

26 June 1960 *William Tell* (ITV)

6 August 1960 *Jazz Session* (BBC TV)

29 August 1960 *Saber of London* (ITV)

13 November 1960 *Danger Man* (ITV)

3 December 1960 *The Third Man* (ITV)

16 June 1961 *Hancock*, 'The Lift' (BBC TV) #

18 June 1961 *The Pursuers* (ITV)

4 November 1961 *Ghost Squad* (ITV)

17 December 1961 *Armchair Theatre* (ITV)

5 February 1962 *Saber of London* (ITV)

31 March 1962 *Danger Man* (ITV)

5 October 1962 *Dial RIX* (BBC TV)

25 January 1963 *Mr Justice Duncannon* (BBC TV)

12 February 1963 *This Is Your Life*, Hattie Jacques (BBC TV)

25 January–15 February 1963 *Mr Justice Duncannon* (BBC TV) (two episodes)

7 March 1963 *Hancock*, 'The Politician' (BBC TV)

5 April 1963 *Galton & Simpson Comedy Playhouse* (BBC TV)

16 April 1963 *The Brimstone Butterfly* (ITV)

5 October 1963 *Casebook* (ITV)

17 November 1963 *Long Past Glory* (ITV)

24 January 1964 *The Avengers* (ITV)

12 February 1964 *The Lady of the Camellias* (BBC TV)

26 February 1964 *The Master of Santiago* (BBC TV)

12 April 1964 *Sunday Story* (BBC TV)

23 November 1964 *The Bachelors* (ITV)

25 March 1965 *Tea Party* (BBC1)

1 April 1965 *Story Parade*: 'The Bachelors' (BBC2)

2 July 1965 *Memoirs of a Chaise Longue* (BBC1)

9 August 1965 *Riviera Police* (ITV)

2 January 1966 *Theatre 625*: 'Dr Knock' (BBC2)

26 February 1966 *The Avengers* (ITV)

2 March 1966 *The Wednesday Play*: 'Macready's Gala' (BBC1)

8 March 1966 *Frankie Howerd* (BBC1)

1 April–13 June 1966 *Pardon the Expression* (ITV) # (four episodes)

25 April 1966 *Thirty Minute Theatre* (BBC2)

6 May 1966 *Marriage Lines* (BBC1)

4 August 1966 *Adam Adamant Lives!* (BBC1)

19 November–24 December 1966 *George and the Dragon* series 1 (ITV) # (six episodes)

3 January 1967 *Hugh and I* (BBC1)

31 January 1967 *All Gas and Gaiters* (BBC1)

22 February 1967 *Thirty Minute Theatre* (BBC1)

17 March 1967 *Mr Rose* (ITV)

20 March 1967 *The Troubleshooters* (BBC1)

20 May–1 July 1967 *George and the Dragon* series 2 (ITV) # (seven episodes)

30 May 1967 *The Further Adventures of Lucky Jim* (BBC2)

29 June 1967 *To Lucifer: A Son* (BBC1)

25 September 1967 *Thirty-Minute Theatre*: An Absolute Treasure (BBC2)

6 January–17 February 1968 *George and the Dragon* series 3 (ITV) # (seven episodes)

25 February 1968 *Call My Bluff* (BBC2)

31 July–11 September 1968 *Dad's Army* series 1 (BBC1) # † (six episodes)

26 September–31 October 1968 *George and the Dragon* series 4 (ITV) # (six episodes)

21 October 1968 *Harry Worth* (BBC1)

25 February 1969 *Two in Clover* (ITV)

1 March–5 April 1969 *Dad's Army* series 2 (BBC1) # (six episodes)

11 June 1969 *The Mind of Mr J.G. Reeder* (ITV) #

17 June 1969 *The Creative Impulse* (BBC2)

25 July 1969 *Tales of Edgar Wallace* (ITV)

11 September–11 December 1969 *Dad's Army* series 3 (BBC1) # (fourteen episodes)

1 October 1969 *The Last Train Through Harecastle Tunnel* (BBC1)

26 December 1969 *The Coward Revue* (BBC2)

3 January 1970 *Saturday Night Theatre* (ITV)

22 March 1970 *Bird's Eye View* (BBC2)

1 April 1970 *Haven of Rest* (BBC1)

13 May 1970 *Shine a Light* (ITV)

25 May 1970 *A Royal Television Gala Performance* (BBC1)

31 July 1970 *The Des O'Connor Show* (ITV)

25 September–18 December 1970 *Dad's Army* series 4 (BBC1) # (thirteen episodes)

8 March 1971 *Dear Mother . . . Love Albert* (ITV)

24 March 1971 *This Is Your Life* Clive Dunn (ITV)

22 April 1971 *The Morecambe & Wise Show* (BBC1) #

9 June 1971 *Paul Temple* (BBC1) #

7 July 1971 *Jokers Wild* (ITV)

28 July 1971 *Jokers Wild* (ITV)

6 August 1971 *Misleading Cases* (BBC1)

22 August 1971 *Doctor At Large* (ITV) #

14 October 1971 *Traitor* (BBC1)

10 December 1971 *The Goodies* (BBC1) #

27 December 1971 *Dad's Army* special, 'Battle of the Giants' (BBC1) #

16 February 1972 *Jason King* (ITV) #

11–15 September 1972 *Jackanory* (BBC1) (five episodes)

13 September–18 October 1972 *A Class By Himself* (ITV) (six episodes)

14–15 September 1972 *Jackanory* (BBC1) (two episodes)

29 September 1972 *Sykes* (BBC1) #

6 October–29 December 1972 *Dad's Army* series 5 (BBC1) # (thirteen episodes)

31 October 1972 *Armchair Theatre* (ITV)

5 January 1973 *Jason King* (ITV) #

1 February 1973 *Comedy Playhouse*: 'Marry the Girls' (BBC1)

22 February 1973 *Blue Peter* (BBC1)

2 June 1973 *Thriller*: 'File It Under Fear' (ITV) #

31 July 1973 *Spotlight*: 'The Sergeant from
  Sandhurst' (BBC1 East)
4 September 1973 *Black and Blue* (BBC1)
31 October–12 December 1973 *Dad's Army*
  series 6 (BBC1) # (six episodes)
28 November 1973 *Great Mysteries*
  (ITV/Anglia)
27 December 1973 *Crown Court* (ITV) #
18 September 1974 *Francis Howerd in Concert*
  (ITV)
25 September 1974 *Late Night Theatre* (ITV)
15 November–23 December 1974 *Dad's Army*
  series 7 (BBC1) # (six episodes)
18 May 1975 *Village Hall* (ITV)
14 July 1975 *Centre Play*: 'The Flight Fund'
  (BBC2)
5 September–10 October 1975 *Dad's Army*
  series 8 (BBC1) # (six episodes)
25 September 1975 *Death of an Old-Fashioned
  Girl* (ITV)
7 October 1975 *Shades Of Greene* (ITV)
26 December 1975 *Dad's Army* special, 'My
  Brother and I' (BBC1) #
1975–1976 *Bod* (BBC1) # (thirteen episodes)
10 March 1976 *This Is Your Life*, Arnold
  Ridley (ITV)
1 April 1976 *Pebble Mill* (BBC1)
26 December 1976 *Dad's Army* special, 'The
  Love of Three Oranges'(BBC1)#
2 October–6 November 1977 *Dad's Army*
  series 9 (BBC1) # (six episodes)
15 October 1977 *Multi-Coloured Swap Shop*
  (BBC1)
24 December 1977 *A Christmas Carol* (BBC2)
25 December 1977 *The Morecambe & Wise
  Show* (BBC1) #
15 January 1978 *Flint* (BBC1)
4 November 1979 *An Honourable Retirement*
  (ITV)
24 October 1979 *Ripping Yarns* (BBC2) #
5 January 1980 *The Dick Emery Show* (BBC1)
6 January 1980 *The Shillingbury Blowers* (ITV)
  #
3 February 1980 *Worzel Gummidge* (ITV) #
21 December 1980 *Night of 100 Stars* (ITV)
17 November 1981 *Brideshead Revisited* (ITV)
  #
15 February 1982 *Dead Ernest* (ITV)
9–23 March 1982 Bognor (ITV) (three
  episodes)
7 November 1982 *Hi-de-Hi* (BBC1) #
10–31 July 1983 *A Married Man* (Channel 4)
  # (four episodes)

MOVIES

1948 *Death in the Hand*
1948 *Escape from Broadmoor*
1949 *Old Mother Riley's New Venture*
1949 *A Matter of Murder*
1950 *Dark Interval*
1951 *The Small Miracle*
1952 *Blind Man's Bluff*
1952 *Old Mother Riley Meets the Vampire* #
1953 *The Pleasure Garden* #
1953 *The Drayton Case*
1953 *The Blue Parrot*
1953 *Black 13*
1954 *Dangerous Cargo*
1954 *Beautiful Stranger*
1954 *Stranger from Venus*
1955 *Police Dog*
1955 *Josephine and Men*
1955 *A Time to Kill*
1956 *Private's Progress* #
1956 *The Battle of the River Plate*
1956 *The Baby and the Battleship* #
1957 *Brothers in Law* #
1957 *The Good Companions*
1957 *The Admirable Crichton* #
1957 *These Dangerous Years*
1957 *High Flight*
1958 *Happy is the Bride* #
1958 *Gideon's Day*
1958 *The Man Who Wouldn't Talk*
1958 *Law and Disorder*
1958 *Another Time, Another Place* #
1958 *The Moonraker*
1958 *Blind Spot*
1958 *Blood of the Vampire*
1958 *Man with a Gun*
1958 *I Was Monty's Double* #
1959 *Our Man in Havana* #
1959 *The Captain's Table*
1959 *Operation Amsterdam*
1959 *Ben-Hur* #
1959 *The Lady is a Square*
1959 *Jack the Ripper*
1959 *The Wreck of the Mary Deare*
1959 *Desert Mice*
1959 *Follow a Star* #
1959 *Too Many Crooks* #
1959 *Carlton-Browne of the F.O.* #
1959 *The Hound of the Baskervilles* #
1959 *I'm All Right, Jack* #
1960 *School for Scoundrels* #
1960 *The Day They Robbed the Bank of England*
1960 *Never Let Go* #

1960 *Doctor in Love* #
1960 *The Bulldog Breed* #
1960 *The Pure Hell of St Trinian's* #
1960 *A Touch of Larceny*
1960 *Let's Get Married*
1960 *Dead Lucky*
1961 *On the Fiddle*
1961 *The Night We Got the Bird*
1961 *Five Golden Hours*
1961 *Mr Topaze*
1961 *Don't Bother to Knock*
1961 *Invasion Quartet*
1961 *The Rebel* #
1961 *Very Important Person* #
1962 *Waltz of the Toreadors* #
1962 *Go to Blazes*
1962 *We Joined the Navy*
1962 *Hair of the Dog*
1962 *Only Two Can Play* #
1962 *Village of Daughters*
1962 *Mrs Gibbons' Boys*
1962 *Jigsaw*
1962 *The Main Attraction*
1963 *The Punch and Judy Man* #
1963 *The Wrong Arm of the Law* #
1963 *The Mouse on the Moon* #
1963 *In the Cool of the Day*
1963 *The Pink Panther* #
1963 *Never Put it in Writing*
1964 *Hot Enough for June* #
1964 *The Moon-Spinners* #
1965 *The City Under the Sea* (aka *War-Gods of the Deep*)
1965 *Where the Spies Are*
1965 *The Early Bird* #
1965 *Masquerade*
1965 *Those Magnificent Men in Their Flying Machines* #
1965 *The Liquidator*
1966 *The Sandwich Man* #
1966 *Our Man in Marrakesh* #
1966 *The Wrong Box* #
1966 *Finders Keepers*
1966 *Eye of the Devil*
1967 *La Vingt-Cinquième Heure*
1967 *Cuckoo Patrol*
1967 *Casino Royale* #
1967 *Mister Ten Per Cent* #
1968 *Salt and Pepper* #
1969 *Midas Run*
1969 *The Italian Job* #
1969 *The Magic Christian* #
1970 *Doctor in Trouble* #

1970 *On a Clear Day You Can See Forever* #
1971 *Dad's Army* #
1972 *Au Pair Girls* #
1972 *The Alf Garnett Saga* #
1974 *Confessions of a Window Cleaner* #
1974 *Brief Encounter* #
1974 *The Culcheth Job* (British Leyland promo)
1974 *Three for All*
1975 *The Adventure of Sherlock Holmes' Smarter Brother* #
1977 *Jabberwocky* #
1977 *What's Up Nurse!* #
1977 *Stand Up, Virgin Soldiers* #
1978 *Rosie Dixon – Night Nurse*
1978 *Who Is Killing the Great Chefs of Europe?* #
1979 *The Spaceman & King Arthur* #
1980 *The Shillingbury Blowers* #
1980 *The Fiendish Plot of Dr Fu Manchu* #
1981 *Late Flowering Love* #
1984 *Facelift*
1984 *The Passionate Pilgrim* #

ALBUMS

Dad's Army: Original Cast Recording
Warner Brothers, 1975 Cat No: K56186

What is Going To Become of Us All?
Warner Communications, 1976 Cat No: K54080

The Velveteen Rabbit
Narrated by John Le Mesurier
featuring Robin Le Mesurier with music by Ed Welch
Columbia Records, 1978 Cat No: SCX6599

Once Upon a World
Narrated by John Le Mesurier
B7 Media, 1977/2008 Cat No: 1906577005

SINGLES

'A Nightingale Sang In Berkeley Square' – John Le Mesurier /'Hometown' – John Le Mesurier, Arthur Lowe and company
Warner Bros, 1975

'There Ain't Much Change From A Pound These Days'/ 'After All These Years'
– John Le Mesurier & Clive Dunn
KA Records, 1982

Notes

Prologue

Epigraph: 'These Foolish Things (Remind Me of You)', words by Holt Marvell (aka Eric Maschwitz), music by Harry Link and Jack Strachey (published by Boosey & Co, 1935).

1 *The Times*, 16 November 1983, p. 26.
2 John Le Mesurier, *Guardian*, 16 November 1983, p. 1.
3 John Le Mesurier, *A Jobbing Actor* (London: Elm Tree Books, 1984), p. 44.
4 John Le Mesurier, quoted in David Croft, *You Have Been Watching . . .* (London: BBC Books, 2004), p. 176.
5 John Le Mesurier, quoted by George Tremlett, *TV Times* (Australian edition), 21 April 1971, p. 8.
6 Le Mesurier, *A Jobbing Actor*, p. 44.
7 Ibid., p. 64.
8 Ibid., p. 72.
9 Ibid.
10 Ibid.

Chapter I Master John

Header quote: John Le Mesurier as Sergeant Wilson, 'The Honourable Man', episode 5 series 6, *Dad's Army* (written by Jimmy Perry and David Croft, first broadcast on BBC1, 28 November 1973).

1 Le Mesurier, *A Jobbing Actor*, p. 1.
2 In 1898, Charles Bailey Halliley, John's paternal grandfather, became a shareholder and director of a company set up to purchase the Bedford Turkish Baths at 18 Ashburnham Road which, after the liquidation of the Bedford Turkish Baths Company Ltd in 1898, was owned by James Walter Hobson and George Henry Martin. The project, however, never came to fruition and the company remained

dormant until it too was dissolved in 1901. (See National Archives: PRO: BT31 8094/58365.)
3 Charles Bailey Halliley would die at his home in Somerset on 15 March 1934, aged 83.
4 The Hereditary Governorship of Alderney began soon after the Restoration in 1660, when Charles II appointed a Jerseyman, Sir George de Carteret, to the post. The position then passed by marriage from the de Carterets to the Andros family in Guernsey, with Charles renewing their 'patent' for ninety years in 1683, and afterwards passed on, de facto, to the Le Mesuriers, another Guernsey family related to the Androses by marriage. Various members of this family acted as Lt Governors for the Andros family until Henry Le Mesurier inherited the patent formally from his Andros mother and was sworn in officially as Governor, in the Alderney Court, on 6 February 1730. The Le Mesuriers remained as Hereditary Governors of Alderney until Lt-General John Le Mesurier (reportedly frustrated at seeing his successful military career stalled by the intrusion of his inherited obligations – see *Gentleman's Magazine*, August 1843, p. 204) sold the patent back to the Crown in 1825 in return for a pension of £725 a year for life. During the Le Mesuriers' rule they brought a great deal of prosperity to the island through means both 'official' and 'unofficial' (including, under the latter category, smuggling and privateering), and, during the several wars against France, America and Spain, they created an efficient militia and defended the island successfully against several French attacks. Many historic Alderney buildings built by the Le Mesurier family – including Government House (now known as Island

Hall), the town school (now a museum), the parish church and Les Mouriaux House – remain as physical reminders of its stewardship.

5 Captain Frederick Le Mesurier – born in 1753 – died young, in his thirtieth year, in 1783. In William Berry's *The History of the Island of Guernsey* (London: Longman, 1815), pp. 152–3, Frederick's epitaph (inscribed on a marble wall inside the family's Guernsey church) reads as follows:

To the memory of Frederick Le Mesurier, late Commander of the Ponsborne East India Ship, Second Son of John Le Mesurier Esq. Governor of the Island of Alderney, who died at Brentford on the third of May 1783, in the thirty first year of his age. In professional Knowledge he had few equals; for the want of longer experience was in him amply supplied by Attention and Activity. His Understanding was sound, his Manners most amiable: simple and modest, he seldom offered himself to the World but when impelled by the necessities of others or his own Duty, his Courage was unaffected: steady, temperate, and inflexible, for it was founded in Religion and Justice. It bore him through many dangers, it supported him in his last moments. Patient and resigned through the course of a painful illness, he seemed only to feel for those friends who wept over him. His Brothers and Sisters have erected this Monument in remembrance of those virtues which assure them of his Happiness in a better State.

6 The Right Hon. Paul Le Mesurier (1755–1805) was Lord Mayor of London 1793–4. During his year as City Sheriff (1786–7), he calmed and relieved the distress in Newgate caused by the delayed sailing of the first convict fleet to Australia. As Mayor, serving at the start of the war against France, he employed a mixture of firmness and expediency to deal with riots directed against the 'crimping' of men into the Army and with unruly protests about assessments under the new Militia Act.

7 Havilland Le Mesurier (1758–1806), youngest son of John Le Mesurier and Mary Dobrée, joined his father and older brother, Peter, in a merchant house involved in privateering in the War of Independence. He later married his distant relation, Elizabeth Dobrée, and established himself among the prospering community of Channel Island merchants in London. He also ventured into military and diplomatic matters with some distinction, setting out the model of a commissariat service in two important and detailed manuals, *A System for the British Commissariat on Foreign Service* (1796) and *The British Commissary* (1798). His stipulations, in particular, on the financial aspects of supply, and on the prompt and full payment of contractors and peasants, proved invaluable to Wellington and other British commanders. In the spring of 1797, with invasion threatening, Le Mesurier was appointed commissary-general of the southern district of England.

8 In 1877, Colonel Cecil Brooke Le Mesurier RA proposed an RML 7-pr (2.5-inch) steel gun that consisted of two parts which screwed together (hence the name 'screw gun'). Twelve guns made by the Elswick Ordnance Company were sent to Afghanistan in 1879 and proved so satisfactory that a much large number were made at the Royal Gun Factory for the service. The screw gun remained the armament of British mountain batteries until after the South African War (1899–1902). It was not, however, a popular weapon among gunners: although cordite had been introduced in 1892, 'screw gun' cartridges were still filled with gunpowder, with the unfortunate consequence that the smoke advertised a gun's position every time it fired. Le Mesurier's design was nonetheless widely considered at the time to be the best mountain gun of its type, and was eulogised by Rudyard Kipling in his poem on the subject (part of which goes: 'For you all love the screw-guns – the screw-guns they all love you!/So when they call round with a few guns, o' course you will know what to do – hoo! hoo!/Jest send in your Chief an' surrender – it's worse if you fights or you runs/You can go where you please, you can skid up the trees, but you don't get away from the guns!').

9 Cannington Manor was established in 1882 when a well-to-do but somewhat embittered Englishman, Captain Edward Michell Pierce, emigrated to Canada after the

sudden loss of his country estate, using his remaining resources to claim five townships 65 km south of Whitewood in the North West Territories (now classed as south-east Saskatchewan). 'Cannington' came from the name of an old English town familiar to Capt Pierce in Somerset; 'Manor' was added later to avoid confusion with another location in Ontario. Knowing relatively little about farming, Pierce nevertheless established an agricultural college for the sons of wealthy Englishmen and set about enlisting a small number of young and suitably idealistic disciples. By 1890, Cannington Manor included an Anglican church, a flour mill, hotel, smithy, carpentry shop, carriage shop and a general store. Failure to adjust to the harsh realities of life in Canada, however, quickly brought business and farm bankruptcies, as well as internal schisms and increasingly fractious debates. In 1901–02, when a new Canadian Pacific Railway line bypassed the village, the remaining businesses moved out and Cannington Manor gradually disappeared. The site is now a provincial historic park, and a number of the original buildings have been reconstructed. Unlike most of the other English settlers, Arthur Swynfer Le Mesurier remained committed to the original ideals of Cannington Manor, stayed in the area for the rest of his life (he died in 1964), marrying there and starting a family; his two younger brothers moved on to more conventional areas, and vocations, elsewhere in Canada (Paul died at a relatively early age and Cecil worked as a teacher in Victoria).

10 The children, in order of birth from 1801 to 1822, were: Thomas; Mary Ann; Margaret; Martha; Henry; James; Henrietta; Charlotte; Anne; John; Ann Elizabeth; Bulkeley George; Julia; Frederick; and Richard Arthur.

11 Established in 1552, Bedford School – not to be confused with Bedford Modern School – was and remains a public school (comprising both a Preparatory and Upper division) for boys aged between seven and eighteen. Henry Le Mesurier began teaching there in the late 1830s.

12 Henry Le Mesurier wrote Bedford School's official song, 'Domus Pater', in 1861; translated from the Latin, the lyrics are:
In Harper's House, O Father, may

Thine honour aye indwelling stay
May ever round its portals be
The guardian angels placed by thee.

The bands of youths look down and see
Restoring here continuously;
And safely on thro' life's rough way
Direct their footsteps day by day.

Strengthen the frail ones with thy word
And guiding discipline, O Lord.
Hold forth thy heavenly food, we pray,
And drive all evil things away.

May they each morn the day begin
With prayer sincere thy grace to win
With grateful hearts at fall of even
May they exalt thy praise to heaven.

To God the Father and his Son,
And God the Spirit, Holy One.
May greatest glory henceforth be
Both now and thro' eternity.

13 Le Mesurier, *A Jobbing Actor*, pp. 6–7.
14 See 'A Visit to Bedford', *The Musical Times*, 1 September 1908, pp. 567–74.
15 Elton Halliley, 'A Short History of The National Society of Conservative and Unionist Agents' (published as a supplement to the *Conservative Agents' Journal*, December 1947), p. 8.
16 The Corrupt and Illegal Practices Prevention Act of 1883 was a continuation of an ongoing process (prompted, in effect, by the first two Reform Acts) designed to make voters in the UK free from the routine intimidation of landowners and politicians. It criminalised attempts to bribe voters and sought to standardise the amount that could be spent on election expenses (thus making the system, at least in theory, less weighted towards the wealthiest operators). The Act called for candidates' expenses to be published so that they could be measured against a maximum sum to be spent on any campaign. Stiff penalties (ranging from heavy fines to a period of imprisonment) were imposed on those found to have broken any of the rules and regulations.
17 Halliley, 'A Short History of The National Society of Conservative and Unionist Agents', p. 3.
18 The Conservative Party's National Society

of agents was formed thanks in large part to the pioneering efforts of such older Tory 'wire-pullers' as Wollaston Pym in Middlesex and Richard William Evelyn Middleton in West Kent. The Liberal Party underwent a similar organisational change, forming the Liberal Secretaries' and Agents' Association in 1882.

19 One breakfast menu prior to a committee meeting at the Angel Hotel in Cardiff, for example, was as follows: 'Soles, Fried Smelts, Kidneys, Mutton Cutlets, Roast Beef, Pressed Beef, Turkey, Roast Chicken and Tongue, Veal and Ham Pie, Pigeon Pie, Pheasants, Partridges and Stewed Fruits' (see Halliley, 'A Short History of The National Society of Conservative and Unionist Agents', p. 5).

20 Halliley, 'A Short History of The National Society of Conservative and Unionist Agents', p. 7.

21 Ibid.

22 Walter Edward Guinness, first Baron Moyne, was born in Dublin on 29 March 1880. He was the third son of the brewer and philanthropist Edward Cecil Guinness, later the first Earl of Iveagh (1847–1927), and his wife, Adelaide Maria Guinness (1844–1916). Educated at Eton College, he passed on an offer to go to Oxford and volunteered instead for service in the South African War with the Suffolk Yeomanry. He married Lady Evelyn Hilda Stuart Erskine, daughter of the fourteenth Earl of Buchan; they had two sons and one daughter. In the early 1890s, after his father bought a sporting estate at Elveden in Suffolk, Guinness stood as Conservative candidate for the Stowmarket division. Although defeated at the general election of 1906, he was returned at a by-election in 1907 for Bury St Edmunds which he continued to represent until 1931. He was appointed Under-Secretary of State for War in 1922 and Financial Secretary to the Treasury in 1923, and again in 1924–5 under his friend and ally Winston Churchill as Chancellor of the Exchequer. He entered the Cabinet in November 1925 as Minister of Agriculture. With the defeat of the Conservatives in 1929, he retired from office, and in January 1932 he was raised to the peerage as Baron Moyne of Bury St Edmunds. Following the outbreak

of the Second World War, Moyne served as Joint Parliamentary Secretary to the Minister of Agriculture on the formation of the Churchill Government in 1940. The next year, he succeeded Lord Lloyd as Secretary of State for the Colonies and Leader of the House of Lords. In August 1942, he was appointed Deputy Minister of State in Cairo, and in January 1944 he succeeded Richard Gardiner Casey as Resident Minister in the Middle East. On 6 November 1944, Moyne was assassinated in Cairo by two members of the Zionist terrorist group LEHI (a Hebrew acronym for 'Fighters for Israel's Freedom' – previously known to its opponents as the Stern gang). Charles Elton Halliley was present at a special service in memory of Moyne held later that month at the Cathedral in Bury St Edmunds, and (as the representative of the Bury St Edmunds Division of the Conservative Association) was one of the mourners at the major memorial service at St Margaret's, Westminster. See *The Times*, 7 November 1944, p. 6; Frederic Mullally, *The Silver Salver: The Story of the Guinness Family* (London: Granada, 1981); and Jonathan Guinness, *Requiem for a Family Business* (London: Macmillan, 1997).

23 The former site of the town's popular horse market, St Mary's Square had become, by the time the Halliley family arrived, a fashionable but extremely expensive residential area, with an appealing patch of green in the middle and only a quiet little winding road passing through. The Hallileys' second house there – number 6 – was next door to the former home of the celebrated anti-slavery campaigner, Thomas Clarkson. Elton and Amy would later move again (circa 1963) to 10 Southgate Street, just around the corner from St Mary's Square, long after their two children had left home. (Sources: 'E. Halliley' appears in the local telephone directories in the late 1910s and 20s with the address '8 St Mary's Square'; by the 1930s, the address has changed to '6 St Mary's Square'; John Le Mesurier returned to the Square in 1973 for a *Radio Times* photo shoot (*Radio Times*, East Anglia edition, 26 July 1973, p. 13), and was pictured with both

houses clearly visible behind him; the only description of either house he provides in his autobiography is of a Queen Anne-style property which corresponds to number 8. The Southgate Street address is recorded in several editions of the telephone book from the early 1960s, as well as on the death certificates of Elton, who died in 1964, and Amy, who died in 1968.)

24 This was the address used by Elton Halliley for Conservative Party correspondence while he was editor of the *Conservative Agents' Journal* from 1920 to 1947 (see, for example, the December 1947 issue).

25 Le Mesurier, *A Jobbing Actor*, p. 3.

26 Ibid., pp. 2–3.

27 William Cobbett, *Rural Rides*, vol. 1 (New York: Cosimo Classics, 2005), p. 47.

28 Charles Dickens, *The Pickwick Papers* (Oxford: Oxford University Press, 2008), p. 190.

29 Ouida disguised the identity of Bury St Edmunds as 'Cantitborough' for the purposes of her fiction 'Blue and Yellow, or How My Brother Fitz Stood for Cantitborough', in *Bentley's Miscellany*, vol. XLVII (London: Richard Bentley, 1860), p. 304.

30 Philip Larkin, 'I Remember, I Remember', *Collected Poems* (London: Faber and Faber, 1988), p. 81.

31 Le Mesurier, *A Jobbing Actor*, p. 4.

32 Ibid., p. 7.

33 Ibid., p. 4.

34 Ibid., p. 6. ('Tommy, Lad!' was written by Edward Teschemacher [lyrics] and E.J. Margetson [music] in 1907 and published by Boosey & Co; 'Drake's Drum' was written by Sir Henry Newbolt in 1897; see Henry Newbolt, *Collected Poems of Henry Newbolt* [London: Thomas Nelson & Sons, 1907].)

35 See Le Mesurier, *A Jobbing Actor*, p. 156.

36 John Le Mesurier, quoted in William Raynor, 'John's East Anglian Womb', *Radio Times* (East Anglia edition only), 26 July 1973, p. 13.

37 Le Mesurier, *A Jobbing Actor*, p. 5.

38 Charles Elton Halliley was awarded the OBE on 1 January 1952 for 'political services'.

39 Le Mesurier, *A Jobbing Actor*, pp. 5–6.

40 See Stephen Leacock, *My Financial Career and Other Follies* (Toronto: New Canadian Library, 1993). The story is included on John Le Mesurier's (sadly long-since deleted) LP entitled *What is Going to Become of Us All?* (Warner Communications, K54080: 1976).

41 Brentwood-born pianist and teacher Kathleen (Ida) Long (1896–1968) was a pupil of Herbert Sharpe at the Royal College of Music in London from 1910 to 1916. Following her professional debut in 1915, she pursued a distinguished career as a soloist with orchestras, as a recitalist and as a chamber music artist. Her tours took her throughout Europe and North America, and she also taught at the Royal College of Music from 1920 to 1964. In 1950 she was awarded the Palmes Académiques of France and in 1957 was made a CBE. An admirably precise and unpretentious interpreter of Bach, Scarlatti, Mozart, Haydn, Schumann, and the French school, especially of Fauré, she also championed the cause of British music. Long made eleven recordings for the National Gramophonic Society between 1927 and 1930; the bulk of her subsequent recordings – dating from the 1940s and 1950s – were released in the UK by Decca. She died in Cambridge.

42 Le Mesurier, *A Jobbing Actor*, p. 5.

43 Ibid., p. 6.

44 Ibid.

45 C.B. Halliley, letter to *The Times*, 12 September 1933, p. 8.

46 Le Mesurier, *A Jobbing Actor*, p. 12.

47 Ibid., p. 7.

48 Ibid., p. 3.

49 Ibid., p. 7.

50 Richard Charkin, 'charkin blog', 16 November 2006 (http://charkinblog.macmillan.com/CommentView,guid,f485f321-e28d-447b-ac81-fe89ef8608db.aspx).

51 Louis de Bernieres, quoted by his fellow ex-pupil John Suchet, 'Oh no, another rotten caning coming up', *Daily Mail* (Weekend section), 7 March 2009, p. 78.

52 John Suchet, ibid.

53 Le Mesurier, *A Jobbing Actor*, p. 7.

54 Ibid.

55 Ibid., p. 8.

56 Ibid., p. 9.

57 Ibid., p. 20.

58 Ibid., p. 9.

59 Ibid., p. 154.
60 See Joan Le Mesurier, *Dear John* (London: Sidgwick & Jackson, 2001), p. 221.
61 P.G. Wodehouse, 'The Man Who Disliked Cats', in *The Man Upstairs and Other Stories* (Rockville: Ark Manor, 2008), p. 90.
62 Le Mesurier, *A Jobbing Actor*, p. 10.
63 Ibid., p. 12.
64 Ibid., p. 154.

Chapter II Sherborne

Epigraph: lines from Noël Coward's poem, 'The Boy Actor', recited by John Le Mesurier on his LP *What Is Going To Become Of Us All?* (Warner Communications, K54080: 1976).

1 Excerpt by Alec Waugh from The Loom of Youth (© Alec Waugh, 1917) is reproduced by permission of PFD (www.pfd.co.uk) on behalf of the Estate of Alec Waugh.
2 Le Mesurier, *A Jobbing Actor*, p. 15.
3 Ibid.
4 Ibid., pp. 15–16.
5 See the memoir by A.H. Trelawny-Ross, *Their Prime of Life* (Winchester: Warren and Sons, 1956), pp. 68, 112.
6 Ibid., p. 170.
7 Le Mesurier, *A Jobbing Actor*, p. 16.
8 Ibid., p. 17.
9 John Le Carré, describing the fictional 'Carne School', which was widely regarded as being modelled closely on Sherborne School, in his novel *A Murder of Quality* (New York: Scribner, 2002), p. 1. Le Carré (whose real name is David Cornwell) hated his time at Sherborne so much that he feigned a nervous breakdown to escape at the age of sixteen.
10 Trelawny-Ross, *Their Prime of Life*, p. 30.
11 See Nowell Charles Smith, *Members of One Another* (London: Chapman & Hall, 1913), p. 341 (although the actual text pre-dates John's stay at Sherborne, Smith's written sermons were repeated with little if any revision every year all the way through to his retirement).
12 Trelawny-Ross, *Their Prime of Life*, p. 71.
13 Ibid., p. 68.
14 Nowell Smith, letter to *The Times*, 13 October 1926, p. 15.
15 The Hallileys sold their old home at number 8 to their friends, Lt-Col B.E. Oliver and his wife.
16 See Halliley, *A Short History of The National Society of Conservative and Unionist Agents*, p. 12. Since becoming a member of the Society himself, Halliley had always regarded the ad hoc manner whereby solicitors would recruit other solicitors as agents as both unjust and unfair in a supposedly modern democratic organisation, and so he began campaigning for change as soon as he was elected as a Representative on the Council in 1917. His first proposed resolution (seconded by the Society's then-Honorary Secretary and future Principal Agent of the Conservative Party, Sir Robert Topping) was debated and voted on in June 1922, but it was blocked by a majority intent on holding on to its own power of patronage. Years of further attempts and debates ensued until Halliley, again backed by Topping, won the rule change at the Society's Annual Meeting at Blackpool in 1932.
17 Trelawny-Ross, *Their Prime of Life*, p. 141.
18 See William Raynor, 'John's East Anglian Womb', *Radio Times* (East Anglia edition only), 26 July 1973, p. 13.
19 Trelawny-Ross, *Their Prime of Life*, pp. 209–10. (Another piece of 'romantic' advice passed on by Trelawny-Ross was: 'Do not write to a woman anything that would sound ridiculous if read out in court.')
20 Le Mesurier, quoted in Raynor, 'John's East Anglian Womb', p. 13.
21 George and Weedon Grossmith, *Diary of a Nobody* (London: Penguin, 1999), p. 57. One of the many recurring jokes in this most wonderful of books is the routine-loving Mr Pooter's love of 'Good old Broadstairs' as his family's holiday resort – and his ignorance, initially at least, not only of how wearied everyone else has become of the place but also of his wife's growing irritation whenever he uses the epithet 'Good old . . .'
22 Le Mesurier, *A Jobbing Actor*, p. 19.
23 Trelawny-Ross, *Their Prime of Life*, p. 35.
24 Ibid., p. 210.
25 Ibid., p. 82. The only excursions to the local cinema that were allowed, it seems, were for those movies that were deemed to contain an 'uplifting', and preferably 'religious', message. See Le Mesurier, *A Jobbing Actor*, p. 19.
26 Ibid., p. 100.

27 Ibid., pp. 110–11.
28 Ibid., p. 173.
29 Ibid., p. 100.
30 Ibid., p. 173.
31 Ibid., p. 123.
32 Ibid., pp. 328–33.
33 Le Mesurier, *A Jobbing Actor*, p. 18.

Chapter III Delaying Tactics

Epigraph: from Oscar Wilde, *The Importance of Being Ernest*, in *The Works of Oscar Wilde* (Ware: Wordsworth Editions, 1998), p. 713.

1 Le Mesurier, *A Jobbing Actor*, p. 18.
2 Ibid.
3 The firm of Greene & Greene moved to its current address in Bury St Edmunds, at 80 Guildhall Street, in 1937, four years after John left its employment.
4 Le Mesurier, *A Jobbing Actor*, p. 18.
5 Ibid.
6 Ibid., p. 19.
7 Ibid.
8 Ibid., p. 1.
9 Ibid., p. 21.
10 Ibid., p. 21.
11 Tessa Borner (née Osborne Durling), a niece of Dorothy Tollemache, told me: 'Yes, it could well be my Aunt Tolley, who married my uncle Arthur Durling in 1921 when she was 26 so it would fit with the mystery woman who was 36 in 1931. She was also very attractive and was born in Bury St Edmunds in 1895' (correspondence with the author, 20 May 2009). The current Lord Tollemache of Helmingham Hall, when contacted for this book, agreed that the evidence, though limited, 'certainly points to the lady being a member of the Tollemache family', but acknowledged that 'it is difficult to pinpoint exactly which one, if any'. Lord Tollemache suggested two other possible candidates:

(1) Mary Stuart, daughter of Lord Hamilton, who married Wilbraham Tollemache in 1878 and died in 1939 as an old widow and lived at Helmingham Hall during that period; (2) Alice Mary, daughter of John Head, who married Douglas Tollemache in 1887. Her husband built the Felix Hotel in Felixstowe and she and her husband would have often come to Helmingham Hall to visit the said Mary above. She died in 1959 aged 94. (Correspondence with the author, 14 December 2009.)

Neither of these women appears as plausible as the Hon. Dorothy, however, as both of them would have been far too old, by 1931, as well as unavailable for such a flirtatious relationship with John Halliley. Alice Mary Tollemache did have two daughters: Cynthia, who would have been forty-one in 1931, and Angela Mariota Tollemache, who would have been thirty-one, but neither of these seems particularly likely, either, as Cynthia had only recently been widowed (her husband, Lt.-Col. Guy Rattray Dubs, died on 23 October 1930 at their home in Portsmouth) and Angela, although divorced from her first husband (Algernon Henry Strutt, the 3rd Baron Belper), appears to have spent most of her time during this period in London with her two young children.

12 Douglas Tollemache built the Felix Hotel in 1903.
13 Le Mesurier, *A Jobbing Actor*, p. 22.
14 Ibid., pp. 23–4.
15 John Le Mesurier, quoted by Joan Le Mesurier, *Dear John*, p. 16.
16 Arthur Maitland Wilson resigned as leader of the Bury St Edmunds branch of the Conservative Party at the start of 1931, and was replaced Mr Lancelot Lake (see *The Times*, 29 January 1931, p. 11).
17 See *The Times*, 10 August 1931, p. 16; 10 November 1932, p. 4; 23 February 1933, p. 4; and 2 January 1932, p. 4.
18 In his autobiography (*A Jobbing Actor*, p. 24), Le Mesurier would say that he decided to leave his job as a solicitor and become an actor when he was on the verge of turning twenty-one, after being 'in my present business for six years'. He must have mis-remembered: since as he left school aged eighteen in 1930 – the records at Sherborne School confirm this – and turned twenty-one in April 1933, he could only have been in his job as an articled clerk for a maximum of three years.
19 Le Mesurier, *A Jobbing Actor*, p. 19.
20 Ibid., p. 19.

Chapter IV Drama School

Epigraph: lines from Noël Coward's poem, 'The Boy Actor', recited by John Le Mesurier on his LP *What Is Going To Become Of Us All?* (Warner Communications K54080, 1976).

1 John Le Mesurier, *A Jobbing Actor*, p. 34.
2 See *The Stage*, 6 November 1930, p. 17.
3 Le Mesurier, *A Jobbing Actor*, p. 25.
4 Alec Guinness, quoted in Joan Le Mesurier, *Dear John*, pp. 233–4.
5 This remains an unsubstantiated claim, but it is known that Alec Guinness himself encouraged the theory on several occasions, and also joked about it at other times. He told the writer John Le Carré, for example: 'My mother was a whore . . . She slept with the entire crew on Lord Moyne's yacht at the Cowes Regatta and when she gave birth she called the bastard Guinness but my father was probably the bloody cook.' See Piers Paul Read, *Alec Guinness: The Authorised Biography* (New York: Simon & Schuster, 2005), pp. 11–15.
6 Le Mesurier, *A Jobbing Actor*, p. 25.
7 Ibid.
8 *The Stage*, 26 July 1934, p. 11.
9 Dennis Edwards appeared as Lord Gomer in four episodes (three of them grouped together under the title of 'The Invasion of Time' in 1978) of the BBC1 sci-fi series *Doctor Who*; Mr Dryden in a 1985 episode ('Minder on the Orient Express') of the ITV comedy crime series *Minder*; and, also in 1985, as Mr Humphries in three episodes of the BBC1 children's serial *Grange Hill*.
10 Alec Guinness, quoted by Piers Paul Read, *Alec Guinness: The Authorised Biography*, p. 366.

Chapter V A Jobbing Actor

Epigraph: lines from 'Comedy Tonight' (from the play *A Funny Thing Happened on the Way to the Forum*) by Stephen Sondheim, published in *All Sondheim*, Volume 1 (New York: Revelation Music Publishing Corp./Rilting Music, 1992).

1 Bernard Miles, quoted by Barry Cryer, *Pigs Can Fly* (London: Orion, 2003), p. 99.
2 Arthur Lane, quoted by Roy Hudd, *Roy Hudd's Book of Music-Hall, Variety and Showbiz Anecdotes* (London: Robson Books, 1993), p. 56.
3 Le Mesurier, *A Jobbing Actor*, p. 27.
4 See, for example, Derek Nimmo, 'John Le Mesurier (1912–1983)', *Oxford Dictionary of National Biography*, ed. H.C.G. Matthew and Brian Harrison (Oxford: Oxford University Press, 2004). Oddly enough, Le Mesurier does not even mention the change, let alone explain the reasons behind it, in his autobiography and refers to himself as Le Mesurier when recalling a period in which he was still known to all as Halliley (see, for example, *A Jobbing Actor*, p. 36).
5 *The Stage*, 31 January 1935, p. 10.
6 The Millicent Ward Players placed a notice in *The Stage* (p. 13) on 17 January 1935, announcing that, owing to the lease of the Palladium changing hands, the company was 'open to offers for short or long seasons from Monday, January 28. They have played 54 consecutive weeks here [at the Palladium]. 54 different productions staged, including West End comedies, farces, and strong plays.'
7 J.C. Trewin, quoted in Sheridan Morley, *John Gielgud: The Authorised Biography* (London: Applause Books, 2003), p. 133.
8 Le Mesurier, *A Jobbing Actor*, p. 26.
9 Ibid.
10 Ibid., p. 27.
11 Ibid., p. 28.
12 Ibid.
13 Ibid., p. 29.
14 Kathleen Long's recital was broadcast by the BBC on 6 June 1935 via its regional Home Service.
15 *The Stage*, 5 September 1935, p. 2.
16 Le Mesurier, *A Jobbing Actor*, p. 30.
17 *The Stage*, 21 November 1935, p. 3.
18 Le Mesurier, *A Jobbing Actor*, p. 30.
19 Le Mesurier wrote (*A Jobbing Actor*, pp. 30–3) that he was recruited from Sheffield by a repertory company in Scotland, where he stayed 'for the six months leading up to the Munich crisis', and then went on to a company in Croydon. As the Munich crisis was in September/October 1938, and reviews and listings of the era clearly show that he was appearing with Croydon Rep in the autumn of 1936, one can conclude that he misremembered the sequence of events.
20 Le Mesurier, *A Jobbing Actor*, p. 34.

21 Anna Wing, speaking in *The Unforgettable John Le Mesurier*, first broadcast by ITV on 9 September 2001.

22 Le Mesurier, *A Jobbing Actor*, p. 36.

23 Ibid., p. 34.

24 Ibid., p. 35. (See also the review in *The Stage*, 17 September 1936, p. 7.)

25 Ibid., p. 35.

26 Ibid., p. 6.

27 See, for example, *The Times*'s review of *The Private Secretary*, 28 December 1937, p. 10.

28 J. Baxter-Somerville, letter to John Le Mesurier, undated, quoted in Joan Le Mesurier, *Dear John*, p. 22.

29 Source: BBC Written Archives Centre (BBC WAC), John Le Mesurier TV Artist File 1: 1938–62, actor's contract.

30 See Asa Briggs, *The History of Broadcasting in the United Kingdom* (Oxford: Oxford University Press, 1961–79), Volume 3; Kate Dunn, *Do Not Adjust Your Set: The Early Days of Live Television* (London: John Murray, 2003).

31 Le Mesurier, *A Jobbing Actor*, p. 33.

32 Ibid., p. 32.

33 See the summaries in *The Times*, 2 February 1939, p. 10, and 8 February 1939, p. 12.

34 Le Mesurier, *A Jobbing Actor*, p. 37.

35 Ibid.

36 Ibid.

37 *Manchester Guardian*, 24 October 1939, p. 4.

38 Le Mesurier, *A Jobbing Actor*, p. 38.

39 Ibid., p. 39.

40 Le Mesurier, *A Jobbing Actor*, p. 40.

41 See the 1939 National Service (Armed Forces) Act. Women aged between eighteen and sixty were brought into the scope of conscription in the spring of 1941, but as all women with dependent children were exempt, and many women were left – informally – in occupations such as nursing or teaching, the number appearing before tribunals was relatively few. In December 1941, the National Service Act (no. 2) made the conscription of women legal. At first, only single women aged between twenty and thirty were called up, but by mid-1943 almost 90 per cent of single women and 80 per cent of married women were employed in essential work for the war effort.

42 Consider, for example, the letter by E.H.M. Clutterbuck published in *The Times* (19 November 1940, p. 5): 'I came down from Oxford in June, and reached the age of 20 in July, when I had expected to be called up. I have been waiting ever since. Each week I felt I was certain to be called up [and] because of this I could not undertake any regular war work. Had I, and several of my friends, known that we should have these months free we might have undertaken work of some use to the national war effort. I am sure our case must be typical of many.'

43 Sir Oswald Stoll, letter to *The Times*, 4 September 1940, p. 6.

44 Le Mesurier, *A Jobbing Actor*, p. 41.

45 Ibid., p. 40.

46 Ibid.

47 John Le Mesurier's own recollections, in his autobiography (see *A Jobbing Actor*, pp. 40–2), are muddled on the chronology at this point: he remembers being married to June when war was declared in 1939. Their marriage certificate, however, clearly states the year as 1940, and the wedding was reported in several newspapers (e.g. *The Stage*, 18 April 1940, p. 6).

48 *The Stage*, 2 May 1940, p. 8.

49 Le Mesurier, *A Jobbing Actor*, p. 43.

50 See, for example, *The Stage*, 4 December 1941, p. 4.

51 Le Mesurier, *A Jobbing Actor*, p. 45.

52 Ibid.

Chapter VI The Army Years

Epigraph: a line from the *Dad's Army* episode 'The Deadly Attachment', written by Jimmy Perry and David Croft, first broadcast on BBC1 on 31 October 1973.

1 See *The Times*, 9 September 1940, p. 2 and Gavin Mortimer, *The Longest Night: The Worst Night of the London Blitz* (London: Phoenix, 2006).

2 Le Mesurier, *A Jobbing Actor*, p. 46.

3 Ibid.

4 Ibid., p. 47.

5 Ibid., p. 48.

6 See Winston Churchill, *Hansard*, 11 June 1941.

7 Le Mesurier, *A Jobbing Actor*, p. 49.

8 See *The Times*, 10 March 1941, p. 4 and Joshua Levine, *Forgotten Voices of the Blitz and the Battle of Britain* (London: Ebury Press, 2006), p. 400.

9 Le Mesurier, *A Jobbing Actor*, p. 52.

10 See *The Times*, 17 April 1941, p. 4.
11 Le Mesurier, *A Jobbing Actor*, p. 55.
12 Ibid., p. 57.
13 Ibid., p. 58.
14 Ibid.
15 Ibid., p. 59.
16 The Central Pool of Artistes – and Stars in Battledress (SIB), as its touring productions were known – was instigated by Lieutenant-Colonel Basil Brown early in 1942. Unlike the civilian company ENSA, SIB was considered a more 'organic' form of military entertainment – by servicemen for servicemen – as well as more integral – it had access to areas prohibited to civilian performers. Among the many future stars who took part at some stage were Terry-Thomas, Spike Milligan, Benny Hill, Reg Varney, Charlie Chester, Ken Platt, Harry Secombe and Norman Vaughan. See John Graven Hughes, *The Greasepaint War* (London: New English Library, 1976), Richard Fawkes, *Fighting for a Laugh* (London: Macdonald and Jane's, 1978) and Bill Pertwee's entertaining anecdotal history, *Stars in Battledress* (London: Hodder & Stoughton, 1992).
17 Le Mesurier, *A Jobbing Actor*, p. 60.
18 Ibid., pp. 59–60.
19 Ibid., p. 60.
20 Ibid., p. 6.
21 John Le Mesurier, speaking to the *Daily Mirror*, 20 August 1970, p. 7.
22 Le Mesurier, *A Jobbing Actor*, p. 61.
23 Ibid., p. 62.
24 Ibid.
25 Ibid.
26 Ibid.
27 Ibid., p. 65.
28 Ibid., p. 63.
29 Ibid., p. 65.

Chapter VII Hattie

Epigraph: 'A Nightingale Sang in Berkeley Square', by Eric Maschwitz and Manning Sherwin (Shapiro Bernstein & Co, 1940: Peter Maurice Music Ltd/EMI Music Ltd).

1 Andy Merriman, *Hattie: The Authorised Biography of Hattie Jacques* (London: Aurum, 2008), p. 2.
2 See *The Stage*, 7 November 1929, p. 22.
3 See Merriman, *Hattie*, p. 40.
4 *The Times*, 10 December 1947, p. 6; Merriman, *Hattie*, p. 47.
5 Le Mesurier, *A Jobbing Actor*, pp. 64–5.
6 Hattie Jacques, quoted in Merriman, *Hattie*, p. 49.
7 Ibid., p. 50.
8 Le Mesurier, *A Jobbing Actor*, p. 65.
9 For a sound account of what is a complicated story, see Merriman, *Hattie*, pp. 21–36.
10 Le Mesurier, *A Jobbing Actor*, p. 70.
11 The 1927 Cinematographic Films Act was introduced to protect the domestic market from the mass of American movies: it controlled advance and block-booking in British cinemas, introduced a quota system to ensure a certain minimum proportion of home-grown products (which was then maintained and refined in a further Act of 1938) and created an Advisory Committee to advise the Board of Trade on the administration of the various rules and regulations. The problem with the Act was that, after a promising run that eventually resulted in an all-time production high of 192 films in 1936, the policy ended up overextending the indigenous industry, causing a crash due to the combination of over-expansion and rapidly diminishing quality. One consequence was that American subsidiary production companies based in the UK had to make a slew of poor-quality movies, on very limited budgets, often just to fill the quotas for the screening of British movies in British cinemas. British feature film production hit rock bottom during the Second World War; only once the conflict was over (and a new Act of 1948 had been passed) did the British cinema industry bounce back, partly (arguably) by encouraging smaller and more competitive entrepreneurs, as well as greater quality, while production levels went up and stabilised for a fairly lengthy period. (For a splendid survey of the phenomenon, see Steve Chibnall and Brian McFarlane, *The British 'B' Film* [London: BFI/Palgrave Macmillan, 2009].)
12 See Roy S. Baker, quoted in Brian McFarlane, *An Autobiography of British Cinema* (London: Methuen, 1997), p. 42.
13 As Roy S. Baker put it (ibid., p. 45): '[Gilling] was very good and very

conscientious; a little bit tough with the actors on the set, but he maintained discipline and turned out some very good pictures.'

14 One reason for Harry Reynolds' unconventional but imaginative approach to independent film production was the fact that, when he had attempted to collaborate with other companies, he had been left out of pocket and sometimes stranded abroad with an unfinished project. In 1950, for example, Reynolds and his crew found themselves alone in Cannes, with unpaid hotel bills, after his partner – a company called Carnegie Films – called in its creditors without warning. Only twenty minutes of his planned movie – *Dangerous Meeting*, starring Michael Redgrave and Anouk Aimée – had been completed. (See *Daily Express*, 3 August 1950, p. 1.)

15 Roy S. Baker, quoted in McFarlane, *An Autobiography of British Cinema*, p. 43.

16 See Le Mesurier, *A Jobbing Actor*, p. 68.

17 Ibid.

18 Ibid., p. 67.

19 Ibid., pp. 68–9.

20 Ibid., p. 69.

21 Ibid.

22 Ibid., p. 65.

23 Ibid., p. 74.

24 Ibid.

25 Ibid.

26 In his autobiography (*A Jobbing Actor*, p. 74), John Le Mesurier would misremember the date, quite spectacularly, as 'April 1952' – almost three years later than the actual event, and not even in the same season.

27 *Daily Mirror*, 11 November 1949, p. 7.

28 See, for example, *The Stage*, 30 November 1950, p. 15.

Chapter VIII Movie Man

Epigraph: John Le Mesurier, *A Jobbing Actor*, p. 72.

1 The letters are preserved in John Le Mesurier's TV Artist Files at the BBC's Written Archives Centre in Caversham.

2 BBC WAC: John Le Mesurier Artist File 1: 1938–62: Audition record, 26 November 1951.

3 Roy S. Baker, quoted in McFarlane, *An Autobiography of British Cinema*, p. 47.

4 *The Times*, 17 January 1952, p. 2.

5 *The Stage*, 30 July 1953, p. 29.

6 The award was given by the *Daily Mail*.

7 Le Mesurier, *A Jobbing Actor*, p. 77.

8 *To-Day's Cinema*, 12 October 1954, p.12.

9 *The Times*, 17 September 1954, p. 11.

10 BBC WAC: John Le Mesurier Artist File 1: 1938–62.

11 See *The Stage*, 12 May 1955, p. 9 and *The Times*, 14 July 1955, p. 7.

12 Le Mesurier, *A Jobbing Actor*, p. 75.

13 Robin Le Mesurier, interview with the author, 27 February 2010.

14 Le Mesurier, *A Jobbing Actor*, pp. 77–8.

15 Robin Le Mesurier, interview with the author, 27 February 2010.

16 Ibid.

17 Ibid.

18 Ibid.

19 Ibid.

20 He had, in fact, worked on certain projects at certain times with agents before he met Freddy Joachim. The first was Gordon Harbord in 1947; the second was Jimmy Thompson at the Shaw & Lang Agency in Monmouth Street, who negotiated a few radio and TV jobs during the early 1950s; and the third was Joan Rees Limited for a few months in the mid-1950s.

21 Joan Le Mesurier recalled: 'Joan was very good – she actually taught me her bookkeeping method when Hattie "handed John over" to me. I still use it to this day' (interview with the author, 18 December 2009).

22 Joachim would go so far, in the case of another actor called Bruce Montague, as to insist on inserting a clause in their contract that prohibited his client from marrying in order to protect his image as an up-and-coming matinée idol.

23 See Richard Stone, *You Should Have Been In Last Night* (Sussex: The Book Guild, 2000), p. 111.

24 Denis Quilley, quoted in John Coldstream, *Dirk Bogarde: The Authorised Biography* (London: Weidenfeld & Nicolson, 2004), p. 160.

25 Frank Harvey, quoted in Le Mesurier, *A Jobbing Actor*, p. 69.

26 Le Mesurier, *A Jobbing Actor*, p. 69.

27 See, for example, *The Times*, 14 November 1955, p. 3.

28 Roy Boulting, quoted in McFarlane, *An*

Autobiography of British Cinema, p. 79.

29 See Le Mesurier, *A Jobbing Actor*, p. 70.

30 See Arthur Marwick, *British Society Since 1945* (Harmondsworth: Penguin, 1982), p. 165.

31 Roy Boulting, quoted in McFarlane, *An Autobiography of British Cinema*, p. 79.

32 Le Mesurier, *A Jobbing Actor*, p. 72.

33 Ibid.

Chapter IX Hancock

Epigraph: Ray Galton and Alan Simpson, 'The Lift', *Hancock*, first broadcast on BBC TV on 16 June 1961.

1 A.A. Milne, *Winnie-the-Pooh* (London: Egmont Books, 2006), pp. 39–40.

2 Tony Hancock, quoted in Cliff Goodwin, *When the Wind Changed* (London: Century, 1999), pp. 132–3.

3 Ibid., p. 414.

4 Le Mesurier, *A Jobbing Actor*, p. 75.

5 In his autobiography – which contains several 'misremembered' details of his life – Le Mesurier gives the impression that he only met Hancock when the comedian visited him after a play to offer him an occasional role in his TV series (see p. 92). The reality was that Hancock had been a frequent visitor to John and Hattie's home ever since he began working on *Educating Archie* six years earlier (as, confusingly, John confirmed himself elsewhere in his own book).

6 Ray Galton and Alan Simpson, 'The Lift', *Hancock*, first broadcast on BBCTV on 16 June 1961.

7 Le Mesurier, *A Jobbing Actor*, p. 92.

8 The fact that an inebriated Hancock sometimes passed out in bars associated at the time with London's gay community, and, on one occasion while on tour during 1962, staggered naked into the singer Matt Monro's bedroom, led to otherwise unfounded rumours that the comedian was bisexual (see, for example, Goodwin, *When the Wind Changed*, pp. 459–60, and John Fisher, *Tony Hancock* (London: Harper, 2009), p. 461). These rumours also encouraged some tabloid reporters to speculate that Hancock's close friendship with John Le Mesurier might actually have been a covertly homosexual relationship. There is absolutely no evidence to support such an allegation, and, indeed, there are plenty of John's friends and family members who are quick to ridicule the idea (as one of them told me: 'It was such a bizarre thing for journalists to ask I could only laugh!'), although biographers of Hancock have continued to ask some of their interviewees about the issue.

9 Jeffrey Bernard, quoted in Goodwin, *When the Wind Changed*, p. 249.

10 Cicely Hancock, quoted in Freddie Hancock and David Nathan, *Hancock* (London: BBC Books, 1996), p. 116.

11 Goodwin, *When the Wind Changed*, p. 164.

12 *The Times*, 2 March 1961, p. 4.

13 The influential critic Bosley Crowther, for example, seemed to overreact in spectacular fashion to what he called this 'presumptuous' movie. Writing in the *New York Times* (17 October 1961, p. 47), he snorted: 'Norman Wisdom can move over. The British have found a low comedian who is every bit as low as he is and even less comical.'

14 Le Mesurier, *A Jobbing Actor*, p. 93.

15 Henri Cartier-Bresson, quoted in Goodwin, *When the Wind Changed*, p. 350.

16 Le Mesurier, *A Jobbing Actor*, p. 93.

17 Ibid., p. 94.

18 Ibid.

19 *Monthly Film Bulletin*, Vol. 30, No. 352 (May 1963), p. 61.

20 *The Times*, 4 April 1963, p. 15.

21 Le Mesurier, *A Jobbing Actor*, p. 95.

22 Tony Hancock, quoted in Goodwin, *When the Wind Changed*, pp. 354–5.

Chapter X Ménage à Trois

Epigraph: John Le Mesurier, quoted by his former de facto sister-in-law, Anne Valery, in the documentary *The Unforgettable Hattie Jacques*, first broadcast on ITV on 21 January 2000.

1 John Le Mesurier, *A Jobbing Actor*, p. 77.

2 Anne Valery, in the documentary *The Unforgettable Hattie Jacques*. Joan Le Mesurier, it has to be said, was not overly impressed with this particular anecdote. She told me: 'Granted, I wasn't there, so who knows, but I think that story about

John and Robin staying out for two days was a bit outrageous. Yes, John loved jazz, and, yes, he could be very vague, but in my experience he was always very punctual and he certainly wasn't the kind of person who just would forget to come home at night!' (interview with the author, 10 February 2010).

3 John Le Mesurier, quoted by Ann Valery in *The Unforgettable John Le Mesurier*.

4 Le Mesurier, *A Jobbing Actor*, p. 80.

5 Bruce Copp, in the documentary *The Unforgettable Hattie Jacques*.

6 John Le Mesurier, quoted in Merriman, *Hattie*, p. 103.

7 Hattie Jacques, *Desert Island Discs*, broadcast on the BBC Light Programme on 16 October 1961.

8 John Le Mesurier, *Desert Island Discs*, broadcast on BBC Radio 4 on 17 February 1973.

9 Le Mesurier, *A Jobbing Actor*, p. 78.

10 Ibid., p. 79.

11 Ibid., pp. 85–6.

12 Ibid., p. 86.

13 Ibid.

14 Robin Le Mesurier, interview with the author, 27 February 2010.

15 A.A. Milne, *The House at Pooh Corner* (London: Puffin, 1992), p. 29.

16 Le Mesurier, *A Jobbing Actor*, pp. 86–7.

17 *This Is Your Life*, broadcast on BBC TV on 12 February 1963.

18 Le Mesurier, *A Jobbing Actor*, p. 87.

19 Ibid., p. 88.

20 Ibid., p. 89.

21 Ibid.

22 Ibid., p. 90.

23 Ibid.

24 Ibid.

25 The diagnosis was confirmed to me by John's widow, Joan Le Mesurier (interview with the author, 18 December 2009).

26 Le Mesurier, *A Jobbing Actor*, p. 91.

27 See *The Times*, 2 February 1938, p.14 and *The Conservative Agents' Journal*, November 1947, pp. 239, 252 and 257–8.

28 Le Mesurier, *A Jobbing Actor*, p. 97.

Chapter XI Joan

Epigraph: John Le Mesurier, quoted by Joan Le Mesurier, interview with the author, 18 December 2009.

1 Mark Eden's real name before his professional career began was Douglas Malin.

2 See Joan Le Mesurier, *Lady Don't Fall Backwards*, passim.

3 Joan Le Mesurier, interview with the author, 18 December 2009.

4 John Le Mesurier, quoted in Joan Le Mesurier, *Lady Don't Fall Backwards*, pp. 55–6.

5 Le Mesurier, *A Jobbing Actor*, p. 96.

6 Joan Le Mesurier, *Lady Don't Fall Backwards*, p. 56.

7 Joan Le Mesurier, speaking in the documentary *The Unforgettable John Le Mesurier*.

8 Le Mesurier, *A Jobbing Actor*, p. 97.

9 Joan Le Mesurier, *Lady Don't Fall Backwards*, p. 64.

10 Ibid., p. 59.

11 Ibid., pp. 59–60.

12 Joan Le Mesurier, *Dear John*, p. 45.

13 John Le Mesurier, quoted in Joan Le Mesurier, *Dear John*, p. 48.

14 Le Mesurier, *A Jobbing Actor*, p. 95.

15 Joan Le Mesurier, *Lady Don't Fall Backwards*, p. 64.

16 Ibid., p. 65.

17 Ibid., p. 67.

18 John Le Mesurier quoted by Joan Le Mesurier in the documentary *The Unforgettable John Le Mesurier*.

19 Joan Le Mesurier, *Lady Don't Fall Backwards*, p. 67.

20 Ibid., p. 69.

21 Ibid.

22 Joan Le Mesurier, interview with the author, 18 December 2009.

23 Joan Le Mesurier, *Lady Don't Fall Backwards*, p. 70.

24 Ibid.

25 Le Mesurier, *A Jobbing Actor*, p. 97.

26 Robin Le Mesurier, quoted in Joan Le Mesurier, *Dear John*, p. 64.

27 Kim Le Mesurier, ibid.

28 Hattie Jacques, quoted in Merriman, *Hattie*, pp. 137–8.

29 Joan Le Mesurier, *Lady Don't Fall Backwards*, p. 71.

30 Joan Le Mesurier, in the documentary *The Unforgettable Hattie Jacques*.

31 See the *Daily Mirror*, 28 May 1965, p. 5.

32 Joan Le Mesurier, *Lady Don't Fall Backwards*, p. 71.

33 Hattie Jacques, quoted in Merriman, *Hattie*, p. 137.

34 Ibid.
35 See, for example, Le Mesurier, *A Jobbing Actor*, p. 91; Merriman, *Hattie*, p. 141; *The Unforgettable Hattie Jacques*.
36 Bruce Copp, in the documentary *The Unforgettable Hattie Jacques*.
37 Merriman, *Hattie*, p. 142.
38 Le Mesurier, *A Jobbing Actor*, p. 99.
39 Le Mesurier, *A Jobbing Actor*, p.100.
40 John Le Mesurier, quoted in Joan Le Mesurier, *Dear John*, p. 70.

Chapter XII The Sad Affair

Epigraph: Ray Galton and Alan Simpson, 'Twelve Angry Men', *Hancock's Half-Hour*, first broadcast on BBC TV, 16 October 1959.

1 John Le Mesurier, quoted in Joan Le Mesurier, *Lady Don't Fall Backwards*, p. 68.
2 Joan Le Mesurier, *Lady Don't Fall Backwards*, pp. 68–9.
3 Ibid., p. 69.
4 Ibid.
5 Ibid. p. 72.
6 Kenneth Williams, diary entry 28 July 1965, in Kenneth Williams, *The Kenneth Williams Diaries*, ed. Russell Davies (London: HarperCollins, 1993), p. 261.
7 Joan Le Mesurier, *Lady Don't Fall Backwards*, p. 76.
8 Ibid.
9 Ibid., p. 77.
10 Ibid., p. 78.
11 Ibid., p. 79.
12 Joan Le Mesurier, interview with the author, 4 November 2009.
13 Joan Le Mesurier, *Lady Don't Fall Backwards*, p. 79.
14 Ibid.
15 Ibid.
16 Ibid., p. 80.
17 Ibid., p. 81.
18 Tony Hancock, quoted in Hancock and Nathan, *Hancock*, p. 177.
19 Tony Hancock, quoted in Fisher, *Tony Hancock*, p. 513.
20 Le Mesurier, *A Jobbing Actor*, p. 109.
21 Ibid., pp. 110–11.
22 Joan Le Mesurier, *Lady Don't Fall Backwards*, p. 79.
23 Le Mesurier, *A Jobbing Actor*, pp. 110–11.
24 Mark Eden, speaking in the documentary *The Unforgettable John Le Mesurier*.
25 Le Mesurier, *A Jobbing Actor*, p. 111.
26 Ibid., p. 76.
27 Le Mesurier, *A Jobbing Actor*, p. 112.
28 Vince Powell, interview with the author, 22 May 2007.
29 Le Mesurier, *A Jobbing Actor*, p. 113.
30 Dialogue transcribed from *George and the Dragon*, series three, episode 1, 'The Reunion', written by Vince Powell and Harry Driver, first broadcast by ATV on 6 January 1968.
31 Dialogue transcribed from *George and the Dragon*, series one, episode 5, 'The Royal Letter', written by Vince Powell and Harry Driver, first broadcast by ATV on 17 December 1966.
32 Source: Television Audience Measurement (TAM) weekly ratings.
33 Dialogue transcribed from *George and the Dragon*, series two, episode 5, 'The Old Flame', written by Vince Powell and Harry Driver, first broadcast by ATV on 17 June 1967.
34 Source: Television Audience Measurement (TAM) weekly ratings.
35 Vince Powell, interview with the author, 22 May 2007.
36 Dialogue transcribed from *George and the Dragon*, series four, episode 1, 'Backing Britain', written by Vince Powell and Harry Driver, first broadcast by ATV on 24 September 1968.
37 Joan Le Mesurier, *Lady Don't Fall Backwards*, p. 95.
38 John Le Mesurier, quoted in the *Sunday Express*, 9 September 2001, p. 60.
39 Joan Le Mesurier, speaking in the documentary *The Unforgettable John Le Mesurier*.
40 Joan Le Mesurier, quoted in Fisher, *Tony Hancock*, p. 574.
41 Cicely Hancock, quoted in Fisher, *Tony Hancock*, p. 528.
42 Joan Le Mesurier, *Lady Don't Fall Backwards*, p. 124.
43 Ibid., p. 140.
44 Ibid., p. 141.
45 Ibid.
46 Ibid.
47 Ibid.
48 Ibid.
49 Joan Le Mesurier, interview with the author, 18 December 2009.
50 Joan Le Mesurier, *Lady Don't Fall Backwards*, p. 142.
51 Ibid.

52 Ibid., p. 143.

53 Ibid.

54 Ibid., p. 145.

55 Ibid., p. 146.

56 Ibid., pp. 145, 149.

57 John Le Mesurier, *A Jobbing Actor*, p. 114.

58 Ibid., pp. 114–15.

59 For accounts of the making of this show, see Roger Wilmut's excellent *Tony Hancock 'Artiste'* (London: Methuen, 1983), chapter 12, and Eddie Joffe's *Hancock's Last Stand* (London: Methuen, 1999), passim.

60 Tony Hancock, quoted in Fisher, *Tony Hancock*, p. 545.

61 Joan Le Mesurier, *Lady Don't Fall Backwards*, p. 152.

62 Amy Le Mesurier Halliley had been living at 10 Southgate Street, Bury St Edmunds before being admitted to the nearby St Mary's Hospital. Although her death certificate records her age as eighty-eight, she had been born in 1878, so she was actually ninety.

63 As John admitted as tactfully as he could in *A Jobbing Actor* (p. 7), he never did have much of a relationship with his sister Michelle. Possessing rather different interests and outlooks, they tended to avoid each other politely for much of their adult lives, apart from a few family gatherings and one stiff and stuffy dinner party that John confided to his wife Joan (interview with the author, 18 December 2009) was 'jolly hard work'. Relations worsened in the mid-1960s, when John, who had only recently begun to recover from a serious illness, was obliged to travel from London to the West Country to film a commercial; he was later admonished by Michelle's daughter in a very angry letter for not taking a detour to see her mother in Bury St Edmunds, as Michelle herself was also recovering from a bout of ill-health. John, Joan would recall, found the complaint both hurtful and unfair, and, sadly, the already very frail relationship between him and his sister never recovered: 'They didn't have anything to do with each other after that.'

64 See Fisher, *Tony Hancock*, p. 566.

65 Joan Le Mesurier, *Lady Don't Fall Backwards*, pp. 153–4.

66 Ibid., p. 154.

67 Ibid.

68 Tony Hancock, quoted in Fisher, *Tony Hancock*, p. 559.

69 Ibid., p. 155.

70 Ibid.

71 Le Mesurier, *A Jobbing Actor*, p. 136.

72 See the helpful account in Fisher, *Tony Hancock*, p. 568.

73 Le Mesurier, *A Jobbing Actor*, p. 116.

74 Joan Le Mesurier, *Lady Don't Fall Backwards*, p. 167.

75 John Le Mesurier, quoted by Joan Le Mesurier, *Dear John*, p. 78.

76 Joan Le Mesurier, *Lady Don't Fall Backwards*, p. 167.

Chapter XIII The Dad's Army Years

Epigraph: 'Who Do You Think You're Kidding, Mr Hitler', words by Jimmy Perry, music by Jimmy Perry and Derek Taverner (Veronica Music Ltd.).

1 See my *Dad's Army: The Story of a Classic Television Show* (London: Fourth Estate, 2001), and, for a comparison between the fiction and the facts about the Home Guard, my article on the BBC website: http://www.bbc.co.uk/history/british/brita in_wwtwo/dads_army_01.shtml.

2 David Croft, interview with the author, 23 May 2000.

3 Michael Mills, quoted by David Croft, interview with the author, 23 May 2000.

4 Freddy Joachim, quoted in Le Mesurier, *A Jobbing Actor*, p. 72.

5 Le Mesurier, *A Jobbing Actor*, p. 113.

6 Ibid., p. 117.

7 See Clive Dunn, *Permission to Speak* (London: Century, 1986), p. 196.

8 Ibid.

9 Ibid., p. 197.

10 David Croft, interview with the author, 23 May 2000.

11 Ibid.

12 Ibid.

13 Bill Pertwee, interview with the author, 27 May 2000.

14 David Croft, interview with the author, 23 May 2000.

15 Clive Dunn, quoted in Le Mesurier, *A Jobbing Actor*, p. 118.

16 Ibid.

17 David Croft, interview with the author, 23 May 2000.

18 Dunn, *Permission to Speak*, p. 198.

19 David Jason, correspondence with the author, 1 June 2000.

20 BBC WAC: *Dad's Army* File T12/890/1: the cast was paid, per episode, the following sums for the first series – John Le Mesurier, £262 10s; Arthur Lowe, £210; Clive Dunn, £210; John Laurie, £105; James Beck, £78 15s; Arnold Ridley, £63; Bill Pertwee, £57 15s; Ian Lavender, £52 10s.

21 Jimmy Perry, interview with the author, 27 August 2000.

22 Ibid.

23 Ibid.

24 David Croft, interview with the author, 23 May 2000.

25 John Laurie, quoted in Peter Way, *Dad's Army* (London: Peter Way, 1972), p. 33.

26 Source: BBC WAC: John Le Mesurier Artist File 3: 1963–1970: actor contract.

27 Jimmy Perry, interview with the author, 27 August 2000.

28 Le Mesurier, *A Jobbing Actor*, p. 118.

29 Huw Wheldon, *The Achievement of Television* (London: BBC, 1975), p. 11.

30 Ibid.

31 Ibid.

32 John Le Mesurier, quoted in Way, *Dad's Army*, p. 19.

33 Barry Took, interview with the author, 17 May 2000.

34 See Tom Sloan, *Television Light Entertainment* (London: BBC, 1969), p. 12.

35 Jimmy Perry, interview with the author, 27 August 2000.

36 David Croft, interview with the author, 23 May 2000.

37 Jimmy Perry, interview with the author, 27 August 2000.

38 David Croft, interview with the author, 23 May 2000.

39 Jimmy Perry and David Croft, 'The Man and the Hour', *Dad's Army*, first broadcast on BBC1 on 31 July 1968.

40 The BBC Daily Viewing Barometer for 31 July 1968 put the size of audience at 14.2 per cent of the UK population (50,500,000 at the time); programmes on BBC2 and ITV during this 8.20–8.50 period attracted audiences of 0.5 per cent and 19.4 per cent respectively.

41 Nancy Banks-Smith, *Sun*, 1 August 1968, p. 12.

42 Sean Day-Lewis, *Daily Telegraph*, 1 August 1968, p. 19.

43 Michael Billington, *The Times*, 1 August 1968, p. 7.

44 Mary Malone, *Daily Mirror*, 1 August 1968, p. 14.

45 Philip Purser, *Sunday Telegraph*, 4 August 1968, p. 13.

46 Tom Stoppard, *Observer*, 4 August 1968, p. 20.

47 Ron Boyle, *Daily Express*, 1 August 1968, p. 10. (As often happened with television and theatre reviews, this piece arrived too late to appear in early editions of the paper, although some of them did carry another review of the programme – also positive – by Robin Turner; Boyle's review first appeared in the *fourth* edition of that day's *Express*.)

48 Le Mesurier, *A Jobbing Actor*, p. 122.

49 In a letter to the *Daily Mirror* (17 August 1968, p. 13), shortly after the third episode had been broadcast, a viewer praised the show and singled out the Mainwaring–Wilson relationship as its highlight: 'Arthur Lowe is a fine character actor and with John Le Mesurier as his foil we surely have the ideal pair.'

50 Jimmy Perry and David Croft, 'Command Decision', *Dad's Army*, first broadcast on BBC1 on 14 August 1968.

51 BBC Daily Viewing Barometer, 11 September 1968. The Reaction Index was 64.

52 Richard Last, *Sun*, 12 September 1968, p. 12.

53 BBC WAC: *Dad's Army* File T12/880/1: memorandum from Keith Smith to David Croft, 16 September 1968.

54 Joan Le Mesurier, *Lady Don't Fall Backwards*, p. 167.

55 Joan Le Mesurier, interview with the author, 18 December 2009.

56 Averages calculated from percentages recorded in the BBC Daily Viewing Barometers.

57 In 1971, when David Croft received the award, it was still known as SFTA (Society of Film and Television Arts); it was re-named BAFTA (British Academy of Film and Television Arts) in 1975.

58 BBC1's Christmas compendium featured specially written *Dad's Army* sketches on 25 December 1968, 1969, 1970 and 1972.

59 *The Coward Revue* was broadcast on BBC2 on 26 December 1969, and repeated on

BBC1 on 28 December.

60 *The Royal Television Gala Performance*, which also featured Morecambe and Wise and Dave Allen, was recorded at Television Centre in the presence of Queen Elizabeth and Prince Philip, and was broadcast on BBC1 on 24 May 1970.

61 The 'Monty on the Bonty' sketch (written by Eddie Braben) was featured in the 22 April 1971 edition of *The Morecambe & Wise Show*, broadcast on BBC1.

62 The *Look In* comic strip ran from 1970 to 1980; a *Dad's Army* colouring and dot-to-dot book was published by World Distributors in 1971; a *Dad's Army Activity Book* was published by World Books in 1973; Ovaltine produced a board game in 1971, while Denys Fisher produced another in 1974; Lever Brothers marketed a *Dad's Army* bubble bath in 1972; Primrose Confectionery produced a set of twenty-five sweet cigarette cards in 1971; Peter Way published an 'official souvenir' magazine, *Dad's Army*, in 1972; and a series of six *Dad's Army Annuals* were published by World Distributors between 1973 and 1978.

63 BCNZ (the Broadcasting Corporation of New Zealand) began showing episodes from series three (the first to be filmed in colour) on 20 March 1970. The other countries followed soon after, each one starting from series three (source: BBC Worldwide).

64 *Parsley Sidings* was set in a backwater railway station. Lowe was the station master, Lavender his son and Pertwee his rival. The show ran for two series between December 1971 and December 1973.

65 Lowe appeared on *Desert Island Discs* on 12 December 1970. The movies he made with Lindsay Anderson during this period were *If . . .* (1969) and *O Lucky Man!* (1973); he also appeared in Anderson's *Britannia Hospital* in 1982.

66 'Grandad' entered the charts in December 1970, reaching number one at the start of January 1971, and remained in the top 40 for 14 weeks.

67 The episode of *Sykes* that featured John Le Mesurier as well as Hattie Jacques was called 'Uncle', and was first broadcast on BBC1 on 21 September 1972.

68 *The Culcheth Job* – sponsored by British Leyland and released in 1974 – was a twenty-seven-minute light-hearted 'heist' movie short designed, it appears, to showcase the talent of Brian Culcheth as well as a range of Triumph cars. John appeared as Major Richard Hornby, the boss of a team of hijackers who recruit Culcheth as the unsuspecting getaway driver to assist them in a security van robbery. After setting the plan into action, Hornby spends most of the rest of the time alone in his luxury apartment, either sipping brandy or adjusting – very slowly – his young female friend's *décolletage*. It was the kind of low-key one-off project that John rather enjoyed, and he impressed those on set with his easygoing professionalism. Brian Culcheth would recall: 'I had such a lot of fun making [the movie] and it was such a privilege to work with John Le Mesurier. One that I am sure many professional actors would have wished for. He was so helpful in guiding me with advice and little techniques' (correspondence with Richard McCann, 15 January 2010).

69 John Le Mesurier appeared on *Desert Island Discs* on 17 February 1973.

70 The first animated television series based on Roger Hargreaves' books was produced in 1975 by Flicks Films, with the voices and the narration provided by Arthur Lowe, and broadcast by BBC1 during that and several subsequent years. *Bod* was another BBC1 children's animated television programme, also first shown in 1975, with thirteen episodes (based on four original *Bod* books written by Joanna and Michael Cole) narrated by John Le Mesurier. A DVD of the entire series is commercially available.

71 John appeared on *Jackanory* several times in the 1970s. The *Blue Peter* appearance by Le Mesurier and Lowe was broadcast on BBC1 on 22 February 1973.

72 Jimmy Perry and David Croft, 'Sgt Wilson's Little Secret', *Dad's Army*, first broadcast on BBC1, 22 March 1969.

73 Jimmy Perry and David Croft, 'A. Wilson (Manager)?', *Dad's Army*, first broadcast on BBC1, 4 November 1970.

74 Compiled from references in the following episodes: 'The Man and the Hour', 'Mum's Army', 'A. Wilson (Manager)?', 'If the Cap

Fits . . .', 'The King Was in his Counting House', 'The Godiva Affair' and 'My Brother And I'.

75 Compiled from references in the following episodes: 'The Man and the Hour', 'War Dance', 'A. Wilson (Manager)?', 'Getting the Bird' and 'The Honourable Man'.

76 Quoted in Le Mesurier, *A Jobbing Actor*, pp. 18–19.

77 Arthur Lowe said: 'Oddly enough, it was never my ambition to be a star; I simply wanted to be the best character actor going, but stardom obviously came through television. I don't think I'd have done it without television.' Quoted in Hughes, *The Greasepaint War*, p. 138.

78 See Bill Pertwee, *Dad's Army* (London: Pavilion, 1998), p. 30, and Dunn, *Permission to Speak*, p. 205.

79 Recalled in Bill Pertwee, *The Story of Dad's Army*, Speaking Volumes audiotape (Polygram 1995).

80 John Le Mesurier, quoted in Joan Le Mesurier, *Lady Don't Fall Backwards*, p. 176.

81 See Pertwee, *Dad's Army*, p. 38.

82 Ian Lavender, interview with the author, 29 May 2000.

83 Le Mesurier, *A Jobbing Actor*, p. 119.

84 Arthur Lowe, quoted by Terence Pettigrew, *Photoplay*, August 1978, pp. 54–5.

85 David Croft, interview with the author, 23 May 2000.

86 Ian Lavender, interview with the author, 29 May 2000.

87 Jimmy Perry, interview with the author, 30 January 2010.

88 Arthur Lowe, quoted in Way, *Dad's Army*, p. 18.

89 Jimmy Perry and David Croft, 'Absent Friends', *Dad's Army*, first broadcast on BBC1, 30 October 1970.

90 Jimmy Perry and David Croft, 'When Did You Last See Your Money?', *Dad's Army*, first broadcast on BBC1, 1 December 1972.

91 Le Mesurier, *A Jobbing Actor*, p. 119.

92 Jimmy Perry and David Croft, 'Wake Up Walmington', *Dad's Army*, first broadcast on BBC1, 2 October 1977.

93 Jimmy Perry and David Croft, 'We Know Our Onions', *Dad's Army*, first broadcast on BBC1, 21 November 1973.

94 Jimmy Perry and David Croft, 'Menace from the Deep', *Dad's Army*, first broadcast

on BBC1, 13 November 1969.

95 Jimmy Perry and David Croft, 'High Finance', *Dad's Army*, first broadcast on BBC1, 3 October 1975.

96 Le Mesurier, *A Jobbing Actor*, p. 120.

97 Ibid.

98 Ibid., p. 122.

99 Quoted in Stephen Lowe, *Arthur Lowe* (London: Virgin, 1997), p. 143.

100 Ibid., p. 105.

101 Arthur Lowe, quoted by Jimmy Perry, interview with the author, 21 June 2001.

102 Arthur Lowe, quoted in Lowe, *Arthur Lowe*, p. 144.

103 Ian Lavender, interview with the author, 29 May 2000.

104 In 1971, Arnold Ridley was seventy-five, John Laurie seventy-four, John Le Mesurier fifty-nine, Edward Sinclair fifty-seven, Arthur Lowe fifty-six, Clive Dunn fifty-one, Bill Pertwee forty-four, James Beck forty-two, Frank Williams forty and Ian Lavender twenty-five.

105 Recalled by Ian Lavender, interview with the author, 29 May 2000.

106 See Pertwee, *Dad's Army*, p. 59.

107 Pertwee, *Dad's Army*, p. 102; Bill Pertwee, *A Funny Way to Make a Living* (London: Sunburst, 1996), p. 256.

108 Jimmy Perry, in *Dad's Army: The Lost Episodes* (London: BBC, 1998), p. 36.

109 David Croft, interview with the author, 23 May 2000.

110 Ibid.

111 Ibid.

112 See my *Dad's Army*, Chapter XIII.

113 The radio version of *Dad's Army* consisted of previously broadcast television scripts adapted by Harold Snoad and Michael Knowles. The first series of twenty-six episodes was recorded during June and July 1973 and broadcast on BBC Radio 2 from 28 January to 18 June 1974. A Christmas special went out on 25 December 1974, followed by a second series of twenty episodes between 11 February and 24 June 1975, and a third series of twenty-six episodes between 16 March and 7 September 1976.

114 Le Mesurier, *A Jobbing Actor*, p. 129.

115 Ibid., p. 130.

116 See Pertwee, *Dad's Army: The Making of a Television Legend*, p. 143.

117 Death certificate: dated 7 August 1973.

118 John Bardon appeared as Harold Forster in one episode of *Dad's Army* ('Ring Dem Bells', first broadcast on BBC1, 5 September 1975), but he went on to play Jim Branning in the BBC1 soap opera *EastEnders*.

119 Hamish Roughead's television credits included episodes of *Doctor Finlay's Casebook* and *The Borderers*.

120 John Le Mesurier, quoted in Pertwee, *Dad's Army*, p. 38.

121 Frank Williams, interview with the author, 8 August 2000.

122 John Le Mesurier, *A Jobbing Actor*, p. 139.

123 Ian Lavender, interview with the author, 29 May 2000.

124 Croft, *You Have Been Watching*, p. 206.

125 *The Stage*, 16 October 1975, p. 24.

126 Ibid., 14 September 1975, p. 5.

127 Jimmy Perry, interview with the author, 27 August 2000.

128 Le Mesurier, *A Jobbing Actor*, p. 145.

129 Source: BBC Daily Viewing Barometers, 2 October–13 November 1977.

130 Ian Lavender, interview with the author, 29 May 2000.

131 David Croft, interview with the author, 23 May 2000.

132 Jimmy Perry and David Croft, 'Never Too Old', *Dad's Army*, first broadcast on BBC1, 13 November 1977.

133 BBC Daily Viewing Barometer, 13 November 1977.

134 BBC WAC: Audience Research Report (VR/77/626, 21 December 1977) on *Dad's Army*, 'Never Too Old'. The Reaction Index was 77.

135 Peter Fiddick, *Guardian*, 14 November 1977, p. 10.

136 Bill Pertwee, interview with the author, 27 May 2000.

137 The *Daily Mirror* organised the event (see pp. 16–17 of its 14 November 1977 edition).

138 Dunn, *Permission to Speak*, p. 213.

139 Le Mesurier, *A Jobbing Actor*, p. 145.

140 Dunn, *Permission to Speak*, p. 213.

141 David Croft, interview with the author, 23 May 2000.

142 Dunn, *Permission to Speak*, p. 213.

143 Arthur Lowe, quoted in the *Daily Mirror*, 14 November 1977, p. 16.

144 John Le Mesurier, ibid.

145 Clive Dunn, ibid.

146 Ian Lavender, ibid., p. 17.

147 Arnold Ridley, quoted in Dunn, *Permission to Speak*, p. 213.

148 Ibid.

149 Le Mesurier, *A Jobbing Actor*, p. 145.

150 *The Morecambe & Wise Show* was broadcast by BBC1 on 25 December 1977.

151 Joan Le Mesurier, *Lady Don't Fall Backwards*, p. 172; Michael Whitehall, *Shark Infested Waters* (London: Timewell Press, 2007), p. 206.

Chapter XIV Do You Think That's Wise?

Epigraph: Le Mesurier, *A Jobbing Actor*, p. 149.

1 Le Mesurier, *A Jobbing Actor*, p. 143.

2 Joan Le Mesurier, *Lady Don't Fall Backwards*, p. 184.

3 Le Mesurier, *A Jobbing Actor*, p. 144.

4 David Croft, interview with the author, 23 May 2000.

5 Joan Le Mesurier, interview with the author, 18 December 2009.

6 Letter from John Le Mesurier to Arthur Lowe, date unknown, quoted in Lowe, *Arthur Lowe*, p. 183.

7 See Richard DeLillo's classic memoir, *The Longest Cocktail Party: An Insider's Diary of the Beatles, Their Million-dollar Apple Empire and Its Wild Rise and Fall* (Edinburgh: Canongate, 2005).

8 Derek Taylor, sleeve notes to the John Le Mesurier album *What is Going to Become of Us All?*

9 Joan Le Mesurier, interview with the author, 18 December 2009.

10 See Joan Le Mesurier, *Lady Don't Fall Backwards*, pp. 191–2.

11 Derek Taylor, sleeve notes to the John Le Mesurier album *What is Going to Become of Us All?*

12 Ibid.

13 Le Mesurier, *A Jobbing Actor*, p. 141.

14 Joan Le Mesurier, *Lady Don't Fall Backwards*, p. 180.

15 Ibid., p. 181.

16 Freddy Joachim retired as an agent at the end of May 1972. John Le Mesurier wrote to inform the BBC of Peter Campbell becoming his new agent on 22 May 1972 (source: BBC WAC: John Le Mesurier Artist File III: 1968–72).

17 As Peter Marden, Campbell had played the character of Frank Nugent in the BBC's *Billy Bunter of Greyfriars School* during the 1950s, and also made one-off appearances in a few other TV shows of the era.

18 The recordings – featuring adaptations of Bible stories by Robert Duncan – were called *Once Upon a World* and had a very limited circulation in 1977 until they were redistributed in 2008 by B7 Media in CD and mp3 formats.

19 Joan Le Mesurier, interview with the author, 18 December 2009.

20 John worked with Vincent Price at Pinewood Studios in 1964 on the set of a movie called *City Under the Sea* (released in 1965). Price – who lived at the time in a Spanish-style mansion, midway between Bel Air and Beverly Hills, at 580 North Beverly Glen – said to him one day: 'At home, in California, when I look out of the window, I see your name.' John, somewhat bemused, replied: 'Of course you do, dear boy.' Price then explained: 'It's a totem pole.' John would later say that this detail rang a bell: 'As a child, I had been told of a great uncle who went out west and, working against fashionable mores, declared his sympathy with the Indians. In recognition of his interest in their well-being, they presented him with the totem' (*A Jobbing Actor*, p. 112). This demonstrates John's rather loose grasp of family history, as it was his three maternal uncles who emigrated to Canada from Bedford, and his Uncle Cecil who became close to an aboriginal community in British Columbia.

21 On 20 November 1978, the MP and former Liberal leader Jeremy Thorpe was accused in court of plotting to kill his alleged former lover, Norman Scott, and then dispose of the dead body. Thorpe was charged along with David Holmes (Deputy Treasurer of the Liberal Party), George Deakin (a nightclub owner) and the 'other' John Le Mesurier (a businessman) of conspiracy to murder Scott. Thorpe was also accused alone of inciting David Holmes to murder Scott. Magistrates committed the case to trial on 13 December 1978. Proceedings began at the Old Bailey in May 1979 – just after the General Election in which Mr Thorpe lost his seat. All four defendants were cleared of the charges a month later, but the case destroyed Thorpe's career and

he did not return to politics.

22 John Le Mesurier, quoted by Joan Le Mesurier, interview with the author, 4 February 2010.

23 Source: BBC WAC: John Le Mesurier Artist File III: 1968–72: actor's contract.

24 See Le Mesurier, *A Jobbing Actor*, p. 124.

25 John Le Mesurier might be best described, politically, as a Burkean conservative, in the broad sense that he favoured evolution over revolution, custom and experience over abstract speculation and pure reason, and the prudence of the community over the capriciousness of the individual. In a less pompous-sounding party political sense, he remained a very moderate 'One Nation' Conservative, but, as his wife Joan explained to me, this allegiance tended to be fairly passive and non-committal: 'He never really thought that much about politics. His upbringing had made him what he was, but he wasn't what you'd call "political" at all. Maybe he'd sort of drifted into doing the odd active thing in the past – especially when he was married to Hattie [Jacques], who was right-wing and always told him how to vote at Equity as well as in elections – but I've always been left-wing so he got no encouragement from me at all! I remember one time in the 1970s, Saatchi & Saatchi called, trying to get him to do some commercials for the Conservative Party in the lead-up to a General Election. I'd picked up the extension, heard it and then gone, "What?" I told him, "John, you can't possibly do that!" He said, "Oh, can't I, darling?" I said, "No, you mustn't!" So he didn't!' (interview with the author, 10 February 2010).

26 Dennis Potter, quoted in Humphrey Carpenter, *Dennis Potter* (London: Faber and Faber, 1998), p. 261.

27 Ibid.

28 Joan Le Mesurier, interview with the author, 18 December 2009.

29 Ibid.

30 Dennis Potter, *Traitor*, first broadcast on BBC1 on 14 October 1971.

31 John Le Mesurier, quoted by D.A.N. Jones, *Radio Times*, 9–15 October 1971, p. 6.

32 Nancy Banks-Smith, *Guardian*, 15 October 1971, p. 7.

33 John Lawrence, *The Stage*, 21 October

1971, p. 14.

34 *The Times*, 15 October 1971, p. 12.

35 David Croft, correspondence with the author, 29 October 2009.

36 Croft, *You Have Been Watching*, p. 176.

37 Richard Briers, conversation with the author, 11 November 2009.

38 Annette Crosbie, correspondence with the author, 6 January 2010.

39 Source: BBC WAC: John Le Mesurier Artist File 1: 1938–62: letter by Stuart Burge to John Le Mesurier, 18 November 1957.

40 Anton Chekhov, 'The Grasshopper', in *The Essential Tales of Chekhov* (London: Granta, 1999), p. 105.

41 Le Mesurier, *A Jobbing Actor*, pp. 153–4.

42 Joan Le Mesurier, interview with the author, 18 December 2009.

43 Recalled by Jonathan Cecil, conversation with the author, 7 April 2009.

44 Le Mesurier, *A Jobbing Actor*, p. 156.

45 Joan Le Mesurier, *Lady Don't Fall Backwards*, p. 186.

46 Le Mesurier, *A Jobbing Actor*, p. 156.

47 Joan Le Mesurier, *Lady Don't Fall Backwards*, p. 186.

48 Le Mesurier, *A Jobbing Actor*, p. 147.

49 See Stone, *You Should Have Been In Last Night*, p. 111.

50 John Le Mesurier, quoted in Whitehall, *Shark Infested Waters*, p. 206.

51 Joan Le Mesurier, *Lady Don't Fall Backwards*, p. 174.

52 Ibid.

53 Le Mesurier, *A Jobbing Actor*, p. 154.

54 Robin Le Mesurier, quoted in Merriman, *Hattie*, p. 103.

55 Joan Le Mesurier, writing in Le Mesurier, *A Jobbing Actor*, p. 154.

56 Joan Le Mesurier, interview with the author, 18 December 2009.

57 Le Mesurier, *A Jobbing Actor*, p. 153.

58 Joan Le Mesurier, interview with the author, 18 December 2009.

59 Joan Le Mesurier, *Lady Don't Fall Backwards*, p. 174.

60 Ibid., p. 175.

61 Le Mesurier, *A Jobbing Actor*, p. 155.

62 Robin Le Mesurier, interview with the author, 27 February 2010.

63 *The Velveteen Rabbit*, narrated by John Le Mesurier and featuring Robin Le Mesurier with music by Ed Welch, was released

originally by Columbia Records in 1978 (Cat No: SCX6599). Robin's quotation comes from a report published in the *Daily Express*, 2 February 1978, p. 22. Robin told me: 'I was signed at the time to Billy Gaff, who was Rod Stewart's manager, and their company Riva, and the guy who was in charge of publishing there came up one day with this idea of me writing something inspired by this book and he suggested getting my dad to narrate it. And he did it beautifully, and I'm quite proud of that record' (interview with the author, 27 February 2010).

64 John Le Mesurier, quoted by Peter Dean, *TV Times* (Australian edition), 9 March 1974, p. 5.

65 John Le Mesurier, quoted in the *Daily Express*, 2 February 1978, p. 22.

66 Joan Le Mesurier, interview with the author, 18 December 2009.

67 Mabel Pickles, *Married to Wilfred* (London: Odhams, 1956), p. 40.

68 See Joan Le Mesurier, *Dear John*, p. 97.

69 Joan Le Mesurier, interview with the author, 18 December 2009.

70 In another strange lapse of memory in his own memoirs, John Le Mesurier would claim (*A Jobbing Actor*, p. 148) that the production of *Hay Fever* 'failed' to reach the West End. It did, however, on 30 April 1980, before going out on a provincial tour.

Chapter XV Conking Out

Header quote: John Le Mesurier, quoted in Joan Le Mesurier, *Lady Don't Fall Backwards*, p. 189.

1 John Le Mesurier, quoted in Merriman, *Hattie*, p. 207.

2 Joan Le Mesurier, speaking in the documentary *The Unforgettable Hattie Jacques*.

3 John Le Mesurier, quoted in the *Guardian*, 11 November 1980, p. 3.

4 John Le Mesurier, quoted by Joan Le Mesurier, *Dear John*, p. 203.

5 Derek Taylor, ibid., p. 202.

6 John Le Mesurier, quoted in Joan Le Mesurier, *Lady Don't Fall Backwards*, p. 191.

7 Michael Knowles and Harold Snoad, *It Sticks Out Half a Mile*, pilot episode,

recorded on 19 July 1981, not broadcast until 29 May 2004 on BBC7.

8 Robin Le Mesurier, interview with the author, 27 February 2010.

9 Joan Le Mesurier, interview with the author, 10 February 2010.

10 Joan Le Mesurier, interview with the author, 18 December 2009.

11 Ibid.

12 Jimmy Perry told me (30 January 2010) that the idea for Simon Cadell's fish-out-of-water character in *Hi-de-Hi!* came from his memory of working with a disaffected former academic at Butlin's shortly after the war. Jeffrey Fairbrother was given King's College, Cambridge, as his alma mater because Perry used to have a relation, William Crisp, who owned a heraldic shop directly opposite on King's Parade.

13 Joan Lowe, quoted in Pertwee, *Dad's Army*, p. 176.

14 Michael Knowles and Harold Snoad, *It Sticks Out Half a Mile*, second pilot episode, first broadcast on BBC Radio 2, 13 November 1983.

15 Bill Pertwee, interview with the author, 27 May 2000.

16 John Howard Davies, correspondence with the author, 12 December 2009.

17 Joan Le Mesurier, *Lady Don't Fall Backwards*, p. 187.

18 Robin Le Mesurier, interview with the author, 27 February 2010.

19 Joan Le Mesurier, *Lady Don't Fall Backwards*, p. 187.

20 Ibid., p. 192.

21 Ibid., pp. 187–8.

22 Derek Taylor, quoted by Joan Le Mesurier, *Dear John*, pp. 221–2.

23 Le Mesurier, *A Jobbing Actor*, p. 149.

24 Joan Le Mesurier, ibid., p. 151.

25 Joan Le Mesurier, *Lady Don't Fall Backwards*, p. 152.

26 Ibid., pp. 187, 189.

27 Ibid., p. 189.

28 Ibid., p. 189.

29 Joan Le Mesurier, *Dear John*, p. 227.

30 Le Mesurier, *A Jobbing Actor*, pp. 151–2.

Epilogue

Epigraph: John Le Mesurier, album title; Philip Larkin, 'An Arundel Tomb', *Collected Poems*, p. 110.

1 *The Times*, 16 November 1983, p. 14.

2 *Guardian*, 16 November 1983, p. 10.

3 Robin Le Mesurier, interview with the author, 27 February 2010.

4 Joan Le Mesurier, *Lady Don't Fall Backwards*, p. 190.

5 Joan Le Mesurier, *Dear John*, pp. 235–6.

6 Derek Taylor, quoted by Joan Le Mesurier, *Lady Don't Fall Backwards*, p. 190.

7 'An Indian Prayer', traditional, read by John Le Mesurier, *What is Going to Become of Us All?*

8 Joan Le Mesurier, writing in John Le Mesurier, *A Jobbing Actor*, p. 152.

9 Robin Le Mesurier, interview with the author, 27 February 2010.

10 David Malin, quoted in Merriman, *Hattie*, p. 216.

11 Robin Le Mesurier would recall that, after his younger brother had recovered from an attack of meningitis, Jake had recuperated in Spain, where he stayed with Joan, before moving into an apartment of his own in Barcelona. Shortly after this, however, he met a young woman who persuaded him to try heroin again: 'She gave him an overdose, his heart stopped and she cleared the apartment of everything. She basically killed him and robbed him. She was never found.' (See *Daily Express*, 21 March 2008, p. 25.)

12 Joan Le Mesurier, *Dear John*, p. 244.

13 Joan Le Mesurier, interview with the author, 18 December 2009.

Bibliography

John Le Mesurier

Ableman, Paul, *Dad's Army: The Defence of a Front Line English Village* (London: BBC Books, 1989)

Bean, Colin, *Who Do You Think You Are Kidding!* (London: Minerva, 1998)

Cotes, Peter, 'The quiet man of comedy', *Guardian*, 16 November 1983, p. 9

Croft, David, *You Have Been Watching . . .* (London: BBC Books, 2004)

Croft, David and Perry, Jimmy, *Dad's Army* (London: Sphere, 1975)

—— *Dad's Army: The Lost Episodes* (London: Virgin, 1998)

Dunn, Clive, *Permission to Speak* (London: Century, 1986)

Halliley, Elton, 'A Short History of The National Society of Conservative and Unionist Agents' (published as a supplement to the *Conservative Agents' Journal*, December 1947)

Hart, Ted (ed.), *Dad's Army* (London: Peter Way, 1972)

Jones, D.A.N., 'Playing Potter's traitor', *Radio Times*, 9–15 October 1971, p. 6

Le Mesurier, Joan, *Lady Don't Fall Backwards* (London: Sidgwick & Jackson, 1988)

—— *Dear John* (London: Sidgwick & Jackson, 2001)

Le Mesurier, John, *A Jobbing Actor* (London: Elm Tree, 1984)

Longmate, Norman, *The Real Dad's Army* (London: Arrow, 1974)

Lowe, Stephen, *Arthur Lowe: Dad's Memory* (London: Virgin, 1997)

McCann, Graham, *Dad's Army: The Story of a Classic Television Show* (London: Fourth Estate, 2001)

Merriman, Andy, *Hattie: The Authorised Biography of Hattie Jacques* (London: Aurum, 2008)

Nimmo, Derek, 'John Le Mesurier (1912–1983)', *Oxford Dictionary of National Biography*, ed. H.C.G. Matthew and Brian Harrison (Oxford: Oxford University Press, 2004)

Perry, Jimmy, *Stupid Boy* (London: Century, 2002)

Pertwee, Bill, *Dad's Army: The Making of a Television Legend* (London: Pavilion, 1998)

Purser, Ann, 'Behind the Success of Dad's Army', *The Stage*, 27 November 1969, p. 12

Raynor, William, 'John's East Anglian Womb', *Radio Times* (East Anglia edition only), 26 July 1973, p. 13

Richards, Jeffrey, 'Dad's Army and the politics of nostalgia', *Films and British National Identity* (Manchester: Manchester University Press, 1997)

Ridley, Nicolas, *Godfrey's Ghost: From Father to Son* (London: Mogzilla, 2009)

Webber, Richard, *Dad's Army: A Celebration* (London: Virgin, 1999)

—— *The Complete A–Z of Dad's Army* (London: Orion, 2000)

General

Allen, Steve, *The Funny Men* (New York: Simon and Schuster, 1956)

Askey, Arthur, *Before Your Very Eyes* (London: London, Woburn Press, 1975)

Babington, Bruce, *Launder and Gilliat* (Manchester: Manchester University Press, 2002)

Bale, Bernard, *Jon Pertwee* (London: André Deutsch, 2000)

Barfe, Louis, *Turned Out Nice Again* (London: Atlantic Books, 2008)

Beaton, Cecil and Kenneth Tynan, *Persona Grata* (London: Wingate, 1953)

Bist, David, 'At the Core of Apple with Derek Taylor', *Montreal Gazette*, 31 May 1969, p. 45

Black, Peter, *The Biggest Aspidistra in the World* (London: BBC, 1972)

—— *The Mirror in the Corner* (London: Hutchison, 1972)

Bradbury, David and Joe McGrath, *Now That's Funny!* (London: Methuen, 1998)

Brandreth, Gyles, *Brief Encounters* (London: Politico's, 2003)

Briggs, Asa, *The History of Broadcasting in the United Kingdom* (Oxford: Oxford University Press, 1961–79):

Vol. 1: *The Birth of Broadcasting* (1961)

Vol. 2: *The Golden Age of Wireless* (1965)

Vol. 3: *The War of Words* (1970)

Vol. 4: *Sound and Vision* (1979)

Bygraves, Max, *Stars In My Eyes* (London: Robson, 2003)

Cardiff, David, 'Mass middlebrow laughter: The origins of BBC comedy', *Media, Culture & Society*, vol. 10, no. 1 (January 1988), pp. 41–60

Chibnall, Steve and Brian McFarlane, *The British 'B' Film* (London: BFI/Palgrave Macmillan, 2009)

Coldstream, John (ed.), *Ever, Dirk* (London: Phoenix, 2009)

Cotton, Bill, *The BBC as an Entertainer* (London: BBC, 1977)

—— *Double Bill*, (London: Fourth Estate, 2000)

Cryer, Barry, *You Won't Believe This But . . .* (London: Virgin, 1998)

—— *Pigs Can Fly* (London: Orion, 2003)

Dunn, Kate, *Do Not Adjust Your Set: The Early Days of Live Television* (London: John Murray, 2003)

Fisher, John, *Funny Way to be a Hero* (London: Frederick Muller, 1973)

—— *Tony Hancock* (London: Harper, 2009)

Frith, Simon, 'The pleasures of the hearth: the making of BBC light entertainment', in Tony Bennett et al. (eds), *Popular Culture and Social Relations* (Milton Keynes: Open University, 1983)

Foster, Andy and Steve Furst, *Radio Comedy 1938–1968* (London: Virgin, 1996)

Gambaccini, Paul and Rod Taylor, *Television's Greatest Hits* (London: Network Books, 1993)

Gillett, Philip, *The British Working Class in Postwar Film* (Manchester: Manchester University Press, 2003)

Gilliatt, Penelope, *To Wit* (New York: Scribner, 1990)

Grade, Michael, *It Seemed Like a Good Idea at the Time* (London: Macmillan, 1999)

Greene, Hugh Carleton, *The BBC as a Public Service* (London: BBC, 1960)

Hancock, Freddie and David Nathan, *Hancock* (London: BBC Books, 1996)

Hudd, Roy, *Roy Hudd's Book of Music-Hall, Variety and Showbiz Anecdotes* (London: Robson, 1993)

Hughes, John Graven, *The Greasepaint War* (London: New English Library, 1976)

James, Clive, *Clive James on Television* (London: Picador, 1991)

Jeffries, Stuart, *Mrs Slocombe's Pussy* (London: Flamingo, 2000)

Kumar, Krishan, *The Making of English National Identity: Englishness and Britishness in Comparative and Historical Perspective* (Cambridge: Cambridge University Press, 2003)

Lewis, Roger, *The Life and Death of Peter Sellers* (London: Century, 1994)

Lewisohn, Mark, *Radio Times Guide to TV Comedy* (London: BBC, 1998)

McCann, Graham, *Cary Grant: A Class Apart* (London: Fourth Estate, 1996)

—— 'Why the best sitcoms must be a class act', *London Evening Standard*, 21 May 1997, p. 9

—— 'An offer we can refuse', *London Evening Standard*, 2 December 1998, p. 8

—— *Morecambe & Wise* (London: Fourth Estate, 1998)

—— 'Sit back and wait for the comedy', *Financial Times*, 24 November 1999, p. 22

—— 'Half-man, half-desk: the secrets of a talk-show host', *Financial Times*, 8/9 April 2000, p. viii

—— 'Don't bury your treasures', *Financial Times*, 28 June 2000, p. 22

—— 'Nocturnal transmissions are a turn-off', *Financial Times*, 8 May 2002, p. 18

—— 'You never had it so good or so funny', *Financial Times*, 13 November 2002, p. 17

—— 'How to define the indefinable', *Financial Times*, 20 March 2003, p. 14

—— 'Bob Hope: The master of special delivery bows out', *Financial Times*, 29 July 2003, p. 15

—— 'Steptoe and Son', *British Comedy Greats*, ed. Annabel Merullo and Neil Wenborn (London: Cassell Illustrated, 2003), pp. 157–61

—— *Frankie Howerd: Stand-Up Comic* (London: Fourth Estate, 2004)

—— (ed.) *The Essential Dave Allen* (London: Hodder & Stoughton, 2005)

—— *Spike & Co* (London: Hodder & Stoughton, 2006)

—— *Fawlty Towers: The Story of the Sitcom* (London: Hodder & Stoughton, 2007)

—— *Bounder! The Biography of Terry-Thomas* (London: Aurum, 2008)

McFarlane, Brian, *An Autobiography of British Cinema* (London: Methuen, 1997)

—— *The Encyclopedia of British Film* (London: Methuen, 2005)

Mellor, G.J., *The Northern Music Hall* (Newcastle upon Tyne: Frank Graham, 1970)

—— *They Made Us Laugh* (Littleborough: George Kelsell, 1982)

Miall, Leonard, *Inside the BBC* (London: Weidenfeld & Nicolson, 1994)

Midwinter, Eric, *Make 'Em Laugh* (London: George Allen & Unwin, 1979)

Monkhouse, Bob, *Crying With Laughter* (London: Arrow, 1994)

—— *Over the Limit* (London: Century, 1998)

More, Kenneth, *More or Less* (London: Hodder & Stoughton, 1978)

Muir, Frank, *Comedy in Television* (London: BBC, 1966)

Murphy, Robert (ed.), *The British Cinema Book* (London: BFI, 2001)

Nathan, David, *The Laughtermakers* (London: Peter Owen, 1971)

Parkinson, Michael, *Parkinson* (London: Elm Tree, 1975)

Pedrick, Gale, 'Laughter in the Air', *BBC Year Book 1948* (London: BBC, 1948), pp. 53–6

Pertwee, Bill, *Promenades and Pierrots* (Devon: Westbridge, 1979)

—— *By Royal Command* (Newton Abbot: David & Charles, 1981)

—— *A Funny Way to Make a Living!* (London: Sunburst, 1996)

Pertwee, Jon, *Moon Boots and Dinner Suits* (London: Hamish Hamilton, 1984)

Pertwee, Michael, *Name Dropping* (London: Leslie Frewin, 1974)

Phillips, Leslie, *Hello* (London: Orion, 2007)

Plomley, Roy, *Desert Island Lists* (London: Hutchinson, 1984)

Priestley, J.B., *Particular Pleasures* (New York: Stein & Day, 1975)

Richards, Jeffrey, *Visions of Yesteryear* (London: Routledge, 1973)

—— *Films and British National Identity* (Manchester: Manchester University Press, 1997)

Silvey, Roger, *Who's Listening? The Story of BBC Audience Research* (London: Allen & Unwin, 1974)

Sloan, Tom, *Television Light Entertainment* (London: BBC, 1969)

Stone, Richard, *You Should Have Been In Last Night* (Sussex: The Book Guild, 2000)

Street, Sarah, *British National Cinema* (London: Routledge, 1997)

Sykes, Eric, *Eric Sykes' Comedy Heroes* (London: Virgin, 2003)

Taylor, Alistair, *Yesterday – The Beatles Remembered* (London: Sidgwick & Jackson, 1988)

Thompson, Harry, *Peter Cook: A Biography* (London: Hodder & Stoughton, 1997)

Took, Barry, *Laughter in the Air* (London: Robson/BBC, 1976)

—— 'Whatever Happened to TV Comedy?', *The Listener*, 5 January 1984, pp. 7–8, and 12 January 1984, pp. 8–9

Tynan, Kenneth, *Profiles* (London: Nick Hern Books, 1989)

Viner, Brian, *Nice To See It, To See It, Nice* (London: Simon & Schuster, 2009)

Walker, Alexander, *Hollywood, England* (London: Harrap, 1986)

—— *National Heroes* (London: Harrap, 1986)

Watt, John (ed.), *Radio Variety* (London: J.M. Dent, 1939)

Wheldon, Huw, *British Traditions in a World-Wide Medium* (London: BBC, 1973)

—— *The Achievement of Television* (London: BBC, 1975)

—— *The British Experience in Television* (London: BBC, 1976)

Whitfield, June, *. . . and June Whitfield* (London: Corgi, 2001)

Wilde, Larry, *The Great Comedians* (Secaucus, New Jersey: Citadel Press, 1973)

Williams, Kenneth, *The Kenneth Williams Diaries*, ed. Russell Davies (London: HarperCollins, 1993)

Wilmut, Roger, *Kindly Leave the Stage: The Story of Variety, 1918–60* (London: Methuen, 1985)

Windsor, Barbara, *All Of Me* (London: Headline, 2001)

Wyndham Goldie, Grace, *Facing The Nation: Broadcasting and Politics 1936–1976* (London: Bodley Head, 1977)

Index